ADVANCE PRAISE FOR *VIRGINIA SECEDES*

"This superbly edited documentary history of Virginia's road to disunion in 1861 should end, once and for all, the absurd notion that secession was all about state's rights. It was, as these documents convincingly demonstrate, all about slavery and the racial order the commonwealth of Virginia, along with the rest of the antebellum South, had erected on this benighted institution. Dwight Pitcaithley's skilled editorial hand is present throughout this volume, from his insightful introduction to his masterful presentation of the documents themselves. It is, from start to finish, nothing short of a tour de force."
—**Charles B. Dew,** author of *Apostles of Disunion: Southern Secession Commissioners and the Causes of the Civil War*

"Anyone who wants to understand Southern secession would do well to consult this illuminating volume. Pitcaithley has deftly curated and contextualized Virginia's sprawling secession debates, dramatizing how slavery and white supremacy were at the core of secessionism. Especially valuable is his attention to the various proposed constitutional amendments, all geared to preserving slavery, that failed to effect compromise. An invaluable resource for understanding the Civil War and American political polarization."
—**Elizabeth R. Varon,** Langbourne M. Williams Professor of American History, University of Virginia

"Pitcaithley's valuable collection of amendments to the Constitution of the United States that Virginians proposed during the secession crisis and his judicious selection of some of the many speeches that the state's political leaders made demonstrate that advocates and opponents of secession all wanted to protect slavery and the interests of enslavers in Virginia. Opponents of secession, who were in the majority until mid-April 1861, tried to preserve Virginia as a slave state in the old Union and to bring back the first states that seceded. The secession crisis debates in Virginia were about how best to protect the future of slavery. Nobody advocated abstract theories of states' rights as later apologists for secession and the Confederacy asserted. The few references to states' rights were all actually to the state-created rights of individual White Southern people to own Black people and

(continued)

to empower White Southerners to carry enslaved people throughout the United States and its territories without danger of their being freed, irrespective of the laws of the states without slavery. In fact, many Virginians proposed to restrict the rights of people in the states without slavery to enact and enforce their own antislavery laws and to empower Congress to reenforce those restrictions as well as to protect slavery in the western territories."
—**Brent Tarter,** author of *Constitutional History of Virginia*

"These expertly edited documents clearly demonstrate that slavery and race— rather than economic policy issues like the tariff—provided the central theme in Virginia's debates over secession."
—**Jonathan M. Atkins,** author of *Politics, Parties, and the Sectional Conflict in Tennessee, 1832–1861*

"*Virginia Secedes* is a valuable addition to the literature on the coming of the Civil War. Pitcaithley's comprehensive narrative and choice of documents show Virginia to be a microcosm of the larger conflict, and reinforce the importance of Virginia's secession to the course of the war. We have needed a volume like this for a long time."
—**Anne Sarah Rubin,** University of Maryland, Baltimore County

VIRGINIA SECEDES

A DOCUMENTARY HISTORY

VIRGINIA SECEDES

A DOCUMENTARY
HISTORY

EDITED BY

Dwight T. Pitcaithley

THE UNIVERSITY OF TENNESSEE PRESS | KNOXVILLE

Library of Congress Cataloging-in-Publication Data
Names: Pitcaithley, Dwight T., editor.
Title: Virginia secedes : a documentary history / edited by Dwight T. Pitcaithley.
Description: First edition. | Knoxville : The University of Tennessee Press, [2024] |
Includes bibliographical references and index. | Summary: "This books collects
amendments to the Constitution of the United States that Virginians proposed
during the secession crisis alongside select speeches of the state's political leaders.
Editor Dwight T. Pitcaithley's selection and introduction emphasize that advocates
and opponents of secession alike wanted to protect slavery and the interests of
enslavers in Virginia. Among the documents are Governor Letcher's January 7,
1861, address to the General Assembly; speeches given to the Washington Peace
Conference, US Senate, and House of Representatives; and the state's secession
convention speeches. Chapter 6 contains the sixteen constitutional amendments
proposed by Virginians. The volume also includes a timeline for Secession
Winter and questions for discussion"—Provided by publisher.
Identifiers: LCCN 2023045671 (print) | LCCN 2023045672 (ebook) |
ISBN 9781621908432 (hardcover) | ISBN 9781621908500 (pdf)
Subjects: LCSH: United States—Politics and government—1861–1865—Sources. |
Constitutional amendments—United States—Sources. | Secession—Virginia—
History—Sources. | Virginia—Politics and government—1861–1865—Sources. |
LCGFT: Primary sources.
Classification: LCC E459 .V57 2023 (print) | LCC E459 (ebook) |
DDC 973.7/13—dc23/eng/20231005
LC record available at https://lccn.loc.gov/2023045671
LC ebook record available at https://lccn.loc.gov/202304567

For Catherine

CONTENTS

Introduction
xi

Documents

1

Governor John Letcher's Address to
the General Assembly, January 7, 1861
1

2

Washington Peace Conference, February 1861
27

3

United States Senate, January–March 1861
61

7

Secession,
April–May, 1861

253

INTRODUCTION

"It would be well for anybody who doubts that the Civil War was about slavery to forget everything that the schoolbooks, movies, and popular culture have taught, no matter what the beliefs of the creators of those teaching tools, and to read nothing published later than 1861. If you read what white Virginians wrote and said in 1861, you will find that the postwar pro-Confederate interpretation was an after-the-fact fabrication."

—BRENT TARTER, retired research historian
and senior editor, Library of Virginia

For the past fifteen decades, historians and popular writers have assigned many causes for the Civil War. Most of those written during the first century after Appomattox developed an explanation based on wishful thinking or out of the need to assign honorable motivations to the South's secession. The primary narrative to emerge during the late nineteenth century was one designed to justify the war's loss to southerners. Built on the writings of Alexander Stephens, Jefferson Davis, and Jubal Early and promoted by heritage organizations, that interpretation of secession minimized the role of slavery. In his 1881 history of the war, Jefferson Davis was emphatic: "The truth remains intact and incontrovertible, that the existence of African servitude was in no wise the cause of the conflict, but only an incident." The true cause of secession was "the systematic and persistent struggle to deprive the Southern States of equality in the Union—generally to discriminate in legislation against the interests of their people; culminating in their exclusion from the Territories, and common property of the States, as well as by the infraction of their compact to promote domestic tranquility."[1] A decade later, he refined his justification: "The origin of the sectional controversy was the question of the balance of political power."[2] Davis insisted that the South's slaves were "faithful" and happy in their service to benevolent owners. Thus began the interpretation that the slave states separated from the United States in the defense of states' rights and not slavery.[3]

One hundred years after Appomattox, Virginia's Civil War Commission continued this sleight of hand by emphasizing Virginia's minority status in the country and the state's need to protect its rights "against the press of the majority" as the chief cause of its secession. The small pamphlet published during the war's centennial detailed the movement toward secession in the state's convention called to determine the weighty matter of disunion, and it clearly identified the vote to separate on April 17 and the peoples' ratification of that decision on May 23. It avoided, however, any discussion of the delegates' concern over the future of slavery, or their efforts to craft amendments designed to protect the institution in the United States Constitution. Nor did it include mention of their decision to form an alliance with the Confederate States of America immediately after it passed the ordinance of secession, or of its adoption of the Confederate Constitution a week after that vote, or of its invitation for the Confederate capital in Montgomery to relocate to Richmond. By the time the White male voters were given the opportunity to ratify the ordinance, Virginia had been accepted into the Confederacy and the state was flooded with Confederate troops. The 1964 state's official statement on Virginia's decision to separate from the United States made no mention of the need to preserve slavery or white supremacy as motivating factors.[4] Yet, the discussion among the convention's delegates revolved around, as historian Allan Nevins concluded over seventy years ago, "slavery and the future position of the Negro race in North America."[5] Virginia deliberated longer than any other state before voting for separation and produced more solutions designed to protect slavery. Its steady drift into the gravitational pull of the Confederacy resulted from the determination of resolute secessionists who exaggerated Republican influence and inflated the threat the incoming Lincoln administration posed to the South's peculiar institution.

In 1860, Virginia was the fifth most populated state in the Union and the one with the largest number of slaves. Its 490,865 enslaved Blacks, concentrated in the tidewater and piedmont portions of the commonwealth, contributed to the state being ranked sixth in overall wealth. Yet Virginia had struggled over the idea of slavery from its founding in 1776. With the growth of the institution being concentrated in the eastern section of the state, and its political life dominated by slave owners, tensions gradually arose between the tidewater aristocracy and the northwestern counties where slave owning was much less prevalent. That distinction between the social and economic systems existing between east and west prompted historian William G. Shade to observe that "this sharp division of the Old Dominion into a slave society east of the Blue Ridge and a society with slavery in the west has symbolized the role of intrastate sectionalism in the history of antebellum Virginia."[6]

The source of the unrest was the 1776 state constitution that restricted suffrage to White males owning one hundred acres or more, and a taxation formula that favored the slave-owning eastern elite. Under pressure by reformers, the legislature called a constitutional convention in 1830 that attempted to democratize the state's charter. The resulting document marginally expanded White male suffrage. The new constitution eliminated the one-hundred-acre provision and substituted owners of property valued at twenty-five dollars or more and leaseholders who held leases for at least five years and paid an annual rent of at least twenty dollars. The new definitions, however, did little to calm emotions as almost a third of the adult White male population were denied the vote, and favored the eastern aristocracy by continuing their control over the state's levers of government. Only one delegate from west of the Blue Ridge voted in favor of the new constitution.[7]

The 1831 slave rebellion led by Nat Turner in Southampton County once again resulted in a state-wide conversation about the future of slavery. Surprisingly, the insurrection which resulted in the deaths of over fifty Whites, prompted much support for the abolition of slavery throughout the state. East and west, however, were divided on the issue. Tidewater representatives largely supported a gradual and compensated emancipation with slaves removed to lower South states, while Trans-Allegheny delegates favored gradual emancipation combined with colonization of freed slaves to Africa. No faction envisioned free Black communities in Virginia. As historian Alison Freehling has noted, "Both groups reflected the inveterate Negrophobia of Virginia's white community. Removal of slavery, all agreed, must also include removal of blacks."[8] Given the stark divisions in the state, not to mention growing talk of a division of the state, the best the legislature could manage was the passage of a compromise measure that required the colonization of all free blacks and manumitted slaves.[9]

Two decades later, reformers again pressed for a revision of the state's constitution. Issues of representation and taxation dominated the resulting convention which opened in January 1851. Driving the demands for a constitutional convention was the dramatic increase in White population in the state west of the Blue Ridge over the previous two decades. After four months of intense debate, including threats of state dismemberment, the gathering agreed on a compromise that embraced representation in the house based on universal manhood suffrage (without property qualifications), but qualification for the Senate continued the 1830 district representation that favored the slave-dominated population of the tidewater. As a carrot to the growing trans-Allegheny counties, the constitution authorized a reapportionment in 1865 based on White-basis representation.[10]

Unable to defer majority rule in the house, eastern conservatives responded with a proposal that insisted on special tax privileges for slave property. While the 1830 constitution was silent on the subject of property taxation, the 1851 constitution exempted slaves under the age of twelve from any taxation and imposed a flat $300 tax on slaves over the age of twelve.[11] Property of nonslaveholding Whites was taxed on the *ad valorem* principle. This aspect of the new constitution continued to fuel discontent among westerners. "For as the decade progressed," observes Alison Freehling, "the Trans-Allegheny would increasingly resent eastern control of the senate and, above all, unequal taxation of slaves."[12] That resentment, fed by a waxing proslavery ideology nationally, would have grave consequences for the state following the election of 1860.

From the conclusion of the war with Mexico in 1848 until Abraham Lincoln's victory, debates over the future of slavery worked to divide the nation.[13] Southern anxiety over the future of slavery began to escalate in 1846 when Pennsylvania representative David Wilmot proposed to exclude slavery from any land acquired from Mexico as a result of that country's war with the United States. The "proviso" never passed both houses of Congress, but nevertheless incensed the slaveholding South. If Congress could prohibit its extension into the western territories, slavery would be limited to the fifteen states where the institution currently existed. A number of southern states threatened to secede three years later in response to Henry Clay's proposal to admit California as a non-slave state, thereby upsetting the political balance in the Senate.[14] The Compromise of 1850 temporarily settled the issue and, with the exception of the publication of Harriet Beecher Stowe's anti-slavery novel *Uncle Tom's Cabin* in 1852, sectional animosity abated somewhat until Congress organized the territory west of Missouri in 1854.

Slavery had earlier been prohibited throughout the Louisiana Territory, except for Missouri, as a result of the Compromise of 1820. Although it had been respected for thirty-four years, interest in overturning the Missouri law mounted as southerners became increasingly concerned that slave states would ultimately be surrounded by non-slave states. Pressure from southern delegations in Congress led to the passage of the Kansas-Nebraska Act which organized both territories and dealt with the slavery issue by allowing the settlers in the two jurisdictions to decide for themselves whether the institution would be supported or prohibited. The idea of popular, or territorial, sovereignty had earlier been adopted in 1850 when Congress organized the New Mexico and Utah Territories. In this case, however, fate did not honor the proslavery elements.

Proslavery and antislavery settlers flocked to Kansas hoping to establish political dominance. Following several contested elections, the former developed the Lecompton Constitution while the latter established the Topeka Constitution. Although the majority of settlers were against slavery, President Buchanan strongly supported the proslavery Lecompton Constitution. The resulting debate in Congress produced a compromise that the Lecompton Constitution would be resubmitted to the state for a final vote. Democrats sweetened the deal by providing substantially more acreage for public buildings and education if the proslavery charter was approved. After four years of bitter fighting (political and physical) between pro- and anti-slavery forces, the territory voted ultimately to prohibit slavery in August of 1858.[15] Coming only eighteen months after the Supreme Court's *Dred Scott* decision declaring that slavery must be preserved throughout the territorial period, the Kansas prohibition heightened tensions between advocates for and opponents of slavery. The Lecompton controversy helped convince many southerners that federal, even constitutional, protections for the institution were required to preserve the South's economic engine.

Paralleling the violence in Kansas following the passage of the Kansas-Nebraska Act, sectional antagonism in Congress also increased to the point where it visited the floor of the Senate. On May 22, 1856, a Democratic congressman named Preston Brooks from South Carolina entered the chamber and beat Massachusetts senator Charles Sumner senseless with a cane. A few days earlier, Sumner had delivered a blistering attack on senators who were supporting the proslavery faction in Kansas. In his speech titled "Crime against Kansas," Sumner specifically implicated Stephen A. Douglas of Illinois, James M. Mason of Virginia, and Andrew P. Butler of South Carolina. Butler's advocacy of slavery drew specific fire from Sumner who accused him of being in the thrall of "the harlot Slavery."[16] Incensed by Sumner's vitriol toward his cousin, Brooks retaliated with violence rather than words. The Brooks-Sumner Affair became emblematic of the growing animus between the proslavery and antislavery expansionist factions.[17]

Not only did the Kansas-Nebraska Act precipitate bloodshed in Kansas and in the United States Capitol, it also led to the formation of the Republican Party. Opposition to upending the thirty-four-year-old ban on slavery north of the 36°30' parallel led to the fragmentation of the Whig Party and united some northern Democrats and Free Soil Party members in a new political organization that called for the admission of Kansas as a free state and asserted the right of Congress to prohibit slavery in the territories. The party selected John Charles Fremont as its standard bearer in 1856. A former explorer of the West, army officer during the war with Mexico, military governor of California, and early Democratic senator representing California, Fremont was an avowed opponent of slavery, and won the nomination on the first ballot.[18]

Democrats selected James Buchanan from Pennsylvania who, in contrast to the political neophyte Fremont, had served as representative and senator in the US Congress, secretary of state under James K. Polk, and minister to Russia and later the United Kingdom. The party's platform endorsed popular sovereignty and condemned Republicans for being a "sectional" party that incited armed resistance to law in the territories. Former president Millard Fillmore of New York became the presidential candidate of the Know Nothing/American Party and campaigned on a platform that was anti-immigration and anti-Catholic.[19]

Significantly, the campaign set the tone for the next four years and the South's response to the election of the Republican Abraham Lincoln in 1860. Slavery and Kansas became the focal points of the race. Democrats labeled Fremont and his party "Black Republicans" who they painted as fanatics and disunionists. If elected, Fremont would destroy the Union. The Republican stance against the extension of slavery was widely misrepresented as a stance for abolition and racial equality. The Yankee fanatics, argued their opponents, threatened the existence of slavery in the South and menaced white supremacy in the North. Black equality was anathema below the Mason-Dixon Line and troublesome to many north of it. All of these charges would echo into the next election cycle.[20]

On November 4, 1856, Fremont carried all of the Upper North states, Fillmore captured Maryland, and Buchanan won the White House by taking all the remaining states including California. The election did not result in a political mandate for Buchanan, however, as he entered the presidency with only 45 percent of the White male vote, 22 percent going to Fillmore.[21] Alarming to southern Democrats was the uncomfortable fact that the upstart Republican Party had captured a third of the popular vote with 33 percent in its initial outing on the national stage. The popular vote starkly illustrated the political divisions in the country. In a three-man race, Fremont won an average of 62 percent of the popular vote in New England and no less than 49 percent in Ohio, Michigan, Wisconsin, and Iowa. Among the slave states, Fremont was listed on the ballot only in Delaware, Kentucky, Maryland, and Virginia.[22]

Two other events of the 1850s specifically affected Virginia as it approached the end of the decade: the Lemmon Slave Case and John Brown's misguided attack on the federal arsenal at Harpers Ferry. In 1852, Juliet Lemon and her husband, Jonathan, decided to move from Bath County in the Shenandoah Valley to Texas.[23] Arriving in Norfolk with their seven children, and eight slaves inherited by Juliet from her father, the family boarded a packet to New York City with plans of transferring to another bound for New Orleans. Soon after landing, and unappreciative of the fact that New York, a decade before, had passed a law declaring all slaves brought into the state free upon their arrival, the Lemons were issued a writ of habeas corpus. After several days' deliberation, a local judge declared he had no choice but to free Juliet's slaves who were quickly escorted north into New England and eventually Canada.

Virginia's governor, Joseph Johnson, infuriated by the seizure, requested that the legislature appeal the case, which it did. As the case worked its way through the New York system, the governorship passed from Johnson to Henry A. Wise who enthusiastically pursued the appeal. Believing that

New York's 1841 law was patently unconstitutional and that the issue was of paramount importance to the South, Wise laid plans to take the case all the way to the US Supreme Court. By then aware of the court's 1857 *Dred Scott* decision, the new governor was confident that if Virginia lost in the New York court system, the highest court in the land would uphold his appeal. Losing in both the New York Supreme Court and the New York Court of Appeals (the latter in March 1860), Virginia appeared to be ready to present the case before Chief Justice Roger B. Taney and the US Supreme Court. Politics, however, intervened. In January of 1860, John Letcher succeeded Henry Wise as governor and Letcher, for reasons unknown, declined to push the case to the higher court.[24] Nevertheless, the constitutional right of slave owners to carry their slaves into non-slave states and territories became a rallying cry for southern Democrats and was reflected in dozens of constitutional amendments proposed over Secession Winter.

John Brown's attack on Harpers Ferry Arsenal on October 16, 1859, similarly roiled southern sensibilities. The armed invasion of southern soil to incite a slave rebellion was a failure from many perspectives. The raid ended quickly with the arrival of a force of US Marines led by Colonel Robert E. Lee and Lieutenant J. E. B. Stuart, no slaves rushed to Brown's summons, and six weeks later, Brown was tried and convicted in a Virginia court and hanged. Nevertheless, slave owners throughout the South read larger, sinister motives behind Brown's singular action. The plot to invade a southern state and encourage slaves to revolt against their owners was portrayed as only the initial phase of a plan by northern abolitionists to destroy the institution of slavery. Although abolitionists comprised only 2 percent of the North's voting population and were a very small minority within the Republican Party,[25] the Virginia secessionist Edmund Ruffin (and others) purposely inflated their influence by claiming that the North was filled with abolitionists of the John Brown stripe, and that the Republican Party was, at its core, an abolitionist party.[26] Brown's raid, and the baseless claims of Ruffin and other vocal secessionists, persuaded many southerners that the election of a Republican as president would lead to dire consequences for their peculiar institution.

The future of slavery did indeed become the focus of the election, but not as Ruffin envisioned it. The primary issue became the extension of slavery into the western territories and not the existence of slavery in the fifteen southern states. Democrats differed on the subject, with a northern faction nominating Senator Stephen A. Douglas of Illinois on a platform that embraced popular sovereignty as the solution to the expansion problem while southerners nominated Buchanan's vice president, John C. Breckinridge, with a platform that demanded the federal protection of slavery during the territorial period. Both camps urged the acquisition of Cuba. Proslavery expansionists had long sought the island as a logical expansion of their slave empire. By 1860, the slave-based sugar economy in Cuba produced one quarter of the world's sugar supply.[27]

The Republican Party, in only its second run at national office, nominated Abraham Lincoln. The party reiterated its opposition to the extension of slavery declaring that "the normal condition of all the territory of the United States is that of freedom." While recommending the immediate admission of Kansas as a free state and the construction of a railroad to the Pacific, and denouncing the "lawless invasion by armed force of the soil of any state of territory," the party forcefully rejected southern claims regarding its abolitionist schemes. "The maintenance inviolate of the rights of the states," it pronounced, "and especially the right of each state to order and control its own domestic institutions according to its own judgment exclusively, is essential to that balance of powers on which the perfection and endurance of our political fabric depends." The party of Lincoln had no interest in, and no constitutional mechanism for, ridding the country of the institution of slavery.[28]

The newly formed Constitutional Union Party, made up largely of former Whigs, attempted to claim a middle ground between extreme abolitionists and extreme secessionists. Nominating Tennessean John Bell, the party quoted the preamble to the Constitution and declared it stood firmly on no other principle than "the Constitution of the country, the union of states, and the enforcement of the laws."[29]

On election day, Abraham Lincoln (and his vice president, Hannibal Hamlin of Maine) won an overwhelming majority in the electoral college, but garnered only 39 percent of the popular vote. The Republican was followed by northern Democrat Stephen A. Douglas, then Breckinridge, and finally John Bell who carried three states. In Virginia, Bell narrowly bested Breckinridge by a mere 156 votes; Douglas finished a distant third. As in 1856, the political divide was graphic. New England again voted for the

Republican candidate by an average of 62 percent while among the eleven
future states of the Confederacy, Virginia was the only one to place Lincoln
on the ballot. There, he received a total of 1,887 votes mostly from northwestern counties.[30] Often overlooked in the retelling of the election of 1860
is the fact that Democrats won both houses of Congress and were poised to
control the legislative branch of government for at least the first two years
of the Lincoln administration!

Southern concerns following the election of 1856 turned to outright fear
after the Republican victory. Edmund Ruffin's campaign conflating Republicanism with abolitionism, echoed by secessionists throughout the
South, had the desired effect. Seven Deep South states immediately began
the march toward disunion with South Carolina leading the way on December 20, 1860. It was within this political environment that Virginia's
governor, John Letcher, addressed the general assembly on January 7, 1861.
Aware that several additional states were on the brink of following South
Carolina out of the Union, Letcher urged the assembled, as he had urged
them a year before, to call a convention of all the states to confront the
"vile spirit of faction" that was growing throughout the country. The "ties
of brotherhood" have been severed, he declared, "the sections seem to be as
hostile . . . as if their citizens belonged to unfriendly governments." Ever
the moderate, Letcher believed that peace could be attained, even at this
late date, through compromise and the consideration of amendments to the
United States Constitution. The necessity for amendments to correct the
imbalance created by the election of Abraham Lincoln was "manifest." "Is it
not monstrous," he asked, "to see a Government like ours destroyed, merely
because men cannot agree about a domestic institution?"

Letcher, a native Virginian from the Shenandoah Valley and a slave owner
himself, had advocated the separation of western Virginia from the rest of
Virginia and the gradual emancipation of slaves west of the Blue Ridge
during the late 1840s. Letcher's interest at the time was in forcing concessions for western Virginia from the tidewater-dominated general assembly
and seems to have been driven by simple political expediency. In 1850, he
publicly recanted his antislavery notions and was elected to Congress in 1851.
Letcher spent most of the next decade in Washington supporting southern
rights but never calling for secession, always favoring compromise and restraint over bombast. On January 1, 1860, he assumed the governorship of

the state and, as a conditional Unionist, supported the candidacy of north-ern Democrat Stephen A. Douglas for president.[31] Now, during January of 1861, this complicated man was attempting to mediate a solution to the crisis brought on by Lincoln's election.

The Northern people, he maintained, hated the institution of slavery and "assailed" it "through the press, in the pulpit, in public meetings." Letcher's list of grievances focused on the failure of the northern states to abide by the Fugitive Slave Act of 1850, on the North's commitment to prevent slavery from expanding into the territories—to "confine slavery within its present limits"—and on its efforts to abolish slavery in the District of Columbia.

The governor's solution to the "systematic and persistent warfare upon the institution of slavery" consisted of an amendment to the Constitution with six parts. The first three dealt with the issues of fugitive slaves, the protection of slavery in the District of Columbia and the territories, and the right of transit for owners and their slaves through free states and territories. The unimpeded transportation of slaves under any and all circumstances was important enough to Letcher that he also included a specific article to guarantee the safe "transmission of slaves between the slaveholding States, either by land or water." A fifth clause aimed at the suppression of organized efforts like John Brown's raid on Harpers Ferry to "assail the slaveholding States, and to excite slaves to insurrection." Finally, Letcher suggested that the federal government be deprived of the authority to appoint officials to southern offices who might be "hostile" to the institutions of the South. The governor specified that he intended this section to prevent federal appointees from sowing "the seed of strife and dissension between the slaveholding and non-slaveholding classes in the Southern States." Letcher, like a growing number of White southerners, was sensitive to any threat that might create divisions between the slave-owning elite and non-slave-owners. It would be a "most serious mistake" on the part of the "fanatics in the Northern States," the governor lectured, to assume that nonslaveholders were not loyal to the South and "would not willingly defend the institution" of slavery.[32]

Such were the constitutional guarantees for the institution of slavery re-quired by a southern moderate. A Unionist at heart, Letcher believed that no honor would be lost if the North would simply agree with his terms for settlement. "We ask nothing, therefore, which is not clearly right, and necessary for our protection." Moderate or not, Letcher understood, as did other southern officeholders, that the issue at hand revolved around protecting slavery from the "fanatics" in the North.

Twelve days after Letcher's address, Virginia's general assembly passed a resolution inviting all states — "slaveholding and non-slaveholding" — to gather in Washington, DC, in an effort to "adjust the present unhappy controversies." Finally approving the governor's call for a national convention, the Virginia legislature additionally suggested, with only slight modifications, that the amendment earlier proposed by John J. Crittenden for the protection of slavery would be acceptable to "the people of this commonwealth." On December 18, 1860, Senator Crittenden of Kentucky had introduced a constitutional amendment designed to settle the secession crisis. Crittenden's "compromise" measure consisted of six articles that would have protected slavery in the New Mexico Territory, but prohibited the institution north of it; protected slavery in the District of Columbia and federal installations in the South; strengthened the Fugitive Slave Act; precluded Congress from interfering with the transit of slaves with their owners through non-slave states; and significantly, prevented Congress from interfering with slavery in any of the fifteen slave states.[33] Specifically, the legislature required that Crittenden's first article dividing the western territories along the 36°30' parallel be applied to all territory "now held or hereafter acquired" south of said line. The phrase had been a part of Crittenden's original proposal, but a number of other suggested amendments limited the division to the present territory of the United States. Democratic Virginians were all too aware that the 1860 platforms of both the Douglas and Breckinridge wings of the party had declared the acquisition of Cuba a high priority, and they didn't want to have the "slavery in the territories" argument all over again. With the memory of the Lemmon Slave Case still fresh, the second stipulation aimed at affirming Crittenden's fourth article securing "to owners of slaves the right of transit with their slaves between and through the non-slaveholding states and territories."[34] (It might be perceived as a bit odd that the general assembly favored the Kentucky senator's resolutions over its own governor's, but in truth, the Crittenden amendment was more extensive, more specific, and better conceptualized than Letcher's.)

The resulting Washington Peace Conference, as it came to be called, deliberated from February 4 until the twenty-seventh with representatives of twenty-one states in attendance. The seven Deep South states that had seceded, or were in the process of seceding, did not send representatives; California, Oregon, Minnesota, Michigan, and Wisconsin (for various reasons) also failed to send delegates, as did Arkansas. With the preponderance of delegates representing states that had voted for Lincoln, the gathering was decidedly pro-Union with the Border South representatives interested in finding some sort of constitutional middle ground.

It was an august group that assembled at Willard's Hall in the District of Columbia. Among the 132 delegates were former cabinet members, governors, senators, members of the House of Representatives, ambassadors, and judges. Salmon P. Chase of Ohio, who would soon become Lincoln's secretary of the Treasury, was in attendance as well as Indiana's Caleb B. Smith who was to become Lincoln's secretary of the Interior. Eight of the delegates would later serve in the Confederate Congress, and James A. Seddon from Virginia would become Jefferson Davis's fifth secretary of war. Former president John Tyler, also from Virginia, presided over the convention and, upon its conclusion, became a delegate to the Confederate Provisional Congress in Montgomery. New Hampshire sent the smallest delegation consisting of three members, while Tennessee sent the largest with twelve. Because of the maturity of the members, Horace Greeley, editor of the *New York Tribune*, labeled the gathering the "Old Gentlemen's Convention." While only seven were under forty years of age and seventy-four were aged fifty or over, all were experienced, and none were doddering. It was an important meeting called with all sincerity by Virginia's general assembly.[35]

The conference quickly created a series of committees to expedite its business including a General Committee Upon Proposals to consider formal suggestions for compromise and the settlement of the issues facing the nation. On February 15, delegate James Guthrie of Kentucky reported the findings of the committee in the form of a recommended constitutional amendment consisting of seven parts. It bore similarities to Senator Crittenden's suggested amendment but included several additions. It began, like Crittenden's, by suggesting that the western territory be divided at the Missouri Compromise line of 36°30' with slavery prohibited during the territorial period north of that line and allowed south of it. It also precluded Congress from passing laws that would interfere with the transportation of slaves, slavery in the District of Columbia, or slavery in federal installations located within slaveholding states. And it contained two articles ensuring the return of fugitive slaves or full payment to the owner in those instances when officers were prevented "by violence or intimidation" from arresting a fugitive. Two other provisions allowed for new territory to be acquired only through formal treaties approved by four-fifths of all members of the Senate, and "forever prohibited" the foreign slave trade. To ensure the perpetuity of these articles, the committee, in a variation of Crittenden, suggested that the proposed amendment "shall not be amended or abolished without the consent of all the States."[36] In short, the committee's focus, like Crittenden's, was on the federal protection of slavery.

The committee's proposal promptly drew a negative reaction from Virginia's James Seddon who objected to the committee's amendment because it varied too greatly from John Crittenden's proposal which Virginia had officially established as the basis for the Washington gathering. A graduate of the University of Virginia, Seddon was staunchly proslavery, regretted the outcome of the Compromise of 1850 as harmful to the interests of the South, and secretly hoped for Virginia's secession and the creation of a southern confederacy. A decade before the war he had owned a mansion on Clay Street in Richmond that would later become the White House of the Confederacy. After Virginia's secession, he would become a delegate to the Confederate Provisional Congress and later secretary of war.[37]

To return the debate to Crittenden's original amendment, Seddon reintroduced the Crittenden resolutions "with modifications suggested by Virginia." The Seddon/Virginia amendment repeated the Crittenden proposal but embellished it in two places. To Crittenden's fourth article, Seddon added language strengthening the right of slave owners to transport slaves "from one slaveholding State or Territory to another." Seddon, like so many other southern statesmen, was aware of the Lemmon Slave Case and the importance of preventing slaves from being taken from their owners as they were being transported through free states and territories. The second modification added a seventh article which read, "The elective franchise and the right to hold office, whether Federal, State, territorial, or municipal, shall not be exercised by persons who are, in whole or in part, of the African race."[38] Although preserving and protecting the institution of slavery clearly formed the core of secessionist thought and rhetoric, the maintenance of white supremacy outside the bounds of slavery was equally important.[39]

Ultimately, the Washington Peace Conference approved an amendment not too dissimilar from the one introduced by James Guthrie on February 15. It reestablished the Missouri Compromise line (but without the "now held, or hereafter acquired" phrase); specified precisely how new territory would be acquired; and protected slavery in states where it already existed, in the District of Columbia, and in federal installations within slaveholding states. Evoking the Lemmon Slave Case, it established the "right of transportation" of slaves from one state or territory to another, strengthened requirements for the return of fugitive slaves, and qualified Crittenden's prohibition on future Congresses amending or abolishing the listed amendments by providing that such amending could only be accomplished with "the consent of all the States."[40] After deliberating for nineteen days, the "Old Gentlemen" in Washington had not contributed meaningfully to solving the nation's crisis.

When John Tyler transmitted the approved amendment to the United States Senate on February 27, it provoked considerable resistance. While John Crittenden embraced the Peace Conference amendment, procedurally substituted it for his own, and called it the "best hope of an adjustment," others were not so sanguine.[41] Senator James Green of Missouri labeled the amendment the "merest twaddle that ever was presented to a thinking people."[42] Senator Joseph Lane of Oregon, and recent running mate of southern Democrat John C. Breckinridge, branded the seven articles developed in Washington a "cheat," a "deception," and a "fraud." Virginia representative Shelton F. Leake labeled it a "miserable abortion," while Essex County's Muscoe Garnett viewed it as "conceived in fraud, and born of cowardice."[43]

The last days of the second session of the Thirty-Sixth Congress were fairly chaotic. Members had debated for three months with nothing of substance to show for it, and during that time senators and representatives from seven states had withdrawn from Congress as their states had withdrawn from the Union. Federal property in the form of forts, arsenals, custom houses, and the United States mint in New Orleans had all been seized by state militias.[44] Many anticipated a civil war but were unsure exactly how incoming president Abraham Lincoln would deal with the seceded states and the capture of federal property throughout the South. Emotions had reached the breaking point in a political atmosphere described by one delegate as "madness."[45] With only minor differences between the Peace Conference's amendment and Senator Crittenden's, southern reaction focused on the absence of the phrase "now held, or hereafter acquired" in the article dealing with slavery in the western territory. While Crittenden's wording would allow slavery in any future territory acquired from Mexico or Cuba, the Peace Convention's construction of the 36°30' line would apply only to existing territory held by the United States. The acquisition of any future territory would need the concurrence of a majority of senators from both slaveholding and nonslaveholding states. In such an environment, minor differences of interpretation led to major differences in political positions and rhetoric.

The point of conflict in the Peace Conference amendment was, once again, the status of slavery in the western territories. Rigid Republicans, in accordance with their 1860 platform, could not conceive of voting for an amendment that allowed slavery in any part of the territories. Diehard Democrats could not conceive of voting for an amendment that prevented them from moving with their slaves into any part of the territories as the *Dred Scott* decision decreed. Moderates on both sides argued for a settlement along the Missouri Compromise line. The acceptance of slavery below 36°30' latitude (for Republicans) and a prohibition on slavery north of 36°30' latitude (for Democrats), while a bitter pill, was preferable to secession and war. At the end of the day, compromise on this amendment failed for two reasons. First, it was defeated because, unlike John Crittenden's proposal, it did not protect all future territorial acquisitions south of the 36°30' line. Secondly, it failed because too many southerners agreed with Virginia's Senator Robert M. T. Hunter who argued that the Peace Conference amendment would place the South "in a far worse position than they now occupy under the present Constitution. . . ."[46] The United States Supreme Court, explained Hunter, had decided that slave owners had a constitutional right to "carry their slaves into any Territory of the United States."[47] Any departure from that decision, at least for Hunter and most White southerners, was unthinkable. Only hours before Lincoln's inauguration, the Senate resoundingly defeated the amendment developed by the Washington Peace Conference by a vote of 28 to 7, while three days earlier (March 1) the House of Representative had declined even to receive the proposal.[48]

Adding protections for slavery in the Constitution during the last month of the Thirty-Sixth Congress, after the departure of Democratic senators and representatives from seven states, was out of the question for Republicans who then controlled both houses. The only concession they were willing to make was to approve an amendment proposed by Ohio representative Thomas Corwin (Republican) regarding slavery where it already existed. "No amendment shall be made to the Constitution," it read, "which will authorize or give to Congress the power to abolish or interfere, within any State, with the domestic institutions thereof, including that of persons held to labor or service by the laws of said State." Prohibiting Congress from interfering with slavery in the states had been included earlier in twenty-seven suggested amendments beginning with Virginia representative Shelton Farrar Leake's on December 12, 1860. Thomas Corwin borrowed the language in his compromise proposal from Republican senator William H. Seward who had proposed such protections on Christmas Eve 1860. Having been earlier approved by the House, the amendment earned a favorable Senate vote during the early hours of March 4—only minutes before the Senate rejected the Washington Peace Conference amendment.[49] In the face of charges that its party was dominated by abolitionists, the Republican constitutional guarantee that slavery in fifteen states could not be constrained in any way by Congress served as a clear corrective. A few hours after the Senate approved the Seward/Corwin amendment, President Lincoln referred to it in his Inaugural Address stating he had "no objection to its being made express, and irrevocable."[50]

Efforts to find a political compromise satisfactory to Virginians found greater success in the state's convention. A week after Governor Letcher delivered his state of the state address on January 7, the General Assembly authorized a popular referendum to elect delegates to a convention that would, in turn, determine Virginia's response to Lincoln's election and the subsequent departure of South Carolina, Mississippi, and Florida. Held on February 4, the same day the Washington Peace Conference began its deliberations, the election's results favored remaining in the Union by almost a 2 to 1 majority. Historian William Link has observed that of "the 152 delegates elected, no more than fifty were secessionists, and the overwhelming majority were either conditional or unconditional Unionists."[51] The Unionist bent of the convention was clearly reflected in its selection of a moderate Whig from Fauquier County, John Janney, as its president by a vote of 70 to 54.[52] That moderate or pro-Union majority would control the convention for most of its deliberations until the guns in Charleston Harbor altered the equation.

Virginia's convention was unique among the slave-state secession conventions in that its delegates debated longer than any other and left a more extensive record of its deliberations—over three thousand pages. The gathering convened on February 13 and did not vote for secession until April 17, a few days after the surrender of Fort Sumter. It was, in many ways, similar to the Washington Peace Conference that Virginia had sponsored, in that it was filled with many, varied, and conflicting opinions.[53]

Once Virginia established a date for its convention, Mississippi, Georgia, and South Carolina appointed commissioners to attend and persuade (they hoped) the delegates to favor secession. Fulton Anderson from Mississippi was the first to address the convention on February 18. Voicing concern for events that might happen rather than those that had happened, Commissioner Anderson spoke of the "infidel fanaticism" in the North that taught "hatred and contempt of us and our institutions." Perceiving president-elect Lincoln as an abolitionist aided and abetted by an antislavery Republican Party, Anderson announced that Mississippi had avoided the "irrepressible conflict" between slavery and free labor by "placing our institutions beyond the reach of further hostility."[54]

Georgian Henry Lewis Benning immediately followed Anderson to the podium. An avowed secessionist, Benning would later serve in the Confederate Army as a brigadier general. More direct in his remarks than Anderson, Benning reiterated the notion that the North hated slavery, considering it a "sin and a crime" and that secession was "the only thing that could prevent the abolition of her slavery." Although the 1860 Republican platform declared that states had the constitutional right to support slavery, Benning lectured that northern politicians were dead set on abolishing slavery throughout the country. When that day came, "the black race will be in a large majority, and then we will have black governors, black legislators, black juries, black everything." Warming to even greater hyperbole, Benning continued: "But that is not all of the Abolition war. We will be completely exterminated, and the land will be left in possession of the blacks, and then it will go back into a wilderness and become another Africa or St. Domingo."[55] Political prevarication has a long history.

John Smith Preston was the last of the commissioners to speak. A graduate of Hampden-Sydney College, the University of Virginia, and Harvard University, Preston had been born into a prestigious Virginia family and had married into one of the wealthiest South Carolina families. In his appeal for Virginia to join the Confederacy, he continued the theme of northern opposition to the South's favored institution. "For thirty years or more," he raged, "the people of the Northern States have assailed the institution of African slavery." "African slavery cannot exist at the North. The South cannot exist without African slavery. [Applause.] None but an equal race can labor at the North; none but a subject race will labor at the South."[56]

Anderson, Benning, and Preston all offered passionate and emotional orations to the assembled delegates in hopes of convincing them to deliver Virginia into the Confederate orbit. Like the dozens of other commissioners sent to persuade recalcitrant states to secede and join the Confederate ranks, they conjured up a future dominated by fanatical Republicans who were focused only on the abolition of slavery. Historian Charles Dew has analyzed the speeches and letters of forty-one of the fifty-two secession commissioners and concluded that they collectively argued that the impending abolition of slavery would lead to racial equality and the certain loss of white supremacy. "To put it quite simply, Dew writes, "slavery and race were absolutely critical elements in the coming of the war." William L. Harris, a commissioner from Mississippi to Georgia, could not have been clearer: "She [Mississippi] had rather see the last of her race, men, women and children, immolated in one common funeral pile, than see them subjected to the degradation of civil, political and social equality with the negro race."[57] In spite of the zealousness displayed by the three commissioners, the convention remained pro-Union — at least for a while.

Like all of the border states (with the exception of Delaware), Virginia possessed a mountainous region not dominated by the institution of slavery. Delegates who represented the western, highland portion of the Commonwealth were much less inclined to separate from the Union than their counterparts representing tidewater Virginia. The western voices in Virginia's convention minimized the importance of Lincoln's perceived threat to the institution of slavery in the states. John Baldwin, from Augusta County, for example, feared that the South had "gotten into the habit of exaggerating, grossly exaggerating, the importance of the Executive office."[58] Others, like Sherrard Clemens from Wheeling, believed that slavery was simply safer in the Union than out of it. Clemens correctly defined the territorial issue as the one which divided the "North and South at this moment" but considered secession wrongheaded. If the southern states all left the Union, where, he asked, "is slavery to expand?" "You will never extort by treaty . . . the same guarantees that you now have in this Constitution. . . ."[59] Delegates like Waitman T. Willey, John S. Carlisle, and Chapman J. Stuart insisted that far from being the solution, secession would lead to the end of slavery.[60] If the Union were dissolved, Carlisle asserted presciently, slavery "would not exist in Virginia five years after the separation."[61]

Voices from the slaveholding sections of Virginia, on the other hand, constructed arguments similar to those from the Deep South. The North, according to those members of the convention, was dominated by abolitionists who would not rest until the institution of slavery had been purged from the country. The election of 1860, they argued, had destroyed the equality of the states through the election of a minority president who had received no votes in ten slaveholding states.[62] Because the Republican Party opposed the extension of slavery into the territories, southern constitutional rights, as defined by the Taney court, were being denied. The South was being controlled by a Republican majority "without law and without limit."[63] James W. Sheffey, from Smyth County, argued that sectional peace would not return until northern attitudes against slavery were reformed. Public sentiment in the North must be "revolutionized." Northern men, he enjoined, meaning northern Democrats, must rise up and "crush out the spirit of fanaticism and of abolitionism." That fell spirit had alienated the two sections of the country, "subverted" the federal government, and "brought us now to the very verge of an awful civil war."[64] For delegate John R. Chambliss, of Greensville and Sussex Counties, the issue was clear. The election of Abraham Lincoln by a sectional majority was a "standing menace to the South—a direct assault upon her institutions."[65]

Thomas F. Goode, of Mecklenburg County, was even more hyperbolic. The South, he argued three weeks after Lincoln's inauguration, was confronted by a "sectional, northern, dominate party" whose guiding principle was "hostility to the social organization of the Southern States." The threat for Goode could not have been more real. "We have an Abolitionist at the head of the Government. . . . We have Abolitionists sent as ministers to foreign courts. We have Abolitionists at the head of all the important committees in the Senate of the United States. We have Abolitionists in all the subordinate Departments of the Government." If Virginia stayed in the Union, Goode prophesied, Virginians would become "the mere serfs and bondsmen of a Northern Government."[66] In light of these calamitous predictions, numerous delegates agreed with William H. Macfarland, from Richmond, that "nothing less" than constitutional amendments that "pledge anew the faith of the Confederacy to the South . . . can or ought to satisfy Virginia."[67]

Virginia's convention delegates who favored constitutional amendments were aware of earlier proposals to do just that. Governor John Letcher's address to the General Assembly on February 8 and James Seddon's extensive proposal to the Washington Peace Conference on February 26 had already set the amendment wheels in motion in Virginia. By the time the Virginia convention got down to the serious business of designing compromise solutions, four amendments had been proposed in Congress by Virginia's representatives. In early December 1860, Sheldon Farrar Leake, an Independent Democrat from Charlottesville, offered an amendment to the House of Representatives that lightly echoed Senator Jefferson Davis's resolutions from earlier in the year.[68] Leake's suggested amendment denied any authority of Congress over slavery in the territories except to protect the institution, disallowed any territorial authority from regulating slavery, and emphasized the importance of returning fugitive slaves. In addition, Leake offered an article that protected the property rights of owners traveling through any state or territory with their slaves.[69]

On the same day, December 12, 1860, another representative of Virginia offered a very different proposal for amending the Constitution. Albert Gallatin Jenkins, a resident of far western Virginia, near Huntington, suggested a constitutional amendment that would provide for "better security of the rights of slaveholders in the common territories." More importantly, Jenkins was interested in determining what "constitutional checks" would be needed to ensure the self-preservation of the slaveholding states "against the operation of the Federal Government." With an incoming president "avowedly" hostile to the institution of slavery, Jenkins wondered whether equality for the South might be achieved through the creation of a "dual Executive," or through a division of the Senate into two parts, or by requiring "a majority of Senators from both the slaveholding and non-slaveholding States necessary to all action on the part of that body."[70] Jenkins's proposal was one of a handful of suggested amendments that would have redesigned the structure of the federal government in order to achieve concessions for the slaveholding states. Jenkins, a graduate of Harvard Law School, would shortly be elected to the First Confederate Congress. Resigning from that body in August of 1862, he secured an appointment as a brigadier general in the Confederate Army and was mortally wounded two years later in southern Virginia.[71]

Robert Mercer Taliaferro Hunter had represented Virginia in the United States Senate since 1847 and although he was a champion of states' rights, he was also known for his moderation and pragmatism. During the lengthy debate during January of 1860 in Congress over John Brown's raid on Harpers Ferry, Hunter had staked out political ground as both a pro-Union and proslavery advocate. He observed to his fellow senators that the various geographical sections all contributed differently to the health and welfare of the nation. These various interests, he argued, "are not hostile and rival, but subsidiary," indeed they "mutually contribute to the support of each other." In his oratorical efforts making the case for the interdependence of the northeastern, northwestern, and southern states, Hunter constructed the simile of a "mighty arch" wherein the mutual support of its parts sustained a "social superstructure . . . unparalleled in the history of man." Was it not obvious, Hunter inquired, that the keystone of the arch consisted of "the black marble block of African slavery?" Was it not strange, he continued, that the institution of slavery—the glue that held society together—had been the object of "continual and persistent warfare for more than forty years."[72]

A year later, as Congress was trying to deal with the implications of Lincoln's election and the secession of four states, Hunter again addressed the Senate, this time in an attempt to forge a satisfactory compromise. On the same day that Alabama's convention voted in favor of secession, Hunter expressed no surprise that states were leaving the Union in the face of a political party that had waged "regular warfare upon the system of slavery in the South." Republicans, he explained, denied that slaves were property and maintained that the federal government was bound not only to prevent its expansion, but also to "abolish and suppress it" to the extent allowed under the Constitution.

Reflecting the concerns found in most amendments proposed by slave-state delegates, Hunter's solution to the threat posed by the incoming Lincoln administration came in the form of a constitutional amendment of seven parts designed to protect the "social system of the South." The amendment held that Congress had no power to abolish slavery in the states, in the District of Columbia, or in any of the federal installations located in slave states; nor did Congress have the authority to "abolish, tax, or obstruct" the slave trade between the states. Other "guarantees" for the protection of slavery dealt with the return of fugitive slaves, the suppression of armed invasions of southern states (like John Brown's), and the recognition and protection of slavery specifically "within the Territories, dock-yards, forts and arsenals of the United States, and wherever the United States has exclusive jurisdiction."[73] Following the failure of compromise and Virginia's secession, Hunter became Jefferson Davis's second secretary of state and later spent most of the war as one of Virginia's delegates to the Confederate Congress.[74]

Just days before Lincoln's inauguration, Representative Sherrard Clemens became the fourth member of Virginia's congressional delegation to suggest a constitutional amendment. A moderate Democrat from Wheeling, Clemens introduced his proposal by observing that "serious and alarming dissensions" had arisen between the northern and southern states concerning the rights of the slaveholding states, especially their rights to emigrate into the territories with their slaves. Clemens, who opposed secession, then introduced an amendment consisting of seven articles that was almost identical to James B. Clay's resolution proposed in the Washington Peace Conference the day before. Using language that varied only slightly from Clay's (and John Crittenden's December 18 amendment), Clemens reiterated the Kentucky senator's six original articles and added a seventh article that prohibited those of the African race from voting or holding office. The Virginia representative included, as had Clay and Crittenden, a provision declaring that Congress could not prevent "officers of the Federal Government, or members of Congress" from bringing their slaves into the nation's capital "during the time their duties may require them to remain there."[75]

On March 9, 1861, Robert Young Conrad, representing Frederick County in Virginia's convention and serving as chair of its Committee on Federal Relations, presented the committee's report to his fellow delegates in Richmond. Conrad spelled out the issues facing the country as he and the members of the committee envisioned them. He propounded the idea that the states had been sovereign at the time of the formation of the Constitution and that the federal government must "respect the rights of the States and the equality of the [White] people thereof." Slavery was a vital part of the social system of the southern states, he observed, and the election of a president who entertains "opinions and avow[s] purposes hostile" to the institution places the South in a position of inferiority. The western territories, he continued, constituted a trust to be administered for the "common benefit" of all the people of the United States, and the ownership of federal forts and arsenals located within slaveholding states clearly reverted to the states upon their departure from the Union. To fortify and use them to enforce federal authority was "a perversion of the purposes for which they were obtained." Conrad then proposed that the United States Constitution should be amended wherever "defects" have been found "to restore the Union and preserve confidence." The report concluded with a call for a convention of all the slave states remaining in the Union to meet in Frankfort, Kentucky, in two months.[76]

Almost immediately, former governor Henry Alexander Wise gained the floor to offer a minority report. Wise, the dominant player in the convention, has been described by historian Nelson Lankford as the most active and influential delegate in Richmond. "No one spoke as much," Lankford observes, "evoked as much laughter from the delegates and from the galleries, or won as much attention."[77] For Wise, the majority report was much too tepid, too general. Wise's interpretation of current events was much more direct. For many years, he pronounced, the property of southern citizens had been "assailed and endangered," the Constitution had been "broken," federal laws had been nullified with respect to the protection of property in slaves, the "domestic tranquility and social safety" of the southern states had been "ruthlessly disturbed by actual invasion," and the character of southerners had been "maligned and misrepresented to the world." These "wrongs," he noted, were perpetrated by the federal government, by the nonslaveholding states, and by the people of the North. (Like many secessionists, Wise inflated the historical importance of John Brown's raid and conflated the positions taken by Republicans and abolitionists in order to condemn generally "the people of the North.") By all indications, the country was being threatened "by an unnatural and unnecessary civil war."[78] Wise then listed fifteen points of "difference and dissension" that needed to be addressed not only by "Constitutional amendments . . . but by grants of power to check abuses or wrongs by the majority of the States."[79]

By the time Wise addressed Virginia's delegates in early March, over fifty proposals to amend the Constitution had been suggested in various political venues discussing secession, so his long list of issues was generously comprehensive. He began with an item seeking the "full recognition of the rights of property in African slaves" and ended with one that addressed the suppression of "all organizations" seeking to "incite domestic violence in any of the States or Territories of the United States." In between, he covered issues relating to the protection of slavery in federal installations in the South, the return of fugitive slaves, and, ever mindful of the implications of the Lemmon Slave Case, the transit of slaves with their owners through free states and territories. Concerned that the presidential appointment of federal judges, especially by non-Democratic presidents, might ultimately lead to the appointment of justices hostile to slavery, he suggested that the "mode of appointing the Federal Judges" be changed. Three of his "points" dealt with the suppression of "incendiary assemblages, associations and publications" that threatened the security of the institution of slavery. Even though acutely aware of the failure of the Washington Peace Conference, Wise concluded his address with a plea for a convention of the states remaining in the Union to meet for the purpose of adjusting the aforementioned list of differences and dissensions. In the meantime, the federal government should avoid any acts that might "irritate the causes of civil war," and withdraw all forces from forts, arsenals, dock yards and other federal installations located in the South.[80] Like everyone else in the country, Wise was actively watching the events developing at Fort Sumter in Charleston Harbor.

Ten days after Wise's challenge to the majority report of the Committee on Federal Relations, Robert Y. Conrad presented to his colleagues "Virginia's propositions of amendments to the Constitution, combining . . . all the advantageous features of both of Virginia's schemes that have hitherto been before the public mind." Blending Wise's points with the original offering of the committee, Conrad's new proposal came in the appearance of a formal amendment to the Constitution—a prospective Thirteenth Amendment—consisting of eight sections. Like fifty-nine other such proposals by southern Democrats, the committee's amendment led with an article that regulated slavery in the territories. As John Crittenden had earlier proposed, it divided New Mexico and Utah along the 36°30' parallel with slavery prohibited above and permitted below. Filling the void perceived in the Washington Peace Conference's amendment, Conrad's committee announced that in any territory which may be acquired in the future, slavery would be prohibited north of the line but "shall not be prohibited" south of it. Section 2 specified that new territories would only be acquired for "naval and commercial stations, depots and transit routes" and only by a majority vote of slave-state senators and a majority vote of the non-slave-state senators. The committee also denied Congress the authority to legislate against slavery in any state or territory where it already existed, to interfere with slavery in the District of Columbia or in federal installations in slave states, to interfere with the return of fugitive slaves, or the transit of slaves with their owners. Another section prohibited the "importation of slaves, coolies, or persons held to service . . . from places beyond the limits" of the United States or its territories. The final three sections provided that the United States would pay the full value of fugitive slaves whose return was prevented by "violence or intimidation from mobs," that African Americans would not be allowed to exercise the "elective franchise or the right to hold office," and that none of the previous articles could be "amended or abolished without the consent of all the States."[81]

Once the convention absorbed the committee's formal proposal for an amendment to the United States Constitution, three delegates—Robert H. Turner representing Warren County, Henry A. Wise (again), and William L. Goggin from Bedford County—found it lacking and proposed amendments of their own. For Turner, the committee's version was not sufficiently explicit. He insisted that Virginia speak in "language which cannot be misunderstood, demanding the rights to which she is entitled," that the convention issue nothing less than an "ultimatum" to the states remaining in the Union and "demand guarantees for her future safety." Turner's proposed amendment covered the same ground as Conrad's formal proposal, but within twelve short rather than eight elaborate sections. He also included two points not included in the committee's offering. Turner believed that the seceded states had left not only because of threats to the institution of slavery, but also because of "a question of tariff." To prevent Congress from enacting exorbitant tariffs, Turner suggested a majority of senators from the slaveholding states as well as a majority of those from the non-slaveholding states be required on all "questions relating to the laying taxes, duties, imposts, and excises." Turner's amendment was one of only two (out of a national total of sixty-eight) proposals to amend the Constitution that included references to excessive "imposts" or tariffs. The other substantive change suggested by Turner stated that "Congress shall have no power to interfere with the slave trade between the States."[82]

The irrepressible Henry A. Wise was equally dissatisfied with the committee's suggested amendment and made a last attempt at crafting one that he believed touched on all the salient points of the debate. So far, former governor Wise was the only Virginian to suggest an amendment that would explicitly nationalize slavery. In this his second attempt to find the right wording, he reconstituted his earlier proposal into nine expansive articles, while even more emphatically emphasizing the importance of protecting slavery through the United States Constitution. He began by dealing with slavery in the territories, but instead of dividing the Mexican Cession along the 36°30' parallel, Wise returned to the opinion of Chief Justice Roger B. Taney that slavery could not be prevented from moving into any part of the existing federal territory north or south of the traditional line of demarcation. Harking back to Jefferson Davis's resolutions of early 1860 and John C. Breckenridge's platform during the election, he argued that slavery must not only be allowed in all the territory, but also protected "as other rights, and be subject to judicial cognizance in the Federal Courts." As with Crittenden, however, Wise allowed that any states formed from the territories would be admitted with or without slavery as the "Constitution of the State may provide." In his most direct departure from the committee's language, Wise insisted that property in slaves be protected under the "due process" clause of the Fifth Amendment. The right of property in slaves, he submitted, "shall be recognized and protected by the United States and their authorities as the rights of other property" are protected.[83] Wise, like Jefferson Davis, wanted slavery protected at the federal, not state, level.[84]

While Wise's amendment covered much of the same ground as the committee's version, he recast the language in places to put a sharper point on the issues. To the committee's fifth article dealing with the prohibition on the "importation of slaves, coolies," and others from outside the limits of the United States, Wise added a sentence allowing the slave trade between the United States and "Southern States which have declared, or may hereafter declare, their separation" from the Union.[85] The former governor wanted to ensure that if Virginia did secede it could continue to engage in the slave trade with Kentucky and Missouri, and if it did not secede that it would not be prohibited from selling slaves to states that had seceded.[86] And to the committee's sixth article prohibiting "persons of the African race" from voting or holding elective office, Wise added two sentences. The first echoed the *Dred Scott* decision that "under the Constitution of the United States" persons of the African race were not entitled "to the privileges and immunities of citizens in the several States." The second sentence directly prohibited states from passing "any laws establishing equality of the African with the white race within their limits."[87] For Wise, like most Democrats, north and south, it was as important to maintain white supremacy as it was to protect the institution of slavery. In proposing these clauses, he affirmed his belief that state laws protecting slavery were constitutional while state laws that allowed free African Americans some semblance of equality of access to democratic principles should be unconstitutional. In the debates over slavery and secession, the ideal of states' rights had clear limits for some southern Whites.

William Leftwich Goggin, a delegate from Bedford County, approached secession from a very different angle. His amendment, offered on April 4th, began by formally announcing Virginia's secession from the United States. Virginia was no longer "one of the Union of States known as the United States of America," and the people of Virginia "owe no allegiance or duty to any Government whatever." Goggin provided, however, for a possible reconciliation with the United States through an amendment to the Constitution that would provide "suitable and sure guarantees." Those guarantees must include a "full and unconditional, plain and positive recognition of the rights of property in slaves," the preservation of slavery in the District of Columbia, and protection of slavery in the territories and various other places throughout the country. He provided for the right of transit for owners with their slaves through "any of the States by land or water," and "for protection against unjust taxation in the form of excessive imposts laid upon foreign importations."[88] Over the course of Secession Winter, Goggin's reference to "imposts" marked only the second time any elected official included protection from excessive tariffs in any of the more than five dozen proposed amendments to the Constitution.

While there were many who participated in Virginia's convention who believed the crisis before the nation could be solved by amending the Constitution, there were also many who did not. James Barbour representing Culpeper County was one of those. At thirty-seven years old in early 1861,

Barbour was a former Unionist who by late March had become an ardent secessionist. Two weeks before the surrender of Fort Sumter, this representative of Virginia's piedmont spoke at length in favor of joining the southern confederacy in Montgomery and against further attempts to find solutions in amendments to the Constitution. Labeling the Lincoln administration that "Abolition Government at Washington," Barbour argued that while constitutional solutions might have worked early in the crisis, with seven states already gone, proposals like John Crittenden's would be "utterly impotent to dissolve that Government in Montgomery." Barbour asked the members of the convention would they not be blind to believe that "by sticking into your Constitution some of these little paper amendments," those southern seven would renounce their "independent Empire" and return to the "oppression from which they successfully, manfully walked away?"[89] For the next two weeks, a majority of the delegates continued to hold out hope for compromise through a constitutional amendment. That confidence was bolstered on April 4, when Delegate Lewis Harvie of Amelia County insisted on a referendum on his ordinance of secession. The ordinance was defeated by a vote of 90 to 45. The resounding rejection of secession by a two-to-one margin demonstrated the commitment of the convention to seek a compromise solution until (only a week later) the Confederate guns in Charleston Harbor changed everything.[90]

Having heard and considered the several alternatives to its original proposal to amend the Constitution, the Committee on Federal Relations began considering the specifics of the individual sections on April 12 — only hours after Confederate batteries began the bombardment of Fort Sumter. Having been notified of the drama unfolding to the south, the delegates quickly approved the first three sections largely as Robert Conrad had presented them on March 19.

After the first three sections had been approved, former governor Henry Wise, recognizing that the committee's amendment did not protect slavery in any universal way, proposed the adoption of language identical to the provision introduced by him on March 29. Cast in the form of "just compensation" for slaves taken during time of war, the more direct intent of Wise's proposal was to link property in slaves to all other kinds of private property. If slave property was recognized and protected under the Constitution, as "rights to any other property are recognized and protected," then the ownership of slaves would be fully safeguarded by federal authority. Without discussion, the convention immediately adopted the provision to nationalize slavery. At two o'clock on the afternoon of April 13, the persistent Mr. Wise achieved what he had originally proposed a month earlier—acceptance by Virginia's convention of a proposal to amend the United States Constitution to recognize and protect the right of property in slaves.[91]

After a two-hour break, the delegates reconvened to consider the next section of the committee's amendment which would have strengthened the fugitive slave clause in the Constitution. It, too, was adopted without discussion.[92] The gathering then turned to the section that prohibited the importation of "slaves, coolies, and persons held to service or labor." As the debate commenced and the convention considered alternative language, John Janney, president of the convention, interrupted the discussion to read a dispatch from South Carolina's governor announcing the latest developments at Fort Sumter. "Our shells fall freely in the Fort," he quoted from the governor's letter, the barrage being so intense that the troops within will have "no peace, night or day." Fort Sumter will shortly fall: "the war is commenced, and we will triumph or perish."[93] All efforts to gain concessions for Virginia and other slaveholding states immediately ceased, and four days later the delegates adopted (by a vote of 90 to 55) an ordinance of secession that charged the federal government with perverting its powers "not only to the injury of the people of Virginia, but to the oppression of the Southern slaveholding States."[94]

The decision to separate from the United States came as secessionists throughout the state were becoming more vocal and aggressive. In late March, the spirited and calculating Henry Wise organized an extralegal "Spontaneous Southern Rights" assembly (also termed the People's Spontaneous Convention) with the goal of pressuring the convention toward disunion. A date of April 16 had been set for Virginia's secessionists to gather in Richmond. The Confederate attack on Fort Sumter and, more specifically, Lincoln's call for 75,000 troops to quell the rebellion, however, compelled Wise to delay the assembly.[95] It was, in fact, the president's request for "the militia of the several states of the Union" that altered the balance in the convention. The federal "coercion" secessionists had been expecting, and predicting, for months had finally arrived. The convention delegates' secession vote rendered Wise's popular attempt to influence them moot. The hoped for result, however, had been achieved, but the serious work of separation remained to be done.

Believing that secession was a weighty issue that should only be decided by the citizens of Virginia, the delegates specified that the ordinance would only take effect when ratified by the White male voters of the state in a referendum scheduled for May 23. But five weeks was a long time for Virginia to be in limbo awaiting the final disunion verdict. Time was of the essence, or so thought former governor Henry Wise. Acting decisively (again!), Wise met secretly with militia units on April 16 and ordered the capture of the federal arsenal at Harpers Ferry and the Gosport Navy Yard at Norfolk. On the following day, Wise showed his hand, announcing to the convention that "there is a probability that blood will be flowing at Harper's Ferry before night" and that the harbor at Norfolk was "obstructed last night by the sinking of vessels."[96] A beleaguered Governor Letcher sanctioned his predecessor's instructions and by April 21, both installations were occupied by Virginia's troops.[97]

A week after the secession vote, to ensure that the state would not remain in the Union, the delegates approved an ordinance uniting Virginia with the Confederate States of America. The directive dictated that "the whole military force and military operations, offensive and defensive, of said Commonwealth, in the impending conflict with the United States, shall be under the chief control and direction of the President of said Confederate States. . . ." Also on April 25, the convention adopted and ratified the Provisional Constitution of the Confederate States of America. Although the ordinance stipulated that it would be null and void if the May 23 election results did not sustain secession, technical niceties were ignored as Virginia formally became the eighth state of the Confederacy on May 7, 1861.[98] To further cement Virginia's fate with the rebellious states, the delegates invited Jefferson Davis to relocate his government to Richmond, an offer approved by the Confederate Congress on May 20.[99] Because of the strategic location of Virginia and rumors of the possible move to Richmond, Confederate troops began moving north. By the third week in May, on the eve of the popular referendum on secession, thousands of armed troops from Texas, Arkansas, South and North Carolina, Georgia, and Mississippi were stationed in Virginia's major cities. The die was cast. As the editor of the Fredericksburg *Christian Banner* observed: "Who is so blind and stupid as not to be able to perceive the whole design at a single glance? The design was, to *awe* Virginia at the point of the bayonet into submission, on the day of the election, to vote for the ratification of the ordinance of secession."[100] On May 23, the White male electors of Virginia approved the ordinance of secession by a vote of 86 to 14 percent.[101]

Virginia's decision to withdraw from the Union had implications for the state that would long outlive the war. Following the conference's vote to secede, dozens of delegates from the northwestern section of the state fled Richmond and began organizing political resistance to the Confederacy. John S. Carlile from Clarksburg, one of the thirty-two delegates to vote against secession, and other Virginia Unionists from the northwest, began planning their own secession from the state of Virginia. Conventions in Wheeling in ensuing months denounced the ordinance of secession and formed the loyalist Reorganized Government of Virginia which led, two years later, to Congress admitting West Virginia as the thirty-fifth state.[102]

From mid-December 1860 to early April 1861, elected officials from Virginia attempted to solve the problem of secession by suggesting no fewer than sixteen amendments to the United States Constitution. With the exception of the two references to high tariffs proposed by Robert Turner and William Goggin, the vast majority of the nearly ninety articles (or subsections) found within Virginia's amendments would, if approved and ratified, have protected the institution of slavery throughout the country. When they discussed the problems facing the Union—in Congress, the Washington Peace Conference, and their own state convention—Virginians debated the future of slavery in the United States. Specifically, they considered the degree to which the incoming Republican president would adversely affect the "peculiar institution" and pondered the appropriate political response. Ultimately, after the attack on Fort Sumter and Lincoln's call for troops, Virginians decided to cast their lot with the Confederate States of America.

Forty years after Virginia's convention-delegates decided to secede, Granville Davisson Hall penned a history of the gathering and the subsequent formation of the state of West Virginia as its consequence. A native of northwestern Virginia, Hall witnessed the secession of Virginia from the nation and reported (for the *Wheeling Daily Intelligencer*, in which he later became part owner) on the several conventions that created West Virginia. Writing at the turn of the century—after the South had recouped her political losses, reversed the meaning of the Fourteenth and Fifteenth Amendments for Black citizens throughout the former Confederate states, and had developed an interpretation on the causes of the war that stressed states' rights to the exclusion of slavery—Hall offered his corrective. "Some of the old secessionists at this late day," he wrote, "would like to make the world believe their revolt was solely in vindication of the State sovereignty dogma—dead as that dogma now confessedly is—not in behalf of slavery. . . . But the claim is contradicted by all the facts." "Without going back of 1861," he explained, "it is sufficient to note that every demand on behalf of the South bore the same burden of greater safe-guards for slavery where it existed and the extension of its prerogative into the territories and free States. This pretense insults the public intelligence."[103] Even a cursory review of the secession debates, and the documents Virginia's elected officials produced during the spring of 1861, confirms Hall's explication of secession.

Sources

The political discussions held over Secession Winter were carefully documented in every venue. The debates of the second session of the Thirty-Sixth Congress were captured in the *Congressional Globe* and are easily accessed at: https://memory.loc.gov/ammem/amlaw/lwcglink.html#anchor36. From December 3, 1860, until March 4, 1861, the *Globe* recorded (in two thousand pages) the speeches and debates of United States senators and representatives. The journal of Virginia's state convention which met from February 13 until May 1, 1861, totals three thousand pages presented in four volumes. A searchable version of the convention's proceedings can be found at https://secession.richmond.edu/. Lucius E. Chittenden was a delegate from Vermont to the Washington Peace Conference and became its self-appointed scribe. Chittenden carefully noted the conference's deliberations from February 4 to February 27, 1861, and published the proceedings in 1864. The combined published records of the *Globe*, secession conventions, state legislatures, and the Washington Peace Conference total over nine thousand pages. See bibliography for specific citations of relevant documents.

Editor's Note

Because of the extensive nature of Virginia's secession documents, I have included only the most germane of them. The speeches have been edited to emphasize the salient points of the debate and to omit redundant or incidental material. Instead of simple ellipses, however, I have provided the reader a sense of the omitted material by including explanatory comments within braces, i.e., {}. Many of the documents include brackets in the original to identify individuals or legislative procedures. For clarity, the editor's emendations are therefore included within braces. Some quotes could not be identified. For various reasons, I limited my research to the speeches and proposals of elected officials, and purposely did not include newspaper articles or editorials. The latter have been used effectively in other accounts of secession. Focusing on the words of the senators, representatives, and delegates to the numerous gatherings held over Secession Winter allows an unfiltered examination of the presumptions and reasoning of those ultimately responsible for determining the fate of the nation.

Acknowledgments

Finding, transcribing, and analyzing Virginia's public secession documents has been an interesting and educational journey that, while largely solitary, was not without the assistance of friends. William Eamon assisted with Latin translations, Jane Scott with legal terms, and John Andrews with references to the works of William Shakespeare. Marie Tyler-McGraw and Laura Feller provided most useful comments on an early draft. I am deeply appreciative of the thorough reviews given by William A. Link and Jonathan M. Atkins. Their suggested changes strengthened the manuscript and saved me from several embarrassing mistakes. Scot Danforth and Jonathan Boggs at the University of Tennessee Press have, yet again, served critical roles in bringing my research to the public. I am also deeply appreciative of the staff of the interlibrary loan department at New Mexico State University. Finally, the companionship of Giacomo throughout the effort made the work much more enjoyable.

1

Governor John Letcher's Address to the General Assembly

January 7, 1861

John Letcher (1813–1884) was born in Lexington, Virginia, and briefly attended Washington College (now Washington and Lee University), before setting up his law practice in Lexington. He served as Virginia's governor from 1860 to 1864. His immediate predecessor was Henry Alexander Wise.[1] On January 7, 1861, only South Carolina had broken from the Union, but over the next four days, Mississippi, Florida, and Alabama would follow suit.

A political moderate who had supported Stephen Douglas in the 1860 election, Letcher believed a national convention of all the states was the appropriate response to the secession of South Carolina. Such a gathering, he suggested, should consider the development of constitutional amendments that would protect the institution of slavery from further attack on the part the nonslaveholding states. In introducing his own six-part solution to the secessionist threat that would have protected slavery at the federal level, Letcher counseled that reasonable minds should be able to agree on a peaceful solution to the secession crisis. "Is it not monstrous," he lectured, "to see a government like ours destroyed, merely because men cannot agree about a domestic institution [slavery], which existed at the formation of the government, and which is now recognized by fifteen out of the thirty-three States composing the Union?" Like several of the Border State governors, Letcher expressed irritation that South Carolina would secede without consulting the other slave states.

Gentlemen of the Senate and House of Delegates:

My proclamation, issued on the 15th day of November last, states succinctly the considerations which induced me to convene you in extraordinary session.

Duty, however, requires of me a more detailed exposition of my views upon the subjects therein referred to, as well as the presentation of such recommendations as are demanded by a proper regard for the public interests, and the faithful, prompt and efficient execution of the laws of this great and growing Commonwealth. These views and recommendations will be presented with as much brevity as the extraordinary circumstances of the times will justify.

Entertaining a profound respect for the intelligence, experience and information of the gentlemen constituting the two houses of the General Assembly, I feel that it would be a reflection upon them to accompany each recommendation with an assignment of all the reasons which might be urged in its favor. I will content myself, therefore, with the assignment of a few general reasons in support of my recommendations. You will consider and discuss them, and either adopt or reject them, as your judgment and discretion shall determine. I am responsible to the people, our common constituents, for the recommendations. You are responsible to the same tribunal for the disposition you may make of them.

I regret that I cannot congratulate you on the peace and prosperity, the healthy and flourishing condition of the various branches of business in which our people are so vitally interested, and offer bright and cheering hopes for the future of our country. The times are indeed full of peril and danger, and demand from those who are clothed with representative trusts, coolness, calmness and firmness, united with prudence, wisdom, moderation and patriotism. Indecision or indiscretion, passion or prejudice, heedlessness or recklessness, will precipitate results that may be deplored when too late to be averted. A blunder at such a time is a crime. An error committed now can never, perhaps, be corrected.

With these preliminary remarks, I address myself to the discussion of the most important question that has ever claimed your consideration, and in the determination of which so much of human happiness or misery is involved. I repeat, as applicable to this occasion, the language of Governor Floyd,[2] in his message of January 1833: "Your station is high and responsible;

to you the people will look; nay, do look for security and protection and the maintenance of all the rights of the States. Virginia, the land of our birth, the burial place of our fathers, the peaceful home of our wives and daughters, awaits your decision." The people will review whatever may be done, and the man who fears to trust them, is not a friend to their rights or their safety.

FEDERAL RELATIONS.

The condition of our country at this time excites the most serious fears for the perpetuation of the Union. "Clouds o'erlappingclouds, are weaving o'er our house an evil woof, a fearful canopy."[3] The country is torn by dissension; fierce and angry excitement exhibits itself in all sections; passion and prejudice have taken absolute possession of the minds of the people throughout the land. The vile spirit of faction, "which pollutes the fountain of national honor, and digs the grave of patriotism," shows itself on all sides. Confidence is destroyed; fraternal feeling has been supplanted by intense sectional hate; the spirit of conciliation has been smothered and crushed, and the affections of the people, North and South, East and West, appear to have been entirely withdrawn from their government. The ties of brotherhood have been severed; and though living under the same Constitution, the sections seem to be as hostile, each to the other, as if their citizens belonged to unfriendly governments. Distrust has marred the pleasure of friendship and social intercourse; bitterness and unkindness have crushed out fraternity. Unity of feeling, unity of action is now gone. It is hardly possible for a government to live and flourish under such adverse circumstances. "We must not, however, look mournfully into the past." That is beyond the hope to recall. We must wisely improve the present; correct its errors; reform its abuses; reunite the severed ties of affection, and enkindle anew the fires of patriotism, if we would recover all that has been lost. If this shall be done, a bright and glorious future is yet before us. We should be blessed with power, influence, wealth and prosperity, such as no nation has ever enjoyed in the history of the world. Great as has been our success, as compared with the nations of the earth, heretofore, greater far would it be hereafter.

It is interesting to trace our progress, from the formation of the Constitution up to the present time. The results will be found in the highest degree gratifying to our pride as a people, and immensely important, so far as our power and influence as a nation is concerned. What was the area of our country in square miles, embraced by the original thirteen States? Only 549,615. What is it now? Thirty-three States covering an area of 1,602,000, six organized Territories exclusive of the District of Columbia, covering an area of 1,401,000; and in addition, we have the Mesilla Valley,[4] embracing 78,000, and the Indian Territory, embracing 187,000 square miles. Our territory has been enlarged nearly seven times in extent; our navy has been increased until its canvas whitens every ocean, and our national flag assures protection to the American citizen wherever he may be. Our power, our influence, our prosperity, our agricultural, mechanical and manufacturing wealth have increased far beyond all expectation. That banner which is borne up, and which has been carried forward by the unseen, yet steady hand of progress, has attained a position far in advance of the hopes and anticipations of the founders of our government. Surely no people have been blessed as we have been, and it is melancholy to think that all is now about to be sacrificed upon the altar of passion. If the judgments of men were consulted, if the admonitions of their consciences were respected, the Union would yet be saved from overthrow. Every calm, considerate and reflecting mind is filled with apprehensions of the most painful character; every patriotic heart throbs with anxiety, and all conservative men throughout our extended country are seeking to devise some means of escape from the evils that now threaten our peace and the continued existence of the government. All see and feel and know that the danger is imminent, and all true patriots are exerting themselves to save us from the perils now impending over us. The dark gloom of apprehension is fast gathering around us, and if saved at all, the wisdom, prudence and patriotism of the country can alone (aided by Divine Providence) be relied upon to relieve us in this hour of our extremity.

My inaugural message, presented to you just one year ago to-day, was prepared in anticipation of the occurrences of the past two months, which have cast their shadow like a pall over the business, financial and commercial, of the country. I thought I saw then a storm ahead that threatened to be destructive in its consequences; and, anxious to avert its fury if possible, I made two recommendations, which, if adopted, would (in my judgment) have saved us from the consequences now upon us. In this opinion, however, you did not concur, and no action was taken in regard to either.

Seeing no other hope of averting the threatened danger, I cordially endorsed the proposition presented by Colonel Memminger of South Carolina, and Mr. Starke of Mississippi, for a conference with those States.[5] If that proposition had been accepted, I am entirely satisfied that the results would have been most happy; that it would have tended in a great degree to the settlement and satisfactory adjustment of the painful controversy which had so long existed, and which seemed to be increased by time and untoward circumstances, between the two sections of the Union. The questions would have been presented in a form and shape, and in a manner so imposing, that action must have followed. That action could not have tended otherwise than toward peace.

I now again most respectfully renew the recommendation, presented in my inaugural message, in the following extract:

The only mode, therefore, of remedying the evil, that occurs to me, under the Constitution, is provided in the fifth article thereof. Summon a convention of all the States, that a full and free conference may be had between the representatives of the people, elected for this purpose, and thus ascertain whether the questions in controversy cannot be settled upon some basis mutually satisfactory to both sections. If such a convention shall assemble, and after free and full consultation and comparison of opinions, they shall find that the differences between the slaveholding and nonslaveholding States are irreconcilable, let them consider the question of a peaceable separation, and the adjustment of all questions relating to the disposition of the common property between the two sections. If they can be reconciled, let them adjust the terms, and give them such sanctions as will render them effective.

I suggest, therefore, that you adopt resolutions in favor of the call of such a convention, and appeal to the Legislatures of the several States to unite in the application proposed to be made to Congress, in pursuance of the provisions of the article aforesaid. If the nonslaveholding States shall fail or refuse to unite in the application, such failure or refusal will furnish conclusive evidence of a determination on their part to keep up the agitation, and to continue their aggressions upon us. If the convention shall meet, and the question cannot be satisfactorily adjusted, it will furnish evidence equally conclusive of their determination. In either event, the people of the South will clearly understand what they are to expect in the future.

The article of the Constitution to which reference is here made, is in the following words, and I quote it, inasmuch as it will be referred to hereafter in this communication: "The Congress, whenever two-thirds of both houses shall deem it necessary, shall propose amendments to this Constitution, or, on the applications of the Legislatures of two-thirds of the several States, shall call a convention for proposing amendments, which, in either case, shall be valid to all intents and purposes, as part of this Constitution, when ratified by the Legislatures of three fourths of the several States, or by conventions in three-fourths thereof, as the one or the other mode of ratification may be proposed by the Congress."[6]

Under this article, the Constitution of the United States has been amended on three several occasions in our history, and those amendments have all been exceedingly valuable and important. The first ten amendments were ratified by some of the States, in 1789, by others in 1790, and by the residue in 1791. Another amendment was proposed in 1794, which the President of the United States announced in his message to both houses dated January 8th, 1798, as having been adopted by the constitutional number of States. The last amendment was proposed in 1803, and adopted by the constitutional number of States in 1804. Those amendments were proposed and adopted at periods less alarming, perhaps, than at the present day. Still their adoption was necessary, to insure peace and quiet to our country, and were demanded by a proper deference to public opinion.

In the present condition of public affairs, why cannot such additional amendments as the circumstances now existing require, be proposed for ratification and adoption? The necessity is manifest, and the duty to adopt all constitutional measures, before we resort to the ultimate remedy of secession, is imperative. Is it not monstrous to see a government like ours destroyed, merely because men cannot agree about a domestic institution, which existed at the formation of the government, and which is now recognized by fifteen out of the thirty-three States composing the Union?

In support of my position, I quote from the message of Governor John Floyd, dated January 25th, 1833. He was one of the ablest and most reliable of the State rights men of Virginia. Though he has been taken from amongst us, he has left behind him a record as enduring as time:

> But the call of a general convention of the States, brings at once full before all the parties to the compact, every doubtful or disputed power of the Federal Government in the mode pointed out by the instrument itself, where all amendments could be made, and disputed powers settled, in a spirit of kindness much more congenial to the harmony of our institutions than that which now seems in contemplation. This course ought to be acceptable to all, as it gives full assurance of peaceful days hereafter, and will restore confidence to the mind of the patriot, already too long agitated with the foreseen disasters of the coming conflict.

This recommendation was made at a period in our history not unlike the present. It was made by a statesman of great practical wisdom, and of large political experience. He was a true Virginian, in feeling, sentiment, and principle, jealous of her honor, true to her interests, faithful to her rights and institutions, cool, calm and sagacious.

It becomes our State to be mindful of her own interests, in the present deranged and unsettled condition of public affairs. The cotton States seem to be looking to their own interests alone, and why should we not look to ours? Virginia has immense interests, valuable and important, at stake, and it becomes us to see that these interests are adequately protected. She occupies a position now, as she did in 1833, when she can mediate between the contending parties, North and South, and see that some fair settlement and arrangement of existing differences shall be agreed upon. While I would not have her occupy a position that would require the slightest sacrifice of her honor, her rights or her institutions, she must see that in all her future movements and associations these are securely protected. Now, that guarantees are the order of the day, and each State is earnestly and anxiously enquiring what guarantees are requested for her protection, it becomes us to secure such as will protect and preserve the rights of persons and property of our own citizens. A disruption of the Union is inevitable; and if new confederacies are to be formed, we must have the best guarantees before we can attach our State to either of them.

The late Executive of South Carolina, in his message to the Legislature, devotes considerable space to a commentary upon your action respecting "a conference of the Southern States."[7] That reference does not appear to me to be dictated by a kind spirit. It wears the aspect of dissatisfaction with your decision, and, in connection with other portions of the message, indicates distrust of, and hostility on his part, towards this Commonwealth. The duty which I owe to Virginia demands a notice of so much of this communication as relates to our State, and the action of her Legislature.

Why Virginia alone, of all the southern states, should have been singled out for comment, is to me unaccountable. The resolutions of the South Carolina Legislature, asking the conference, were transmitted to all the Southern States, and none of those states responded, except Mississippi and Alabama. Why no complaint of the other states who decided to accede to the proposal? After a careful examination of your resolutions, since the perusal of the Governor's message, I see nothing that could have entitled them to the special notice that has been bestowed upon them. They declare, "That the General Assembly of Virginia, recognizing in our present relations with the nonslaveholding states an imperative necessity for decisive measures, does not yet distrust the capacity of the Southern States, by a wise and firm exercise of their reserved powers, to protect the rights and liberties of the people, and to preserve the Federal Union. For this purpose, we earnestly desire the *concurrent action of the Southern States*." The authorities of Virginia acted with kindness and courtesy towards the State of South Carolina and her estimable commissioner, and in declining to go into a Southern conference at this time, they intended no disrespect to that State.

South Carolina having determined upon her future course, without consultation with any one of her slaveholding sister States, her late Executive announces in his message, "It is too late to receive propositions for a conference; and the State would be wanting in self-respect, after having deliberately decided on her course, to entertain any proposition looking to a continuance of the present Union. We can get no safer or better guarantee than the present Constitution, and that has proved impotent to protect us against the fanaticism of the North." It may be too late now to confer with her sister States, but there was a time when she could have conferred with them with great propriety, and perhaps advantage to herself and them. The Governor states that Col. Memminger was not sent to Virginia "to plan a dissolution of the Union, but to save it, if possible." Before she determined to precipitate a dissolution, would it not have been wise to let us know what was her determination, and to have made an effort to secure "*the concurrent action of the Southern States.*" As it is, her movement takes her Southern sisters by surprise.

The financial and commercial policy of the Federal Government in past years has, I have no doubt, in a great degree determined her action. The only specific allegation in regard to the slavery question, so far as I have observed, is the conduct of the Northern States in passing personal liberty bills, designed to obstruct the execution of the fugitive slave law. The action of the Northern States in regard to this law, is, beyond all question, a just and proper subject of complaint and even denunciation on the part of all slaveholding States, and especially the border States.

The faithful, prompt and just execution of all the provisions of the present Constitution will not prove satisfactory to South Carolina. Believing she can get nothing more than the Constitution accords to her, without even making an effort through a convention of all the States, her late Executive solemnly announces, "It is too late to receive propositions for a conference;" that "having deliberately decided on her course, self-respect forbids her entertaining any proposition looking to continuance *in the Union.*"

The late Executive of South Carolina is not content to announce this determination, but his recommendations look to the embarrassment of every slaveholding State on the border, which is not disposed to follow her lead. Hence we find in his message an open and undisguised proclamation of war upon the interests of all the border slaveholding States, unless they unite with South Carolina:

> The introduction of slaves from other States, which may not become members of the Southern Confederacy, and particularly the border States, should be prohibited by legislative enactment, and by this means they will be brought to see that their safety depends upon a withdrawal from their enemies, and an union with their friends and natural allies. If they should continue their union with the nonslaveholding States, let them keep their slave property in their own borders, and the only alternative left them will be emancipation by their own act, or by the action of their confederates. We cannot consent to relieve them from their embarrassing situation, by permitting them to realize

the money value for their slaves, by selling them to us, and thus prepare them, without any loss of property, to accommodate themselves
to the Northern free soil ideas. But should they unite their destiny
with us, and become stars in the Southern galaxy—members of a great
Southern Confederation—we will receive them with open arms and
an enthusiastic greeting. Should, then, danger approach their borders,
or an enemy, open or disguised, make war upon them, there is not a
doubt but a living rampart of freemen, from the Atlantic to the Gulf of
Mexico, would line their borders and beat back the invaders.

Here we have the exhibition of a determined purpose to coerce Virginia
and the other border States to follow her example; and if they fail to do so,
then they are to be placed in such a position as will drive them to the emancipation of their slaves! This movement, begun ostensibly for the *protection*
of slave property, for the diffusion and the preservation of the institution
of slavery, is to be so managed and directed now, as to force States holding
slave property to free themselves from it *by emancipation*. This is the avowed
policy of the late Executive of a State interested in an institution sanctioned
by the teachings and precepts of Christianity, and promotive of a higher
degree of civilization and refinement—an institution that ought to be diffused and extended, and the permanency and prosperity of which ought to
be insured. Can it be possible that such suggestions can exert an influence
upon the future action of either of the border States—that they can be coerced into an union with those who thus manifest a determined purpose to
rule or ruin them? They may rest satisfied that such a policy cannot control
the action of Virginia. She has the independence and the ability to think
for herself, and her action, whatever it may be, will be the result of her convictions of duty. She is equally as jealous of her honor as South Carolina or
any other State, and she will guard and protect it, with a purpose as resolute
and determined, and a spirit as firm and undaunted, as unyielding and as
exacting.

I now propose to present, in contrast with these views of the Executive
of South Carolina, the sentiments announced by her Commissioner[8] in this
capitol on the 19th of January, 1860. In his address he declares, "I can confidently affirm that such an interchange of kindly feeling as you have exhibited, *cannot fail to bind together the hearts of our people in closer ties of sympathy*

and fellowship." Does the conduct of the late Executive of South Carolina, in his recent message, show that such has been the result? No observer of events for some months past can fail to have been struck with the numerous evidences of hostility and prejudice which have been exhibited towards Virginia by very many of the leading and most influential public men of that State. We have seen nothing going to show the existence of these "ties of sympathy and fellowship" which bind "together the hearts of our people," so handsomely alluded to by Col. Memminger on that interesting occasion. Distrust of us, and distrust without sufficient cause (a result greatly to be deplored), appears to have sundered the "ties of sympathy and fellowship" which ought to have existed, at this critical juncture in our affairs, not only between South Carolina and Virginia, but between all the slaveholding States. Such taunts as have been indulged in towards this Commonwealth by the late Executive of South Carolina, do not exhibit that spirit of comity which should at all times, and more especially at this time, characterize the intercourse and relations between sister States, with a common domestic institution, that can be best defended and maintained by united counsels and action. Such allusions to Virginia should never have been made by the Executive of a State who feels her "obligation for the large contribution of mind and effort which Virginia has made to the common cause," and who is more largely indebted to her for manifestations of particular concern in her "welfare."

In this address it was also declared, "that when we (South Carolina) propose a conference, we do so with the full understanding that we are but one of the States in that Conference, entitled like all the others to express our opinions, but willing *to respect and abide by the united judgment of the whole*. If our pace is too fast for some, we are content to walk slower; our earnest wish is, that *all may keep together*." These are the noble sentiments, and declare a sound and proper position. In a movement so important, and involving consequences so serious to all the slaveholding States, no one State should have ventured to move without first having given timely notice to the others of her purpose, even if she did not intend "to respect and abide by the united judgment of the whole." Such action on the part of South Carolina would at this moment, in all probability, have enabled "all" to "keep together." What effect her movement may have upon the future, time alone can disclose.

South Carolina, a sovereign State, had a right to adopt the line of policy she has pursued; and I would have made no special reference to her course if I had not been indirectly invited to do so by her late executive in his uncalled for references to Virginia. It has been my rule, as the Executive of Virginia, to exhibit, in my official intercourse with the States of the Confederacy, a spirit of comity, and to manifest all that respect which is due from one state to another. Whenever the motives or the actions of Virginia are arraigned, I will feel it to be my duty to remonstrate; and in doing so, I will observe that moderation, courtesy and kind spirit which become the character of a State whose "large contributions to the Union" have "secured to her the respect and affection of every state of this Confederacy."

In the recent message of the Governor of Mississippi,[9] I find a reference to the border States, of the same character, and manifesting the same spirit which has been exhibited by the late Executive of South Carolina: "As it is more than probable that many of the citizens of the border States may seek a market for their slaves in the cotton States, I recommend the passage of an act prohibiting the introduction of slaves into this State, unless their owners come with them and become citizens, and prohibiting the introduction of slaves for sale by all persons whomsoever."

These references to the border States are pregnant with meaning, and no one can be at a loss to understand what that meaning is. While disavowing any unkind feeling towards South Carolina and Mississippi, I must still say, that I will resist the *coercion* of Virginia into the adopting of a line of policy, whenever the attempt is made by Northern or Southern states.

For the present condition of public affairs, the nonslaveholding States are chargeable; and if the Union shall be destroyed, upon them will rest the solemn responsibility. Their systematic and persistent warfare upon the institution of domestic slavery, as it exists amongst us — their fierce and un-qualified denunciation of it, and all who recognize or tolerate it, have done much to create the present state of exasperation existing between the two sections of the Union. Hatred to slavery and slaveholders is instilled into the minds of their children, as part and parcel of their education, through-out the infected district of New England. The institution is constantly assailed — through the press, in the pulpit, in public meetings, in private associations, in their legislative assemblies, in their statutes, on all occasions — as morally, socially and politically wrong. The slave owner is painted as the great criminal of the age, deserving death. Money is raised and has been expended in hiring desperate and depraved men, in arming and supporting them, in order that they may make raids into Southern States, and excite the slaves to insurrection and murder. Arms peculiarly suited to the use of the slave have been fabricated, and sent into the slave States, to be placed in the hands of this class of our population, after they have been stimulated to such a degree of madness as will qualify them for the commission of murder, arson, and every species of cruelty. The results of these teachings were seen in the Harpers Ferry raid.

Such an outrage ought to have provoked the unqualified and universal condemnation of good and law-abiding citizens in every State of the Confederacy. In atrocity, it stands without parallel in the history of our country, and all right thinking men would suppose that neither the authors nor the act would find apologists anywhere. Is it so? Did we not find numerous apologies for the conduct of John Brown and his flagitious associates, throughout many of the Northern, but more especially in the New England States? The fountain of New England sympathy was broken up to its depths, and gushed forth, when John Brown and his followers were condemned, after a fair trial, and expiated their crimes upon the gallows. Though they are dead, New England sympathy for them still survives. But a few weeks ago a John Brown sympathizer was elected to the Gubernatorial chair of the state of Massachusetts,[10] one of the original thirteen. The Executive chairs of the States of Ohio and Iowa[11] are also filled with the same description of men, holding the same general views, advocating the same principles and measures, and exhibiting deep sympathy and strong partiality for these heartless malefactors: both elected, however, prior to the Harpers Ferry raid.

The people of the Northern States, as their statutes show, and it is confirmed by their speeches and addresses, their resolutions in public meetings, and indeed in almost every conceivable mode, have been endeavoring to confine slavery within its present limits, by excluding it from all the Territories belonging to the government. They have been endeavoring "to draw a line around the Southern States," with the purpose of then declaring that slavery shall not go beyond the limits thus determined by them. The statutes and resolutions of many of the nonslaveholding States, from the time Texas sought admission into the Union, up to this day, confirm this view of the design and purposes of the free States.

Who can have forgotten the attempt made by the Northern people to use the mails for the transmission of the vilest papers, illustrated by pictorial representations, calculated and intended "to produce dissatisfaction and revolt amongst the slaves, and to incite their wild passions to vengeance" against their masters and others in slaveholding States. The objects they then had in view, and towards the accomplishment of which their efforts were directed, were the abolition of slavery in the District of Columbia, and the exclusion of slave States from admission into the Union.

Since the formation of the government, composed of the original thirteen States, twenty new States have been added to the Union, making now the number of thirty-three. Of the number so added, eleven have been free States, and nine slave States. For many years the policy was to admit States *pari passu*,[12] so as to preserve the equilibrium in the Senate between the North and the South. In carrying out this policy, Vermont and Kentucky, Tennessee and Ohio, Indiana and Mississippi, Illinois and Alabama, Maine and Missouri, Arkansas and Michigan, Florida and Iowa, came in together, or near the same time. When the State of Missouri was admitted, the State of Maine was cut off from the then State of Massachusetts, for the purpose of preserving the equilibrium between the North and South, in the Senate. A Northern State was divided, with a view of keeping up the equipoise, and that division gave an additional free State to the Union. That equipoise is now destroyed, and we stand fifteen slave and eighteen free States.[13] Even in this state of the case, the South has been so forbearing and unselfish, that she has never asked for the division of her States, that the equipoise might be restored.[14]

An advantage has been gained over us in another respect, equally important. The organized territories (with the exception of New Mexico) are destined to become free States; and it may be that even this territory will be of like character.[15] All of these territories will come into the Union near about the same time; and while the North has the advantage over us now of six senators, that advantage must, in the ordinary course of events, if the Union shall survive, be greatly increased. Besides, the territory of the slave States is generally large; the territory of the free States generally small. Rhode Island is made equal to Missouri in the Senate; Connecticut is a counterpoise to Virginia; Vermont, with its wild fanaticism, is an offset to Georgia, the empire State of the South.

Can it be surprising that the people of the South should be restive and uneasy under such circumstances? In addition, a candidate has just been elected to the Presidency, who gave utterance to the following atrocious sentiments, indicating his bitter hostility to the South and her institutions: "In my opinion, it (the slavery agitation) will not cease until a crisis shall have been reached and passed. A house divided against itself cannot stand. I believe this government cannot endure permanently, half slave and half free. I do not expect the Union to be dissolved; I do not expect the house to fall; but I do expect it will cease to be divided. It will become all one thing, or all the other. Either the opponents of slavery will arrest the further spread of it, and place it where the public mind shall rest in the belief that it is in the course of ultimate extinction, or its advocates will push it forward until it shall become alike lawful in all the states, old as well as new, North as well as South."[16] And again, he says: "I embrace with pleasure this opportunity of declaring my *disapprobation* of this clause of the Constitution which denies to a portion of the colored people the right of suffrage."[17]

When a President is elected, entertaining and boldly avowing such sentiments—when, to this moment, they have never been retracted or qualified, have we not reason for alarm and resentment?

The Union is now disrupted; let the North bear the blame. They have brought these sad and deplorable results upon the country, and the candid and honest men of the world will hold them responsible for the destruction of a government that has challenged the admiration and commanded the respect of the nations of the earth. Before God and the world, they will be held answerable for this calamity.

They yet have the power to end the strife and excitement, and restore confidence to the country. Will they do it? I await their response, but not without apprehension. Time, however, will soon furnish the answer. The present state of things cannot continue long. A change for the better or the worse, must soon come.

Can it be supposed that a dissolution of the Union can end in the organization of a Northern and Southern Confederacy, embracing the States and Territory on this side of the Rocky Mountains? I entertain no such opinion. I consider it not only possible, but highly probable, that when disunion shall come, we will have four organizations, independent and distinct. The States and Territories on the Pacific, by reason of their loyalty and isolation, will form one. The New England States, with New York, in consequence of their identity of opinions on the subject of African slavery, and their other fanatical ideas of like kind, will constitute the second. The border slave States, with Pennsylvania, New Jersey, Missouri, and the northwestern States and Territories, will form the third. The Ohio river, a great highway, owned by Virginia, furnishes a common bond of union between several of them—the Missouri river, another great highway, is a bond of union between others—and as these make up the Mississippi, that great valley will sooner or later form a union with those with whom they trade, and whose interests are therefore common. For this organization, New Orleans would be its chief city. It would be the exporting and importing city for the States in existence, and those which may be hereafter formed out of the immense unsettled territory which it would possess. Besides, the unsold public lands would invite population, and their sales would furnish the means to defray governmental expenses, in part at least. Kentucky and the northwestern territory originally formed a part of the domain of Virginia. This organization will keep her united with what formerly belonged to her, and constituted a part of her territory. The cotton States would form the fourth. All these confederacies being thus formed, although Louisiana, Arkansas, Texas and Mississippi might at first attach themselves to a cotton State organization, a very short time would elapse before they would find it to be their interest to connect themselves with the border and northwestern States. Their trade, their interests, their business relations, are with those states, and all upon the waters of the Mississippi and its tributaries must necessarily be united. If Louisiana remained in alliance with the cotton states, her great city of New Orleans would have to compete with Mobile and Charleston, for the export and import trade, and the most she could hope for, would be a third of it.

Such an arrangement would be followed by a struggle for the key of the Gulf (Pensacola;) and the third organization would have it, cost what it might in treasure and blood. It would be too important an acquisition to the cotton State Confederacy, without a desperate struggle. These are my speculations as to the results that are to follow a dissolution of the Union. These results are bad enough, but may be much worse. It is not given to us to read the future. We may, however, speculate about it.

When the Union was formed, it was not expected or believed that the domestic institutions of all the States should be alike. The institutions of

Maine and Louisiana were never intended to be the same. The people of each were invested with full power to determine whether slavery should exist, and the former decided against the institution; the latter determined in its favor—as each had the undoubted right to do.

In the list of grievances against the North, it is somewhat remarkable, that in our own State so little has been said in regard to the conduct of the Governors of Iowa and Ohio, in refusing to surrender fugitives from justice who participated in the Harpers Ferry raid. They were regularly indicted; the Governors of those States were applied to in due form to deliver them up; the application was refused; and our people, instead of taking a stand, and making an issue upon this practical question, seem inclined to ignore it, and unite in the complaints of the cotton States. The complaints of those States are rather against the financial and commercial policy of the Federal Government, than any action or want of action on the subject of slavery.[18] The slave-owners of Virginia have suffered seriously; the wrongs inflicted upon us by the conduct of these executives, have been great: still, we have heard but little complaint in our own State. The grievances complained of mainly, are those which the cotton States plead as a justification for their action. Would it not be well for us to redress the wrongs our own people have suffered, before we undertake to redress the wrongs of others, who have suffered much less, so far as slavery is concerned, than we have done? Our action should be based upon the wrongs done to our own people.

The proposition for the call of a State convention, to determine the position which Virginia shall take, in view of passing events, appears to have been received with very general favor. As the subject has been much discussed by the people in their primary meetings, it is not only proper, but it is doubtless expected that I should refer to it in this communication. It is pleasant, alike to the private citizen and the public officer, to know that his views and opinions are endorsed by those around him; that he is backed by the popular sentiment of the day; but there are times and occasions, in the history of every man, when it is imperative upon him to adhere to his convictions of duty, maintain his opinions firmly, but courteously, even at the hazard of being found in a minority. I have no hesitation in expressing my opinion upon this or any other question of public concern.

I have my convictions upon this question, and I give expression to them, in declaring my opposition at this time, to the call of a State Convention. I see no necessity for it at this time, nor do I now see any good practical result that can be accomplished by it. I do not consider this a propitious time to moot the question, and I apprehend, from indications that have been exhibited, that serious difficulties and embarrassments will attend the movement. Subsequent events may show the necessity for it.

In 1833 and 1850, when the existence of the Union was seriously threatened, when the danger was imminent, the Legislature accomplished everything desired, in a manner as satisfactory as it would have been accomplished, if the mode now suggested had been adopted. On neither occasion was the Legislature chosen, with reference to the events which subsequently occurred, and which devolved upon them the necessity for such action as was taken, and which gave so much satisfaction to the people of Virginia and the whole country.

In my inaugural message I made this recommendation, which, if adopted, would perhaps have relieved us, to some extent, from the complications with which we are now embarrassed:

> I also suggest that a commission, to consist of two of our most intelligent, discreet and experienced statesmen, shall be appointed, whose duty it shall be to visit the Legislatures of those States which have passed laws to obstruct the execution of the fugitive slave act, and insist, in the name of Virginia, upon their unconditional repeal. In support of the suggestion of the appointment of a commission, a precedent is to be found in the history of our own State, in the appointment of the distinguished Benjamin Watkins Leigh, who was commissioned to visit the Legislature of South Carolina, at the time of the controversy between that State and the Federal Government.[19] The existence of the Union was then greatly imperiled, and the action of Virginia exerted a most happy influence in bringing about a settlement that averted the danger and restored peace to the country. That crisis in public affairs was almost as serious and alarming as the present.

In renewing the recommendation at this time, I annex a modification, and that is, that commissioners shall not be sent to either of the New England States. The occurrences of the last two months have satisfied me, that New England puritanism has no respect for human constitutions, and so little regard for the Union that they would not sacrifice their prejudices, or smother their resentments to perpetuate it.

I further recommend, that commissioners be sent to the Legislatures or Conventions of all the slaveholding States, to confer with them, with a view of ascertaining what demands, in the nature of amendments to the Constitution, or otherwise, will be satisfactory in this exigency. The adoption of this plan will in all probability tend to secure harmony and produce unity of action.

The controversy now has reached a point when *it must be settled* on some fair, just and permanent basis, if we are to be reunited, and peace, quiet and order restored to the country. The excitement now existing is ruinous to the financial and commercial business, and to the agricultural, planting, mechanical, mercantile and manufacturing interests of all sections. Unless a settlement of the controversy shall be speedily effected, every species of property must fall to merely nominal prices, and a scene of general and ruinous bankruptcy, far exceeding, in intent and severity, any that has preceded it, must be the inevitable result. Even now, hundreds and thousands have been thrown out of employment, and at this inclement season, poverty, want and misery must be the portion of them and their dependent families. It is time the conservative spirit of the country was aroused and stimulated to energetic action. No time is to be lost in putting into immediate requisition all fair, honorable and constitutional means that promise to secure a satisfactory and permanent adjustment.

What, then, is necessary to be done? The Northern States must strike from their statute books their personal liberty bills, and fulfill their constitutional obligations in regard to fugitive slaves and fugitives from justice. If our slaves escape into nonslaveholding States, they must be delivered up; if abandoned, depraved and desperately wicked men come into slave States to excite insurrections, or to commit other crimes against our laws, and escape into free States, they must be given up for trial and punishment, when lawfully demanded by the constituted authorities of those States whose laws have been violated.

Second—We must have proper and effective guarantees for the protection of slavery in the District of Columbia. We can never consent to the abolition of slavery in the District, until Maryland shall emancipate her slaves; and not then, unless it shall be demanded by the citizens of the district.

Third—Our equality in the States and Territories must be fully recognized, and our rights of person and property adequately protected and secured. We must have guarantees that slavery shall not be interdicted in any territory now belonging to, or which may hereafter be acquired by the General Government; either by the Congress of the United States or a Territorial Legislature: that we shall be permitted to pass through the free States and Territories without molestation; and if a slave shall be abducted, that the State in which he or she shall be lost, shall pay the full value of such slave to the owner.

Fourth—Like guarantees must be given, that the transmission of slaves between the slaveholding States, either by land or water, shall not be interfered with.

Fifth—The passage and enforcement of rigid laws for the punishment of such persons in the free States as shall organize, or aid and abet in organizing, either by the contribution of money, arms, munitions of war, or in any other mode whatsoever, companies of men, with a view to assail the slaveholding States, and to excite slaves to insurrection.

Sixth—That the General Government shall be deprived of the power of appointing to local offices in the slaveholding States, persons who are hostile to their institutions, or inimical to their rights—the object being to prevent the appointing power from using patronage to sow the seeds of strife and dissension between the slaveholding and non-slaveholding classes in the Southern States.

These guarantees can be given without prejudice to the honor or rights, and without a sacrifice of the interests, of either of the nonslaveholding States. We ask nothing, therefore, which is not clearly right, and necessary to our protection: And surely, when so much is at stake, it will be freely, cheerfully and promptly assented to. It is the interest of the North and the South to preserve the government from destruction; and they should omit the use of no proper or honorable means to avert so great a calamity. The public safety and welfare demand instant action.

Many of the fanatics in the Northern States are constantly calling attention to the fact, that the number of slave owners, as compared with the white population in the slave States, is small; and hence the inference that the non-slaveholder is not loyal to the State, and would not willingly defend the institution. This is a most serious mistake, and is well calculated to make an erroneous impression upon the northern mind. Such a representation does serious injustice to that loyal and patriotic class of our citizens. It is a reflection upon them, not warranted by their conduct, now or heretofore.[20]

The number of persons in this State, in the year 1860, charged with taxes on slaves was 53,874. The number of persons charged with taxes on lands in the same year, was 159,088. Most of the persons charged with taxes on slaves, are the owners of lands also; and others who own lands, own no slaves. The number of persons charged with taxes, other than owners of lands and slaves, is 201,000. All these parties have a common interest in the protection of persons and property, and each feels that in protecting the rights and property of the others, he is securing and protecting his own, whether of little or great value. As the chief magistrate and as a citizen of Virginia, it is a source of pleasure to me to know that there is no jealousy or distrust, and that harmony and confidence exist between these classes. If the Northern people entertain the opinion that the nonslaveholders of the South are not reliable and trustworthy in all respects, they are most grossly mistaken and deceived.

I have seen it stated that in the empire city of New York the owners of real estate numbered less than 15,000. Do those who are not owners of real estate feel no interest in the property of the 15,000? Would they be willing to defend or protect it, if it were in danger of destruction? It might be charged, with the same propriety, and with as much truth, in this instance, that feeling no interest in common with the owner, they would not risk their lives for the protection of his real estate, worth millions of dollars. They are interested — deeply interested in all that relates to the public prosperity. Their prosperity, their comfort, and the comfort of their families are dependent upon the protection of the rights of property of every individual in the community in which he lives.

I have always reverenced the State rights doctrines of Virginia, as inculcated in the Resolutions of '98 and the Report of '99.[21] I believe the doctrines therein asserted, and the principles therein affirmed, to be worthy of all acceptation. I cordially endorse them, and in so doing, endorse the doctrine of secession. I do not propose to go into an argument in support of my opinion upon this question. The subject has been ably discussed for years, on both sides, and those arguments are familiar to all reading and well informed men. I am content to rest the question upon the discussions which have taken place, and leave the people to form their own opinions and draw their own conclusions. I refer to it, in this connection, to declare my unqualified hostility to the doctrine of *coercion* by the Federal Government.

In my canvass for the office I now hold, I declared my opinion frankly and fearlessly on this question, and every man in the State had the amplest opportunity to be informed of my position. In a written address "to the voters of Virginia," issued on the 12th of May, 1859, I stated, "Should it be the pleasure of the people to elevate me to the office of the Governor, I will endeavor in my administration to carry out the time-honored State rights principles of Virginia. If at any time during my administration the Federal Government shall attempt to interfere with the rights and institutions of Virginia; if it shall at any time interfere with the rights of slavery or the rights of slaveholders in our State, I will be prepared, with the aid of the people, to resist any efforts to coerce us into submission. I will resist any attempts of Federal troops to cross our line to execute such unjust, iniquitous and unconstitutional laws, either in Virginia or any other Southern State." My position now on this question, is what it was then. It has not been changed or modified. I will regard an attempt to pass Federal troops across the territory of Virginia, for the purpose of coercing a southern seceding State, as an act of invasion, which should be met and repelled. The allegiance of every citizen of Virginia is due to her; and when her flag is unfurled, it is his duty to rally to its support and defense. The citizen of Virginia who will not respond to her call, is a traitor to her rights and her honor.

I am not without hope that the present difficulties will find a satisfactory solution in the end. Let the New England States and western New York be sloughed off. In the last war with Great Britain, the New England States entertained the treasonable design of forming an alliance with Canada. Let them now consummate it. At the time the Hartford Convention met,[22] the most treasonable body that has ever assembled in our country, it was declared in their report, "Whenever it shall appear that these causes (of our calamities) are radical and permanent, a separation, by equitable arrangement, will be preferable to an alliance by constraint, among nominal friends, but real enemies, inflamed by mutual hatred and jealousy and inviting, by intestine divisions, contempt and aggression from abroad." The cause of our calamities "are radical and permanent," and we are indebted to New England for them. They are our "nominal friends, but real enemies;" they have originated more trouble, caused more strife, and created more hatred, dissension and division in our country, than all the other States combined. They have uniformly opposed the acquisition of territory, and consequently the organization and admission of new states into the Union. If their policy had prevailed, we should have had at this day the original thirteen States, and no more. All those States carved out of the Louisiana territory, the northwestern territory, Spanish territory and Mexican territory, would have been excluded from association and union with us. They have shown themselves the uncompromising enemies of progress; they have sternly resisted every attempt to extend our empire, under the fear that "*the Western States, multiplied in number and augmented in population, will control the interests of the whole.*" Existing difficulties furnish abundant reasons and the best opportunity for severing our connection with them; and we ought not to permit the occasion to pass unimproved.

A Confederacy, composed of the remaining States, can arrange terms under which they can live harmoniously and happily together; and now that the Union is disrupted, we should avail ourselves of this favorable opportunity to commence the work of reconstruction. In commencing and prosecuting this important work, we must look to our security, the protection of our institutions, and our domestic peace. Let the fabric be reared, discarding all rotten and unsound material, and exhibiting an ordinary share of prudence and wisdom in its fabrication, and there is but little reason to doubt that it can be constructed upon fair and satisfactory terms, and the rights and interests, the institutions and honor of all its members can be satisfactorily secured. We can form such a Confederacy as will draw to it the affections and sympathies of its citizens, thereby securing for it a foundation on which it can rest in safety.

Such is my plan for relief from the difficulties, the perplexities and the complications which now environ us, and I present it for the consideration of my countrymen. Every consideration of duty to ourselves and those who are to succeed us, *demands that the controversy shall be settled finally. It can be no longer delayed.*

The times require prudence, wisdom and patriotism; union, harmony and conciliation. Every man should be willing to risk himself and his future prospects to quell the strife and restore peace to the nation, torn as it now is by dissension, and threatened with anarchy, trusting to the people to do justice to his intentions, even if they should think his judgment in error.

In the present posture of affairs, it becomes us to cast about and ascertain in what way the interests of Virginia can be preserved and advanced. It is neither politic nor wise to neglect our *material prosperity*, and permit it to be sacrificed and destroyed by political or sectional broils. This obligation upon us is imperative whether the Union shall continue to exist or be destroyed. In either event, our material prosperity should be with us an object of the first importance, and to its advancement our efforts should be steadily directed.

We have the best port in the country, and no man can doubt, if direct trade were established between Norfolk and Europe, it would give increased prosperity to every interest in the Commonwealth. It would secure for us a commercial independence that would prove of immense value in any contingency that might occur. The present and prospective system of railroads in the State already points to the great northwest, and must soon become an important part of the immense network of roads which now reach Kansas, and are fast progressing towards the Pacific; and the system, when complete, will be entirely, or almost so, within the central belt from the Atlantic to the Pacific. Virginia then, whether in or out of the Union as it stands at present, has it in her power to place herself in the position, in reference to this great interior and exterior trade, which really belongs to her.

With ships sailing directly to Europe, at regular intervals from the port of Norfolk, an import trade could be established, and importers in the interior cities throughout the West, and some portions of the Southwest, would receive their supplies through this channel. These importations would all pass over our railroads to their intersection with the railroads of other States, especially those of Tennessee, Kentucky and some of the northwestern States. The export and import business would be concentrated upon the Virginia roads, and would thus assure to them controlling power in the arrangement, securing great benefits to the State, and good profits to the stockholders. It may be added that this commerce is already in existence, and only awaits the easiest, cheapest and most expeditious means of reaching the Atlantic, to be conveyed there to all points of destinations, both outward and inward.

I am entirely satisfied, that if direct trade were established between Norfolk and Europe, it would result in the enlargement of our cities, the increase of our agricultural products, the development of our resources, the creation of manufactures, the enhancement of the value of lands, the opening of the coal and mineral beds, make the stock which the State owns in her railroads productive—and the end would be, a diminution of the State debt, and a reduction in the rate of taxation. If such would be the results, the subject is eminently deserving of the most serious consideration. The attention of the people has been directed to the question, and the time is therefore favorable for decisive action upon it. I leave it to your wisdom to digest a plan that will secure the great end.

I have thus presented my reflections on Federal relations, frankly and with that independence which is becoming the position I occupy at this interesting and dangerous epoch in our history. It is only by a free comparison of opinions, and a manly examination of the question in issue, that we can hope to evolve the true state of facts, and provide a remedy for existing troubles and threatened dangers. Having performed my duty, the whole matter is with you, for such action as the wisdom and patriotism of the Legislature may adopt. Be your conclusions what they may, I am satisfied they will be results of your convictions as to what is best to be done in this emergency, for the honor and interests of our beloved Commonwealth and our country.

In conclusion, I have but to add, that the will of Virginia will furnish an inflexible rule for the direction of my own action. My destiny is linked indissolubly with hers. In the expressive language of Ruth, "Whither thou goest I will go, and where thou lodgest I will lodge: Thy people shall be my people, and thy God, my God."[23]

Source: *Journal of the Senate of the Commonwealth of Virginia: Begun and Held at the Capitol in the City of Richmond, on Monday, the Seventh of January, 1861, in the Year One Thousand Eight Hundred and Sixty-One—Being the Eighty-Fifth Year of the Commonwealth. Extra Session* (Richmond: James E. Goode, Senate Printer, 1861), 9–27.

2

Washington Peace Conference
February 1861

Although several states called for a national convention to resolve the crisis created by the secession of South Carolina, it was Virginia's invitation that produced results. On February 4, 131 delegates representing twenty-one states assembled at the Willard Hotel hoping to craft a solution that would stem the secessionist tide. In its summons, the general assembly announced that Senator Crittenden's proposed amendment would satisfy Virginians if slightly modified so that protections for slavery would exist in all territories "now held or hereafter acquired" and that the rights of slave owners would be respected as they traveled to and through non-slave states and territories. Southern interests in acquiring Cuba were evident in the former, and the memory of the legal battle between Virginia and New York in *Lemmon v. The People* prompted the latter. The large number of northern delegates, however, prevented the conference's final proposed amendment from reflecting either requirement.

Call for a National Convention
January 19, 1861

Whereas, it is the deliberate opinion of the general assembly of Virginia, that unless the unhappy controversy which now divides the states of this confederacy, shall be satisfactorily adjusted, a permanent dissolution of the Union is inevitable; and the general assembly, representing the wishes of the people of the commonwealth, is desirous of employing every reasonable means to avert so dire a calamity, and determined to make a final effort to restore the Union and the constitution, in the spirit in which they were established by the fathers of the Republic: Therefore,

Resolved, that on behalf of the commonwealth of Virginia, an invitation is hereby extended to all such States, whether slaveholding or non-slaveholding, as are willing to unite with Virginia in an earnest effort to adjust the present unhappy controversies, in the spirit in which the constitution was originally formed, and consistently with its principles, so as to afford to the people of the slaveholding states adequate guarantees for the security of their rights, to appoint commissioners to meet on the 4th day of February next, in the city of Washington, similar commissioners appointed by Virginia, to consider, and if practicable, agree upon some suitable adjustment.

Resolved, that Ex-president John Tyler, William C. Rives, Judge John W. Brockenbrough, George W. Summers, and James A. Seddon, are hereby appointed commissioners, whose duty it shall be to repair to the city of Washington, on the day designated in the foregoing resolution, to meet such commissioners as may be appointed by any of said states, in accordance with the foregoing resolution.

Resolved, that if said commissioners, after full and free conference, shall agree upon any plan of adjustment requiring amendments to the federal constitution, for the further security of the rights of the people of the slaveholding states, they be requested to communicate the proposed amendments to congress, for the purpose of having the same submitted by that body, according to the forms of the constitution, to the several States for ratification.

Resolved, that if said commissioners cannot agree on such adjustment, or if agreeing, congress shall refuse to submit for ratification such amendments as may be proposed, then the commissioners of this state shall immediately communicate the result to the executive of this commonwealth, to be by him laid before the convention of the people of Virginia and the general assembly: provided, that the said commissioners be subject at all times to the control of the general assembly, or if in session, to that of the state convention.

Resolved, that in the opinion of the general assembly of Virginia, the propositions embraced in the resolutions presented to the senate of the

United States by the Hon. John J. Crittenden, so modified as that the first article proposed as an amendment to the constitution of the United States, shall apply to all the territory of the United States now held or hereafter acquired south of the latitude thirty-six degrees and thirty minutes, and provide that slavery of the African race shall be effectually protected as property therein during the continuance of the territorial government, and the fourth article shall secure to the owners of slaves the right of transit with their slaves between and through the non-slaveholding states and territories, constitute the basis of such an adjustment of the unhappy controversy which now divides the states of this confederacy, as would be accepted by the people of this commonwealth.

Resolved, that Ex-president John Tyler is hereby appointed, by the concurrent vote of each branch of the general assembly, a commissioner to the president of the United States, and Judge John Robertson is hereby appointed, by a like vote, a commissioner to the state of South Carolina, and the other states that have seceded or shall secede, with instructions respectfully to request the president of the United States and authorities of such states to agree to abstain, pending the proceedings contemplated by the action of this general assembly, from any and all acts calculated to produce a collision of arms between the states and the government of the United States.

Resolved, that copies of the foregoing resolutions be forthwith telegraphed to the executives of the several states, and also to the president of the United States, and that the governor be requested to inform, without delay, the commissioners of their appointment by the foregoing resolutions.

Source: *Journal of the House of Delegates of the State of Virginia, for the Extra Session, 1861* (Richmond: William F. Ritchie, Public Printer, 1861), 65–66.

James Alexander Seddon
February 18, 1861

James A. Seddon (1815–1880) graduated with a degree in law from the University of Virginia in 1835 and served as a US representative 1845–1847 and 1849–1851. Following the conclusion of the Peace Conference, he participated in the Provisional Confederate Congress before being

appointed Confederate secretary of war in November 1862, a position
he held until January 1865. During the war his former mansion in Richmond functioned as the White House of the Confederacy.

Seddon began his remarks by commenting on the draft amendment proposed by the Committee Upon Propositions three days earlier which he found unacceptable. To Seddon's mind, the committee's
amendment did not address Virginia's basic concerns regarding the impending Republican threat to slavery. Most importantly, he lectured,
the draft amendment did not contain the "provision as to future territory," that is, did not contain Senator Crittenden's clause that in all
territory "now held, or hereafter acquired" slavery would be protected
south of the 36°30' parallel. After describing the rise of the Republican party and the threat it posed for the institution of slavery, Seddon
warned his fellow delegates that if Virginia were to stay in the Union
"fuller and greater guarantees," for the protection of slavery must be
built into the United States Constitution. Four days later Seddon introduced a slightly modified version of Crittenden's amendment including
the latter's added seventh article prohibiting persons of the "African
race" from voting or holding elective office.

Mr. SEDDON:—It is very clear to me that I ought not to make a prolonged
address upon a question which I favor. The only question now before us
is: Shall this amendment be made plain? We should deal honestly among
ourselves; there should be no cheat—no uncertainty—no delusion here.
Our language should be so clear that it will breed no new nests of trouble.

But the address of the gentleman from Maryland[1] requires a brief notice
from me. I listened with sadness to many parts of it. I bemoan that tones so
patriotic could not rise to the level of the high ground of equality and right
upon which we all ought to stand.

I appeal not to forbearance—I ask not for pity. I feel proud to represent the grand old commonwealth of Virginia here, and prouder still that
I only come here to demand right and justice in her behalf. Aye! and it is
more complimentary to you to have it so. I ask for such guarantees only as
Virginia needs, and as she has the right to demand. It is far more complimentary to you to appeal to your sense of justice, to your sense of right, than
to your forbearance or pity.

Virginia comes forward in a great national crisis. When support after support of this glorious temple of our Government has been torn away, she comes—proud of her memories of the past—happy in the part she had in the construction of this great system—she comes to present to you, calmly and plainly, the question, whether new and additional guarantees are not needed for her rights; and she tells you what those guarantees ought to be.

Nor does she stand alone. She is supported by all her border sisters. The propositions she makes are familiar to the country. They were made by a patriot of the olden time, a time near to that of the foundation of our Government. They were such as he thought suited to the exigencies of his time. They have since then received a larger meed of approval, north and south, than any other plan of arrangement.

My State offers these resolutions of her Legislature as a basis for our action here, with certain modifications acceptable to her people. One of these modifications has since been accepted by the mover of these resolutions himself. Most important among them is the provision as to future territory. The gentleman seems to think that Virginia would not insist on this provision as applicable to territory we may never have. It behooves not me to answer such a momentous question. I am only the mouthpiece of Virginia. She insists on the provision for future territory. She and her sister States plant themselves upon it. What right have I to strike out a clause which she makes specific? What right have I to esteem it of so little weight that it may be thrown aside and disregarded? I do not propose to give my reasons, though they would not be troublesome to give. It was an element in the Missouri Compromise that it should apply to future as well as to existing territory.[2]

Does not the gentleman assert that under the laws as they now stand, we have the right to go north of the compromise line with our slaves? What, then, is our position? Under the decision of the Supreme Court we are entitled to participate in *all* the territory of the United States. We are offering to give up the great part and the best part of it, and in payment we are to take the naked chance of getting a little piece of the worthless territory south of the proposed line! Such an idea was never entertained by those who made the Compromise. The idea which governed their action was, beyond all doubt, not that present territory alone should be thus divided, but that the question should be removed from doubt and difficulty for all time, and to give us at the South a chance whatever change might come.

Shall we be rewarded for all we give up, and find full compensation in a clause which itself prevents the acquisition of future territory? The statement is in itself a sufficient answer to the question.

But there was another element in the propositions of the Legislature of Virginia. That, was security against the principles of the North, and her great and now dominant party; it was intended to put an end to the discussions that have convulsed the country and jeopardized our institutions.

It was the policy of our fathers to settle these questions. They determined to make a final and decisive line of demarkation, and to let that be conclusive. But this young people could not be restrained, and when new territory was acquired the same question arose again. It now comes up once more. Virginia early saw the seeds of trouble in it, because she saw that the tide of emigration would continue to press toward the fertile lands of the South. She saw and she acted. In consequence of her action we are here. Would it not be wise and well as statesmen and as patriots, that you should do what you can for adjustment? do what you can to bring back your sisters of the South who have departed? It is the part of wisdom to settle. Virginia was wise to ask it.

There is another thing. A great and mighty party has arisen at the North that is determined to exclude the institution of slavery, not only from all future, but from all *present* territory. We know that in all ways this party has declared that it would not consent to let slavery go where it does not now exist. More heated zealots, also animated and sustained by this same party, have determined that this natural and patriarchal institution of the South should be surrounded by a cordon of free States, and in the end be extinguished altogether.

Is it not wise in Virginia, that she should see that this project of surrounding the South with free States should be guarded against — most effectually guarded against now and in time to come, and so preserve her dignity and power?

This amendment adopted, and the proposition to Virginia will be a farce. Gentlemen, we hold that as the soul is to man, so is honor to a nation. Honor is the soul of nations. Without it, no nation can have a place in history or among the nations. We of Virginia must have in this Confederation the position of an equal. Equal in dignity — equal in right. In the Congress of the States of this Union, we insist on this as our right. We must have the same protection as the States of the North. Otherwise we are a dishonored people. We might live for a time otherwise, but we should be unworthy a place among the nations. We hold our *property*, yes, *our property in slaves*, as rightful and as honorable as any property to be found in the broad expanse between ocean and ocean.

We feel that in the existence, the perpetuity, the protection of the African race, we have a mission to perform, and not a mission only, but a right and a duty.

Upon this subject I have a word to say in all seriousness. Think not, gentlemen of the North, that we propose to deceive or mislead you. We of the South are earnest in what we say. This is a question which we answer to ourselves. We hold that these colored barbarians have been withdrawn from a country of native barbarism, and under the benignant influence of a Christian rule, of a Christian civilization, have been elevated, yes, *elevated* to a standing and position which they could never have otherwise secured. In respect to the colored race we challenge comparison with San Domingo, with the freed regions of Jamaica, with those who have been transferred to the coast of Africa. Ask the travellers who have visited those distant shores to contrast the condition of the colored people there with that of those on our Southern plantations, and they will give you but one answer—they will say, we have redeemed and kept well our high and our holy trust.

But this is a matter with our own consciences, not with yours. We appeal to you to leave it where it is, to leave the colored people where they are. Why should you undertake to interfere with the policy of a neighboring State concerning a people about which you know nothing? We feel, we know that we have done that race no wrong. Deep into the Southern heart has this feeling penetrated. For scores of years we have been laboring earnestly in our mission. In all this time we have contributed far more to the greatness of the North than to our own. Yet all this time we have been assailed, attacked, vilified and defamed, by the people of the North, from the cradle to the grave, and you have educated your children to believe us monsters of brutality, lust and iniquity.

I tell you, that from the time the abolition societies aroused the latent anti-slavery spirit of the North until now, nothing but evil has come of the excitement and discussion. It has spread a horrid influence far and wide; it has for years distilled, and is now distilling its poison and venom all over the land.

It was under English, yes, British, Anglo-Saxon instigation that it first commenced. By this instigation it has been fed, been given life, continuity and power. Think you the English authors of this instigation had any purpose but to disrupt this Republic? They professed to regard slavery as an evil and a sin. The fruits of their action were first manifested in religious societies—first in the largest churches in New England, in the Presbyterian or Congregational churches, next the Methodist, then the Baptist, and finally, the venom spread so widely, its influence separated other churches. What has the moral influence of this power done? It has made the abstraction of our slaves a virtue. Societies have been formed for that very purpose, inciting their members and others, by the vilest motives, to steal our slaves, to destroy our property.

Nor have they been sufficiently modest to cloak their designs under the veil of secrecy. These people advocated their pernicious doctrines openly in your leading cities, even within the consecrated walls of Faneuil Hall.[3]

Openly among your people, in the very light of day, these efforts were carried on for the destruction of your sister States. There has not been an effort of the law nor an exertion of public opinion to put them down.

These efforts culminated in the actual invasion of my own old honored State, and your people thought they were doing GOD service in signing a petition to our authorities for mercy to John Brown and his ruffian invaders of our soil. And when these men met the just reward of their crime, there was, throughout the North, in your meetings and your public prints, expressions of sympathy for these robbers and murderers. They were looked upon as the victims of oppression, as martyrs to a holy and religious cause. Gentlemen, consider these things, and tell me, is there not to-day reason for suspicion; on the part of the South for grave apprehension?

But the half is yet to be told; I have looked only at the moral aspect of the question. Dangerous enough hitherto, it becomes far more dangerous when it culminates on the arena of politics, and asks, with the powerful aid of a majority, the interference and the aid of the Government.

As soon as it became the party of one idea it began to draw to it, first the support of one, then another political party. It went on securing the assistance of one after another until it demoralized, until it brought each to ruin. It destroyed the grand old Whig party. Fanatic enough before, when it had brought that party to its grave, it thrust upon the arena of politics this question of slavery in the territories. Then for the first time it raised the cry of "Free Soil," and brought to its support the hearts of a majority of the people of the northern States.

The people of the North and Northwest have long been noted for their acquisitive disposition, especially for the acquisition of lands. This has been manifested in every form. Carried into effect it has made them powerful, until, not long since, they thought they might get entire dominion at no distant day. Then arose in their hearts a desire greater than the greed of land—the greed of office and power. They then saw that perhaps the North alone might control the national government, and with it the South. Then, too, the great class of protected interests at the North—always greater at the North than at the South—joined with them. All these protected classes, whose advantages had been diverted from other classes to which they belonged, joined with landseekers to secure power. Influence after influence of this sort combined, until it produced your great Republican party; in other words, your great Sectional party, which has at length come to majority and power.

I do not wish to dwell upon the principles of that party, or to discuss them; I simply assert that their principles involve all the sentiments of abolitionism. They may be summed up in this: you determine to oppose the admission of slave States in the future.

You say that the whole power of the country, the whole power of the administration, shall be used in future for the final extinction of slavery.

This, now, is the ruling idea of your great sectional party. It is simply the rule of one portion of the country over another. There is no difference between attacking slavery in the States and keeping it out of the territories. It is only drawing a parallel around the citadel at a more remote point.

Now, see how the South is placed. The South has forborne as long as it can, just as long as party organization existed, and as long as the South could keep it in existence. It was only when we saw that the whole united Government was to be turned against us, that we began to think of taking the subject into our own hands.

What are we to expect now, when the power, direct and indirect, of this great Government is to be used in the most effective manner against us? A power which claims that we shall not exercise the rights of States even, a power which seeks to coerce us, when we propose to protect ourselves against this lowering and impending danger. You of the North are descended from men who honored the scaffold for the very rights we now seek to exercise. So are we. You would deserve to be spurned by the maids and matrons among you, if you refused to protect yourselves against the dangers thus drawing around you. Can you expect less of us?

Do you tell me that this is an artificial crisis? Would seven States have abandoned all the grand interest they possessed in a glorious and happy Confederacy like ours, but for more serious and vital interests, the interests of safety, security, and honor? Think well of these things, gentlemen!

I have hastily endeavored to show you where I conceive we of the South stand. The feelings which I express are entertained likewise by the border States, by all the citizens of the South, by every householder of my State in a greater or less degree.

The State to which I refer, Virginia, is now met in solemn convocation to consider whether she shall remain in the Union or go out of it; and with the most earnest desire to secure to herself a longer connection with the American Union, a Union of so much honor and pride, and with an equally earnest desire to bring back the wandering States of the South which have already left us, she, my own, my native State, comes here to ask for these guarantees. In my deliberate judgment, the Union and the Constitution, as they now stand, are unsafe for the people of the South, without other guarantees which will give them actual power instead of mere paper rights. Her stake in this controversy is too deep. In my judgment she has asked too little; I think fuller and greater guarantees ought to be required, and that this Convention should not stand upon ceremony, but in a free and liberal spirit of concession should yield to us all that we ask. Be assured we shall ask none but adequate guarantees.

But I am told that Virginia is content with the Crittenden Resolutions — I say this because I am instructed to say so — that is, if we are to treat these resolutions, not as the principles of the man who offers them, but as the principles of the great party just come into power.

Gentlemen, remember that we of the South are already stripped of one-half our sister States; our system is dislocated; the Union is disrupted.

How can you expect now to retain Virginia, to retain the border States, when they stand in the face of such a great, such an immense party? How can you expect Virginia to remain in the Union without these added guarantees?

I told you I would make no appeals to your pity. If we are not entitled to the guarantees we ask, according to the principles of sound philosophy, of right and justice, then we do not ask them at all.

Source: Lucius E. Chittenden, ed., *A Report of the Debates and Proceedings in the Secret Sessions of the Conference Convention, for Proposing Amendments to the Constitution of the United States, Held at Washington, D.C., in February, A.D. 1861* (New York: D. Appleton & Company, 1864), 91–98.

William Cabell Rives
February 19, 1861

William C. Rives (1793–1868) attended Hampden-Sydney College and graduated from the College of William and Mary in 1809. He studied law with Thomas Jefferson and began his law practice in Charlottesville in 1814. He was a member of the house of delegates (1817–1820, 1822–1823), and served as a US representative (1823–1829). President Andrew Jackson appointed him minister to France in 1829, a post he held until 1832. He then served in the US Senate on three occasions: 1832–1834, 1836–1839, and 1839–1845. He represented the US again as minister to France from 1849 until 1853 having been appointed by President Zachary Taylor. A Unionist until Virginia seceded on May 23, Rives then participated in the Confederate Provisional Congress and was a member of the Second Confederate Congress.

Rives condemned secession while believing that slavery was threatened by the incoming Lincoln administration. Arguing that the New England states had been responsible for "fastening slavery upon us," he suggested that it would cost the North nothing to simply write into the Constitution that the government would not interfere with slavery in the states, the territories, or the District of Columbia. Remembering the Lemmon Slave Case, Rives also asked that such a revision of the Constitution should "permit the transit of our slaves from one State to another."

To emphasize the importance of finding a solution to the secession crisis for White southerners, Rives asserted that the primary issue at stake was the maintenance of white supremacy. "In fact, it is not a question of slavery at all. It is a question of race. We know that the very best position for the African race to occupy is one of unmitigated legal subjection." Slavery constituted the best possible position for the "negroes of the United States . . . both for the superior and inferior race."

Mr. RIVES:—I rise for the purpose of answering some of the observations of the gentleman from New York;[4] and first of all I wish to say a word about the motives and purposes of Virginia in calling this Convention. She has called this Convention together because she believed it would exert a powerful influence for the safety and honor of the country, and the perpetuity of its institutions. She is met *in limine*[5] with the reproach that her action is unconstitutional. How unconstitutional?

Is not our Government based upon the sovereignty of the people? Is not that the idea upon which this Government rests? And when the people act, are they to be told that their action is unconstitutional or improper? Cannot Virginia and her people, acting through their representatives, suggest the means of amendment or improvement in our Constitution to Congress?—the Congress which represents the people, and whose members are servants only of the people? Can she not call together a convention of this kind and suggest measures to be considered by it for the purpose of saving an imperilled country? Virginia knew well that this was to be an advisory Conference merely. She invited commissioners from all the States to come here and present their views, to compare and discuss them, to devise measures for the benefit of the country, in the same way that any assemblage of the people may lawfully do. Has the gentleman looked into the history of our present Constitution? Virginia did the same thing previous to the adoption of the Constitution, which she is doing now.

Some State must invite a Conference if one is to be had. If it was proper that Virginia should do it before the adoption of our present Constitution, it is eminently proper that she should do it now. There are occasions, sir, in the history of nations, when men should rise far above the rules of special pleading. This is one of them. Let the gentleman look into the history of the old articles of Confederation; let him read the debates which arose upon their adoption. Virginia originated measures then, far more important than any before us now; and there were gentlemen then, who took the same ground that gentlemen do now, who sought by the use of dilatory pleas, by interposing objections, temporary in their nature, to prevent and delay action upon the great national questions then under consideration. Now, in a time of great peril, when the whole country is convulsed, when the existence and perpetuity of the Government is in danger, Virginia has invoked her sister States to come here and see whether they cannot devise some method to avoid the danger and save the country.

In the preamble to the first ten articles of Confederation, there is to be found an express reference to the action of the State Legislatures in initiating proposals of amendment. Every amendment that has hitherto been made to our Constitution originated with the people, and directly or indirectly through the action of State Legislatures. What purpose can gentlemen have in interposing these dilatory pleas, objections merely for delay, when we all know that Congress is now waiting for—actually inviting the action of this Conference?

Senator COLLAMER,[6] in his speech already referred to, makes the distinct proposition, that when any considerable portion of the people (certainly a much smaller portion than is here represented) desire to have amendments submitted, it is the duty of Congress to propose them, and to do so without committing that body either for or against them. Governor {Thomas} CORWIN, also of the Congressional Committee of Thirty-three, having this subject in charge, is understood to have stated that the committee desire to consider the propositions which may here be adopted.

Now, as I said, these dilatory objections were interposed previous to the adoption of our present Constitution.

Mr. NOYES:—Are we to understand that Virginia then asked for a General Convention to consider amendments to the Constitution?

Mr. RIVES:—No! The Annapolis Convention met.[7] The invitation under which that body was convened was addressed to all the States. Five only responded, and they proposed a General Convention of all the States, to meet at Philadelphia. Virginia was the first to act and appoint her delegates. I repeat, that the same objection was then urged, that Congress *or* the States should propose the amendments. The first Convention was just as unconstitutional as this. The two cases were perfectly alike. The crisis is infinitely more important now than it was then. Then, there was no disintegration of the States. They still held firmly together. How are we now? Seven States are out of the Union. *The Union is dissolved!* Virginia loves the Union. She cherishes all its glorious memories. She is proud of its history and of her own connection with it. But Virginia has no apprehension as to her future destiny. She can live in the Union or out of it. She can stand in her own strength and power if necessary. Her delegates come here in no spirit of supplication, nor do they propose to offer any intimidation. She has called you here as brothers, as friends, as patriots. If the future has suffering in store for Virginia, be assured all her sister States must suffer equally.

Mr. PRESIDENT {John Tyler of Virginia}, the position of Virginia must be understood and appreciated. She is just now the neutral ground between two embattled legions, between two angry, excited, and hostile portions of the Union. To expect that her people are not to participate in the excitement by which they are surrounded; to expect that they should not share in the apprehensions which pervade the country; to expect that they should not begin to look after the safety of their interests and their institutions, were to expect something superhuman. Something must be done to save the country, to allay these apprehensions, to restore a broken confidence. Virginia steps in to arrest the progress of the country on its road to ruin. She steps in to save the country. I am here in part to represent her. I utter no menace; intimidation would be unworthy of Virginia, but if I perform my duty I must speak freely. The danger is imminent, *very* imminent.

Our national affairs cannot longer remain in their present condition; it is impossible, absolutely impossible that they should. My Republican friends, will you not take warning? Were there not pretended prophets of old, who cried, "Peace! Peace! when there was no peace"? Political prophets to-day say there is no danger. Have their counsels been wise heretofore? Can you not see that there is danger, and imminent danger in them, now?

Look, sir, at our position! I mean the position of the loyal South. By the secession of these States we are reduced to an utterly helpless minority; a minority of seven or eight States to stand in your national councils against an united North! It is not in the nature of the Anglo-Saxon race to stand in the face of a dominant and opposition party. Were the case reversed, you would not do it yourselves. We cannot hold our rights by mere sufferance,

WILLIAM CABELL RIVES, FEBRUARY 19

41

and we will not; we do not ask you to hold yours in that way. If the other States had kept on with us—had remained in the Union—we might have secured our rights in a fair contest. Now other paths are open to us, and one of these we must follow.

I desire to say a word in answer to the propositions of my honorable friend from Connecticut.[8] What did he tell us? He said that this was a self-sustaining Government; a Government that possessed the power of securing its own perpetuity, and one that must not yield or make concessions. Sir, let me say that ideas, that principles, that statements of that kind have led to the downfall of every Government on earth which has ever fallen. What but ideas and language of this kind, forced our colonies into rebellion, and lost America to the British crown?

Sir, I have had some experience in revolutions in another hemisphere—in revolutions produced by the same causes that are now operating among us. What causes but these led to the two revolutions in France? One of them I saw myself, where interest was arrayed against interest, friend against friend, brother against brother. I have seen the pavements of Paris covered, and her gutters running with fraternal blood! God forbid that I should see this horrid picture repeated in my own country; and yet it will be, sir, if we listen to the counsels urged here.

It is too late to theorize, too late to differ theoretically. I do not believe in the constitutional right of secession. I proclaimed *that*, thirty years ago in Congress. I have always adhered to my opinions since. But we are not now discussing theories; we are in the presence of a great fact. The South is in danger; her institutions are in danger. If other excuses were necessary, she might justify her action in the eyes of the world upon the ground of self-defence alone.

I condemn the secession of the States. I am not here to justify it. I detest it. But the great fact is still before us. Seven States have gone out from among us, and a President is actually inaugurated to govern the new Confederation.

With this fact the nation must deal. Right or wrong, it exists. The country is divided. Wide dissensions exist. A people have separated from another people. Force will never bring them together. Coercion is not a word to be used in this connection. There must be negotiation. Virginia presents herself as a mediator to bring back those who have left us.

The border States are not in revolt; and by border States I mean States on both sides of the border. They are here, and they came here to unite with you in measures that will reunite the country, and save it from irredeemable ruin.

There was one observation of the gentleman from Massachusetts that surprised me. He complained of Virginia for thrusting herself between the Republican party and its victory. It is not so.

Mr. BOUTWELL:[9]—I said that Massachusetts thought her action had that appearance.

Mr. RIVES:—Let me say to you, Republican gentlemen, we wish to make your victory worthy of you. We wish to inaugurate your power and your administration over the *whole* Union. We wish to give you a nation worth governing. Do us at least the justice of supposing we are in earnest in this. We are laboring to relieve you from the difficulties that hang over you. War is impending. Do you wish to govern a country convulsed by civil war? The country is divided. Do you wish to govern a fraction of the country? Behold the difficulties that you must encounter. You cannot carry on your Government without money. Where is the capitalist who will advance you money under existing circumstances?

Gentlemen, believe me, as one who has given no small amount of time and careful reflection to this subject, when I tell you that you cannot coerce sovereign States. It is impossible. Mr. HAMILTON'S[10] great foresight made him assert that our strength lay in the Government of the States—of the undivided States. Look at New York. She herself is a match for the whole army of the United States. Look at the South. She stands now almost upon an equality with you. You may spend millions of treasure, you may shed oceans of blood, but you cannot conquer any five or seven States of this Union. The proposition is an utter absurdity. You must find some other way to deal with them. In the wisdom of the country some other way must be found.

Several gentlemen have referred to our army and our navy. As a citizen of the United States, I am proud of both. I am proud of the country they serve. I have enjoyed at times her honors, at others endured her chastisements. I respect the power which our army and our navy give to our nation, but our army and navy are impotent in such a crisis as this.[11]

Mr. PRESIDENT, even England herself has been shaken to her centre by rebellions in her North with which she has been forced to contend. In Paris, too, I have myself seen regiment after regiment throw down their arms and rush into the arms of the people, of their fellow-citizens, and thus oppose, by military strength, the government under which their organization was formed. Will you repeat such occurrences here? Will you 'destroy the imperishable renown of this nation'? No! I answer for you all—you will not. Now, we, representatives of the South and of Virginia, ask of this Convention, the only body under heaven that can do it, to interpose and save us from a repetition of the scenes of blood which some of us have witnessed.

Our patriotic committee have labored for two weeks—have labored earnestly and zealously. Their report, though not satisfactory to Virginia in all respects, will yet receive her sanction, and the sanction of the border States. The representatives of Virginia know they are yielding much, when they tell you that they will support these propositions. We will do it because they will give peace to the country. Now, sir, when we are just in sight of land, when we are just entering a safe harbor, shall we turn about and circumnavigate the ocean to find an unknown shore? No, sir! no! Let us enter the harbor of safety now opened before us.

Mr. PRESIDENT, I know Massachusetts well. She is a powerful Commonwealth. She has added largely to the wealth, the power, and glory of this Union. I respect the gentleman[12] who has addressed this Convention in her behalf; but when he went out of his way and stated that he abhorred slavery, the statement grated harshly on my ears. We of the South, we of Virginia, may not and do not like many of the institutions of Massachusetts, but we cannot and we will not say that we abhor them.

Let me recall to the gentleman from Massachusetts who has addressed us, a fact from history. Let me show him that his own State was powerful in colonial times in extending the time for the importation of slaves! Let me tell him that his State has helped to fasten the institution of slavery upon a portion of this nation. Is it for a son of Massachusetts now to complain of the result of the acts of his own State? Is it for him to use these reproaches, which, if not ungrateful, are at least wanting in charity? It was a representative of Massachusetts, Mr. Gorham,[13] through whose motion and influence the time for the importation of slaves was extended in that period of our colonial history. Virginia ever, in every period of her colonial existence, exerted herself to close her ports against the importation of slaves. It was the veto of her Royal Master alone that rendered her efforts nugatory. It was New England that fastened this institution upon us. Shall she reproach us for its existence now?

Mr. BALDWIN {Roger S. Baldwin of Connecticut}:—At the time of the adoption of our present Constitution, it was well understood that Georgia and South Carolina would not enter the Union without slavery. The only question then was, should slavery have an existence inside the Union or out of it.

Mr. RIVES:—No, sir! The gentleman is mistaken. In the Constitution, as first proposed to the Convention, an unlimited right was given to import slaves. Mr. ELLSWORTH {Oliver Ellsworth of Connecticut} declared that it would be an infraction of *State rights* to prohibit this importation. New England, engaged in commerce, found an advantage in the right of importation, and she endeavored to force it upon the South.

I regard the present course of New England as very unfair. She is herself responsible for the existence of slavery—she is now our fiercest opponent; and yet New Jersey and Pennsylvania, who have not this responsibility, have always stood by the South, and I believe they always will.

It is not by *abhorring* slavery that you can put an end to the institution. You must let it alone. We are responsible for it now, and we are willing to stand responsible for it before the world. We understand the subject better than you do. It has occupied the attention of the wisest men of our time. In fact, it is not a question of slavery at all. It is a question of race. We know that the very best position for the African race to occupy is one of unmitigated legal subjection. We must deal with them as our experience and wisdom dictate; with that you have nothing to do. The gentleman from Massachusetts may congratulate himself that there are no negroes in that Commonwealth. I ask him what he would do, if he had the race to deal with in Massachusetts as we have it in Virginia?

I said, twenty years ago, in the Senate of the United States, and my whole experience since having confirmed the truth of the statement I repeat it now, that candid minds cannot differ upon this proposition, that the present position of the negroes of the United States is the best one they could occupy, both for the superior and inferior race.

And to the people of New England I have this to say: Your ancestors were most powerful and influential in fastening slavery upon us. You are the very last who ought to reproach us for its existence now. We do not indulge reproaches toward you. It is unpleasant for us to receive them from you. Their use by either can only serve to widen the unhappy differences existing between us. Let us all drop them, so far as we can, let us close up every avenue through which dissensions may come. We call upon you to make no sacrifices for us. It will cost you nothing to yield what we ask. Say, and let it be said in the Constitution, that you will not interfere with slavery in the District, or in the States, or in the Territories. Permit the free transit of our slaves from one State to another, and in the language of the patriarch, "let there be peace between you and me."

Let us all agree that there shall be landmarks between us; the same which our fathers erected. Let us say that they shall never be removed. I think upon this point I can cite an authority that will command universal respect. I discovered it in my researches into the history of the very Constitution we are now considering. {Editor Chittenden here inserted the following:}

[Mr. RIVES here read an extract from a letter written by Mr. {James} MADISON after his retirement from public life. I have not a copy of his letter, but the substance of the portion read by Mr. RIVES was a statement by Mr. MADISON, that upon the passage of the Missouri Compromise, President MONROE was much embarrassed with the question of the constitutionality of the prohibition clause; that he took counsel with Mr. MARTIN, who declared that, in his judgment, Congress had no power over the subject of slavery in the territories.]

Mr. JAMES {Amaziah B. James of New York}:—Will you leave that question just where the Constitution leaves it, upon your construction of that instrument? If so, we will agree to give you all the necessary guarantees against interference.

Mr. RIVES:—No! I will not leave it there, for it would always remain a question of construction. I prefer to put the prohibition into the Constitution.

The gentleman from Massachusetts speaks for the North,[14] Massachusetts does not constitute the North. I venerate the Commonwealth of Massachusetts. I have many friends there. I look with pride upon her connection with the Revolution; upon her public men, her manufactures, her public institutions. Her people who have accomplished so much, will not turn a deaf ear to our wants now. We wish to go to her people and obtain their judgment upon our propositions. But Massachusetts is not all the North. Rhode Island constitutes a part of it. She has always spoken for us. She will speak for us to-day. What does New Jersey say? What does the great State of Pennsylvania and the greater Northwest say? Surely they do not echo the sentiments of the gentleman from Massachusetts. They are with us, and we will trust to them.

I dislike this way of answering for sections of the country. I have heard similar language from Mr. {John C.} CALHOUN. He was fond of saying, "The South says—The South thinks—The South will do," this or that. I did not like it then. It stirred up all the rebellious sentiments of my nature; for I knew the statement was not true. I do not like such language better now. Let the *people* of Massachusetts speak. I know they will not refuse to fulfil the compact of their fathers.

We are brothers. I feel we can settle this important question which portends over us like an eclipse; we can leave this glorious country to our posterity. Once more let me refer to the noble and eloquent counsels of MADISON, and I am done. As children of the same family, as fellow-citizens of a great, glorious, and proud Republic, he invoked the kindred blood of our people to consecrate our common Union, and to banish forever the thought of our becoming aliens.

Source: Lucius E. Chittenden, ed., *A Report of the Debates and Proceedings in the Secret Sessions of the Conference Convention, for Proposing Amendments to the Constitution of the United States, Held at Washington, D.C., in February, A.D. 1861* (New York: D. Appleton & Company, 1864), 133–41.

George William Summers
February 19, 1861

George W. Summers (1804–1868) was born in Fairfax County, attended what would later become Washington and Lee University, graduated from Ohio University in 1825, and opened his law practice in Charleston two years later. He served in Virginia's House of Delegates (1830–1832; 1834–1836), in the US House of Representatives (1841–1845), and represented Kanawha County as a Whig in the 1850 Virginia constitutional convention. The following year, he ran unsuccessfully for governor, losing to Joseph Johnson. He later served as circuit judge (1852–1858) for the Eighteenth Judicial Circuit. He again represented Kanawha County as a Unionist in Virginia's state convention from which he resigned when the convention voted to secede on April 17.

Representing the western part of the state, Summers arrived at the conference prepared to defend the Union and accept any compromise that would prevent the breakup of the nation. He believed Senator John Crittenden's proposed amendment as reinterpreted by James Seddon on February 18, was "an acceptable way of settling our present difficulties." But above all, he lectured: "The Union is our inheritance — it is our pride," and "*I will never give up the Union!*" Should war come, "I will gather the last handful of faithful men, carry them to the mountains of Western Virginia, and there set up the flag of the Union." Following his resignation from the state convention, Summers played no role in the ensuing war.

Mr. SUMMERS: — Well, then, let it be eight o'clock. But let me ask you, gentlemen, not to protract or unnecessarily delay our action here.

Mr. President, my heart is full! I cannot approach the great issues with which we are dealing with becoming coolness and deliberation! Sir, I love this Union. The man does not live who entertains a higher respect for this Government than I do. I know its history — I know how it was established. There is not an incident in its history that is not precious to me. I do not wish to survive its dissolution. My hand or voice was never raised against it. They never will be. The Union is as dear to me as to any living man; and it would be pleasant, indeed, if my mind to-day could be as free from fear and anxiety about it, as the minds of other gentlemen appear to be. But, Sir, I cannot shut my eyes to events which are daily transpiring among a people who are excited and anxious, who are apprehensive that their rights are in danger — who are solicitous for — who will do as much to preserve their rights as any people. They must be calmed and quieted. It is useless now to tell them that they have no cause for fear. They are looking to this Conference. This Conference must act. If it does not, I almost fear to contemplate the prospect that will open before us.

Sir! This Conference has now been in session fifteen days. While I have felt reluctant to do anything which should have the appearance of precipitating our action, of cutting off or limiting debate, I have all the time been pressed with this conviction; that if we are to save this country we must act speedily. I have been in constant communication with the people of Virginia since I have been here. I know that this feeling of apprehension which existed when I came away, has been constantly increasing in my State since; and even last night I received letters from members of the Convention now in session in Richmond; gentlemen who are as true to this Union as the needle to the pole, informing me that every hour of *delay* in this Conference was an hour of *danger*.

I do not agree with some of my colleagues in their construction of the resolutions of the Virginia Legislature inviting this Conference. I understand that she suggests the resolutions of Mr. CRITTENDEN as *one* acceptable way of settling our present difficulties. She says that she will be satisfied with a settlement on the basis of those resolutions. But she has not made them her *ultimatum*. She has not said she will not consent to any other plan of arrangement. Her purpose was not to draw up certain articles of pacification; to call her sister States together, and say to them, "These or nothing! We have dictated the terms upon which the matter between us may be arranged. We will have these or we will not arrange at all!" I understand her as offering no restrictions whatever. She invites a conference—she asks the States to *confer* together. She expects reasonable concessions, reasonable guarantees, and with these she will be satisfied.

Nor do I know why the gentleman from Maine[15] places Virginia in a position he described, nor upon what authority. I reply to him that he makes a grave assumption when he attributes to Virginia a dictatorial position. I have come here, and I trust my colleagues have also, animated by a single purpose:—that purpose is to save the Union. Virginia claims no greater rights than any other State. She would not take them if they were offered.

Let me say here, that it is my purpose to carry out the wishes of the people of Virginia; that exercising the best judgment I have I shall try to ascertain what that purpose is, and shall do all I can to accomplish it. When the proper time comes I shall cast my vote for the proposals of amendment offered by my colleague (Mr. SEDDON): I shall do so for several reasons.[16] The first and most important of them all is this: The Union is our inheritance—it is our pride. To preserve it, what sacrifice should we not make?

Its preservation is the one single desire that animates me. Can I not be understood by my Northern friends? Will you not yield something to our necessities—to our condition? Will you not do something which will enable us to go back to our excited people and say to them, "The North is treating us fairly. See what she will do to make our Union perpetual!"

Again; I shall vote cheerfully for Mr. SEDDON's propositions, because the Legislature of my State has said that such amendments will satisfy the people of Virginia. I think the Legislature is right. I think in this respect it reflects the will of the people of Virginia. Remember, sir, that these propositions have been for some time before the country, that they have been discussed and commented upon by the public Press—that they will probably settle our difficulties, now and forever. They were introduced into Congress by a distinguished and an able man—a statesman, whose integrity and fidelity no one has ever questioned, and no one will question.[17] It is my firm belief that the States can adopt them without any material sacrifice, and that they will adopt them if they have the opportunity.

But if the CRITTENDEN resolutions—if the propositions of my colleague cannot be recommended by this Conference—do not find favor with the majority here? What then? Shall we dissolve this body, and go home? Shall we risk all the fearful consequences which must follow? No, sir! No! We came here for *peace*. Virginia came here for *peace*. We will not be impracticable. You, representatives of the free States, will not be impracticable. Therefore, I tell you that it is my firm belief that the people of Virginia WILL accept the proposals of amendment to the Constitution as reported by the majority of the committee. I believe these propositions would be acceptable to our people. I believe if we should pass them here, that the Convention now in session in Richmond would at once adopt them and recommend them to the people of that honored member of the Federal Union. Can you not? Will you not give us one chance to satisfy our people, and to save us from that other alternative which I almost fear to contemplate?

I feared when the result was announced, that the late election in Virginia of the delegates to the Convention now in session, would be misapprehended and misunderstood at the North: that the North would regard it as a triumph of the Union sentiment in Virginia.[18] In one sense it was such a triumph. The advocates of immediate and unconditional secession were defeated, were defeated by a heavy majority.

But the members comprising that Convention represent the true feeling of the people who elected them, and they represent the present feeling of Virginia. The people of that State are full of anxiety. They fear that the new administration has designs which it will carry into execution, fatal to their rights and interests. They are for the Union, *provided* their rights can be secured; provided, they can have proper and honorable guarantees. It is useless to discuss now whether they are right or wrong. Such is the condition of affairs now, and it is too late to enter into the causes which produced it. We must deal with things as they are.

I have known many gentlemen who have represented the interests of New England long and well. I know what sentiment filled their hearts years ago, and I do not believe those sentiments are changed now. I appeal to Vermont. Among her representatives here, I see a gentleman with whom, for a long time, I was upon terms of peculiar intimacy. In the whole course of that intimacy I cannot recall a single occurrence which did not impress me with his integrity, his ability, his justice. I appeal to him. I appeal to him by every consideration which can move a friend, which can influence a patriot, which can govern the action of a statesman. I appeal to Massachusetts, to all New England, which I know possesses many like himself; and I ask you to consider our circumstances, to consider our dangers, and not to refuse us the little boon we ask, when the consequences of that refusal must be so awful. Can you not afford to make a little sacrifice, when we make one so great? Can you not yield to us what is a mere matter of opinion with you, but what is so vital with us? Will you not put us in a position where we can stand with our people, and let us and you stand together in the Union? I have no delicacy here. The importance of our action with me, transcends all other considerations. I do not hesitate to appeal to New England for help in this crisis.

If New England refuses to come to our aid, it will not alter my course or change my conviction. In no possible contingency which can now be foreseen shall these convictions be changed. *I will never give up the Union!* Clouds may hang over it, storms and tempest may assail it, the waves of dissolution may dash against it, but so far as my feeble hand can support it, that support shall be given to it while I live!

When the dark days come over this Republic, and there is nothing in the future but gloom and despondency, I will do as WASHINGTON once said he would do in similar circumstances: I will gather the last handful of faithful men, carry them to the mountains of Western Virginia, and there set up the flag of the Union. It shall be defended there against all assailants until the friends of freedom and liberty from all parts of the civilized world shall rally around it, and again establish it in triumph and glory over every portion of a restored and united country.

Sir, the questions which now agitate and alarm the country do not affect the interests of all sections of the Union, or if they do affect all sections, certainly not in the same proportion. The farther sections are removed from each other, the less do the interests and the principles of their people assimilate. Maine and Louisiana, far distant from each other, differ widely. Approaching the line between the slave and free States all these differences grow less. This is shown by the action of this Conference. The border States can settle these questions. They will settle them if you will let them alone. Pennsylvania and Virginia, Maryland and New Jersey, States along the line, whose people are most vitally interested can have no difficulty in coming to an agreement. With all the possible political interests, which you may have, not only are the relations of society, of business, and commerce, to be interrupted, but these States are to form the long frontier between two foreign nations, if that fearful contingency is to happen, so often and so confidently referred to here.

Why, then, should remote sections interfere to prevent this adjustment? If they cannot aid us, why not let us alone? Let them look along the valley of the Ohio River, one of the most fertile sections of the continent, in itself great enough and fruitful enough to support a nation. It has already a large population, and that population is increasing every day. The people are attached to each other by every tie that binds society together. They now live in harmony and friendship; their property is secure. They are prosperous and happy. Such a *people cannot be, must not be divided*.

And therefore, I say, if we are driven to that alternative; if the representatives of the two extremes will not give us the benefit of their counsel and assistance, the Central States, and the great Northwest, must take the matter into their own hands. North Carolina, Virginia, Kentucky, Tennessee, with Pennsylvania, New Jersey, and other States near them, must unite with Ohio and the Northwest to save the country. They have the power to do it—they must do it.

Remember, sir, that I only refer to this as a last alternative. It is one to which I hope and pray we may never be driven. I cannot yet give up the hope, that all we need here is patient and thorough discussion and examination of the subject; that when the true condition is understood, we shall unite together to restore confidence to the country. It must be so. The consequences of farther disagreement are too great, the crisis is too important to permit mere sectional differences, mere pride of opinion, party shackles or party platforms to control the action of any gentleman here. The Republic shall not be divided. The nation shall not be destroyed. The patriotism of the people will yet save the country against all its enemies.

Source: Lucius E. Chittenden, ed., *A Report of the Debates and Proceedings in the Secret Sessions of the Conference Convention, for Proposing Amendments to the Constitution of the United States, Held at Washington, D.C., in February, A.D. 1861* (New York: D. Appleton & Company, 1864), 150–56.

John White Brockenbrough
February 22, 1861

John W. Brockenbrough (1806–1877) was educated at the College of William and Mary and the University of Virginia. He practiced law in Hanover County and Lexington. President James K. Polk appointed him a federal judge for the Western District of Virginia. He served as a representative to the Confederate Provisional Congress, and later as Confederate judge for western Virginia.

For Judge Brockenbrough the political equation was quite simple: a president had been elected who was hostile to the institution of slavery. Constitutional guarantees were therefore necessary to protect the economic engine of the South, and Virginia had agreed that the Crittenden amendment, slightly altered, would provide the security desired. "Give us the guarantees we ask," he concluded, "and my word for it, you will see the seceded States coming back one by one, and we shall see ourselves once more a happy and a united people!"

I represent an old and honorable Commonwealth. I speak, remembering the maxing [*sic*] that "a soft answer turneth away wrath," But I should disregard my duty if I did not reply to what was said a few days ago, in arraignment—in unfair and improper arraignment, of Virginia.

Virginia occupies no menacing position, no attitude of hostility toward the Union or her sister States. Virginia knows that there is good policy in the maxim, "In peace prepare for war." Her action is only such as is dictated by a prudent foresight. How unkind, then, are such taunts against Virginia, the mother of us all. She comes here in a paternal spirit; she desires to preserve the Union; she disdains to employ a menace; she knows that she never can secure the coöperation of brave men by employing menaces. No! She wishes to use all her efforts to perpetuate the reign of peace.

Another says we are seeking to secure an amendment of the Constitution by the employment of unconstitutional means, and that this meeting is a revolutionary mob—that those eminent men of the country assembled here, constitute a mob. No, sir! No!

{Here Delegate Brockenbrough, Roger S. Baldwin (Connecticut), and Lucius E. Chittenden (Vermont) had a conversation regarding the constitutionality of the gathering. Chittenden remarked that the conference "could pledge them (the delegates) *to abide by the Union, whatever* the result might be. That is the pledge we ask from the South."}

Well, that is a pledge we have no authority to give. We cannot accept these propositions as a boon from any section. We must have them as a right, or not at all.

But let me address myself at once to the momentous question. It seems that we can agree upon every thing but this question of slavery in the Territories. So far as that subject is concerned, Virginia has declared that she will accept the Crittenden resolutions. She and her southern sisters will stand upon and abide by them. If gentlemen will come up to this basis of adjustment with manly firmness, the electric wires will flash a thrill of joy to the hearts of the people this very hour. Why not come up to it like men?

The Supreme Court has already established the rights of the South, so far as this question is concerned, upon a basis which is satisfactory. Under the Dred Scott decision, the people of the South have the right to go into any portion of the Territory with their slaves. You, gentlemen of the North, will not abide by that decision. You have declared in your platform that it is a miserable dogma. How can we be satisfied with such a guarantee for our rights as that?

But it is said that this part of the Dred Scott decision is only an *obiter dictum*;[19] that the question was not presented by the record. This is not so. As was said by Governor WICKLIFFE,[20] the other day, there were two questions in that case. The judgment of the court was upon them both, and both were presented by the record.

We know that the dominant party has elected a President on a purely sectional issue, and in deadly hostility to our institutions. We believe, from all the indications of the times, that our institutions are utterly insecure. Therefore we ask these guarantees. Give them to us, and from that time you will restore peace and quiet to the country. You at once attach the Border States firmly to you forever. I hope you will do so; but I tell you that the Border States cannot be retained unless you will consent to give such guarantees as will bring back the seceded States, and unite us all in a glorious confederation.

Sentiments have been uttered here that grate harshly on the minds of Southern gentlemen. It is said that this is a war of ideas. If so, then there is certainly that irrepressible conflict about which we have heard so much. But it is not true that slaves exclude free labor. Come to the harvest homes of Western Virginia. There you will see the union of white and black labor—see the two races working harmoniously together. The mechanics are white, the field hands are black. Those only make such assertions who know nothing about it.

You insist at the North that slavery is a sin. If it is as you claim it to be, a sin, the sum of all villanies,[*sic*] then we may as well separate. We cannot live together longer.

If we cannot have the aid of other sections, the Border States must take the subject into their own hands, and settle it for themselves. These States, with one exception, have shown a most excellent spirit. Let them all come up to the work today; on this natal day of WASHINGTON,[21] of whom it was said that nature had denied him children, in order that he might be indeed the Father of his Country. New Jersey has most nobly responded, through her distinguished sons, but especially through the voice of that eloquent man, who swept with a master hand the chords of the human heart, in his remarks here, and tones of heavenly music responded to the touch.[22]

The whole nation stands on tiptoe awaiting the final result of the action of this Conference. All sections are ready to make sacrifices, but sacrifices are not required. Let us act, and then go home. A grateful people will bind the wreath of victory around your brows, for "Peace hath her victories not less than War."

We make no appeal to the sympathies of gentlemen. We ask you to do justice, simple justice to the South. Do it, and you will do honor to yourselves. Give us the guarantees we ask, and my word for it, you will see the seceded States coming back one by one, and we shall see ourselves once more a happy and a united people!

Source: Lucius E. Chittenden, ed., *A Report of the Debates and Proceedings of the Secret Sessions of the Conference Convention, for Proposing Amendments to the Constitution of the United States, Held at Washington, D.C., in February, A.D. 1861* (New York: D. Appleton & Company, 1864), 278–81.

James Alexander Seddon
February 22, 1861

Delegate Seddon's short speech is illustrative of the hyperbole often employed by southern elected officials over Secession Winter. Passing over the fact that proslavery Democrats would control both houses of Congress for the next two years and that Republicans would not control "all the powers of the Government," but only the executive branch, Seddon pronounced that the Lincoln administration would prohibit slavery from the western territories and declare that the "Government shall be on the side of freedom." In closing, he reiterated the importance of slavery to the South as a "democratic and a social interest, a political institution, the grandest item of our prosperity."

It is important to note that earlier in February, both houses of

Congress had organized the Colorado Territory without any restrictions on slavery. By the time of the vote, seven southern states had seceded and recalled their delegations from Washington, leaving Congress in control of Republicans. Ironically, when the Republican Party had the opportunity to prohibit slavery from a western territory it moderated its views, turned its back on its 1860 platform, and placed no limitation on the importation of slaves into Colorado. By March 4, the Republican-controlled Congress had also organized the territories of Dakota and Nevada in a similar manner.

Mr. SEDDON:—My voice has failed me to-day, and I do not know that I can speak in audible tones, but I will try.

I understand the gentleman who last addressed us to say, that there are to be incorporated into the administration of the Government two new principles: one is, that there shall be no slavery in the territories; the other is, that the action of the Government shall be on the side of freedom. And furthermore, that slavery is to be regarded as a purely local institution, and that slaves are not to be regarded as property anywhere except in the slave States. Now, that was just the way in which I interpreted the action of the North in the last election, and it is precisely this view which has led to the secession of the States. The gentleman well understands that a different view of their rights under the Constitution prevails among the Southern people. Will he also understand and recognize the fact, that the Supreme Court has clearly given the sanction of its opinion to the Southern construction?

Mr. WILMOT[23]—Ought not the action of the Government under WASHINGTON to be a precedent of some weight in our favor?

Mr. SEDDON:—I cannot accede to that. Now the North has inaugurated this policy. We of the South say it is a subversion of the Constitution. The gentleman must as freely submit that the party just coming into power must of necessity be a Northern party. It can have no affiliation with any party at the South. Now I ask, can we, as a matter of policy or justice, whose rights are so vitally involved, sit by and see this done? Slavery is with us a democratic and a social interest, a political institution, the grandest item of our prosperity. Can we in safety or justice sit quietly by and allow the North thus to array all the powers of the Government against it?

Source: Lucius E. Chittenden, ed., *A Report of the Debates and Proceedings in the Secret Sessions of the Conference Convention, for Proposing Amendments to the Constitution of the United States, Held at Washington, D.C., in February, A.D. 1861* (New York: D. Appleton & Company, 1864), 284–85.

Final Proposal from the Conference
February 27, 1861

After three weeks of deliberation, the conference issued its final compromise amendment. Due to the influence of northern state delegates, it differed in substantial ways from Virginia's proposal for an amended Crittenden amendment. Generally it substituted the phrase "persons held to labor" in lieu of "slavery" and "slaves" reflecting the language in the United States Constitution. It included neither of the specific requirements of Virginia's General Assembly. The conference's amendment did not adopt the phrase "now held, or hereafter acquired," in section 1 regarding slavery in the territories, nor did it protect the property rights of slave owners traveling through non-slave states and territories. Section 3 specifically prohibited Congress from interfering with state or territorial law regarding the transit of slaves in or through those domains.

Section 1. In all the present territory of the United States, north of the parallel of 36°30' of north latitude, involuntary servitude, except in punishment of crime, is prohibited. In all the present Territory south of that line, the status of persons held to involuntary servitude or labor, as it now exists, shall not be changed; nor shall any law be passed by Congress or the Territorial Legislature to hinder or prevent the taking of such persons from any of the States of this Union to said Territory, nor to impair the rights arising from said relation; but the same shall be subject to judicial cognizance in the Federal courts, according to the course of the common law. When any territory north or south of said line, within such boundary as Congress may prescribe, shall contain a population equal to that required for a member of Congress, it shall, if its form of government be republican, be admitted into the Union on an equal footing with the original States, with or without slavery, as the constitution of such new State may provide. (Approved by a vote of 9 to 8; Virginia voted "No.")

Section 2. No Territory shall be acquired by the United States, except by discovery and for naval and commercial stations, depots, and transit routes, without the concurrence of a majority of all the Senators from States which allow involuntary servitude, and a majority of all the Senators from States which prohibit that relation; nor shall territory be acquired by treaty, unless the votes of a majority of the Senators from States from each class of States herein-before mentioned be cast as a part of the two-thirds majority necessary to the ratification of such treaty. (Approved by a vote of 11 to 8; Virginia voted "Yes.")

Section 3. Neither the Constitution nor any amendment thereof shall be construed to give Congress power to regulate, abolish, or control, within any State, the relation established or recognized by the laws thereof touching persons held to labor or involuntary service therein, nor to interfere with or abolish involuntary service in the District of Columbia without the consent of Maryland and without the consent of the owners, or making the owners who do not consent just compensation; nor the power to interfere with or prohibit Representatives and others from bringing with them to the District of Columbia, retaining, and taking away, persons so held to labor or service; nor the power to interfere with or abolish involuntary service in places under the exclusive jurisdiction of the United States within those States and Territories where the same is established or recognized; nor the power to prohibit the removal or transportation of persons held to labor or involuntary service in any State or Territory of the United States to any other State or Territory thereof where it is established or recognized by law or usage, and the right during transportation, by sea or river, of touching at ports, shores, and landings, and of landing in case of distress, shall exist; but not the right of transit in or through any State or Territory, or of sale or traffic, against the laws thereof. Nor shall Congress have power to authorize any higher rate of taxation on persons held to labor or service than on land.

The bringing into the District of Columbia of persons held to labor or service, for sale, or placing them in depots to be afterwards transferred to other places for sale as merchandise, is prohibited. (Approved by a vote of 12 to 7; Virginia voted "Yes.")

Sec. 4. The third paragraph of the second section of the fourth article of the Constitution shall not be construed to prevent any of the States, by appropriate legislation, and through the action of their judicial and ministerial officers from enforcing the delivery of fugitives from labor to the person to whom such service or labor is due. (Approved by a vote of 15 to 4; Virginia voted "Yes.")

Section 5. The foreign slave trade is hereby forever prohibited; and it shall be the duty of Congress to pass laws to prevent the importation of slaves, coolies, or persons held to service or labor, into the United States and the Territories from places beyond the limits thereof. (Approved by a vote of 16 to 5; Virginia voted "No.")

Section 6. The first, third, and fifth sections, together with this section of these amendments, and the third paragraph of the second section of the first article of the Constitution, and the third paragraph of the second section of the fourth article thereof, shall not be amended or abolished without the consent of all the States.[24] (Approved by a vote of 11 to 9; Virginia voted "No.")

Section 7. Congress shall provide by law that the United States shall pay to the owner the full value of his fugitive from labor, in all cases where the marshal, or other officer, whose duty it was to arrest such fugitive, was prevented from so doing by violence or intimidation from mobs or riotous assemblages, or when, after arrest, such fugitive was rescued by like violence and intimidation, and the owner thereby deprived of the same; and the acceptance of such payment shall preclude the owner from further claim to such fugitive. Congress shall provide by law for securing to the citizens of each State the privileges and immunities of citizens in the several States. (Approved by a vote of 12 to 7; Virginia voted "No.")

[Note: This amendment was first proposed on February 15, 1861 (see Chittenden, 43–45) in a different form. Also *Congressional Globe*, 36th Cong., 2nd Sess., Senate Resolution No. 70, February 28, 1861, 1269–270. The House of Representatives declined to receive the Washington Peace Conference amendment by a vote of

93–67 on March 1, 1861; *Congressional Globe*, 36th Cong., 2nd Sess., 1333. The Senate rejected the Washington Peace Conference amendment by a vote of 28–7 on March 4, 1861; *Congressional Globe*, 36th Cong., 2nd Sess., 1405.]

Source: Lucius E. Chittenden, ed., *A Report of the Debates and Proceedings in the Secret Sessions of the Conference Convention, for Proposing Amendments to the Constitution of the United States, Held at Washington, D.C., in February, A.D. 1861* (New York: D. Appleton & Company, 1864), 440–45.

3

United States Senate
January–March 1861

Robert Mercer Taliaferro Hunter
January 11, 1861

Robert M. T. Hunter (1809–1887) graduated from the University of Virginia in 1828 and began his law practice in Lloyds in 1830. He served in Virginia's general assembly (1834–1837) and in the US House of Representatives (1837–1843; 1845–1847) before being elected to the US Senate in 1846, serving there from 1847 to 1861. He was formally expelled from the Senate on July 11, 1861, for engaging in a "conspiracy for the destruction of the Union and Government." He was elected as a delegate to the Confederate Provisional Congress and briefly served as Confederate secretary of state (1861–1862) before being elected to the Confederate Senate where he served from 1862 until 1865.[1]

By January 11, South Carolina, Mississippi, and Florida had seceded; Alabama would vote in favor of disunion that very day. A staunch defender of slavery— "the very foundation of the social system of the South"—Hunter argued that if protections for slavery were not added to the US Constitution and if Virginia did not secede, White men would gradually be "reduced to the level of the negro." To prevent that eventuality from becoming a reality, the senator proposed a constitutional amendment that would protect slavery and the interstate slave trade from congressional intervention, require states to suppress armed invasions of neighboring states (a clear reference to the 1859 John Brown raid on Harpers Ferry), and strengthen the fugitive slave clause of the Constitution. In addition, Hunter proposed a dual executive to prevent one section from dominating the other, and advocated in favor of expanding the Supreme Court to ten justices on the presumption that North and South would be equally represented.

Mr. HUNTER. Mr. President, I have not sought to speak hitherto on the momentous question of the day, because I did not believe that any good would be accomplished by speaking. The disease seemed to me to be so deeply seated that none but the most radical remedies would suffice; and I had no hope that the public mind of the North was in a condition to receive any such proposition. I do not know that it is even now prepared to weigh carefully such a suggestion; but surely none can longer doubt the imminence or the extremity of the danger. All must see that the bonds which have hitherto bound together the members of this Confederacy are parting like flax before the fire of popular passion. Our political fabric is reeling and tottering in the storm; so that, if it were not based on the solid foundations of State organization, there would be every reason to expect its entire destruction. Before the end of this month, it is almost certain that six or seven of the States will have seceded from this Union. It is therefore now no more a question of saving or of preserving the old Union. We cannot recall the past; we cannot restore the dead; but the hope and the trust of those who desire a Union, are that we may be able to reconstruct a new Government and a new Union, which perhaps may be more permanent and efficient than the old. I know, sir, that there are difficulties in the way; but I put my trust in the good sense and in the instincts of empire, which have heretofore characterized the American people, to accomplish that great work. If we would do it, we must not sit idly, bewailing the condition of public affairs; but in the heroic spirit of the mariner who is cast away on a distant shore, see if we cannot find materials to build another ship, in which we may once more take the sea, and rejoin our kindred and friends. But, Mr. President, to do this, we must face and acknowledge the true evil of the day. To-day we must deal wisely with the mighty present, that we may be ready for perhaps the still more eventful future which will be on us tomorrow. New ideas, like new forces, have entered into our system; they are demanding the legitimate expression of their power, or they threaten to rend and destroy it in their wild and irregular play. There are now portions of this Union in which population already begins to press on the means of subsistence. In all of the States there is a desire—in some of them a necessity—for further expansion. It is that which has led to the warfare between the two social systems which have been brought together in our Constitution; a war waged with a bitterness and asperity that has reduced us to the sad pass in which we now find ourselves.

This Constitution was designed to unite two social systems, upon terms of equality and fairness, different in their character, but not necessarily hostile. Indeed, the very differences in these systems, it would seem, ought to have formed causes of union and mutual attraction, instead of giving rise to the "irrepressible conflict"[2] which, it is said, some law of nature has declared between them. What the one wanted, the other could supply. If the carrying States did not make their provisions, the provision-growing States, on the other hand, had not the ships in which to transport their surplus productions. If the manufacturing States did not raise the raw material, the planting States, on the other hand, did not have the manufactories to convert that material into useful and necessary fabrics. Thus, what the one wanted, the other could supply. The only difference of products would seem to have afforded the means for forming a perfect system of industry, which should have been stronger by the mutual dependence and support of the parts. Unfortunately, however, as those who represented the non-slaveholding system of society grew into power, they commenced a warfare upon the other system which was associated with it under the Constitution. It was commenced in 1820, when it was declared that the social system of the South was founded upon sin, was anti-republican in its character, and deserved to be repressed and suppressed by the General Government wherever it had exclusive jurisdiction. The claim was made, that so far as the Territories of the United States were concerned, they were to be given up to the exclusive expansion of one of the systems at the expense of the other. Unhappily, in that first contest, the weaker system went by the board; a law was passed which did put it under the ban of the Empire; which did exclude the South from a large portion of the domain of the United States.[3]

After that sprang up a party, at first not so large as it now is, which commenced a regular warfare upon the system of slavery in the South; upon the social system of the States which tolerated the institution of slavery. They commenced a system of agitation through the press, the pulpit, and the common halls of legislation whose object it was to wound the self-respect of the slaveholder, and to make him odious in the eyes of the rest of the world. They denied that there could be any property in slaves—the very foundation of the social system of the South—and, as a consequence, they maintained that this Government was bound to prevent its extension, and to abolish and suppress it wherever it had exclusive jurisdiction. They sought, by petition, to put an end to the slave trade between the States, that the institution might be pent up, and made dangerous and unprofitable.

In process of time, they either evaded or they denied the constitutional obligation to return fugitive slaves, and at last it was proclaimed here in these Halls that there was a law higher than the Constitution, which nullified its obligations and its provisions. Practicing upon this preaching, the majority of the non-slaveholding States, as was shown by my friend from Georgia [Mr. TOOMBS][4] in his able argument on this subject, passed personal liberty bills, the practical effect of which was to nullify the fugitive slave law, which was passed in pursuance of the Constitution of the United States.

It is but a year since there was an armed invasion of my State for the purpose of creating servile insurrections; and yet not a State—and it is with the State alone that effectual remedies can be applied—has interfered, to make any such combination penal in time to come. We have heard it pronounced, sir, by a distinguished leader of that party, that there was to be an "irrepressible conflict" between the two social systems, until one or the other was destroyed. A President has been nominated and elected by a sectional majority, who was known to have avowed and to entertain such opinions; and a party has come into power, with full possession of this Government, which has elected a President and a standard-bearer who has made such declarations in regard to the rights of the South.[5]

Is it surprising, then, that the southern States should say: "It is not safe for us to remain longer in a Government which may be directed as an instrument of hostility against us; it is not safe for us to remain longer under the rule of a Government whose President may misuse his patronage for the very purpose of stirring up civil strife among us, and also for the purpose of creating civil war in our midst?" For it is known that a large portion—and that was but a year ago—of the Republican leaders and members of the

House of Representatives indorsed and recommended a book which proposed the extinction of slavery by such means.[6] Under such circumstances,
I ask, is it surprising that the southern States should say: "It is unsafe for
us to remain under a Government which, instead of protecting us, may be
directed against us, as an instrument of attack, unless we can be protected
by some new constitutional guarantees, which will save our social system
from such a warfare as this?"

Mr. President, the southern people number now some thirteen million,
and cover between eight hundred thousand and nine hundred thousand
square miles of territory. They have within themselves all the capacities of
empire. Is it to be supposed that when they are threatened in the common
Government with an attack upon their social system, upon which their very
being depends, they will not withdraw from that Government—unless they
can be secured within the Union—for the purpose of establishing another,
which they know can and will protect them? Why, sir, what people is it that
can stand a constant warfare upon their social system, waged for the purpose
of dwarfing and suppressing and destroying it? The social system of a people
is its moral being; and the Government which would dwarf or suppress it is
like the parent who would consign his child to vice and ignorance. I know of
instances in which nations have thriven under bad laws; I know of instances
in which nations have thriven when their allegiance was transferred by force
from one country to another; I know of none which survived the sudden
and total prostration of its social system. To reduce them to that is to reduce
them to anarchy, which is the death of a nation or a people.

I say, therefore, sir, that the South is bound to take this course unless it
can get some guarantees which will protect it in the Union, some constitutional guarantees which will serve that end; and I now ask, what should be
the nature of the guarantees that would effectually prevent the social system
from such assaults as these? I say, they must be guarantees of a kind that
will stop up all the avenues through which they have threatened to assail the
social system of the South. There must be constitutional amendments which
shall provide first, that Congress shall have no power to abolish slavery in
the States, in the District of Columbia, in the dock-yards, forts, and arsenals of the United States; second, that it shall not abolish, tax, or obstruct
the slave trade between the States; third, that it shall be the duty of each
of the States to suppress combinations within their jurisdiction for armed

invasions of another; fourth, that States shall be admitted with or without slavery, according to the election of the people; fifth, that it shall be the duty of the States to restore fugitive slaves when within their borders, or to pay the value of the same; sixth, that fugitives from justice shall be deemed all those who have offended against the laws of a State within its jurisdiction, and who have escaped therefrom; seventh, that Congress shall recognize and protect as property whatever is held to be such by the laws or prescriptions of any State within the Territories, dock-yards, forts, and arsenals of the United States, and wherever the United States has exclusive jurisdiction; with the following exceptions: First, it may leave the subject of slavery or involuntary servitude to the people of the Territories when a law shall be passed to that effect with the usual sanction, and also with the assent of a majority of the Senators from the slaveholding States, and a majority of the Senators from the non-slaveholding States. That exception is designed to provide for the case where we might annex a Territory almost fully peopled, and whose people ought to have the right of self-government, and yet might not be ready to be admitted as a State into the Union.

The next exception is, that "Congress may divide the Territories, to the effect that slavery or involuntary servitude shall be prohibited in one portion of the territory, and recognized and protected in another; provided the law has the sanction of a majority from each of the sections as aforesaid," and that exception is designed to provide for the case where an unpeopled Territory is annexed and it is a fair subject of division between the two sections.

Such, Mr. President, are the guarantees of principle, which, it seems to me, ought to be established by amendments to the Constitution; but I do not believe that these guarantees alone would protect the social system of the South against attack, and perhaps overthrow, from the superior power of the North. I believe that, in addition to these guarantees of principle, there ought to be guarantees of power; because, if you do not adopt these, the South would still be subjected to the danger of an improper use of the patronage of the Executive, who might apply it for the purpose of stirring up civil strife and dissension among them. The southern States might, too, notwithstanding these provisions, find themselves in a position in which the stronger party had construed them away, and asserted, perhaps, that there was some higher law, which nullified and destroyed them. To make the South secure, then, some power ought to be given it to protect its rights in the Union—some veto power in the system, which would enable it to prevent it from ever being perverted to its attack and destruction.

And here, Mr. President, if the Senate will bear with me, I will proceed to suggest such remedies in this regard as I think ought to be applied, premising that I do not mean, by any means, to say that I suppose I am suggesting the only means on which a settlement may be made. I know there are others—others on which I would agree to settle it—but I am suggesting the means on which I think the best and the most permanent settlement can be made; and I do not think that any permanent peace can be secured, unless we provide some guarantees of power, as well as of principle.

In regard to this guarantee of power, in the first place, I would resort to the dual executive, as proposed by Mr. Calhoun,[7] not in the shape in which he recommended it, but in another form, which, I think, is not obnoxious to the objection that may be fairly taken against his plan. I would provide that each section should elect a President, to be called a first and a second President; the first to serve for four years as President, the next to succeed him at the end of four years, and to govern for four other years, and afterwards to be reëligible. I would provide that, during the term of service of the first President, the second should be President of the Senate, with a casting vote in case of a tie; and that no treaty should be valid which did not have the signature of both Presidents, and the assent of two thirds of the Senate; that no law should be valid which did not have the assent of both Presidents, or in the event of a veto by one of them, the assent of a majority of the Senators of the section from which he came; that no person should be appointed to a local office in the section from which the second President was elected, unless the appointment had the assent of that President, or in the event of his veto, the assent of a majority of the Senators from the section from which he came.

{Here Senator Hunter explained the advantages of his proposal for a dual executive mostly in preventing one section from dominating governmental affairs and in that elections would be held only once every eight years. The senator did not explore the possibility of California and Oregon considering themselves a section which might lead to the formation of a triadic executive. He concluded by voicing a concern that the Constitution assigned a "large class of rights" to states "for which there are no remedies, or next to no remedies."}

I believe, myself, that it was intended, by the framers of that instrument, that the States should have been mainly instrumental in restoring fugitives from labor, or, to speak more plainly, fugitive slaves. We know that it is in their power, not only to refrain from discharging this duty, but actually to obstruct and impede the Government of the United States in its effort to execute the law. There are certain rights for which there are no remedies. It is provided, for instance, that no State shall maintain an army; and yet, if it does so, there is no remedy to prevent it.

Now, sir, I propose, in order to secure the proper enforcement of these rights for which, as I say, there are no adequate remedies, that the Supreme Court should also be adjusted. It should consist of ten judges—five from each section—the Chief Justice to be one of the five. I would allow any State to cite another State before this tribunal to charge it with having failed to perform its constitutional obligations; and if the court decided a State thus cited to be in default, then I would provide, if it did not repair the wrong it had done, that any State might deny to its citizens within its jurisdiction the privileges of citizens in all the States; that it might tax its commerce and the property of its people until it ceased to be in default. Thus, I would provide a remedy without bringing the General Government into collision with the States; and without bringing the Supreme Court into collision with them. Whenever international stipulations in regard to the duties imposed on the State, as laid down in the Constitution, are violated, I would remedy the wrong by international remedies. I would give a State the right, in such cases, after the adjudication of the court, to deny to the offending State the performance of the mutual obligations which had been created for its benefit. In this way I believe that those wrongs might be remedied without producing collision in the system. A self-executing process would thus provide a remedy for the wrong, without a jar to the machinery of Government.

In order to make this check efficient, it should be provided that the judges of the Supreme Court in each section should be appointed by the President from that section, and this is the only original appointing power which I would give to the second President.

I have presented this scheme, Mr. President, as one which, in my opinion, would adjust the differences between the two social systems, and which would protect each from the assault of the other. If this were done, so that we were made mutually safe, I, for one, would be willing to regulate the right of secession, which I hold to be a right not given in the Constitution, but resulting from the nature of the compact. I would provide, that before a State seceded it should summon a convention of the States in the section to which it belonged, and submit to them a statement of its grievances and wrongs. Should a majority of the States in such a convention decide the complaint to be well founded, then the State ought to be permitted to secede in peace. For, whenever a majority of States in an entire section shall declare that good cause for secession exists, then who can dispute that it ought to take place? Should they say, however, that no good cause existed, then the moral force of such a decision, on the part of the confederacy of those who are bound to the complaining State by identical and homogeneous interests, would prevent it from prosecuting the claim any further. I believe that the system thus adjusted would give us a permanent Union, an efficient, a useful, and just Government. I think our Government would then rank among the most permanent of human institutions. It is my honest opinion that, with a Government thus balanced, and with such capacities for empire as our people possess, we should build up a political system whose power and stability and beneficial influences would be unparalleled in all the history of the past.

I know, Mr. President, it may be said that such a distribution of power does not accord with the principle of distributing power according to numbers; but I say if that be the true principle at all, it applies only to States which have a single government; it does not apply to confederacies; and if it were left to me to amend this Constitution, I would stamp upon this Government a character still more distinctly federative than that which it now bears. I say, then, that the distribution of power which I propose would be entirely just upon the federative principle. Nor would my proposition be at all more inconsistent with the principle of distributing power according to numbers than the arrangements of the present Federal Constitution. Nothing in my scheme is more unequal than the provision which gives the six New England States twelve Senators while New York has only two, although the population of that State is as great, and I believe greater,

than that of all the New England States together. There is nothing in the
scheme now proposed, inconsistent with the federative principle; and if the
slaveholding and the non-slaveholding States had been standing apart for a
dozen years in different confederacies, and there was a proposition to unite
those confederacies in one, no man would think it extreme, or be surprised
if each of the confederacies insisted upon such powers and such guarantees
as would enable it to defend its own social system and to secure equality,
together with the opportunity for expansion according to the peculiar law
of its development.

But, Mr. President, as I said before, I do not mean to declare that this is
the only scheme upon which I will settle. I say I believe it to afford the best
basis of settlement which has yet been devised. There are other schemes
upon which I would settle. I would settle upon something which would
give only a truce, provided it promised to be a long truce, and then trust to
public opinion and the progress of truth to remedy future evils when they
might arise. But I would prefer, when we do settle, after all this turmoil and
confusion, that we should do so upon some principle which promises us a
permanent adjustment, a constant and continuing peace, a safe, an efficient,
and a stable Government.

Mr. President, I have founded my suggestions upon the fact, which I
take to be an accomplished fact, that some of the States of this Union have
already withdrawn, and that the old Union has been dissolved, and has
gone. I believe there is no way of obtaining a Union except through a reconstruction, because I utterly repudiate and deny that it can be done through
the system of coercion, which some have proposed. Sir, I say, if you were
to attempt coercion, and by conquest to restore the Union, it would not be
the Union of our fathers; but a very different one. I say it would be a Union
constructed in entire opposition to the true American spirit and American
principles; a Union of a number of subjugated provinces with others who
governed them and wielded the whole power of the Confederacy.

{Here Senator Hunter devoted a considerable amount of his time to
address the issue of northern coercion against the seceded states. A
civil war between the sections, he argued, would "produce immense
disasters in both sections of the country." He added that a blockade of

southern ports in order to collect tariffs would equally be impossible to imagine. "Is it to be presumed that Great Britain, which has millions of human beings whose very existence depends upon cotton, that the great interests of civilization, would allow this grand material of human industry to be thus shut up and denied to them? Why, sir, it is not to be supposed for a moment. There are other Powers which would prevent such a blockade, in addition to the resistance which might be expected from the section that it was attempted thus to coerce."}

I say, then, Mr. President, that it is idle to think of coercion. You may, if you choose, if such be your feeling, inflict evils by waging civil war; but will you inflict more on others than you will receive in return? Will you be benefited by the operation when you come to sum up its results and effects? I think not. But suppose you could succeed—I put the question to you now—suppose you had succeeded according to your utmost wishes; suppose you had conquered the South; that you had subjugated the entire section; that you had reduced those States to the condition of dependent provinces: how then would you exercise your power? Would you apply your doctrine, that there can be no property in slaves? In that community of eight or nine million white men and four million slaves, would you turn them loose together, and set the slaves free? Would you repeat the experiment of the British West Indies—of the Island of Jamaica?[8] Would your people stand by and see the cultivated fields return to the bush, the white man being gradually reduced to the level of the negro, and the negro remitted and restored to his primitive condition of barbarism? Would the great interests of civilization and humanity permit such a result? Would your own interests, your manufacturers, your shipowners, agree to it? Sir, it is not to be supposed that such a thing would be permitted; and what then would be the result? You would have to maintain the social system; you would have to recognize property in slaves; and what would follow from that? If you recognize property in slaves, you must cause fugitive slaves to be restored. If you recognize a property that is under the jurisdiction of your Government, you must protect it, and if you do protect it, you must punish persons who attempt to make raids upon it, and to incite servile insurrections. And, sirs, if you once commit yourselves to the duty of protecting it throughout all these conquered States, you would find that it followed, as a necessary consequence, that you must protect it wherever you had the exclusive jurisdiction. What, then, would become of your dogma of excluding it from the Territories? What would be the effect of such an experiment? You pen them up until there comes to be a surplus population in the old States; you pen up the negroes, and say the negro shall not move, but the white man may. What is the effect of that? The white man does move when the wages of labor are low; the negro remains and gains the preponderance in population until you give him the best part of the continent, and remove the white man to the worst. Could such an absurdity as this be tolerated, Mr. President? No, sir; not for a moment.

Then, if you would be forced to accede to all these things, if you succeeded according to your wishes, and conquered and subdued us, after a bloody and harassing civil war, why not do it beforehand, when it would save the Union? Why not do it now, when it would avert all these calamities? Why not avail yourself of the present opportunity, when you may do so without the dreadful inconsistency which will be charged upon you, when you may be forced to do these very things after you have carried on this cruel and harassing and distressing system of civil war?

I say, then, Mr. President, that it is impossible to coerce the southern States, if you were to attempt to do so. If you had the constitutional right to do so, it would be impossible. Why create a civil war wantonly, without purpose, without use or benefit to any one? If this be so, why not adopt the proposition in my resolution—why not cede back the forts to those States that claim to have seceded, and to have withdrawn from this Confederacy? What do you want with them? What do you want with the forts in the harbor of Charleston? If you do not mean to coerce South Carolina, they are of no use to you; if you do not mean to coerce her, you ought not to have them. The whole thing lies in a nutshell; because, if you do mean to use them for the purpose of coercion, you light up the flames of civil war, and there is no telling when those flames will be extinguished; if you do attempt to use them for the purpose of coercion, you destroy the chances of the construction of another Union, which I still hope and trust may take place, and which may prove to us a more permanent bond of alliance and fraternity than that one which is passing away from us.

I say, too, sir, that you have no right, when you came to weigh the question

of right, to hold on to these forts. You could not have obtained them without the consent of the Legislature of the State; that is the provision of the
Constitution. Upon what was that consent given? Not for pecuniary considerations. It was given upon the consideration that they were to be used for
the defense of the State. Now, sir, you keep them when they can no longer
be used for the defense of the State, but are proposed to be used for offensive
purposes against her. The consideration, therefore, in my opinion, has failed;
and in justice and equity, you ought to restore them.

{Senator Hunter continued here to plead with Republicans to respect
the wishes of the South, avoid civil war, and plant the seeds for a re-
construction of the Union. "Secession does not necessarily destroy the
Union, or rather the hopes of reunion; it may turn out to be the necessary path to reconstruction." But reconstruction, warned Hunter, will
not be possible if the North forces the country into a civil war. The
South will prefer death "in any and every form rather than submission
to such oppression and tyranny."}

But, Mr. President, I do not wish to pursue this line of argument. I do
not desire to engage in any discussion which so much stirs the blood as the
supposition that such rights as these are to be denied to any portion of my
countrymen. I choose rather to stand in the character in which I appear this
day. I stand here to plead for peace; not that my State, in my opinion, has
any reason to fear war more than another, but because it is the interest of
all to preserve the peace. In the sacred names of humanity and of Christian
civilization; in the names of thirty million human souls, men, women, and
children, whose lives, whose honor, and whose happiness, depend upon the
events of such a civil war as that with which we are threatened; in the name
of the great American experiment, which, as I said before, was founded by
Providence in the wilderness, and which, I insist, has not yet failed; I appeal
to the American people to prevent the effusion of blood. It is said that the
very scent of blood stirs up the animal passions of man. Give us time for
the play of reason. Let us see, after the southern States have secured themselves by some united action, if we cannot bring together once more our

scattered divisions; if we cannot close up our broken ranks; if we cannot find
some place of conciliation, some common ground upon which we all may
rally once more; and when the columns come mustering in from the distant
North and the furthest South, from the rising and from the setting sun, to
take their part in that grand review, the shout of their war-cry shall shake
the air until it brings down the very birds in their flight as it ascends to the
heavens to proclaim to the world that we are united once more, brothers in
war, and brothers in peace, ready to take our wonted place in the front line
of the mighty march of human progress, and able and willing to play for the
mastery in that game of nations where the prizes are power and empire, and
where victory may crown our name with eternal fame and deathless renown.

Source: *Congressional Globe*, 36th Cong., 2nd Sess., 328–32.

James Murray Mason
March 7, 1861

James M. Mason (1798–1871) graduated from the University of Pennsylvania in 1818 and the law department of William and Mary in 1820
before setting up his law practice in Winchester. He served in the Virginia House of Delegates (1826–1832), the US House of Representatives
(1837–1839), and the US Senate from 1847 until 1861. Along with his colleague, Robert M. T. Hunter, he was formally expelled from the Senate on July 11, 1861. He was a delegate to the Confederate Provisional
Congress prior to being appointed commissioner of the Confederacy to
Great Britain and France, a post he held throughout the war.[9]

Continuing the secessionist mantra that the Republican Party had
"the political power of the country in their hands," Senator Mason
claimed in this speech that President Lincoln's inaugural address was
clearly a "proclamation of war" and that the positions proclaimed in
the Chicago Platform would be the law of the land. He also voiced the
commonly expressed fear that the Lincoln administration was planning to coerce the departed states into submission in spite of the fact
that the Republican controlled Congress had debated two force bills

earlier in the year and had declined to pass either. Mason specifically
found the president's message vague when it came to the "great question of African slavery, which has already rent the Union and keeps
other slave States trembling in the balance."

Mr. President, so far as I recollect, in a service of now some fourteen years
in the Senate, I do not remember on any former occasion a motion to print
the inaugural speech of the President. I may be mistaken in the fact, but
such is my recollection. It would not seem appropriate for the Senate to
print the speech, only because it is not a paper addressed to the Senate, or
to Congress, of which the Senate is a part. It is an address that is made to
the American people, the constituents of the new President, and is intended
usually to give to them a general idea, but an intelligible idea of the manner
in which the public affairs of the country shall be administered while he is
their President. When, however, I heard the motion of the honorable Senator from Connecticut,[10] that this paper should be printed, I received it as an
intimation of a purpose on the part of the political friends of the President
to make an opportunity through the Senate of giving to all the States an
exposition of the views of the President set out in that paper. I have been
disappointed in that. The debate has continued now for some two days, and
no purpose has been evinced on the other side of the Chamber to make a
single comment upon this document.

The honorable Senator from Illinois,[11] soon after the motion was
made, took the floor, and showed, by his exposition of the meaning of the
inaugural—whether it was right or wrong—that he had made it the subject of careful study. He so announced; and if he had not announced it, his
manner of treating it would have evinced the fact. But on the other side of
the Chamber, where, if at all, we were to look for any commentary, or any
interpretation of any hidden meaning in the message, the whole body is silent. Now, sir, why this motion to print? I shall avail myself of it very briefly
to give to my constituents, from my place here, my interpretation of this very
strange document—strange, considering the condition of things in which
it was pronounced.

Sir, the honorable Senator from Illinois, yesterday, proclaimed, with some
apparent emotion, that after a careful, and, as he expressed it, a critical

analysis of the various texts—and there are many texts in the document—
he had at last attained the great and consoling conclusion that the purpose
of the President was to proclaim a peace. I was surprised to hear it. I had
read the document with some care; I had heard a very general expression of
opinion upon it in many circles, political and social; I had seen the rever-
beration of the public press, not in the South alone, but elsewhere, on the
document; and the Senator from Illinois was the only source from which
there was any declaration that it should be interpreted as a measure of peace.

Mr. President, what is meant by peace? What is the condition of the
country? The Union, in a process of disintegration, has already lost seven
of the States; they have confederated and formed a new government. The
progressive process of that disintegration was officially made known to the
Senate by Senators who filed—and you have now in your archives—the or-
dinances of separation. It is known as a historical fact, that those States have
confederated and formed a new government, established a flag, established
a revenue, organized a complete government in all its parts, provided for a
military force by sea and land, and that there is not absent one single feature
necessary to constitute a perfect, and stable government, and a government
comprising within its limits five million people, bond and free; nearly three
million of whom are white. In that condition of things the President, in
his inaugural, as it is called, his introductory message to the people of the
United States, tells them that, notwithstanding that existing fact, the Union
is unbroken. That is his language. Now, sir, I am not going very far into the
policy of his message; but what I want is, to ascertain what the southern
States are to expect as the policy of this Administration,—what they are
to look for. I mean not only those States that have confederated, but I mean
those States that have not yet confederated, but who necessarily sympathize,
from affection, from intercourse, from alliance, more than all from that great
bond which can never be broken, (holding in common with them the same
social fabric on which their institutions rest,) for the policy of the President
of the United States is equally interesting to my State, on this question of
force, as it is to the confederated States, where the force is to be exercised. I
have looked, therefore, carefully to see what that policy is; and I say again,
that if there be one man or one press who has found in that message what
the Senator from Illinois has found, (a policy of peace,) I have yet to hear
who that man or that press is. It has not been announced on the other side.

They have put no such interpretation on it, so far as they have spoken, and if they could speak it, would they not? Why, sir, if there was the peaceful solution in that message which the Senator from Illinois has found, it would be proclaimed in the tongue of a trumpet, that it might go forth and give peace to the land and restore the prosperity which has been destroyed, and under which the country has been suffering. It is the want of that assurance which causes, as we are informed, thousands of the honest, laborious, industrious population of the country now to be suffering for bread; and it is the want of that assurance which places the country in the depressed condition that it is; and will anybody tell me, that if the policy of the President here was what the Senator from Illinois has found to be, peaceful policy, it would not be proclaimed and joyously proclaimed, by the representatives of that suffering population? But they are silent, and they must be silent, because the message is a proclamation of war—not of peace.

How did the Senator find it? He has gone through various paragraphs in the message; admitted that they were not very explicit or direct; that they might be susceptible of a doubtful interpretation on this question of peace or war; but at last he discovered what he calls the great key to the meaning of the message, and which he proclaims as evincive of a peaceful solution of the whole question. He discovered the key to the President's meaning; and that key proclaimed to him, as he says, that the whole intent of the message was one of peace. Now, let us look at it. The message says that, under the Constitution and the laws, the Union is unbroken; that he came to the Presidency of the Union in that condition, and that it is his duty to preserve the Union by enforcing the laws in all the States, making no exception whatever. He says that he has no purpose of violence, or of bloodshed; and I have no doubt that violence and bloodshed would be as abhorrent to the nature of that new President as it is to ours; but does he say he can avoid it? No; he says that he is required by his constitutional duty to enforce the laws in all the States, and that he will do it. Well, how is it to be done? He says, in the inaugural:

> I therefore consider that, in view of the Constitution and the laws, the Union is unbroken; and, to the extent of my ability, I shall take care, as the Constitution itself expressly enjoins upon me, that the laws of the Union be faithfully executed in all the States. Doing this I deem to be only a simple duty on my part; and I shall perform it, so far

as practicable, unless my rightful masters, the American people, shall withhold the requisite means, or, in some authoritative manner, direct the contrary. I trust this will not be regarded as a menace.

Certainly not. The President here proclaiming what he considers his constitutional duty; and it would be a very extraordinary thing that, when he declares his determination to perform that duty, anybody should consider it a menace. No, sir; it rises far above a menace; it is a declaration of the purpose of political power, and it is to be regarded in that light alone. It is a declaration of the possession of political power, and a duty to exercise it, and a purpose to discharge that duty. But why did he ask us not to consider it as a menace? Who looks upon it as a menace? What thrust that into the mind of the President? A menace? A menace is a threat, a threat which comes from one who possesses power and intends to exercise it at discretion, not as a duty. There is no menace in a declaration of discharging a duty. The word is out of place. A power of discretion may be exercised rightfully or wrongfully; and a declaration how that discretion may be exercised, if construed wrongfully, may be a menace. No, sir; this is not a menace; the President need have no apprehension that in the South it will be looked at as a menace; it will be looked at, as it is intended, as a declaration that he is in possession of political power, that it is his duty to use it in a certain way, and that he will use it. That is enough. It places him exactly where he intended to place himself. Now, what is the power? There is no menace in it. The power is to execute the laws; and his purpose is to do it. Common sense would tell him, and common sense has told him, as we shall see presently in the message, that there are seven States out of the Union. You say they are not out; that the Constitution and laws are still extended over them. They say the contrary. You say you will execute the laws in all the States, including those that have abandoned the Union; and common sense tells us if you attempt it, it will be resisted by force. He knows that. Who that is present in this Senate-house doubts that, if the President of the United States attempts to collect revenue in one of the seceding States, it will be resisted? The President knows it. He says, therefore, following out the idea, and speaking of his duty to execute the laws: "In doing this, there need be no bloodshed or violence." No, sir; there need be none, provided those States that have seceded permit him to execute the laws. "There need be no violence or bloodshed;" and that is the idea of peace, I suppose, that possesses the mind of the honorable Senator from Illinois. The President carries it still further: "The power confided in me will be used to hold, occupy, and possess the property and places belonging to the Government, and to collect the duties and imposts; but beyond what may be necessary for these objects, there will be no invasion—no using of force against or among the people anywhere."

Now, Mr. President, looking at the condition of things in the country, unless there be some men who labor under the extraordinary hallucination that the abandonment of the Union by these five million people and seven States, their confederating themselves into a government which is most rapidly hardening from the gristle into the bone, who have established a public revenue, who have established a public credit, who have an army in the field, who have constructed forts and fortifications around those in possession of this Government—unless there be some men laboring under the hallucination to believe that that is all a mere stage trick, a mere piece of painted paper, to deceive and delude the government from which they have detached themselves, there can be no man who can tell me that the President does not intend force, war, by this message, if necessary to execute the laws there.

I am not quarreling with the message; I am only seeking to get its true interpretation, that there may be no mistake about it amongst my people. He is the President of the United States; he is clothed with the whole executive power; he is the commander-in-chief of the Army and Navy; they are disposable at his will. He has taken an oath to support the Constitution; he has taken an oath to execute the laws; and he tells us here what is the interpretation he puts upon the Constitution, so far as regards his duty in these respects. I should be very unreasonable, insensate, if I were to quarrel with him because of the interpretation that he puts upon his duty. Far from it. The responsibility is with him; let him exercise it. But what I challenge him for is, that he has not more explicitly told us what he means to do; that he has left it to inference, to construction, to interpretation that may possibly mislead these people as to his actual purpose. He has said he will execute the laws, will collect the revenue, will occupy, hold, and possess the forts and arsenals, and other places that belong, as he says, to the Government; and that he will use no force, nor will he commit any invasion, beyond what may be necessary to execute these objects. Everybody knows that he cannot get possession of those forts and arsenals and navy-yards that are out of his possession and out of his occupation, without the exercise of public force. He says that he will use the public force, and send it there, thus invading for the purpose of taking possession; but he will not use more force, or have more invasion, than is necessary to execute the purpose.

The great key, however, which the Senator from Illinois found to make all this a peaceful solution at last, is in the concluding paragraph of this part of the message, in which the President says: "The course here indicated will be followed, unless current events and experience shall show a modification or change to be proper; and in every case and exigency, my best discretion will be exercised, according to circumstances actually existing, and with a view and a hope of a peaceful solution of the national troubles, and the restoration of fraternal sympathies and affections."

That is the key that the Senator from Illinois says unlocks the true intent and meaning of this message; and it has been done in the view and hope of a peaceful solution. If that Senator thinks that, because the President has a peaceful view of this armed invasion of a foreign Territory, or a hope of a peaceful solution, notwithstanding the armed invasion which he declares he will exercise, I can only say to that Senator he is more credulous than any of those around him. That is the whole solution; that is, as he expresses it, the great key to the meaning of the President. Now, sir, there is but one thing left unsaid in the message, so far as this question of force is concerned, and that is the time when the force is to be exercised. He cannot get possession of one of these forts without the exercise of force. He cannot take force there without invading a Territory that claims to be foreign to this; and he says he will use that invasion, and he will exercise that force, but only so far as it is necessary to hold, occupy, and possess the forts.

I do not know, by the way, why there was a necessity for using these three words. There seems to be a most extraordinary pleonasm. Hold, occupy, and possess, would seem to be, in regard to the subject to which they were applicable, almost synonymous; but still, unless there was some purpose to mystify or mislead, I know not why they were used.

I say, sir, the message is silent only as to the question of the time when it is to be done. The President has told us that his duty requires him to do it. We know that he is in possession of the military power, and all the public force, and can direct it at his pleasure at any moment upon any point; and he tells us that he is not only stimulated by his sense of duty, but he is under the obligations of an oath to perform that duty. I should infer, therefore, that he would consider it his duty at once, or with reasonable speed, at any rate, to discharge that duty. I so to-day understand the Senator from Illinois. If I understand him aright in what he said a few minutes ago, he said that, in relation to one of these forts—Fort Sumter—there would be very soon a pressing necessity for taking position, on the part of the Federal Government. The Senator said that there was information that the garrison would not have provisions to last them beyond thirty days; that they would have neither bread nor salt; that they would be in a starving condition in that time. I know nothing about the fact. If the Senator is right, however, that they will be short of provisions, he is right in his conclusion that this peaceful policy which he found in the message is to be converted into war within the next thirty days; for again I say none can doubt, I presume—if there be a doubter I do not know who he is—that Fort Sumter can never be reinforced by the Federal Government, who claim to be its owners, without a struggle of thousands and tens of thousands of armed men spilling their blood on the sands and on the sea; and if the Senator is right, that whatever may be the policy will be expedited, because of the necessity, within the next thirty days, whatever of peace the Senator saw in this message, will then be converted into war, real war, stern war.[12]

No, Mr. President, there is a solution of peace, one only—a solution that is not only not held out in this message; but that is carefully avoided, sedulously avoided; there is a solution of peace of this great question, between the contending sections, and there is but one; and so far from that being contained in this inaugural, it is repelled and repudiated by its whole tenor and purpose. The solution is to admit the Union is broken; to yield to the existing fact; to admit that the Union is at an end by the separation of the seven States which have gone out; and whether they are acknowledged as an independent Power or not; to admit the fact of their separate and independent existence; and then withdraw the troops. That is the peace policy; and none other. So far from that being even hinted or intimated in the message, the whole tenor and purpose of it repudiates it; because it declares that the Union is unbroken, in the language quoted from it by the Senator, that in the contemplation of the Constitution and the law, whatever the fact is, it is unbroken, and that he will execute the laws within the separated States;

and that he will hold, occupy, and possess, the fortifications within them. Sir, there is no peace in that. You cannot get it in that way, in any shape or form. There is but one mode, and that is to admit the fact that these States are out, whether rightfully or not, and to withdraw the troops. I can see no reason why that should be longer denied, even among those statesmen who look upon this Government, as the inaugural expresses it, as a thing so peculiar, God-given, or otherwise, that it is insusceptible of being broken. The President says, by the universal law it is presumed to be perpetual. What he means by the universal law, I am quite as much at a loss to understand, as I was the cabalistic meaning of a phrase used by the Senator from New York of a higher law.[13] What is the universal law? I know what the law of the Constitution is; I know what the laws of the United States are; I know what the international law is; but what this universal law is, unless it be the law of the universe, that law which keeps the spheres in place, and directs their motions, and provides for their rotation upon their axes and in their orbits, I am at a loss to know. But it is by terms like these, not only general, but unmeaning and inapplicable, that we are to be deluded into the idea that there is no mode by which this Government, as he calls it, however oppressive it may become, however odious to the people under it, however cruel in its exactions, however perverse in its infractions of constitutional duty, can be got rid of, because of some law of the universe.

Sir, the people of the southern States, at least, are not to be deluded out of their rights, or out of their remedies, by this sort of hidden, cabalistic meaning. I say the only way to preserve the peace of the country is to admit the fact that those States are out, that your laws are inoperative within them, and that so far as they are concerned, they are as much foreign to this Government as England or France, and to withdraw your troops, and give up the strong places. Unless that is done, there is no more possibility of averting a war than there would be of shutting out from the world the light of heaven.

I have thought it a matter of moment that the policy of this message should be eviscerated, wherever its meaning was indirect or dark, because my own people, the people of Virginia, who are yet in the Union, are banded together upon the fixed, unchangeable purpose of making themselves a party to that war when the first gun is fired. There is no mistaking that. Whatever difference of opinion there may have been as to the policy of immediately abandoning the Union, the policy of remaining in the Union to negotiate for securities, as was attempted by the late peace congress, the policy of going out of the Union and forming an intermediate confederacy, or the policy of remaining in the Union under abject submission, whatever forms of difference of opinion there may have been as to what it became Virginia to do, on this question there is almost a unit; that if there is any attempt by public force exercised on the part of this Government, under the plea of executing the laws, or under the plea of taking possession of the forts and arsenals as public property, or under any other plea, to march a hostile army into those States, Virginia will become, by the unanimous consent of her people, a party to that war when the first gun is fired. I say we have evidences of that, at least, which are unmistakable. It is due that this message should be clearly understood, not only in its purpose, but in the time that purpose is to be executed, that the proper preparation should be made to meet the great occasion.

There is another part of this message that I wanted to comment on, which I think discloses, but discloses again in a rather occult way, what the policy of this Administration is to be in reference to that great question of African slavery, which has already rent the Union and keeps other slave States trembling in the balance. I said here a few days ago, in debate, that the resolution which passed the House of Representatives, proposing an amendment to the Constitution, which was subsequently adopted in the Senate, took its origin in the Chicago platform.[14] I have not read the platform, probably, since it was promulgated; I had a vague recollection of it; but I was struck with the coincidence; and the message shows that what I accidentally stumbled upon was a preconcerted purpose of the Republican Party, under the lead of the President, to throw that sop to Cerberus,[15] in the form of such an amendment to the Constitution, and with the explicit denial of any other. It shows more: that this new President, in his inaugural, adopts that as the only permissible amendment to the Constitution, for two reasons: the first is, as stated in the inaugural, because already it is the implied law of the Constitution, and therefore he could have no objection to make it the express law; and secondly, for the still more remarkable reason that this proposed amendment to the Constitution constituted a part of the Chicago platform, and that platform is his law. I will read what he says: "I do but quote from one of those speeches" —

Alluding to one of his own speeches —

when I declare that "I have no purpose, directly or indirectly, to interfere with the institution of slavery in the States where it exists. I
believe I have no lawful right to do so, and I have no inclination to do
so." Those who nominated and elected me did so with full knowledge
that I had made this, and many similar declarations, and had never
recanted them. And more than this, they placed in the platform for
my acceptance, and as a law to themselves and to me, the clear and
emphatic resolution which I now read.[16]

And then he reads the third resolution of the Chicago platform. That he
says was placed in the Chicago platform for his acceptance as a law to those
who framed it and to him, and therefore he adopts it! There is the declaration that whatever is in the Chicago platform is his law; because, if this
declaration that they are not to interfere with slavery in the States is a law
to him for the reason that it is in the Chicago platform, it follows, not as a
logical sequence only, but it follows, by any rule of interpretation, if the one
resolution is a law the whole is a law. Now, what are they? In that Chicago
platform I find, in the fifth section, denouncing the Democratic Administration for various of its measures, this: "In construing the personal relation
between master and slave to involve an unqualified property in persons."
That is one of the offenses of the Democratic Administration. That is one
of the laws of this platform which the President in his inaugural has told
the American people is law to him because it is there, and the policy of the
Administration is here declared to be the inexorable law of party allegiance;
a law admitted by the President to be obligatory upon him. One part of
the policy of the Administration is to be, whenever the occasion permits it,
to deny property in slaves. What further? In the seventh section the platform recites that—"The new dogma that the Constitution, of its own force,
carries slavery into any or all of the Territories of the United States, is a
dangerous political heresy, at variance with the explicit provisions of that
instrument itself, with contemporaneous exposition, and with legislative
and judicial precedent; is revolutionary in its tendency, and subversive of the
peace and harmony of the country."
That is, the political doctrine that the Constitution recognizes property
in man within the Territories is to be declared to be a dangerous political
heresy. They call it carrying slavery into the Territories. There seems to be

a settled purpose in this Republican party, to use phrases susceptible of all sorts of meanings. I never heard of a law that carried slavery anywhere. I know a slave can be taken anywhere; but he carries no law of slavery with him. A slave is taken anywhere, as an ox or a horse is, because he is property, and he remains property, unless there be some law there to prohibit that sort of property. That is the doctrine which the platform says is a dangerous political heresy.

But again: in the eighth section, we find—"That the normal condition of all the territory of the United States is that of freedom."

This is another of those occult modes of speaking. "Free territory" and "slave territory" are catch-words used—useful, perhaps—in getting up party combinations, but here made a part of that law which is to control the President of these United States, and bind his conscience, by his own declarations in his inaugural. "Free territory!" Sir, there is no meaning in the phrase. Take the State of Pennsylvania: they have declared that involuntary servitude, or slavery, shall not exist there. That is nothing on earth, in the language of the jurist, but prohibiting that sort of property, or, in the language of the politician, prohibiting that element of political power; but what on earth has it to do with the soil, the land? It can find its base, I think, nowhere but in the necessities of urgent politicians to get up catch-words to combine political parties; and yet it is put in here in the platform, and made a law to the President, by his own admission. It concludes by saying: "We deny the authority of Congress, of a Territorial Legislature, or of any individuals, to give legal existence to slavery in any Territory of the United States."

That is binding on the President. This, to use the language, and the appropriate language, of the Senator from Illinois, is the key to the whole meaning of the utter failure, after every effort during this winter to get any amendment proposed to the Constitution, to secure what the southern States know are their rights under the Constitution. "The platform," says the President, "is my law. On the subject of slavery it has declared only that there shall be no interference with slavery in the States; and it being my law, I therefore approve of the amendment which was passed; but all the rest is a law to me. It is a law to me that there shall be no slaves carried into the Territories."[17] Thus, notwithstanding the struggle that we saw in the committees of the two Houses, and in the peace conference, the subject, in the hands of those who had charge of it from the free States, was insusceptible of adjustment, because they never intended to give any security of any kind to those rights, the denial of which has driven seven States out of the Union, and which my State, by its commissioners, came here to demand should be recognized. The only thing is, that joint resolution that passed the other day; and that the President says he acquiesces in, because it was already a part of the Constitution, in the contemplation of everybody, and because the Chicago platform said it should be done; and that is his law.

If any further proof were wanting, look at the extraordinary fact that the President, after admitting in the inaugural that the great struggle upon the question of slavery was in the Territories, not only refrains from expressing any policy in regard to the Territories, but passes over the whole subject in two lines. He says: "One section of the country believes slavery is right, and ought to be extended, while the other believes it is wrong, and ought not to be extended. That is the only substantial dispute."

And there he leaves the question. He is right in saying, not that it is the only substantial dispute, but that it has been the greatest question in dispute, because upon it depended, not the measure of political power alone under the Constitution, but upon it depended the very safety and integrity of the southern States where slavery is; and yet, although he declares it to have been the great subject of dispute, how does he dispose of it? He disposes of it thus, in another part of the message: "*May* Congress prohibit slavery in the Territories? The Constitution does not expressly say. *Must* Congress protect slavery in the Territories? The Constitution does not expressly say."

The Chicago platform said that slavery should be prohibited in the Territories; and the President says in his inaugural that is a law with him, and one that he must obey.

I have thought proper, Mr. President, to bring to the notice of the country these views in the inaugural in connection with the Chicago platform, for the purpose of elucidating the strange fact that, with the country in the convulsed condition which it is, with the Union broken, with a confederation formed out of a portion of the States in the southern section, with the necessary result, attending these political events, of a depression and almost ruin of the public credit, and stagnation in every branch of industry, and commerce almost at an end, thousands of people suffering for employment, the Congress of the United States, aided by commissioners from twenty or twenty-one States, were unable to bring forward any mode by which the American people could again be united. The Republican party are in the ascendant; they have got the political power of the country in their hands; the Chicago platform has laid down the law by which that power is to be administered; and the President declares that the platform is law to him. I am sorry to have detained the Senate so long; but I really thought the occasion and the position of my State, in reference to this matter, required that I should give my views somewhat at length.

Mr. DOUGLAS. The Senator from Virginia is under a strange misapprehension in regard to the view that I took in relation to the condition of Fort Sumter, when I stated casually what I supposed was well known to everybody, that the provisions of the garrison would be exhausted in thirty or thirty-one days, and that it would take a very large land force, besides all the naval force we have, to reinforce it, or place supplies in it. I certainly did not draw the inference that therefore war was to come within the thirty days. On the contrary, I thought the inference was irresistible that war would not come, in relation to Fort Sumter, for the simple reason that it is not possible for you to raise an army in thirty days. Congress is not in session, and you cannot bring them together in that time; you cannot concentrate an army in that time. I take it for granted, therefore, that no attempt will be made to reinforce Fort Sumter, for the simple reason that it is impossible to do it, if even there was a disposition to do it.

Then, while I have no knowledge of the views or purposes of anybody connected with the Government and having control of this question in regard to Fort Sumter, I take it for granted that an army which we have not got, and which cannot be raised in many months, for the reason that it would require a session of Congress first, is not to be collected for the purpose of relieving Fort Sumter in the next thirty days.

Mr. MASON. I ask the Senator, then, what is to be done with the garrison if they are in a starving condition?

Mr. DOUGLAS. If the Senator had voted right in the last presidential election I should have been in a condition, perhaps, to tell him authoritatively what ought to be done. [Laughter.][18] Not occupying that position, I must refer him to those who have been intrusted by the American people according to the Constitution with the decision of that question. I am only pointing out facts which I think tell us more clearly than language what must be done.

I apprehend the same is true in regard to the collection of revenue. We are told that the collection of revenue in the seceding States is going to lead to collision and war. That cannot be done without further legislation. Does any one suppose that the President is going to send a collector of the port to New Orleans to collect revenue — a city with nearly two hundred thousand inhabitants, situated two hundred miles from the Gulf, where nobody acknowledges allegiance to our Government? You must capture the city of New Orleans before you can collect revenue there; and yet the laws of the land, which require the collection of the revenue, locate the custom-houses in the city, and do not authorize you to collect the duties anywhere else. Hence it is very clear that the President did not mean New Orleans when he spoke of collecting the revenue. So it is with Mobile, thirty miles inside of the bar, up in the State of Alabama. No one expects that he is going to appoint a collector of the port there to collect the revenue, unless he raises an army and takes possession of the city. The same is true in regard to Savannah, situated a long distance up the Savannah river in the interior of the country, where no duties can be collected until you have captured the place.

The same is true of Charleston. Since this controversy has commenced, the city of Charleston and the authorities of South Carolina have erected a large number of batteries, for miles below Fort Moultrie and Fort Sumter, upon Sullivan's and Morris islands, and the other bars and islands there, that close every channel but one, and that having only eight feet of water. The President has no authority by law to remove the custom-house from Charleston outside of the harbor; none to remove the custom-house from Savannah down to the ocean; none to remove it from Mobile down into the Gulf; none to remove it from New Orleans down to the Belize; and, therefore, you cannot collect customs or maintain your custom-houses at any of these places, unless you first send a military force to take possession of them. Not having the power, no law on the statute-book authorizing it, it is very clear that the President could not have contemplated the using of military force to collect revenue there, until Congress should meet and make it his duty, and give him the power to do so.

{Senator Douglas concluded the discussion by pointing out that once
the representatives and senators from the seven Deep South states that
left the Union departed from Congress, the Republican Party held
a majority in both houses. Furthermore, he continued, the House of
Representatives debated a force bill giving the President authority to
raise an army, but "for patriotic purposes," consciously decided against
approving it. He also observed that he had never met a "military man
who made an estimate of less than two hundred and fifty thousand
men as being necessary to reduce the southern States into submission."}

Source: *Congressional Globe*, 36th Cong., 2nd Sess., 1443–446.

4

United States House of Representatives

January 1861

Muscoe Russell Hunter Garnett
January 16, 1861

Muscoe R. H. Garnett (1821–1864) graduated from the University of Virginia in 1839 and three years later received a law degree from the same institution. He established his law practice in Loretto, Essex County. He served in Virginia's house of delegates (1853–1856) and as a Democrat in the US House of Representatives (1856–1861). He was elected as a delegate to the First Confederate Congress.

As Representative Garnett spoke on the floor of the House of Representatives South Carolina, Mississippi, Florida, and Alabama had all seceded, leaving control of Congress to the Republican Party. Envisioning a dangerously dominant Republican Party in the near future, Garnett spoke of eventualities rather than current realities. Dominated by the "extreme men" of the party, the northern antislavery party would soon be in possession of the "entire legislative as well as the executive department of the Federal Government." Republican power would then seek to abolish slavery in forts and navy yards, and prohibit the interstate slave trade. "The inevitable end is the emancipation of the African race at the South." And emancipation, he lectured, would lead to "social and political equality and ultimate amalgamation with the free blacks." The only solution could be found in a constitutional amendment that would redistribute political power between the sections. "To secure this, the South must have an absolute veto in every department of the Government."

Garnett's address was typical among Democrats over Secession Winter who feared what a Republican controlled government might do in the future, rather than what the federal government had done in the past. It should be noted that as he spoke, the proslavery Democratic Party had controlled the executive branch of government for the past decade, and had held a majority in both houses of Congress except in the House of Representatives during the Thirty-Fourth and Thirty-Sixth Congresses.

Mr. GARNETT. Mr. Chairman, on the first day of this session, the House ordered the appointment of a committee, to be composed of one member from each State, to consider the alarming condition of the country. Since then, it has been contented to stand with folded arms and silent lips, while the flames of civil discord daily burst more fiercely, though it has long since been apparent that the committee can do nothing to arrest them. And when the history of these times comes to be written, I think the stolid indifference of the American House of Representatives to the dissolution of the American Union will be recorded as one of their strangest phenomena. State after State secedes; and yet, though the minute guns successively announce that spar by spar, and timber by timber, the mighty ship gives way before the storm, we still stand, like mere spectators on the shore, in helpless bewilderment. I think it time to address ourselves earnestly to the danger; not with anger, or bitterness, or exaggeration, but with a frank, truthful interchange of views, ascending above the horizon of party, as men upon whom Providence has cast the fearful responsibilities belonging to those exceptional occasions in a nation's life, which determine its destinies, and affect the course of the world's history for generations yet unborn. It is in this spirit, sir, that I enter the debate.

He who traces back the present troubles only to the 6th day of November last, would be but a shallow observer. Their causes are to be found, not in the mere election of Lincoln and Hamlin, but in the fact which that election disclosed; that this once equal Union of sovereign Republics had changed into the dominion of one section over another section, into which it was divided by differences of character, of institutions, and in some sort of race, coinciding with a geographical line. This revolution is not the less complete, because, as in Rome under Augustus, the old forms and names of the Constitution are preserved. Such great historical changes are never sudden; nor is this an exception.

In years past, the anti-slavery party had, after many vicissitudes of fortune, broken down the great historic party of the Whigs, and the even stronger, though more ephemeral, organization of the Know Nothings;[1] but now it has burst through the last line of our defenses, and, routing the Democratic forces, it has seized the scepter of American empire—the object of its long ambition, of its patient toil. Under the name of Republicans, it has obtained every electoral vote, except three, in the eighteen non-slaveholding States, against and over the unanimous voice of the fifteen slaveholding States. Nor is its majority in electoral votes only. Its popular vote is one million eight hundred and thirty-one thousand one hundred and sixty-eight, against one million five hundred and seventy-four thousand and ninety-one.[2] It has a plurality of the popular vote in Oregon and California, and an absolute majority in every northern State this side of the Rocky Mountains except gallant New Jersey, where alone it was beaten. Nor is this strength a thing of yesterday—a summer cloud which we may hope will pass away as rapidly as it gathered. Since the anti-slavery candidate, Birney,[3] received seven thousand and fifty-nine votes in 1840, each presidential election has shown a steady growth in the party vote, except in 1852, when it met an accidental and temporary check.[4] The intermediate State elections show the same progression.

This party, then, now calling itself Republican, has steadily advanced for many years, until it has gained possession of all the northern States, in every department of their State governments, with very few exceptions. It controls this House of Representatives; and after the 4th of March there will be thirty avowed Republican Senators, besides two from Kansas, if admitted—within two or five, as the case may be, of a majority of the Senate, were all the southern States still in the Union. Nor can there be a doubt that nothing but the accidental length of the terms of the remaining six Democratic Senators from the North prevents our then seeing every northern State represented by Republicans. It cannot be long before the entire legislative as well as the executive department of the Federal Government is in possession of this party, unless some mighty change occurs in northern sentiment. Nor can we expect such a change from ordinary causes; for schools, pulpits, and books, have trained the northern mind to a strong and fixed hostility to African slavery; and this is precisely the feeling on which the Republican party is founded. Anti-slavery: this is its central idea, its vital principle, without which it never could have come into being, and without which it would now dissolve. Here is its tower of strength, and it has flourished just in proportion as it has been true to this flag. Around it may be grouped camp followers and mercenaries, always attendant on victory; the various factions, each with its individual purpose, which it hopes to promote under the shadow of its great leader. But the heart of the party, its active, progressive element, which interpenetrates all others, and molds and controls them to its purpose; which gives it vigor in the fight, and rallies popular enthusiasm to its cause, is the anti-slavery sentiment. As Mr. SEWARD said: "The secret of its success lies in the fact that it is a party of one idea; but that idea is a noble one, an idea that fills and expands all generous souls—the idea of equality, the equality of all men before human tribunals and human laws, as they all are equal before the Divine tribunal and Divine laws."[5]

Yes, sir, the Republican party is made up from the disbanded cohorts of the former Whig and American parties, and deserters from the Democratic, brought together by this one common feeling. As Mr. Lincoln himself said, "the Republican party is made up of those who, as far as they can, peaceably oppose the extension of slavery, and who will hope for its ultimate extinction." "It is made," he says, "of strange, discordant, and even hostile elements," all fused and disciplined into one strong body by enmity to slavery. More emphatically still, Mr. Lincoln says:

> The real issue in this controversy—the one pressing upon every mind—
> is the sentiment on the part of one class that looks upon the institution
> of slavery as a wrong, and of another class that does not look upon it
> as a wrong. The sentiment that contemplates the institution of slavery
> in this country as a wrong, is the sentiment of the Republican party.
> It is the sentiment around which all their actions, all their arguments,
> circle; from which all other propositions radiate. They look upon it
> as being a moral, social, and political wrong. * * * * They insist that it
> should, as far as may be, *be treated* as a wrong; and one of the methods
> of treating it as a wrong, is to *make provision that it shall grow no larger.*

They also desire a policy that looks to a peaceful end of slavery at some time, as being wrong.[6]

The official platforms of the party confirm these declarations of its leader. It was first organized because no existing party made anti-slavery opinions a test in its nominations. The Abolition or Liberty party of 1840–44 was succeeded by the so-called "Free Democratic party," or Buffalo men of 1848–52. Meantime the Whig party had been dissolved by dissension between its northern and southern wings on this same question of slavery; and a like fate befell its successor—the American party. Its northern elements, uniting with this "Free Democracy" on the anti-slavery idea, cast over one million three hundred thousand votes, as Republicans, in 1856;[7] and have now elected their President. Like every great party, it contains men of various shades of opinion, more or less extreme; but, as in all such cases, the extreme men, those who carry the leading idea of the party to its logical consequences, and are truest to it, must ultimately govern and control the others. Even the most moderate are determined to prevent the extension of slavery into any Federal territory, because they consider it a moral, social, and political wrong and evil, which they are bound, to the extent of their power, to limit and discourage. As Mr. Lincoln says, any man "who does not think the institution of slavery wrong;" who does not "desire a policy that looks to a peaceful end of slavery at some time, as being wrong;" who does not "insist that it shall be treated as a wrong," is "misplaced, and ought not to be with the Republicans."[8]

Now, sir, it will be admitted that it is impossible for the people of any southern State to adopt these opinions without at the same time making up their minds to the emancipation, more or less speedy, of their slaves. In other words, it is impossible for any southern people to join the Republican party without commencing a total revolution in their internal State polity and social organization. Therefore it is, sir, that we justly charge the Republicans with sectionalism. That surely is a sectional party, which the people in fifteen States of the Union cannot join without committing themselves to a radical change in their State constitutions, and a complete overthrow of the entire structure of their society. So long as there are slaveholding States which mean to continue slaveholding States, so long must the domination of this party be the domination of the non-slaveholding over the slaveholding section. The former will enjoy all the offices and honors of the Confederacy, except such inferior places as may be bestowed on time-servers or traitors in the South. The sectional majority will wield the entire power of the Union, direct its foreign alliances, levy its taxes, hold the keys of the Treasury, and the gates of war and peace—the purse and the sword—command its armies and navies, govern its Territories, and control its destinies. The minority section will pay its taxes, but direct neither their kind, their amount, nor their appropriation. It will help to fight your battles, and to extend the boundaries of your confederacy; but yours will be the sole gain, for the new territory will be appropriated by the majority section for its emigration and settlement, and the new States whose stars appear in the constellation of the Union will do homage to the institutions of that section, and be so many pillars of its political supremacy. Meantime, the minority section will be in a minority more and more hopeless. Southern civilization will be walled in and isolated beyond hope of escape, and the enormous pressure of this huge Federal machine, its patronage and power and moral influence, brought down on southern society to bring about the extinction of slavery.

I think I do not color the picture too highly. I will suppose that the so-called *moderate* wing of the Republican party prevails in its councils. I will suppose that no direct attack is made on the sale of slaves between the States, or on slavery in the States or even in the forts, navy-yards, or District of Columbia. I will admit, for the argument's sake, that the Republican party is content to confine slavery within its present limits, and prevent its extension into any new territory. It necessarily follows that there can never be a new slave State. Our present territory, over one million two hundred thousand square miles, is large enough for twenty States; and we must expect moreover, large acquisitions from Mexico. The chief present restraint on the lust of acquisition is sectional jealousy, and this would not be felt when one section is all-powerful. Its ambition would scarcely be checked by the cost, whether in blood or treasure, of wars and treaties whose fruits were to be exclusively its own; for it would levy the greater part of the expense from the subject and minority section. Mr. SEWARD, in the recent canvas, repeatedly foreshadowed this policy of acquisition for the exclusive occupation of northern society. The time is not far distant when you would have three fourths of the States, and could amend the Constitution at pleasure.[9]

But the moderate Republicans tell us that they interfere with slavery only where they have the power, because conscience commands the abatement of this wrong wherever the power exists. How then, when future extensions invest you with a power over the institution in the States themselves? That same conscience will not allow you to rest until you have taken measures for its ultimate extinction. You are eager for the day when you shall have filled up the western territories with free States, and you may number the requisite three fourths. When, in 1820, you interdicted slavery in all the territory north of 36°30', you simultaneously reduced the price of the public lands from two dollars to a dollar and a quarter, in order to stimulate emigration and hasten the formation of new States. Now, when you think you have finally secured all the Territories, present and future, you incorporate into your platform, as practical measure of your party, the homestead bill. You invite all the nations of Europe to take possession of the Federal lands without cost; and by this donation you encourage and increase to the utmost foreign immigration, already numbering annually more than enough for a new State every year.

Meanwhile, the Republican party is necessarily confined to the non-slaveholding section; since, as I have remarked, no slaveholding community can join it without ultimately surrendering its institutions. But how long can any people maintain a struggle which it feels daily more hopeless? How long keep up its spirit under the degrading influence of subjection to a Government from whose power and honors it is perpetually excluded? The strength of the defense, the spirit of resistance, would gradually weaken. Ambitious and active tempers—some, allured by the power or distinctions others by the mere emoluments of office—would first profess a policy of acquiescence, and then an adoption of those Republican principles which open the door to preferment. Anti-slavery doctrines and emancipation parties would appear in the slave States, and the dominant and sectional party in the Federal Government would, of necessity, aid and strengthen them by its patronage and influence. Meantime the dominant section, selfish as all unchecked power must be, would, by protective tariffs and sectional expenditures, encourage its own labor, and render the labor of the slaves comparatively worthless. Thus the institution of slavery in the minority section would be "localized and discouraged," to use the Republican phrase. Undermined and weakened, and its defenders dispirited or divided, it would probably give way, even before the increase in the number of the free States placed its constitutional defenses at their mercy.

Thus far I have traced the results of Republican rule, on the assumption that it is exercised by the most moderate members of the party. But such an assumption is contradicted by all history. The law of life in every party is fidelity to the idea which gave it existence. If the leaders falter, aspirants for place thrust them aside with professions of more extreme opinions. The responsibility of power, it is true, moderates its possessors; but in a popular Government, based on universal suffrage, such moderation is short lived. The real power is in the popular masses, who feel none of its responsibilities. At the North the old Federalist leaven is widely diffused, and is especially strong in the Republican ranks. Accustomed to construe the Constitution most liberally for power, they will perpetually press their Representatives to use it against what they deem the monstrous evil of slavery. They claim power to abolish it in the forts and the navy-yards, and to prohibit the sale of slaves between the States, or their transportation on the high seas; and excited by victory, and goaded on by a fanatical pulpit, this power will surely be used—used when the southern people, discouraged by subjection and divided by patronage, are too weak to resist.

The inevitable end is the emancipation of the African race at the South. When will this happen? Thirty years hence, when the slaves number eight million; or sixty years, when they are sixteen million; or ninety years, when their thirty-two million outnumber the present total population of all the States? Be it when it may, (and the longer it is delayed the more numerous the slaves, the worse will be the consequences when it occurs,) the destruction of southern wealth and industry will be almost complete; for the experiment in the British West Indies has proved beyond controversy—what indeed well-informed persons knew before—that the African will not work without compulsion. You may substitute the slavery of the law—bondage to the community, a system of labor enforced and regulated by legal enactment—for slavery to individual masters; but you will get not half work; and in destroying the personal and hereditary tie between master and slave, you have destroyed not only that which makes the industry profitable, but still more, you have broken up the essential condition on which all that is humane or good in the relation depends. I will not dilate on the incalculable loss to the North or to the world involved in the ruin of the cotton culture and southern commerce and industry. My interests are nearer home, where I see a country once animated by peaceful industry, once blessed with happy homes, once advancing under the control of the white race, men proud of their position as peers of any under God's heaven,—I see this country, its industry extinguished, its homes deserted by the rich, its fields overgrown by the thicket, and abandoned to the improvident laziness of the emancipated African, while the poorer class are left to reconcile themselves as best they may to social and political equality, and ultimate amalgamation with the free blacks. In one word, I see the southern States, I see Virginia and her southern sisters and daughters, reduced to the condition of Jamaica and Hayti, and blotted from the roll of nations.

I ask you, sir—I ask any fair man, whether from North or South—can we, ought we to acquiesce in this result? or shall we try to avert it while there is yet time? Yet this ruin is the legitimate, the inexorable consequence of acquiescence in Republican rule, as I have shown.

How can we avert the danger? Shall we trust to a change in the northern mind? But on what grounds shall we hope for such a change? A change means, really, not the mere overthrow of the Republican party, but in that anti-slavery sentiment which created it, and which would then create another in its stead, as Mr. SEWARD truly said.

Truth is mighty, and will prevail; but the truth is proverbially a slow traveler, and before you can hope to work such a change at the North by ordinary causes, the evil will have been done, and our ruin accomplished. Past history shows that the present working of our political machinery has been favorable to the growth of this anti-slavery power. Twenty-five years ago it was not tolerated at the North itself; its public meetings were broken up by mobs; its printing offices burned down; and northern Governors recommended its repression by legal enactment. How changed the scene now, when it controls nearly every department of the Government, State and Federal; and when conspiracies are formed for the armed invasion of sister States, and neither laws proposed nor indictments found to punish the conspirators! Here is a change indeed, but a change against, not for us—the only change, I fear, we can hope. I ask no better proof of the firm hold this anti-slavery feeling has on the northern heart, than the recent disruption of the Democratic party, which was clearly due to the general aversion to slavery, and the determination that it shall not be extended to any new territory.

How could it be otherwise? Or how can we hope to obtain even a hearing there? A few in the cities may listen to us; but the rural millions, how can we reach them? The schools, the pulpits, and the press, all their literature and all their teachers, daily impress on their minds the impolicy and sinfulness of slavery. Some urge active measures to remedy this wrong; others would separate the practice from the principle — a caution not easily taught to a conscientious and active people of the Puritan stock. These sons of the Mayflower will never rest easy under a conviction of their neighbor's sins, without aggressive efforts for his compulsory salvation.

{Representative Garnett here continued to decry the growth of antislavery sentiment in the northern states. He took aim at the corrupting nature of northern politics in which, in his words, the "educated and conservative classes" become disenchanted with political processes which results in the "vulgar concerns of Government" being "left for the most part, to political intriguers, and corrupt caucuses, who control the rowdies and the ignorant." He then shifted to the corruption of the federal government "in nearly all its branches," noting "how little northern constituencies seem to care for it!" Congress, to his mind, was tainted as it was "reduced to the open shame of accusing and expelling its own members for corruption, to be reelected, however, soon after." Although Representative Garnett's intent here was to undermine faith in northern democratic processes, his rambling delivery also cast aspersions on the federal government generally, then, except for the House of Representatives, under the control of the Democratic Party.}

It is vain, therefore, to expect safety from a change of parties at the North. Still less is the remedy for our present troubles to be found in any mere legislation by Congress, or even in a repeal of the obnoxious personal liberty statutes of the northern States, except it were evidence of a change of opinion as to slavery. The present fugitive slave law is stringent enough, were the hearts of the people inclined to obey it. How far they are the contrary, the obnoxious personal liberty bills, the forcible rescue of captured fugitives, the personal peril of masters who claim their property, and the continual retreat of slave population from the border line, where it is exposed to increasing hazards, all witness. Nor can we hope for the peaceful and regular return of our fugitives, or the suppression of organized conspiracies to aid and stimulate their escape, so long as the northern heart and conscience are so deeply impressed with the anti-slavery idea.

But, sir, I go further, and assert that it is not for the interest of either party or section to leave this question open. The continual struggle cannot longer be endured. It swallows up all others; makes wise legislation on other subjects impossible; paralyzes every department of the Government; and breeds hatred, overpowering in intensity, between the sections. For the interest of both, it ought now to be finally settled. And for the South especially, it is neither safe nor honorable to depend for security on the mercy of the North, or the vicissitudes of party warfare. The fifteen southern States cannot safely or honorably hold their four million African slaves, their social and political institutions, by the forbearance of the eighteen northern. I think, that the people of the South have judged wisely, when they accept the recent election as proof that the time, long foreseen, has at last arrived, when, the machinery of party having become impotent for their protection, they must look elsewhere for safety. And in pronouncing this judgment, I would say to our conservative friends at the North, whether of the Democratic or Bell party, that we fully appreciate their gallant services in defense of our rights under the Constitution. We admire their constancy under defeat, and their moral courage in boldly fighting against increasing odds; and we shall regret that our safety does not permit us to await the chances of other and future battles in conjunction with such noble allies. But we plainly see—and we are sure their own candor will admit—that the game would be too hazardous for such momentous stakes. Even an occasional party success would but delay for a short time the inevitable crisis now upon us; and it would then be likely to find us weakened, divided, and less able to meet it. On the contrary, we beg them to see that it is the part of prudence to be timely bold, and now, once and forever, to remove these vexed and dangerous interests from the slippery arena of party strife.

The public mind, agreeing with these views, is evidently disposed to seek a remedy in amendments to the Constitution, which would place the whole subject outside of Federal control. There are two kinds of amendment possible—the one, consisting of declarations that Congress shall or shall not exercise certain powers; the other, making a new distribution of power between the sections.

I do not look very hopefully on the former. For the most part, promises without the power to enforce their performance, are not worth much. And if such amendments succeed in closing the controversy on the issues now prominent, yet who can foresee the various forms in which the anti-slavery feeling will make its future attacks? How can amendments of this character secure the South effectually against the malign influences of the patronage of the anti-slavery party? How can they obtain for her a fair share in the honors, the influence, and the expansion of our empire? Yet I do not commit myself against a present settlement on this basis. It is the part of practical statesmanship to meet questions as they arise; and though the settlement might be only a truce, yet if good as far as it goes, and if the end of the truce on such a basis would probably find the relative strength of the parties unchanged, if its terms did not demoralize the spirit of my own section, I would be disposed to accept it.[10] At the same time, I believe a more radical and therefore more permanent adjustment would be better for both sections, the North as well as the South.

The present Constitution, as our fathers made it, was all sufficient while it protected kindred and friendly States, and would be so still, were all disposed to fulfill its obligations with a good faith inspired by mutual good will and respect. There is danger that new declaratory clauses or promises would be regarded no more than the old. What the minority section needs is *power*—power to secure its rights against a majority section, differing in opinions and institutions, and animated by fixed hostility to those of the minority. The danger to the minority is not only in hostile legislation, but in a hostile use of Federal patronage and influence; and in the absence of such positive protection as its interests may require, whether in our foreign relations, in expansion by territorial acquisition, or in forming new States by colonization in such acquisition. To secure all this, the South must have an absolute veto in every department of the Government. The Union was once a Union of equal States. It has now become, by the force of events, a Union of sections. It is to be determined whether this shall be a Union of superior and inferior sections, or of equal sections. Any permanent radical settlement of the present difficulties must recognize the fact, now manifest to all the world, whether we choose to recognize it or not, that this Union is composed of two widely-differing sections; and to secure to each its rights and its fair share of the benefits of the Union, every act of the Government must depend on the consent of both. For a self-protecting power in every great interest of the community is the fundamental principle of every free Government that has ever endured. Neither the North nor the South can require the other to abandon its opposite opinions on the subject of slavery. Let each enjoy its own sentiments. Let the North condemn and the South approve African slavery. But let both remember that the only safe Union between powerful States, where such opposite opinions exist, is an absolute equality. And in conceding such a change, what would the North concede? Nothing—literally nothing, but the right to govern us. It would not even involve that *quasi*-recognition of slavery, which the Republicans make a chief objection to various moderate propositions, Mr. CRITTENDEN'S and others. Surely in the nineteenth century, and here among this chosen people, "foremost in the files of time" in vindicating for every nation the right of self-government, there can be no great sacrifice in a settlement which secures that inestimable privilege to either section of the Confederacy.

{Representative Garnett here argued that any amendment to the Constitution would take a great deal of time and that there was no guarantee that Republicans would agree to one. Postponing action until the fall's northern legislative election cycle, in hopes of a change in sentiment among the nonslaveholding states, would only "expose herself [the South] to all the chances of division and discouragement at home," and "abandon the only course that can convince the North of her sincerity, or give to conservative men there the strength to carry those measures which the extreme men in power would a short time since have refused even to consider."}

Meantime Virginia, my own State, has called a convention of her people in their sovereign capacity, for the 13th of February, which will decide her future course. She has been, she still is, sincerely attached to the Union; and she would gladly have preserved it; she would willingly reconstruct it. Not long since, she would have accepted, and advised her southern sister States to accept, a most moderate basis of settlement. But events daily strengthen the feeling for secession. Your defiant speeches, and still more insulting indifference; your threats of military coercion, inflame her people; your rejection of all compromise induce the belief that you are determined to rule, if need be, by the sword; and as this belief grows into conviction, so rises Virginia's estimate of the conditions which would make this a safe Union for the South. And let no man doubt where she would be in the final disruption.

She will join no border State confederacy, with two frontiers to defend, instead of one, cut off from the natural outlet for her emigration in the South, and with all the territorial and slavery controversies in the new Union, which drove her out of the old.

Still less can she, or the border slave States, remain in the northern confederacy. If the fifteen southern States were unsafe in the old Union, how would the eight border States fare in the new Union, with nineteen free States? How then would they resist the sectional taxation and appropriation, the commercial and fiscal systems, which, even in the former Union, have built up northern cities, and fostered northern industry at the expense of the agricultural labor of the South? If permitted to keep her slaves, what would become of their increasing population, shut out from the Territories by the northern government, and perhaps from the South by its confederacy?

The picture would be reversed for these States in a southern confederacy, and especially for Virginia, the oldest and the largest, whether she considers her material interests or the ties of blood which bind her to her children, scattered in thousands over the entire South. Virginia can never hesitate between being the leading State of a southern confederacy, or the dependent follower of a northern. The great statesman of the Republican party traced its lineage to Plymouth rock, and celebrated its victory as the triumph of the Massachusetts school of politics. He was right, Plymouth and Jamestown, the Puritans and the Cavaliers, Massachusetts and Virginia, are the great origins of the opposite systems of American policy and society. You of the North seem to prefer the Massachusetts school, as you have a right. It rests on the infallibility of majorities — the divine right of the greater number to rule absolutely the lesser. It cares more to strengthen the community than it fears to dwarf the individual. Its ultimate tendency is to depend more on

Government and less on individual wisdom or energy; and its final word must be a despotism of mere numbers under a military dictatorship, after the French model. The Virginia school, on the contrary, is more English. It reduces government to its *minimum* of power, and relies upon the powers of the individual man for its strength, its prosperity, and its glory. Its motto is, not the Benthamite heresy[11] of the greatest good of the greatest number, but the greatest good of all. Founding its society on the subordination of an inferior to a superior race, it would combine lofty spirit and culture of an aristocracy with the equality of a democracy. If Virginia could forget her material interests, she could never forego, for her sons, the interests of empire. She will never consent to close for them the possibility of playing their equal part in the drama of civilization. She knows that to her school of politics this Union owes its Constitution and its noblest achievements; and that whenever the Massachusetts school prevailed, whether under the elder or younger Adams, as at present, the country was brought to the verge of ruin. Hers were the Eastern portals whence the dawning day called forth that morning of American greatness—

—whose brightness broad hath blazed;
Whose glorious, glittering light hath all men's eyes amazed.

She will never abandon her principles, or those southern States which, sprung from her loins and formed in her similitude, have multiplied her honors, and endowed the Old Dominion with a youth ever new.

But, sir, I have wandered from the strict line of my argument. I have endeavored to show that the real cause of the present difficulties is the difference between the social systems of the North and South, and the aggressive character of the anti-slavery sentiment that controls the former, and which has made the Union the Union of a dominant and a subject section; that the South would have sought a remedy in constitutional amendments had you of the Republican party shown any disposition to give them. But your hearts are hardened like Pharaoh's in your pride; and the South could not safely await the slow and uncertain chances of new and distant elections. Some of her States have resorted to the only remaining course—an exercise of the right of secession, withdrawing from the Union in the same manner and by the same authority they entered it. And thus, whether you acknowledge it or not, the Union is dissolved. For, even if you resort to civil war, that very war is in itself an end of the Union as a union between equal States; but with peace; reunion becomes possible.

{Representative Garnett concluded his address with a long discussion of the advantages of a peaceful separation of the two sections. Garnett believed, theoretically, that a reconstruction of the Union would be possible, but only after the North recognized a southern confederacy. "Negotiation between such confederacy [the South] and this would soon determine the conditions of reunion, which each could submit to its several States, according to the provisions of its own Constitution." Personally, however, he concluded that the better solution would be the formation of two separate governmental entities, each governed according to their own special interests. "Nay, sir, would it not be a great advance in the American idea of perfect self-government, which consists chiefly in so decentralizing and dividing the functions of government that each shall be administered by those only who have the same interest in its exercise."}

Source: *Congressional Globe*, 36th Cong., 2nd Sess., 411–16.

John Singleton Millson
January 21, 1861

John S. Millson (1808–1874) was born in Norfolk, and studied for and was admitted to the bar in 1829. He was elected as a Democrat to the US House of Representatives and served from 1849 until 1861. He gained notoriety in 1854 when he became only one of two Democrats to vote against the Kansas-Nebraska Act. (The other was Missouri representative Thomas Hart Benton.) After leaving Congress, he resumed his law practice in Norfolk.

An opponent of the extreme southern agenda, Representative Millson carefully dismantled secessionists' claims of abuse by the non-slaveholding states and the Republican Party. The proper response to northern personal liberty laws, he lectured, was not secession, but legal action. They should be challenged in the courts which would logically, he reasoned, "annul them as unconstitutional." Regarding slavery in the territories, Millson admonished his southern colleagues, the issue was well settled: "settled by the existing laws of the land, settled by the Constitution, settled by the supreme judicial tribunal of the country, and settled in favor of the South." Dissolution is urged, he observed, not because of any real or imminent jeopardy, but "because of appre-hended danger; because of peril in the future." Millson also chided his Democratic colleagues for arguing slaves were property only and should thus be protected as such by the Constitution's Fifth Amend-ment as all other forms of property were protected. In a perceptive and logical passage, he observed that the recognition of slaves in the Constitution was as "persons held to service" and not solely as prop-erty. If they were property, "and nothing but property, they would not be represented in Congress" as allowed by the three-fifths provision in Article I, Section 2. Millson's calm refutation of the arguments of southern extremists emphasized that it was only fear of future even-tualities that was driving the secessionist fervor, "fear that something may be done hereafter—some wrong attempted, or committed, which her sons may not have the spirit or the power to resist."

The House having under consideration the report from the select committee of thirty three—

Mr. MILLSON said:

Mr. SPEAKER: I feel that I ought not to be silent in this debate. Great events are happening every day. Great questions are every day presented for our decision. I have some views to submit; I do not know how sound they are, how just they are; but this I know, that if we would all frankly and fairly express our real sentiments, without any weak concession to what we believe to be error, for the sake of conciliating an adverse sentiment, this collision of opinion would be apt to strike out the truth.

Mr. Speaker, we have a grave controversy, and I acknowledge the obliga-tion to approach its discussion in a temperate and conciliatory spirit. I will imitate the temper and moderation—I cannot equal the eloquence—of the gentleman from Ohio [Mr. CORWIN][12] who has just closed his speech. I will say nothing that may rankle the prejudices of any political party. Sir, I have, perhaps, as frequently and as earnestly as any of my colleagues, combated the positions assumed by our political opponents from the northern States. But this is no time for altercation and recrimination, and I have no purpose now of reviving those discussions.

Sir, what was the state of things which led to the formation of the committee whose report we are now considering? The Union in imminent danger of dissolution! The Government threatened with overthrow! Is it desirable to preserve the Union? Do we want the Union to continue such as the Constitution made it? Does any man say no? Sir, I know there are some gentlemen who do not desire a continuation of the American Union. There are others, perhaps, who would not acknowledge a wish to destroy it, yet regard the dread results of a dissolution of the Union with a degree of lightness which, to me, is absolutely shocking. Yes, sir, the worst sign of all is the levity with which the whole subject is viewed by many of those upon whom the people have devolved the responsibility of administering their affairs. They do not seem to understand the dread significance of the proposed disruption of our Government. Sir, I do not expect the statesmen of the present day to attain to the wisdom of the founders of our Constitution; but I did suppose they might at least aspire to the capacity of comprehending its results. One ignorant of the mechanism of a watch, and incapable of putting its parts together, might still admire it when done, and understand its uses. But some of those to whom is assigned only the humble duty of keeping it going, seem to be so unconscious of its objects that they would break it into pieces to escape the annoyance of its ticking. If there be those here who desire the dissolution of the Union as an end, as a consummation to be wished, I have no argument to make to them.

If the Union is to continue, is it desirable that there shall be a reconciliation of the differences which have so long disturbed its harmony? I suppose, sir, the very appointment of the committee, by so large a vote of the House, implies that such a result is sought and wished. But if there be those who want no reconciliation, who court strife and would perpetuate discord, to them I have no argument to make.

I approach, then, the consideration of the question before the House.

In one respect I will not imitate the example of the gentleman from Ohio, unless I shall unconsciously wander from my purpose. I do not propose to discuss any of the controverted questions of the day, either to defend the Democratic or southern policy, or to assail that of the Republican party. We are trying to find out whether anything has yet happened, or is likely to happen, which requires, or would justify, a dissolution of the Union. We are trying to settle existing difficulties; and the first step in the settlement of any difficulty is to understand precisely what it is that is to be settled.

Is it the election of Lincoln that is to be brought into the settlement? Is it the election of Lincoln that is to be adjusted? No, sir, that is now beyond our reach. It has been asked, "shall Virginia submit to Lincoln?" I reply, Virginia submit to Lincoln! No! Virginia submit to Lincoln! Never! It is Lincoln who shall submit to Virginia. It is Lincoln, who, as the servant of Virginia and her sister States, must do their bidding. It is Lincoln, who, as President of the United States, will fulfill the functions and discharge the duties imposed upon him by Virginia in common with the other States of the Union which made the Constitution and prescribed and limited the authority and powers to be exercised by their agents. It is not Lincoln ruling Virginia. It is the States, of whom Virginia is one, the Constitution—the work of Virginia—which control, it may be, the unwilling will of Lincoln, and oblige him to do what Virginia has made it his duty to do. What though the people of Virginia gave their vote against Lincoln? What though the people of Virginia, through their Representatives here, give their vote against the passage of a law enacted by Congress? It is still Virginia that says the law shall be obeyed. It is Virginia that says that her will is potential, and that whoever may receive a majority of the electoral votes of the Union shall be the President. Instead of submitting to Lincoln, I am submitting to the sovereign will of Virginia.

What, then, is the evil to be remedied? Is it the personal liberty bills that are assigned as a justifiable cause of secession? So far, I have seen no other cause involving a breach of the Constitution assigned for secession but the passage of personal liberty bills. The gentleman from Ohio very properly remarked—although he would have saved me some labor in the illustration of the subject if he had followed up his own suggestion to its proper consequences—that those laws were passed by northern Legislatures. It is true, I consider the whole subject from rather a different point of view from that taken by the gentleman from Ohio. I stand here a State-rights man. I stand here now what I have ever been—a State-rights man of the straitest sect. I do regard the Constitution as a convention or compact between the States of the Union; and I do believe that a deliberate, palpable, and dangerous violation of the Constitution by some of the parties to it would release the other parties from their reciprocal obligations. But, sir, is the Legislature of a State one of the parties to the compact? The Legislature of a State is but a subordinate agency of one of the parties. And if the passage of an unconstitutional law, if the assumption of unconstitutional power by a State Legislature, may be regarded as an infraction of the Constitution, by one of the parties to it, then so would be the assumption of unconstitutional power by the President, by the Governor of a State, a State or Federal judge, a postmaster, or collector of the customs.

But here, sir, I am compelled to leave the gentleman from Ohio. If the act of a State Legislature be deliberately approved and ratified by the people, if, after remonstrance, the people sanction the act of their agent, then, sir, it is the privilege of the States that are the parties to the Constitution to regard the acts of the Legislature as the acts of the State they represent, and hold the compact of Union to be broken. I do not see that any such resort has yet been made to the States; nor do I enter on the inquiry how far the violation of the compact by one or two States, or by four or five States, will justify any State in severing the ties that connect her also with States that have not offended. I will not go into the consideration of that question. Let it suffice to know, although it may be the privilege of a State to avail herself of the broken faith of another, if it be her interest or her wish to do so, yet it is but a privilege, and cannot be considered a duty. If so, the passage of a personal liberty bill by Connecticut would compel Massachusetts to secede; for Massachusetts is a party to the Constitution as well as South Carolina. The refusal of one State to comply with a single Federal engagement would, on such a supposition, instantly destroy the Union as to all, and resolve the Federation into as many separate and independent nations as there were States composing it. If these States derive great advantage from the Union, it would be strange if they were held to forfeit it by the faithless act of another State.

That the passage of these bills by northern Legislatures is a grievous wrong, ought not to be denied. That we will silently submit to them, cannot be supposed. What then? Can no redress be had? Must we either submit to this wrong, or sacrifice, by secession from the Union, the most important rights and interests belonging to us as members of this Union? Sir, we will do neither. We may bring these laws before the courts, and annul them as unconstitutional; or we may, by retaliatory legislation, as Virginia has done, show our sense of the injustice done us. I do not, then, Mr. Speaker, see anything in the passage of the personal liberty bills that requires a dissolution of the Union; more especially as evidence has been so plainly and clearly supplied, within the last few weeks, of the purpose on the part of the northern Legislatures themselves to strike these offensive laws from their statute books.[13] No one, till very lately, seems to have supposed that dissolution was demanded for such a cause; no one would now suppose it, had Mr. Breckinridge been elected President; and as no other wrong, either on the part of the Federal Government, or by any State government, has been assigned in justification of secession, I am forced to conclude that there is nothing in the *past* which invokes a remedy so extreme.

But dissolution is urged because of apprehended danger; because of peril in the future; and what is it? Gentlemen tell us that the territorial question—the power to prohibit slavery in the Territories—must be settled. Must be settled? Why, sir, it seems to be strangely overlooked by many that the question is already settled; settled by the existing laws of the land; settled by the Constitution; settled by the supreme judicial tribunal of the country; and settled in favor of the South. And yet the overthrow of the Government is sought, and disunion, with all its attendant horrors, invited, because a very large number of the northern people are trying to unsettle it—with less prospect of success, perhaps, than at any time before. We are in the possession of all that we claim. There is no Territory into which we have not the right to go now with our slaves. And yet we must throw away all that we have, because it is possible it may be taken from us. Let us do what we may, how can we prevent other people from attempting to undo it?

I cannot, then, see, Mr. Speaker, that there are any well-founded apprehensions of future danger that afford any justification for giving up our present security, and rushing headlong into disunion.

But we are urged to do this in the name of State-rights. Gentlemen who are neophytes in the State-rights school address me, a veteran State-rights man, with the argument that we must vindicate the rights of our State. And what are those State rights which some are so forward to defend? Why, it would seem that gentlemen suppose there are no other rights of a State but those which involve her own destruction; the right to sacrifice her interests; the right to lay heavy burdens on her own people; the right to expose herself to extreme peril; the right to throw away all her rights.

But, gentlemen, I stand with you there, too. I too will defend these rights of my State, if she choose to exercise them. I, too, will defend her right to commit suicide, if she be tired of prosperity and renown, and of life itself. But the rights belonging to Virginia, which I, as one of her sons, reared in the school of State rights, am most eager to maintain, are those which concern her welfare and safety—her commerce, her industry, her peace, her consideration at home and abroad, the property, the happiness, the lives of her people; in short, all those inestimable blessings and benefits which the Constitution has secured to her as a member of this Union, and of which she is now, or was but lately, in the actual enjoyment. These are State rights which I would have her defend at every hazard. These are State rights which, if all the other States should attempt to take them from her, I would have her defend against their united power. And these are the State rights which some State-rights men want her to throw away, only to show her right to do so.

And what is it that should make her do so? Is it honor? No, it is only fear; fear that something may be done hereafter—some wrong attempted, or committed, which her sons may not then have the spirit or the power to resist.

Still, Mr. Speaker, it is undoubtedly true, that the people feel apprehensions of future aggression, of coming danger; and I regret that I must dissent from the conclusion to which the gentleman from Ohio brought his argument—that these apprehensions of danger may be wholly allayed by congressional legislation, and without some new guarantees in the Constitution. Gentlemen, my constituents do not believe the declarations of their political opponents. Gentlemen, my constituents will not believe the explanations of their own Representatives, when they inform them what are the designs, and what are not the designs, of the Republican party; and you cannot expect them to repose greater confidence in your assurances than in the statements of those whom they have constituted their Representatives.

It is proper that there should be some guarantees. It does not involve the objection just now presented by the gentleman from Ohio, that the members of the Republican party entertained constitutional views which they could not yield. We are not asking any surrender of constitutional views, founded on their construction of the Constitution as it is. We do not ask them to give up their construction of the existing clauses of the Constitution; but we ask an addition—a stipulation. We ask that the Constitution may interpret itself. There can be no objection, then, on the ground of a surrender of constitutional views; because such a stipulation would simply determine doubts and differences. It proposes no concession of privileges to the South. It proposes no new grant of rights to the slaveholding States. It requires no surrender of power or advantage by the northern States. It would serve only as a declaration of existing rights.

Gentlemen, in another point of view, this territorial question has been settled. The battle has been settled. The battle has been fought, and it has been won by both parties; it has been lost by both parties. You have lost the principle on which your party is founded. You cannot, under existing laws and the existing Constitution, as interpreted by the Supreme Court, prohibit slavery in a Territory. You have lost the battle; we have gained it. But you know that, if your purpose has been to exclude slavery from the Territories, there is not the least probability that slavery will ever be carried into any one of them. Thus, in all that respects practical results, you have gained the battle, and we have lost it. You have lost the principle, we the substance. You have gained the substance, we the principle. We are, then, on equal terms. We are both victims; we are both vanquished. There is nothing, then, to prevent us from making an end of the whole quarrel now, and preclude all controversy on the subject hereafter. Let us restore that harmony and good fellowship which ought to prevail amongst confederated States.

{Here Representative Millson reflected on South Carolina's secession observing that he wished she had, instead, called "together the confederated States," and informed them, and the federal government, of her grievances, and then announced her intention to secede. Millson informed his colleagues that he had "little sympathy, and hardly any respect with her (South Carolina), as to the causes assigned for her secession," and termed her leaving "misguided," "rash and reckless."}

Let me say a word upon a subject which the gentleman from Ohio [Mr. CORWIN] discussed with so much ability and so much frankness; and that is, the idea of property in slaves. The gentleman from Ohio has taken a philosophical view of this question. Nothing, in my judgment, has been more senseless than the silly controversy which has been carried on so long between northern and southern men as to whether the Constitution recognizes the existence of property in man. One would suppose the phrase "property in man" was to be found in the Constitution, and that gentlemen were quarreling as to the proper interpretation to be given to it; but, as there is no such language there, it is wholly unnecessary to inquire whether that description of domestic servitude—that personal relation which is described in the Constitution in the words "persons held to service or labor under the laws of any State"—can be called property or not. Southern gentlemen sometimes say, in public debate, that slaves are property, and nothing but property. I cannot understand why they said so, except that they supposed they were claiming most for the South, when they expressed themselves in language which they thought would be most offensive to the North. That the claim of the master to the slave constitutes property, is undoubtedly true; but to suppose that there is nothing in the relation between them but property, is to lower and degrade the southern position. It is the weakest ground upon which the institution of slavery, in its constitutional relations, can be placed. There is a personal relation that is much higher. The Constitution recognizes and describes these men as persons held to service. I have heard it said by members of the Republican party that the framers of the Constitution refused to use any terms that would indicate a recognition of the right of property in man; that they excluded the word slave, or slavery, from the Constitution, because of their reluctance to disclose the fact that there was any such personal relation acknowledged or established by the laws of any of our States.

Sir, such an argument does great injustice to the framers of the Constitution. They were moved by no such sentimentalism. It is a reproach to them, to say that they were so intensely hypocritical that they were not ashamed to do what they were ashamed to talk about. It is an aspersion upon them to suppose that they were so intensely hypocritical as to consent to the continuance of the slave trade for twenty years, with all its attendant horrors and atrocities, and yet, like timid maidens, to shrink from the words "slave" and "slavery," as recognizing property in a human being. No, sir; they had stronger and better reasons for the adoption of the language they put in the Constitution. They knew—and the gentleman from Ohio [Mr. CORWIN] has relieved me from much of the discussion by the able and lucid manner in which he has illustrated this subject to-day—they knew the word slave, or slavery, was a word of vague and indefinite signification, having a variety of meanings. Had they used the word slave, it would have led to infinite cavil and dispute as to the precise meaning intended. Some Abolitionists might have argued that it did not apply to Africans held to servitude under the laws of Virginia and Maryland; that a negro servant, escaping from his master, was not such a slave as the Constitution required to be delivered up, because the master had not the power of life and death over him, as under the Roman law, which authorized the master to take the life of his slave. They might have argued, moreover, that the word slavery, in the Constitution, was one, and to be taken in one sense alone; that is, that two different interpretations could not be given to it; and therefore, if the laws of domestic servitude in South Carolina differed from those in Virginia, the word slavery might be applied to one or the other of them, but it could not be applied to both; because you could not give different interpretations to the same word. The framers of the Constitution, then, sir, wisely substituted a description for a word. They said "persons held to service or labor under the laws of any State." It embraced every kind of servitude. It comprehended the servants of Virginia, of North Carolina, of South Carolina, of Georgia, and of all the States. It excluded all cavil and all doubt. But they were guilty of no such miserable hypocrisy as that sometimes attributed to them—that they were unwilling to introduce into the Constitution any phrase which might imply that there could be property in man. To insist that they are persons, as well as property, is to take the highest position on which the South can rest her claims. To say that they are property, and nothing but property, is not true in any sense of the word. It is not true in physics; it is not true in morals; it is not true in religion, it is not true in politics. A slave is a man. He is a responsible man; responsible to our laws, responsible to God. He is a person; a person held to service; and it is because he is a person, that the position of the South before this Congress and in the Constitution is impregnable. I say it is because he is a person, that gentlemen of the Republican party are forbidden to pass a law prohibiting his emigration into the

Territories. As mere property, you might set us a plausible claim to exclude him. Ay, as mere property there would be a color of argument in favor of its exclusion; but as a person, a person held to service, a man holding a personal relation to another, a member of the household, a part of the family, you have no more right to exclude him from the privileges of going into the Territories with his master than you have to exclude a wife from going into the Territories with her husband. The wife, too, by law, owes service and labor to the husband. The relation existing between husband and wife is the relation established by the laws of the States; and the gentleman from Ohio cannot say that these laws which are local, and do not extend beyond the limits of the States where they were enacted; because the same argument would force him to the conclusion that it is within the power of Congress to exclude from a Territory a wife bound to her husband under the laws of any State, and that the husband cannot carry a wife occupying that relation with him into the Territories, because the law under which that relation was established or recognized does not extend beyond the territory of the State in which it was enacted.

This, then is the very highest position which the South can occupy in relation to their slaves. And permit me, sir, to say that, if they were property, and nothing but property, they would not be represented in Congress; for there is no description of property represented in Congress as property—neither lands, nor money, nor stocks, nor any other kind of property. If they were property, and nothing but property, then we deprive ourselves of the right of representation of three-fifths of their whole number, except upon the condition that an equal representation be given to property of equal value in other States of the Union.[14]

Mr. Speaker, I know that very many of these false theories, really detrimental to the South, have been supported because of that natural harmony of action between them arising from their relative weakness, which sometimes inclines the southern Representatives to acquiesce in almost any pretension set up by a Representative from their own section. I have sat in my own seat and seen gentlemen from the South inconsiderately pressing propositions, and heard them use arguments, which they supposed involved a very large claim of right for their own section; when, in truth, they were not only calculated to excite a prejudice against them with those they were trying to convince, but, in point of fact, they sometimes involved a surrender

JOHN SINGLETON MILLSON, JANUARY 21

of the safeguards which the Constitution had secured to them. And when they would move to suspend the rules to introduce their propositions, other southern gentlemen would sometimes vote with them, because of the natural disinclination of those from one section of the country to refuse to support what was brought forward to sustain a common cause. Hence this acquiescence of gentlemen has sometimes impressed the popular mind of the South with the belief that those pretensions were right and just; because they were seemingly favored by the most intelligent of their Representatives. In that way it has come that some unsound and impracticable theories have been pressed in the name of the South; which, like that I have been discussing, actually involved a surrender of many of the strongest positions which the South ought to occupy.

And now a word or two in relation to the views suggested by the gentleman from Ohio [Mr. CORWIN] upon the subject of the admission of New Mexico as a State. I regret to have to differ with the gentleman upon this subject. The House will perceive that I have not disagreed with him on many points; and I am happy now to express my admiration of the temper and tone which pervaded the whole of his speech. Much of it I heartily approve; and I regret that I am under the necessity of dissenting from some of the conclusions to which the gentleman arrived. I cannot give my consent to the admission of New Mexico at this time as a State, and for reasons wholly unconnected with the sectional controversy which is now agitating the country. Sir, if I believed, as some of my southern associates appear to do, that the people of the South were in any such danger as justified disunion, in order to escape it; if I believed that the Republican party could, if they would, exclude slavery from the Territories; if I believed that any such aggression could be consummated, why, I might then accept the tender of New Mexico as a State, in order that I might take away from them the inducement and the opportunity to accomplish any such promise. Whether they have the purpose or not, I know they have not the power. I say here now what I said more than a year ago to the Republican party: "Gentlemen, I do not fear you. I do not fear that you will have the power to do what you declare it is your wish to do. I do not believe you will be able to command a majority for the purpose of prohibiting slavery in the Territories of the United States." I should, perhaps, be doing you injustice if I supposed that it was your purpose now to attempt the exercise of this power. If, in the present condition of the country, for the sake of a wanton exercise of power, from which you could reap no advantage, you should undertake to prohibit slavery in any part of the Territories of the United States, you would put yourselves beyond the pale of any sympathy—I was about to say of all respect—of the country. Should this be attempted, I do not believe you could succeed; and should you succeed here, I should rest secure in the decision of the supreme judicial authority of the country—a barrier which you can neither leap over nor break down. I am under no apprehension; and I will not attempt to increase the present unhappy excitement in the country by stimulating the fears of others, when I am altogether free from them myself. It is for that reason that I am unable to vote to admit New Mexico as a State. I do not think she is now in a condition to become a State; and I will not consent to admit her as a State merely for the purpose of avoiding the shadowy and unreal danger of which I have spoken. But if I did believe it, I should then take her as a State. If I did believe that the safety of the Union depended upon it; if I believed that was the only escape from the exercise of a power to prohibit slavery in the Territories, I should feel myself wholly inexcusable for not guarding against all these dangers by the admission of New Mexico.

[Here the hammer fell.]

Source: *Congressional Globe*, 36th Cong., 2nd Sess., Appendix, 76–79.

Sherrard Clemens
January 22, 1861

Sherrard Clemens (1820–1881) was born in Wheeling, Virginia (now West Virginia), graduated from Washington College in Pennsylvania, and admitted to the bar in 1843. After setting up his law practice in Wheeling he served in the US House of Representatives from 1852 to 1853, and again from 1857 until 1861. He was elected as a Unionist from Ohio County to Virginia's state convention. After voting against secession on April 17, he left Richmond to attend the First Wheeling Convention in May 1861 which began the process of separating western Virginia from the rest of the state.

In September 1858, Clemens challenged O. Jennings "Obie" Wise (son of then governor Henry A. Wise) to a duel after Wise attacked Clemens in an editorial regarding the upcoming gubernatorial election. On the fourth volley, Clemens suffered a serious injury to a thigh bone. Wise walked away unscathed.[15] Clemens was a distant cousin of Samuel Clemens, the renowned author more commonly known as Mark Twain.

Like many southern moderates, Representative Clemens believed that secession would lead to the demise of slavery. After announcing that the "great superinducing cause of all difficulty has been that very territorial question," and suggesting that secession would lead to the resumption of the African slave trade, he observed that the slave South was not all that unified. While the "ruling interest" of the Gulf and Atlantic states was slavery, the "other states *have great interests besides slavery, which cannot be lightly abandoned.*" Clemens expressed concern that the southern antipathy toward protective tariffs would work against the "mechanical and manufacturing and mining industry and capital of Missouri, of Kentucky, of Virginia, of North Carolina, of Maryland, and Delaware." Pleading for less thoughtless rhetoric that simply repeated hackneyed political phrases, he encouraged his fellow representatives: "Let us feel we have a country to save, instead of a geographical section to represent."

The House having under consideration the report from the select committee of thirty-three—

Mr. CLEMENS said:

Mr. SPEAKER: For two years and more, my voice has rarely resounded in this Hall. On questions of high debate my vote has even been wanting. Contending with physical anguish, on a bed of languishment and disease, the dependent mind could be but wearily exercised. I know, sir, I have done nothing worthy of the high place to which I have been so generously called. I know I have not justified the expectations of the noble constituency whose sympathy has soothed, and whose support has smoothed, the thorny path which sickness always brings. Sacred silence is, perhaps, the proper meed for these sacred matters; but I would feign believe, that, by a benign ordination of God, at the very period when my services are needed by my people most, I have, in the precarious boon of renovated health, the power to represent them. I would speak in *their* cause, this day, living, as they do, upon the very confines of what may be hostile confederacies. I would speak as one who has never known anything from them but the beneficence with which they have sustained me, and the good offices by which they have overflowed my heart with gratitude. Sir, I would not speak in passion. It befits not the solemn and portentous issues of this hour. We are in the midst of great events. We are making history. We may be in the dying days of this Republic; and I should undo my deeds, I should unknow my knowledge, before I would, as the traveler in the Alps, utter, even in a whisper, one word which might bring down the avalanche upon the quiet homes of my people. I would speak as a southern man, identified by birth, by education, by residence, by interest, by property, by affection, with her population. Sir, on a bayou of the Mississippi, reposes now in quiet the inheritance of my children—an inheritance which, even in slaves, amounts to one half of the whole number in all the eleven counties which compose my congressional district in Virginia. I would speak as a western Virginian, and as the custodian of the property of those children, who are not old enough to know the peril to which it is exposed by those who are riding on the very crest of the popular wave, but who are yet destined to sink in the very trough of the sea, to a depth so unfathomable that a bubble will never rise to mark the spot where they went so ignominiously down! Well may those who have inaugurated the revolution which is now stalking over the land cry out, with uplifted hands, for peace, and deprecate the effusion of blood. It was the inventor of the guillotine who was its first unresisting victim; and the day may not be far off before we may find those among our own people who will be compelled to rely upon the magnanimity of the very population they have outraged and deceived. The authors of revolutions have often been their victims.

Sir, at this hour, I have no heart to enter into the details of this argument, or to express the indignant emotions which rise to my lips and plead for utterance. Before God, and in my inmost conscience, I believe that slavery will be crucified, if this unhappy controversy ends in a dismemberment of the Union. Sir, if not crucified, it will carry the death rattle in its throat. I may be a timid man; I may not know what it is to take up arms in my own defense. It remains to be seen, however, whether treason can be carried out with the same facility it can be plotted and arranged. There is a holy courage among the minority in every slave State, that may be for the time overwhelmed. Lazarus is not dead, but sleepeth. Ere long, the stone will be rolled away from the mouth of the tomb, and we shall have all the glories of a new resurrection.

{Here Representative Clemens spoke of the great "political paradox" that had befallen the nation, where "expansive love of country, has become a diseased sentimentality." He expressed dismay that a statesman "can take an oath to support the Constitution of the United States, but he can enter with honor into a conspiracy to overthrow it." He invoked the words of George Washington who advised citizens to "indignantly frown upon the first dawning of every attempt to alienate any portion of our country from the rest, or to enfeeble the sacred ties which now link together the various parts."}

Sir, that great man penetrated, as with the acumen of a seer, into the crowning bane of this disastrous period, when he warned his countrymen against the consequences of geographical parties. Extremes in the North and extremes in the South have at last met. Parties have been organized and carried on by systematic perversions of each other's aims and objects. In the North it has been represented that the South desired and intended to monopolize with slave labor *all* the public territory; to drive out free labor; to convert every free State into common ground for the recapture of colored persons as slaves who were free; and to put the Federal Government, in all its departments, under the control of a slave oligarchy. These and all other stratagems that could be resorted to to arouse antagonistic feelings were wielded with turbulent and tumultuous passion. As we planted, so we reap. Now, that victory has been obtained by the Republican party, and the Government must be administered upon national policy and principles, the fissures in the ground hitherto occupied become apparent; and hence there must necessarily be a large defection in its ranks among the more ultra of its adherents, who are, as a general thing, ideal, speculative, and not practical men.

Out of power, a party is apt to be radical; vest it with power, and it becomes conservative. This is the ordeal through which the Republican, like all other parties, is now passing; and it is to be hoped, for the peace of the country, it will result in the triumph of practical and national, rather than ideal policy and sectional measures. Herein consists the almost insuperable difficulty of coming to any feasible adjustment upon the existing discontents. The bulk of politicians, North and South, are bound by a past record and past professions. They are thinking all the while of what Mrs. Grundy will say.[16] The people understand the cause of the difficulty, and are moving. If they could interpose, the country might yet be saved.

Sir, what is that difficulty now; what has it always been? I appeal to every unprejudiced man's experience to say, whether it has not been that, in the hands of ultraists North and ultraists South, the slaveholder has been used as a shuttledore,[17] and, for purposes utterly dissimilar, has been banded from South Carolina to Massachusetts, and from Massachusetts to South Carolina, until now the last point of endurance has been reached. Every virulent word uttered North has been sent South, and the South has responded in the same virulent spirit. Nay, the Abolitionist himself has been granted an audience in every southern city, at every southern political meeting, and the most violent, insulting, agrarian speeches repeated in the hearing even of slaves themselves. Is it not a humiliation to confess, that the very people who would burn in effigy, if not at the stake, a postmaster who would dare to distribute a copy of ultra abolition speeches, honor as among their chief defenders, the candidates who can quote the most obnoxious passages from all? Who has made of southern politics, a vast hotbed, for the propagation of abolition sentiments, but ultra southern men themselves? Who has indoctrinated the northern people with dissimilar sentiments, expressed by the most ultra southern men, but northern zealots themselves?

{Representative Clemens continued on the theme of abolitionism and the South's unrealistic reaction to it. "The Abolitionist revels in the madness of the hour. He sees the crack in the iceberg at last. For *him* the desert and the battlefield are both alike welcome." For Clemens, however, secession would only lead to disaster for slavery and the South. "Defeated, stigmatized, insulted, scoffed at, ostracized, gibbeted

by his countrymen, he now gloats over the most fearful of all retribu-
tions. His deadliest foes hitherto in the South, have now struck hands
in a solemn league of kindred designs, and with exultant tramp, stol-
idly march, adorned like a Roman ox, with the garlands of sacrifice, to
their eternal doom." He then quoted speeches of abolitionists William
Lloyd Garrison and Wendell Phillips in which they proclaimed that
they were themselves "disunionists" and that they "would get rid of this
Union, to get rid of slavery."}

We have, then, before us, these knights of a new crusade. The Constitution of the United States is the sanctified Jerusalem, against which their deluded cohorts are arrayed. They contend the only mode to overthrow slavery
is to overthrow the Constitution. They refuse to take office under it, because
it recognizes slavery. They will not take an oath to support it, because it pro-
tects slavery. They claim their allegiance is due to the State, and to the State
alone. They are State-rights men of the straightest sect; and they wield the
legislative power of the State for the extinction of slavery, as South Carolina
professes to wield her's for the perpetuation of slavery.

Sir, is there not left among us statesmanship sufficient to control these
issues, and apply the corrective in time, and save this great country, now
convulsed from its center to its circumference? Standing in the midst of
these troubles, and looking into the future with the most inexpressible apprehensions, I acknowledge, with pleasure, one patriotic move in the right
direction. It is one of the cheering signs of this most disastrous time, when
"an airy devil's in the sky, and rains down mischiefs," that the descendant
of two former Presidents, who bears an ancestral fame now greater than
any man in America, should step forward with an offering of peace to an
afflicted people.[18] Sir, grant it was nothing more than a covenant declaratory
of the spirit of the Constitution. It was meet that Massachusetts, so largely
partaking in our common glory in the past; Massachusetts, for the first
blood for American liberty was shed—should rise superior to the convul-
sions of the hour, and give an earnest, at least, that the spirit of conciliation,
of inter-State comity, of fraternal affection, was not yet wholly lost. As the
worn traveler in the midst of the snows of the Alps lingers, with delighted
gaze, upon the friendly light which peers from the windows of the distant

convent, where, from the desolation of the storm around him, he may at last find repose, so do I hail that little gleam of hope in the midst of all the darkness of this hour.

{Clemens encouraged his southern colleagues to graciously accept the Adams proposition. He reminded his listeners that Massachusetts representative Harrison Gray Otis had supported slavery in the formation of the Mississippi Territory in 1798. Clemens stated, "He (Otis) thought it was not the business of those who had nothing to do with *that kind of property, to interfere with that right.*"}

What divides the North and South at this moment? Is it the personal liberty bills? No, sir! Not so much them. Is it the fugitive slave law? No, sir; not so much that. The great superinducing cause of all difficulty has been that very territorial question which was settled so quietly by the policy of Mr. Otis in 1798, and is now settled on the same principle by the Supreme Court.[19]

{At this point, Representative Clemens entered into a lengthy portion of his address explaining the growth the South's slave population over the past thirty years and the concomitant escalation in the value of slaves. Slavery could not, he argued, expand quickly because of the heightened value of slaves. In order to bring the price for a slave down so that more southerners could become slaveowners, Clemens presented quotes from various representatives stating under certain circumstances they would be in favor of reopening the importation of slaves from Africa. He concluded: "Now, sir, if one so humble as myself may venture an opinion upon these and kindred matters, I must be allowed to say that the border slave States may as well be prepared first as last for the realization of the truth, that the coast States are aiming not so much at expansion *within* as expansion *without* the Union. Visions of conquest, visions of military glory, float before the southern enthusiast, in the glowing speeches of a Peter the Hermit[20] of a new crusade, whose declared policy it was 'to inflame the southern mind, fire the southern heart, and precipitate the cotton States into a revolution.'"}

But where is slavery to expand? The South goes out of the Union, and will never touch as much earth of the territory that now belongs to it as I can grasp thus. Never! Never! A war of thirty years will never get it back. If you fight, you will never extort by a treaty from the North the same guarantees that you now have in this Constitution emblazoned on those shields above us — the very type of national strength and national unity.

{Clemens here argued that if the South abandoned its claims on the western territories of the United States, slavery could not expand to Mexico where the institution had been abolished, nor to Central America where slavery had also been abolished through British influence. To that end, he reminded his fellow representatives that a slave uprising in Tennessee in 1835 had been encouraged by the English abolitionist George Thompson.[21]}

I dismiss this unwelcome theme. Let me pass to another. It is evident that, in the event of the formation of a southern confederacy, there will be, besides the African slave trade, another element of discord and agitation, in which the Gulf and border States will have interests entirely dissimilar. Slavery is the great ruling interest of the extreme Gulf States; the other States *have great interests besides slavery, which cannot be lightly abandoned.* I admit it is to the advantage of the coast States to have a direct exchange of staple commodities for the manufactured articles of England and France. That this is proposed to be realized, we have the fullest proofs. Charleston, Savannah, Mobile, and New Orleans will become great marts of trade. Export duties and direct taxation will be to them a prosperous policy; but how will it operate upon the mechanical and manufacturing and mining industry and capital of Missouri, of Kentucky, of Virginia, of North Carolina, of

Maryland, and Delaware, if *they* should form part of the confederation? I know it is asserted that a mutuality of purposes and a community of interest in slavery will avoid this result. How is it to be avoided? Sir, when it involves a contradiction of the avowed designs of South Carolina for the last thirty years, and is in perfect correspondence with the declared plans of the people of the cotton States themselves, how, I say, will you avoid it?

An examination of the census of 1860 will disclose the astounding fact that if the Constitution of the United States is taken as a provisional form of government under this new convention which they have called to meet in Montgomery, Alabama, the cotton States, with those abutting upon them, will have, under the fixed ratio of representation, the legislative power over the border slave States, and they will be bound by a policy which may be, as to their great material and mechanical interests, as oppressive as it will be ruinous. If these causes should exist, we shall have an antagonism in that union quite as great; fifty fold intensified, it may be, beyond anything we have ever had in *this*. But if the other view is taken, and the border States are encouraged and protected in manufactures, the white population of those States will be so vastly increased that they will be but nominal slave States, finally becoming free States by the very necessities of their existence under that inexorable law of population to which I have referred. What principle in free-trade, or any other principle for which they are now contending, will the cotton States have gained by this most disastrous revolution? What time it may take to effect these results, no human sagacity can foretell; but that they will follow, if any reliance at all can be placed upon past experience, is at least my own fixed and solemn conviction. With a tier of free States along the whole northern border of Texas, the western borders of Louisiana and Arkansas, the northern and western portions of Missouri, of Kentucky, of Virginia, and of Maryland, a distance of nearly four thousand miles, this inevitable law of population, operating from its geographical center in the North west, and with the facilities for settlement which a Pacific railroad will give, a branch of which the South voluntarily and most fallaciously relinquishes, the great hog-eating Teutons of these vast plains will bear down even upon Texas and Mexico, and ultimately bear them away from any confederacy into which they may enter. In the Union there is at least a fair prospect that Mexico, by the very necessities of our position, will fall into our hands, and in the providence of God it may yet be that this now distracted land, cursed with civil feuds, and racked with internecine wars, may yet be reserved for the purpose of working out the great problem under which the brain of this vast nation is now overwhelmed and reels.

Mr. Speaker, gentlemen from the North shrink back in dismay at the very mention of a proposition to protect slavery south of the line of 36°30', either as applied to territory now existing, or which may be hereafter acquired, when it is perfectly demonstrable, on the law of population to which we have referred, that every slave State erected within the tropics can only be had at the ultimate sacrifice of a kindred State along the borders of the free States. The policy is the policy of Saturn feeding on the bodies of his own children.[22] It is time the North, as well as the South, appreciated this state of facts. The field for argument and illustration thus presented is inviting indeed; but within the limits of the hour I can but make suggestions, rather than maintain any extended line of remark. The question for the statesman to decide is: whether the South shall not be guarantied by constitutional en-actments, if need be, in the principle secured to her by that instrument itself, by the decision of the Supreme Court; a principle which may not only be barren of any practical advantage to her, but, if rendered effective, can only be so on the basis of a compensating benefit to the free States themselves, of opening up new fields in a temperate and genial clime for the increase of white population.

I would fain hope, in the determination of this vast question, we may rise above the silly prejudices and splendid shams of the hour. *Let us have no more cant. Let our eyes not blink under the truth as it is.* Let us enlighten, as best we may, the people of this great country, not only as to their duties in the present, but as to their destiny to come. Let us feel we have a country to save, instead of a geographical section to represent. Let us act as men, and not as partisans; and the old Constitution, now in the very trough of the sea, with battered masts and sails in shreds, rolling at the mercy of every breaker, will again, with her dark and weather-beaten sides, loom from the deep; will again skim over the waves like the sea-bird, that scarce wets his bosom on their snowy crests, ringing with glad shouts, and the rapture of anticipated triumph, as when she ranged, like a mighty monster of the deep, beneath the castles of Tripoli, striking them dumb as she passed, or, as when she spread her broad and glorious banner to the winds, and rushed, like a strong man rejoicing to run a race, on the Guerriere and the Java.[23]

Mr. Speaker, I have necessarily left much unsaid. My last hope upon this most distracting question is upon the action of Virginia. Heed her voice while yet you may! I would now conclude all I have to say in the solemn warning of one of her noblest sons, the author of the Declaration of Independence himself, who, in 1798, in a period not unlike the present, appealed to erring sisters to cling to the sanctuary of their fathers.

"In every free and deliberative society," says he, "there must, from the nature of man, be opposite parties and violent discussions and discords; and one of these, for the most part, must prevail over the other for a longer or shorter time. Perhaps this party division is necessary to induce each to watch and delate to the people the proceedings of the other. *But if, on a temporary superiority of the one party, the other is to resort to a scission of the Union, no Federal Government can ever exist.* If, to rid ourselves of the present rule of Massachusetts and Connecticut, we break up the Union, will the evil stop there? Suppose the New England States be alone cut off: will our natures be changed? Are we not men still, with all the passions of men? Immediately we shall see a Pennsylvania and Virginia party arise in the residuary confederacy, and the public mind will be distracted with the same party spirit. *What game, too, will one party have in their hands by eternally threatening each other, that unless they do so, they will join their northern neighbors?* If we reduce our Union to Virginia and North Carolina, immediately the conflict will be established between the representatives of these two States; and even *they* will end by breaking into their simple units. Seeing, therefore, that an association of men, *who will not quarrel with one another*, is a thing that never yet existed, from the greatest Confederacy of nations down to the town meeting or vestry; seeing that we must have somebody to quarrel with, *I had rather keep our New England associates for that purpose than to see our bickerings transferred to others.*" A little patience, mark you, Mr. Speaker—*"a little patience*, AND WE SHALL SEE THE REIGN OF WITCHES PASS OVER, THEIR SPELLS DISSOLVED, AND THE PEOPLE RECOVERING THEIR TRUE SIGHT, RESTORING THEIR GOVERNMENT TO ITS TRUE PRINCIPLES."[24]

Source: *Congressional Globe*, 36th Cong., 2nd Sess., Appendix, 103–6.

Shelton Farrar Leake
January 25, 1861

Shelton F. Leake (1812–1884) was born in Albemarle County, admitted
to the bar in 1835, and established his law practice in Charlottesville.
He served in Virginia's house of delegates (1842–1843), as a Democrat
in the US House of Representatives (1845–1847), as lieutenant governor
(1852), and as an Independent Democrat to the US Congress where he
served from 1859 until 1861. He spent the war practicing law in Charlottesville. Representative Leake was the first Virginian to propose a
constitutional amendment as a solution to the sectional crisis.

In an effort to rebut the comments of Representative Millson of a
few days earlier, Leake asserted that he did not believe the mere election of Lincoln was sufficient cause for disunion, but argued that the
reasons for his election were evidence of sectional incompatibility. The
growth of the antislavery movement from the Missouri Compromise
to the present, specifically the passage of personal liberty acts aimed
at preventing the constitutionally required return of fugitive slaves
had sanctified northern crime against the South. The Black Republican party had "control of this Government," he proclaimed, and on
March 4 the country would not inaugurate a president, but a "miserable
king of shreds and patches" who would preside over a nation "sundered
by petty politicians."

Mr. LEAKE. We have fallen upon evil times. But yesterday, as it were,
there was not a solitary gentleman, a member of this House, not a citizen of
the then United States of America, who could not have boasted that, in the
face of the world, he belonged to a country whose flag was an ample guarantee of all his rights; and that, in all sections of the world, that flag carried
with it a passport to respect in the eyes of all foreign officials. But yesterday,
and our country was floating in the full tide of successful experiment. In
all branches of its industry, it was unusually prosperous and extraordinarily
happy. There was nothing, as far as human ken could see, to mar the prospect which a brilliant future seemed to offer to the history of this great and

glorious country. But now, Mr. Speaker, how changed the picture! We are no longer sailing upon this great ocean of prosperity to a haven of success- ful repose and an eminent prosperity. We are involved in the horrors of a revolution, and evil convulsion, which, whatever may be its result, portends mischief, permanent, enduring, and irreparable, to one section or the other, or to one of the many sections of this glorious Confederacy.

It becomes us, then, surrounded by these difficulties, to pause, in order to inquire, for a single moment at least, why it is that this blight has so suddenly come over all the prospects of this country; that we should pause to inquire, for a moment, what causes are we to look to for results so unex- pected but a brief year since? I know we shall differ in the different sections of the Confederacy. I know well that, on the one section or the other will be charged the evils which have fallen upon us. I know well that that evil is upon us; and I, for one, am accepting it as a fact, and dealing with it as such, whoever may be to blame. But whence comes it? I cannot say, nor can any man upon this floor; least of all can any member of the Republican party of this House, or of this country, say that he has not had premonitions of the storm which has now burst in all its fury upon the devoted head of this country. Warning upon warning has been given. Statesman after statesman, for long years, has raised his voice and told you that there were dangers, deep, serious, and irreparable, ahead, which, if not warded off, would ul- timately result in precisely the state of things which we are now in. They have been unheeded. The Republican party—that party which has lately swept into power, overriding all that was dear and sacred in the Consti- tution, the laws, and history—that party has seen the breakers ahead for long years past; nay, more, not only did these breakers lift their heads above the surrounding waters, but we, of the South, had erected our lighthouses to warn you of the dangers. You heeded not the warning; you headed your ship upon the rocks; and now, when the old ship of State has gone to pieces upon the rocks, and is floating in broken fragments upon the dread ocean of public opinion, you demand that we shall gather them up, and reconstruct her in all her fair and majestic proportions. Sir, it cannot be done. You have wrecked the ship, and you are entitled to no salvage; at least, we of the South are unwilling to pay it.

Now, sir, upon what ground is it that I come to this conclusion? Mr. Speaker, there have been crimination and recrimination upon all sides of

this Hall. Gentlemen from the non-slaveholding States have charged upon
the South that we are the cause of all the mischief which has come upon
us. We, of the South, have charged back upon them that the true source of
all the evil is in the very organization which now constitutes the dominant
party of this country, so far as the popular will seems to be concerned.
Where lies the truth? Sirs, our Government, in its earlier, its purer, its hap-
pier, and its better days, did encounter questions which were in conflict
with the very institutions under which we live, and which it was necessary
to settle in order to secure the peace, the prosperity, and the happiness of
the country. We had the alien and sedition laws; we had the question of
war with Great Britain, when one whole section arrayed itself against the
Union; we had the tariff acts of 1828 and 1833. All those questions we settled;
not, perhaps, in the manner which my conscience approved; and yet, they
were so settled as to secure the peace, if not the prosperity of the country.
Whence sprung this difficulty? Where was its origin? From 1788 down to
1819–20, we had no controversy upon this subject of slavery. There was no
serious difficulty. It is very true, in 1797, a member from Massachusetts proposed to restrict slavery in the Territory of Mississippi; but another member,
long since gone to his reward, (Mr. Otis,) opposed it; and the proposition
was rejected.[25] We had no serious difficulty, I repeat, until Missouri applied
for admission into the Confederacy, as a free, sovereign, and equal member
of this glorious galaxy of States. How, then, did this difficulty originate?

Sir, let me premise, at this point, by saying—what has often been said
upon this floor as a part of the history of the country, and is therefore not
to be controverted—that, at the formation of this Government, every State
but one was a slaveholding State, and that, at the time of the Declaration
of Independence, every State was a slaveholding State. And yet, in 1820,
owing to the magnanimity and liberality of the South, and particularly of
Virginia, you had gathered strength enough upon the floor of this very body
to interpose a restriction, not only upon southern rights, but equally upon
the rights of sovereign States which might thereafter be admitted into the
Union. Mr. Jefferson declared that the "Missouri restriction came upon him
like a fire-bell in the dead of night"[26]—language expressive of the profound
peace, calm, and repose in which the country then was, when the North
sprang this question of ill omen upon the people of the South. There is the
source of all the mischief under which this country now labors.

Sir, my colleague from the Norfolk district, [Mr. MILLSON,] whom I do not see now in his seat, declared, in the able and eloquent speech which he delivered two or three days since, that every question between the North and the South had been settled in favor of the South; although, he added, that while we got the principle, they got the substance. My friend from Missouri, here, says we got the shadow. It was less than the shadow. We got the principle? When did we get it? In the Missouri question? I know that when it was proposed to interpose an anti-slavery qualification as a condition of the admission of Missouri, it was compromised. But how compromised? By agreeing to draw an imaginary line through the then territory of the United States, and positively prohibiting slavery in all that part of the territory north of that line, while that part south might come in with or without slavery, as the people of the Territory themselves might prescribe when they applied for admission into the Union. How was that controversy settled in favor of the South? On the contrary, it was, as I said just now, the source of all the ills under which this country labors. It was settled against the South; because then the right of Congress to interdict slavery in the Territories was conceded by an act of this body. You assumed jurisdiction over the question at that time, and have recognized it since, whenever it has been necessary, in your opinion, to exercise it.

But, Mr. Speaker, I appeal to my colleague again upon a point on which I am inclined to think he will agree with me when he understands what I mean. I am willing to take this question upon his own basis, and to argue it upon the idea that, so far as the action of this Government is concerned, every question has been settled in favor of the South; and I am forced to come to a conclusion diametrically opposite to the one at which my distinguished and respected colleague arrived in his argument. Admit that we have all the guarantees that the Constitution can give us, and that we have settled every controversy that has risen, so far as this Government can settle it, in favor of the South; and yet we know that the South is now the oppressed section, and that we have not derived one solitary jot or tittle of benefit from the settlements of which my colleague so proudly boasts. The question has been settled practically and morally against us. The Government has utterly failed in the great end and object of its creation; and the southern people have been entirely deprived of those rights which I know my colleague wants, which I want, and which the South demands. It has failed—utterly failed; your legislation is worthless; your compromises are not worth the paper upon which they are written. I repeat, that the experiment is a failure; and when the people of my section of this country wish to derive adequate protection for their rights from the Government and the Constitution, and the laws made in pursuance thereof, then, sir, Virginia holds the remedy in the hollow of her hand; and I tell you that she will apply it in the manner she may deem best for her own good.

Mr. MILLSON. Will my colleague allow me to interrupt him?

Mr. LEAKE. Certainly, sir.

Mr. MILLSON. I want to correct an error. He is answering an argument I never made. I never did say that every question had been settled in favor of the South. I said that the present territorial question, involving the right to carry slaves into the Territories had been settled in favor of the South; settled by the repeal of the Missouri restriction, to which my colleague has referred; settled by the Supreme Court; and if we have derived no benefit from it, it is only because we have no slaves to carry into the Territory, and no territory suitable for them.

Mr. LEAKE. I think that if my colleague will read the written report of his speech, which I read very carefully last night—and I may say that I heard every word he uttered—he will find there excuses for the misapprehension (for I doubt not there is misapprehension) into which I have fallen. I know he will not suspect me of a disposition to misrepresent him.

Mr. MILLSON. Certainly not.

Mr. LEAKE. The argument comes back to the same point; but I must pass rapidly from it, because I have other matters to deal with. Let me say here that it strikes me that this whole controversy is even now not well understood by the people of either section of the country. I know well that certain legislation on the part of northern States is constantly referred to, and certain action upon the part of this Government; and I know also that the question has been again and again asked—a question which was answered in his way by my colleague from the Norfolk district—whether the election of Lincoln was a *casus belli*,[27] for which we ought to sever the relations existing between the different sections? Sir, I pause to remark that the election of Lincoln was no cause of a dissolution of the Union. I tell you that the *mere election* of a President of the United States, under the forms of the Constitution, never can be a justifiable cause of a dissolution of the

Confederacy. I say, however, at the same time, that whilst the constitutional form is there, you have to "create a soul under the ribs of death." You have furnished us with the ribs of death; it is for you to inquire whether you have given us the soul under those ribs. What I believe, and what I believe the whole South thinks, is, that the election of Lincoln is evidence that cause for the dissolution of the Union exists. It is not cause itself; but it is evidence that that cause exists. That cause underlies it; it reaches far behind it — so far behind that very few, perhaps, have taken the pains to look into it.

Another colleague of mine, whom I see in his seat, [Mr. CLEMENS,] — and he will pardon me for observing that he seemed to take especial pleasure in administering to the delectation of his northern friends upon the other side of the House — thought proper, in the course of the remarkable speech which he delivered, to quote from the farewell address of the father of Virginia's liberties.[28] In that address he warned us against sectional controversies. As though he possessed the power of omniscience, of looking into the human heart, of penetrating that darkest and most mysterious of all labyrinths, and subjecting its motives to the test of infallible analysis, that immortal man warned you, in the language quoted by my colleague, against the dangers of sectional strife. I wonder that the member from Virginia should apply the quotation to the people of the southern section of this Confederacy. I wonder that he should have attempted to draw us within the admonition of that great, and illustrious man. Sir, had he attempted then to describe, with more than prophetic vision, the present position, aims, and objects of the Republican party, he could not have better done it. Who have created this sectional controversy? Who are its authors? Who have prosecuted it until there is, perhaps, no hope left for the South but in the *ultima ratio*[29] of nations? The North. Did the South begin the fight? I appeal to my colleague to know whether Virginia ever attempted to create sectional strife within the limits of this Confederacy? He shakes his head. I am glad he does it. Even that slight assent to the southern view of the question will be gratifying to his constituents. Where did it begin? I have alluded to the Missouri compromise. What next. You may go back to the history of this Confederacy from 1821–22 down to this day, and you will find that history but the history of a series of aggressions upon the part of the North on the just constitutional rights of the South; new agitations in both branches of Congress, and attempts to interfere with the relations between master and slave. You need not talk to me about legislation, when you have organized your societies and set the machinery at work to sap the foundations upon which our whole society rests. What have the North done? You have sanctified crime; you have canonized murder; you have offered a premium upon perjury; and you have made it a high crime and misdemeanor to obey the Constitution of the United States, and the laws passed in pursuance thereof. I except, of course, from this statement, the gallant Democracy of the North. Sir, if you wanted to find the man within the broad limits of this Confederacy who has done more to sap the foundations upon which the Government has, until of late years, reposed in peace and quiet; who has laid the foundation of this whole controversy, broadly and deeply; who has done it in a way that shows that he would not comply with his own constitutional obligations, but would punish all who complied with theirs, and protect those who violate the Constitution and the laws, you will find him, I thank God, not within the limits of the sunny South. I cannot allude, I believe, to anything which has been said in the Senate of the United States. It would be unparliamentary to do so, and I mean to violate no parliamentary law if I can avoid it. But that man is now in the Senate of the United States, representing the greatest State of this Confederacy. I allude, sir, to William H. Seward, who, as Governor of New York, as far back as 1839, asserted doctrines fatal to the rights of all the States of this Confederacy.

At that time, three men went to the city of Norfolk, in Virginia, and stole three negroes. They escaped with them to New York. William H. Seward was then Governor of the State of New York. The proofs were made out, the evidence filed, every requirement of the law complied with, and the acting Governor of Virginia[30] made his requisition in solemn form for the surrender of the criminals; but the Governor of the State of New York refused to comply with the obligations of the Constitution. And on what ground? On the naked ground that, according to the laws of New York, there could be no property in slaves. Sir, would it not be a novelty, in a system of government constituted as ours is, if every State of the Confederacy had a right to supervise the laws of every other State of the Confederacy? Would it not be a novelty, if not only the State, through her regularly constituted legislative authorities, but that the Governor of each State, should have a right to supervise those laws? Yet Mr. Seward did it. The crime was not a felony in New York, and therefore he was not bound to surrender a fugitive accused of committing that crime. Now let us examine that for a moment.

Not long ago, the State of New York came very near abolishing the law inflicting the punishment of death for murder; and it is contended by some that she did absolutely make it impossible to punish murder in the first degree. Suppose she had said by her legislation that murder should not be a crime within the limits of the State of New York; and suppose a man committed a murder in the State of Virginia and escaped to New York; would the Governor of New York be justified in saying, in response to a requisition made upon him, "No, sir; we do not regard murder as a crime in New York, and therefore we are not bound to surrender this person?" Now, is that law?

I am merely giving a rapid sketch of these things. What has the Governor of Ohio done? Governor Dennison[31] refused to surrender a man accused of aiding and abetting others to commit murder.

Mr. SHERMAN.[32] Will the gentleman allow me to make a statement about this matter?

Mr. LEAKE. Certainly, sir.

Mr. SHERMAN. I simply desire to state that whenever any citizen of Ohio goes within the limits of the State of Virginia, and there commits a crime against her laws and flees to Ohio, no Governor of Ohio has ever refused to surrender such person. The case referred to was a case where a citizen of Ohio was accused of having committed a crime, not within the limits of Virginia, but of Ohio. The papers showed on their face that the presence alleged in Virginia was a mere constructive presence, and not an actual presence. I know the Governor of Virginia very well; and I verily believe that he himself would not surrender a citizen of Virginia to the Executive of Ohio when that citizen of Virginia had not left the soil of his native State.

{Here ensued a lengthy discussion among Leake, John Sherman (Ohio), Samuel S. Cox (Ohio), Clement Vallandigham (Ohio) and others regarding the comity provisions of the Constitution, the rendition of the members of John Brown's raiding party who escaped Harpers Ferry into nearby states, and the mechanics of the 1850 Fugitive Slave Law.}

Mr. LEAKE. I must interrupt the gentleman, and resume my remarks.

I may be pardoned here, if, while upon this issue in regard to the repudiation of the fugitive slave law, I allude to the conduct of Virginia upon a question of a similar character. In a question between New York and Virginia, in 1839 and 1840, when the Governor of New York was, as I think, plotting against the Constitution, and the whole tone of our fraternal system of Government, by refusing to surrender up men who had stolen negroes, a man, who had committed an offense in New York, escaped into Virginia. T. M. Gilmer,[33] my own trusted and honored friend, was then the Governor of that State. Mr. Seward, then Governor of New York, made a requisition upon him for the man, and Governor Gilmer immediately notified him that he would hold the man in custody for six months, to see whether New York would comply with her constitutional obligations. He wanted to show that he thought this compact between the States ought to be carried out. When the fact came to the knowledge of the Legislature of Virginia, they, with great unanimity, passed a resolution in which they declared that the State of Virginia would comply with the constitutional obligation to surrender fugitives, although New York had refused to do so. That is but a specimen of the mode in which Virginia complies with her obligations under the Constitution and the laws of the land.

Again: I refer to the action of a foreign Government—Canada—and the mode in which they execute their extradition treaties, which are not as of high solemnity and sanction as the Constitution of the United States. The courts of Canada, instead of imitating the examples of the Government of New York, Ohio, and Iowa, have, upon solemn deliberation, remanded a slave who had committed murder and fled to Canada.

But I pass to another point. I want to show northern men where it is that this controversy finds its true origin and source. Hence my allusion to this difficulty. You have broken up the comity of States. You have refused compliance with constitutional obligations, in the cases to which I have alluded, and many others. And I have alluded to them for the purpose of turning again to the fact of the passage of your personal liberty bills. I said at the outset of my desultory speech—made more desultory than I thought it would be, by repeated interruptions—that they had sanctified crime at the North. You have done it through the instrumentality of your State authorities, by declaring that what we in the South regard as crime, is entitled to immunity, if not to protection, at the North. What more have you done? Why, you have offered a premium on perjury, by declaring, in your personal liberty laws, that you will make it a high crime and misdemeanor to obey the Constitution and the laws of the land. Eleven, if not twelve, of your States have imposed pains and penalties upon the man who undertakes to execute the law of Congress for the recovery of fugitive slaves, passed in pursuance of the precise terms of the Constitution. That is the amount of your personal liberty bills, and they amount to nothing more and nothing less. The whole six New England States have passed such laws. Ohio has a kindred measure, but not so strong. New York has a pretty strong one; and Pennsylvania, too, has an enactment upon her statute-book looking to the same results. While these eleven or twelve States thus come forward and solemnly nullify that law, and the Constitution which they are sworn to support, and refuse compliance with its obligations, gentlemen get up here and prate about South Carolina and Georgia and Florida and Alabama and Mississippi and Louisiana very soon, and old Virginia before the 4th of March, not consenting longer to be subject to a Government to all the burdens of which they are bound to submit without deriving any of its benefits.

As I told you in the outset, it is not the election of Lincoln which is the cause of the dissolution of the Union. There is evidence, and conclusive evidence, to my mind, that the cause exists behind Lincoln's election. It is the sectional party of which my colleague spoke. Where is it, and what is it? It is easy for you now to repudiate the Garrisons and Giddingses and Phillipses,[34] and the old Abolition organization; but history proves that those old Abolitionists were the sappers and miners of the Black Republican party, and prepared the way for that tremendous organization which has at last marched into power, strewing its pathway with the broken columns and crumbling pillars of the Union. This sectional party has got into power. You have the control of this Government. Your organization is based upon the one idea of hostility to the South and to her institutions. But, being forewarned, we should be worse than fools not to be forearmed. We are armed; and if there shall be any mad attempt to coerce us, may God defend the right! But we want no war or bloodshed. You have got the control of the Government; you have won your victory; but I warn you now that upon the 4th of March next, instead of inaugurating the President of a mighty Republic, you will instal a miserable king of shreds and patches;

and when installed, instead of standing like a conquerer exultant upon the field of his victory, he will sit like Caius Marius,[35] brooding amid the ruins of Carthage. He will have exchanged the laurel for the cypress. Instead of shouting *Io triumpe*,[36] you will chant your jeremiads.

Mr. Speaker, time was when I looked forward to the continuance of this Union—this glorious Union as we call it—as the only means to preserve, to perpetuate, to conserve the liberties of the great and imperious people of these States. I did think that the very mountains which grasp in their giant embrace the sister States of this Confederacy would to-day, in the eloquent and expressive language of nature, have proclaimed, that what God himself had joined together should not be sundered by petty politicians. But, it has been done; the ruin has been brought about; the mischief has been consummated, and upon your heads, as well as ours, be the consequences. What is the remedy? Sir, the gentleman from Tennessee, [Mr. NELSON,][37] if I understood him correctly, almost ridiculed the idea of secession. Did it occur to that amiable, most excellent, and talented gentleman, that in denying the right of secession—

Mr. NELSON. Will the gentleman give way to me for a moment?

Mr. LEAKE. I will, sir, if I can have my time extended.

Mr. VAN WYCK.[38] I object to that.

Mr. NELSON. I gave way, I think, to the gentleman from Virginia, and it was not taken out of my time.

Mr. LEAKE. If it is anything personal, he shall have the rest of my time. I yield to the gentleman from Tennessee.

Mr. NELSON. I am obliged to the gentleman from Virginia for his kindness in yielding the floor to me, and I shall endeavor not to abuse his courtesy. What I have to say in regard to secession is this: it was condemned by Madison; it was condemned by Jackson; it has been repudiated by the fathers of the Republic. The doctrine of peaceable secession is inconsistent with the Constitution, for the Constitution is in the nature of a partnership between equal States; and no one State has a right to destroy its obligation without the consent of the others. Mr. Howell Cobb,[39] if I am not mistaken, also sustains the doctrine which I have advocated here today.

Mr. LEAKE. The gentleman refers to the venerated name of Madison, whose bones repose quietly within twenty-five miles of my own residence, but whose bones, I doubt not, would turn over in the very grave at the use now made of his authority. His language has been quoted again and again on the other side of the House. Sir, I will do no injustice to the memory of that pure patriot. A better man, a nobler statesman, this country has never produced.

Mr. POTTLE[40] obtained the floor.

Mr. LEAKE. My time is not up.

The SPEAKER *pro tempore.* The time of the gentleman from Virginia has expired.

Source: *Congressional Globe*, 36th Cong., 2nd Sess., 564–68.

Roger Atkinson Pryor
January 28, 1861

Roger A. Pryor (1828–1919) was born in Dinwiddie County, graduated from Hampden-Sydney College and the University of Virginia, and established his law practice in Petersburg in 1849. He turned to publishing, establishing the (Petersburg) *Southside Democrat* and briefly becoming the editor of the Washington *Union* during the Franklin Pierce administration before moving on to the Richmond *Enquirer* in 1853. In 1855, President Pierce appointed him special commissioner to Greece to settle a land dispute. Pryor later served one term in the US House of Representatives (1859–1861). During the 1850s, editor Pryor fought a number of duels leading the historian Douglas Southall Freeman to label him, "perhaps the most notorious duellist of his day."[41]

After Virginia's secession, Pryor served in the Confederate Congress before joining the Confederate Army rising to the rank of brigadier general in 1862. He moved to New York City following Appomattox and became a law partner with Benjamin B. Butler (known throughout the South as "Beast Butler" for his treatment of southern ladies while serving as military governor of New Orleans). Pryor was appointed as judge of the New York Court of Common Pleas in 1890 and as justice to the New York Supreme Court in 1894.

By the time of Pryor's address to Congress, six states had seceded, Lincoln's inaugural was five weeks in the future, and the pro-southern

James Buchanan still occupied the White House. Unlike Shelton Leake who believed Lincoln's election was not cause for disunion, Pryor thought otherwise: "Sir, in our judgment, a proclamation of war is an overt act; and such proclamation we find in the election, by an exclusively sectional vote, of a President pledged to put our rights and our property 'in course of ultimate extinction.'" In a speech prepared before the new administration had been formed, Pryor charged that the "dominant section of this Confederacy claims and exercises absolute power" and it was "in resistance to this despotic rule, that the people of the South have taken up arms." Pryor's biographer a century later termed the words Pryor chose for his remarks over Secession Winter, "the most intemperate of his career."[42]

STATE OF THE UNION.

The House resumed the consideration of the special order, being the report of the special committee of thirty-three, on which Mr. PRYOR was entitled to the floor.

Mr. PRYOR. Mr. Speaker, the resolutions before the House invite discussion of all the issues involved in the present unhappy controversy. The rapid march of events, outstripping the dilatory movements of procrastinating politicians leaves no question to consider but the alternative of peace or war. While your committee of compromise have been painfully elaborating plans of adjustment—all "mean reparations upon mighty ruins"[43]—the dispute has become incapable of accommodation; and the results their wisdom was to intercept are now accomplished and irrevocable facts. Of the thirty-three States which composed the Confederacy, at the beginning of this session, six are no longer members of the Union. Not many days will elapse before others will follow their example. Sir, it is an idle and unmeaning mockery to talk of preserving the Union; and they who indulge in this strain of declamation betray little of the candor demanded by the urgency of the occasion. In the presence of so tremendous a catastrophe as that which now oppresses us—the overthrow of Government, the partition of a great empire, and the imminent hazard of civil war—we owe it to ourselves and to the country to be done with the expedients of a timid and temporizing policy, and to address ourselves to the emergency without reserve and without equivocation.

The issue before the country, I repeat, sir, is the simple question of peace or war. Acting, as they conceive, from the impulse of abundant provocation, and exerting a power which they derive from the fundamental principles of this Government, the States of South Carolina, Mississippi, Florida, Alabama, Georgia, and Louisiana, have renounced the Confederacy and assumed the attitude of independent republics. The party into whose hands the control of the Administration is passing, so far from a recourse to conciliatory measures and a recognition of the rights of secession, obdurately reject all overtures of compromise, and avow a purpose to employ all the resources of Government for the subjugation of the retiring States.[44] And so it is that the calamities of civil war are about to be precipitated upon the country.

Mr. Speaker, in the suspense of this dreadful expectation, the people of the South are sustained by the conviction that, after the passions and prejudices of the moment have passed away, impartial history will acquit them of responsibility for the consequences of the impending conflict. Whenever, in after times, men shall revert to the events of this period, they will curse the madness of those by whom humanity was so deeply wounded; but not upon us will fall their maledictions. In what obligation of confederate duty, I demand, have we of the South been found delinquent? Do we not contribute more than an equal proportion of the support of your Government? Has not southern statesmanship successfully guided the councils of the Republican peace? Has not southern valor gloriously illustrated its arms on the field of battle? To what pledge of confederate faith have we been recreant? Nor is it only in a literal compliance with the obligations of the constitutional compact that the South has exhibited its patriotic fidelity. In our conception, something more was exacted by the association of fellow-citizenship; and we have denied the people of the North no facility in trade, and no advantage of policy which might promote their prosperity. With whose acquiescence, and to whose detriment, were measures of protection enacted for the aggrandizement of your manufacturing interest? Upon the productions of whose industry does your splendid commerce subsist? Until the demon of sectional discord was roused by your invasion of our rights, we willingly bore the burden of unequal tariffs and exclusive bounties, to assist the development of your resources; and your marvelous opulence we contemplated with the pride of fraternal sympathy. In this spirit of unselfish patriotism, Virginia contributed a princely domain to the ascendancy of the North, little dreaming that the States to be born of her bounty would repay her munificence with more than the ingratitude of Lear's unnatural offspring.[45]

Sir, in what manner have the loyalty and devotion of the South been requited by our confederates of the North? I propound the inquiry in no spirit of vindictive accusation. Indeed, sir, I would despise myself no less than the public would reproach me, if, at this august moment, I should contribute anything to the exasperation of passions already too much inflamed. I advert to the wrongs which the South has endured, with no other view than to vindicate the position she has assumed in this controversy. In what manner, I repeat, has the North repaid the fidelity with which the South has redeemed all the pledges of confederate faith and discharged all the duties of common citizenship?

At the epoch of the Revolution, and, indeed, when the Federal Government was organized, slavery prevailed in the North as well as in the South. If not the chief, it was at least conspicuous among the interests for the protection of which our present system of Government was established. The Constitution distinguishes it by express and repeated recognition, in each case fortifying it by particular guarantees.

Now, sir, against this great and vital interest — an interest of which the pecuniary value is indicated by countless millions,[46] and the importance of which, in the more essential aspect of social and political relation, no form of expression can adequately represent; an interest on which subsists the material prosperity of the southern States, and with which their security and independence are inseparably associated, — this interest, so vast and so vital, is the object of organized and incessant assault by those who are bound by every obligation of written covenant and confederate faith to protect it. They have launched against it the anathemas of moral and legal outlawry, and have canvassed Christendom for recruits in the crusade of Abolitionism. They have burdened it with iniquitous and oppressive impositions. They have denied it the development without which it cannot long endure. They have attacked it in detail by every variety of criminal expedient. And, finally, they have essayed, through the instrumentality of servile insurrection, to involve the South in total and irreparable ruin.

These wrongs, I know, appeal in vain to the men by whom they are inflicted; but I can imagine a case analogous in all essential particulars, in the contemplation of which they will not be likely to exhibit so much insensibility. The manufacturing interest, if not the main, is among the most important of the industrial pursuits of New England. Now, sir, suppose the other States of the Confederacy should combine for the spoliation of this interest, and to that end should hold it up to universal execration, should invoke upon it the vengeance of Heaven, and proclaim it beyond the protection of society; suppose they should employ the agency of the Government for its destruction, should organize conspiracies to ravage it, and, to impart the last touch of enormity to the outrage, should inflame the passions of your operatives in bloody and incendiary revolt; who believes the people of New England would patiently endure this accumulation of injuries? If they be capable of so abject a submission, they possess not the spirit of those ancestors of theirs, with whom the most trivial exaction of illegal power was an insufferable oppression. Yet these and greater grievances are endured by the people of the slaveholding States; but you only mock our complaints and tighten the grasp of oppression. Why marvel, then, that the day of resistance and retribution is come at last?

But, sir, we do not rest the vindication of the South on the slavery issue alone, or mainly. Our adversaries, availing themselves of the prevalent prejudice against slavery, have diligently represented that the secession of the South has no other object than the perpetuation of bondage; and the effect of the misstatement is visible already in the unfriendly criticism of the foreign press. It is time our cause were placed upon the true grounds of defense; upon principles which, instead of insulating it from the sympathies of the world, will command respect wherever justice rules and the maxims of republican liberty are revered. True it is that the grievances of which the South complain affect chiefly the interests of slavery; but it is a narrow and unphilosophical view of the controversy to represent the South as protesting only against these grievances. There, indeed, the weight of oppression is most heavily felt; but its source must be sought elsewhere. We commit an error in reasoning, and what is more, a blunder in policy, when we confound the practical effect with the radical principle of tyranny. If we mean to apply the resources of true statesmanship to the disorders of the country, we must discover and correct the organic derangements of the system; otherwise, all our pretentious prescription is but the quackery of the empire.

Sir, for fifty years the interests of the South reposed and prospered under the sacred safeguards of the Constitution. By that compact the equality of the States was guaranteed, their right of self-government recognized, and each member of the Confederacy mutually pledged to the others in a spirit of fraternal alliance. The States of the South acceded to the Union on these conditions: on the condition that they were to be the peers of their sovereign associates, that their rights were to be inviolable, and their property secure under the protection of the common Government. This sacred covenant was the bond of union between the confederate Republics. The Constitution imposed reciprocal obligations on the States, and pledged them to mutual offices of goodwill. In what manner are these pledges redeemed, and these obligations fulfilled, by the northern States?

Foremost in the catalogue of southern grievance is the complaint that the fundamental principle of the Confederacy, the equality of the States, is subverted by a combination between a majority of States to exclude other States from an equal participation in the common domain, and so to deny them equal advantages of expansion and development under the operation of the Federal Government. Nay, this Government itself is abused to the consummation of that iniquity.

To all candid men I appeal, if this single fact of the exclusion of the South from any share and enjoyment of the joint territory of the States, does not involve every circumstance that can rouse the indignation of freemen—a breach of constitutional compact; a stigma of inferiority; a principle of civil disability; and a measure of practical oppression. In private life, individuals resent no grievance sooner than an invasion of their rights of property. Among nations, an encroachment on their territorial possessions is an affront which war alone can redress. But the exclusion of the South from the common domain of the Confederacy, besides these circumstances of insult and aggression, implies a breach of the most solemn stipulation, and a reflection of the most offensive on the southern character. For you cannot deny the South equal rights in the Territories, without subverting the principles of the Constitution; and in justification of this wrong, the social system of the South is denounced as the "sum of all villainies." What other or greater grievance need the South urge in vindication of its conduct?

But this is not all. In respect of another essential of Federal Union—the guarantee of State sovereignty, the right reserved by each State to administer its own affairs and to develop its own destinies, in harmony with the general interests of the Confederacy,—whatsoever of this right may have survived the systematic encroachment of Federal usurpation, has vanished before the threat of military coercion. Already sovereign States are reduced, in contemplation, to the condition of provincial dependencies; and that doom they would speedily realize, but for the indomitable spirit which quails not before all the "pomp and circumstance" of your martial preparation.

Perhaps even these radical violations of the Constitution, in its spirit and essence, you may repel as the vague refinements of a temper alert to discover material of sectional crimination. Let us descend, then, for a moment, to a single instance in illustration of the perfidy by which the South is defrauded of its covenanted rights. An explicit provision of the constitutional compact exacts the restitution of fugitive slaves; yet that provision, albeit so essential that without it the South originally refused to join the Confederacy, is shamefully annulled by the northern States; and by the default millions of southern property have been confiscated.[47] So flagrantly has the South been cheated of its constitutional rights and denied the advantages of the Union, all the burdens of which, however, it bears in enormous disproportion!

What stronger argument than this, of violated faith and broken engagements, of the invasion of chartered rights and the usurpation of forbidden power, can be required in vindication, if you please, of revolutionary measures? All writers, except the partisans of divine right and passive obedience, are agreed that an infraction of the implied contract between sovereign and subject absolves the latter from his allegiance. It is this principle of constitutional liberty which distinguishes the great rebellion and the revolution of 1688 as the most glorious epochs in British history.[48] Say, then, is there less obligation in a solemnly ratified and written compact, than in a tacit and disputed engagement; and are sovereign States denied a redress which the genius of free government guarantees to individuals?

But, the defense of the South rests upon still stronger grounds; and her secession from the Confederacy is justified by even higher principles than the right to vindicate a violated covenant. Absolute power is the essence of tyranny, whether the power be wielded by a monarch or a multitude. The dominant section of this Confederacy claims and exercises absolute power—power without limitation and without responsibility: without limitation, since all the restrictions of the Constitution are broken down; and without responsibility, because, in the nature of things, the weaker interest cannot control the majority. Of all species of tyranny, the South is subjected to the most intolerable. Under the rule of a despot, we might hope something of his impartial indifference between the sections; but to be exposed to the unbridled sway of a majority adverse in interest, inimical in feeling, and ambitious of domination, is to be reduced to a condition more abject than that of the slaves whose emancipation is the pretext of all this controversy.

It is against this sectional domination, this rule of the majority without law and without limit—a rule asserted in subversion of the Constitution, and established on the ruins of the Confederacy—it is in resistance to this despotic and detestable rule, that the people of the South have taken up arms. This, sir, is the cause of the South; and tell me if cause more just ever consecrated revolution? It is the cause of self-government against the domination of foreign power—the very cause for which our fathers fought in 1776. Sooner than submit to the irresponsible rule of alien interests, they tore themselves from the embrace of the mother country, and staked all in the triumph of *secession*. Washington and Jefferson were the most illustrious of secessionists; and we of today are but walking in the light of their glorious example. They held it unworthy of freemen to bear the burden of arbitrary imposition; and they were not conciliated by the deceptive tender of partial representation in the British Parliament. The South has her Representatives in this Capitol; but their voice is of no avail against the northern majority. She is taxed not with her own consent, but by the votes of delegates whom she cannot control.

I repeat, it is against the rule of a sectional despotism that the South demands protection; and it is to assert the cause of civil liberty, that she declares her independence. You of the North lavished your sympathy on the people of Hungary in their revolt against Austrian absolutism;[49] but our cause is identical in principle and purpose. At this moment, while you bestow admiration and applause on the revolutionists of Italy,[50] I would remind you that the people of the South are moved by the same impatience of alien ascendency, and the same aspiration of self-government, which, after ages of slumber, have at last awakened the Italians to a recollection of their long-lost liberties.

The cause of the South solicits recognition and regard by yet another consideration, by a consideration which appeals to the interest of every section.

To-day, it is slavery which suffers from the overthrow of constitutional guarantees, and the irresponsible reign of the majority. But, the principle of absolute power once ascendant in the Government, no interest is secure; and circumstances will determine against what object it may be directed. If, in contravention of the compact of Union, slavery may be oppressed by Federal action, the navigation of New England, or the iron interests of Pennsylvania, will be exposed to the same ruin, whenever they shall incur the displeasure or invite the rapacity of other sections. The only safeguard of American liberty is in maintaining the integrity of the Constitution, and preserving intact the limitations of the Government. For that the South contends; and all are alike concerned in the success of her cause.

If, after the endurance of so many wrongs, and the menace of others still more intolerable, anything were wanting to justify the South in the public opinion of the world, it would be supplied by her solicitude to avoid violence, and redress her grievances within the Union. We are reproached, I know, with precipitancy in not awaiting an *overt act* of hostility from the sectional Administration. Sir, in our judgment, a proclamation of war is an overt act; and such proclamation we find in the election, by an exclusively sectional vote, of a President pledged to put our rights and our property "in course of ultimate extinction"—a President who admonishes us in advance of his aggressive designs by the sententious but significant declaration, that "they who deny freedom to others do not deserve it themselves, and, under a just God, cannot long retain it." We could not agree to await inactively the development of the disposition of the President elect; for we claim to hold our rights by some higher and more solid tenure than the capricious temper of any individual. Indeed, the argument of our opponents involves a concession of our case, inasmuch as it implies that the rights of the South are no longer secured by constitutional guarantees, but are suspended on the accident of an unfriendly Administration.

A more imperative consideration still determined the South to act at once, and to act decisively. If negotiation might avail, we thought to strengthen negotiation by a demonstration of our spirit. If the sword alone can reclaim our rights, we were resolved not to be unprepared for the issue.

Mr. Speaker, since the fatal 6th of November to the present hour, the Representatives of the South have invariably exhibited an accommodating disposition. The first day of our session was signalized by a proposition by a colleague of my own, [Mr. BOTELER.] which contemplated a pacific adjustment of our difficulties.[51] A similar movement, likewise originating with a southern man, was initiated in the Senate.[52] Meanwhile various schemes of settlement have been submitted in one or the other House of Congress, of which, without much regard to their intrinsic efficacy, we have uniformly avowed our support; while on the other side they have been as uniformly rejected with a contemptuous disdain of compromise. Thus, while the South are willing to remain in the Union with an assurance of their rights, the North declare, by a refusal of all concession, that they will destroy the Union rather than renounce their aggressive designs. In the perverted patriotism of the dominant party, the Constitution of Washington is substituted by the platform of Lincoln; and rather than be reproached with logical inconsistency, they choose to incur the guilt of civil war.

And not in the negative sense of rejected compromise only, do this party betray a purpose to push the dispute to the arbitrament of the sword. Instead of a proclamation of conservative policy that should give assurance of peace to a distracted country, their leader announces that his Administration is to be directed by the counsels of the champion of the "irrepressible conflict." Instead of the sense of justice and patriotic spirit which, we were told, still animate the masses of the northern people, northern Legislatures vote men and munitions of war to chastize the resistance roused by their own perfidious violations of a constitutional covenant. And here, while with the one hand Republican Representatives spurn all overtures of peace, with the other they grasp the sword. No measure of conciliation will they pass; their energies are engrossed in contriving schemes of coercion. Day after day developes the completeness of their system of force. Now it is a bill denying South Carolina the facilities of postal communication; anon a bill for the compulsory collection of the revenue at Charleston. In the South, frowning fortresses threaten the subjugation of sovereign States; in this District a hireling soldiery are concentrated to impose an obnoxious ruler on an unwilling people. Auspicious inauguration of a Republican President! Happy presage of a liberal Administration! If the conclusion be but consistent with this encouraging commencement, no doubt the next four years will reconcile the South to the rule of the dominant party.

In aggravation of circumstances, themselves sufficiently exasperating, the rumor, too monstrous for belief, that all these measures of coercion against the South are stimulated and directed by a son whom the South has de-lighted to honor, in proportion even to his own conceit of his own merit, imparts a tone of deeper indignation to the murmurs of an outraged people.

Thus, Mr. Speaker, by a series of aggressions, of which I have at-tempted nothing more than an imperfect sketch, the dominant party in the North have effected that which the world in arms could not have accomplished—the overthrow of this once glorious Confederacy. And not content with an achievement that will burden their memory through all coming ages, they now propose to consummate their work by afflicting the country with the calamities of civil war.

Mr. Speaker, we of the South maintain that among the fundamental and essential articles of the Republican faith is the doctrine that the States, having subscribed the constitutional compact on their own independent volition and in the exercise of an inherent sovereignty, have the right, per-fect and inviolable, to renounce the Union whenever, in their judgment, the Constitution is annulled and the Union abused to their oppression. Nay, in the very act of assent to the league of confederation, Virginia, and other States, by express stipulation, reserved to themselves, the right to resume their original sovereignty whenever, in their opinion, the conditions of al-liance might be violated. As we understand it, this is an association of co-equal sovereignties, held in fraternal embrace by the sweet influences of reciprocal confidence and regard; not a system of reluctant and oppressive connection, bound together by the fetters of Federal force. Nor have the people of the South contemplated the right of secession as a vain speculative proposition, but have cherished it as an actual and inestimable muniment of republican liberty. It is precisely in this particular that the citizens of the United States have the advantage of the people of all other countries; in that, when the checks and balances of the central Government are overthrown, there remains the rampart of State sovereignty, behind which they may rally and maintain their rights; and in the still more important particular, that, through the instrumentality of secession, they may recover their liberties by the organic operation of the system, without recourse to the dreadful extremity of revolution.

These principles, it appears by too many distressing indications, are not prevalent in the councils of the dominant party. Their cry is for coercion. They present the South no other alternative than submission or subjugation.

Sir, it is no easy effort to debate an issue of this sort; and the impulse of a gallant people is to answer menace by defiance. But we owe it to the solemnity of the occasion to repress every ebullition of resentment, and to discuss even an offensive topic in a spirit of moderation.

What, then, I would entreat of gentlemen on the other side, do they propose by kindling the flame of civil war? No matter what may be the issue, liberty cannot survive the conflict. The frail fabric of a system constructed for the abode of peace, would perish under the shocks and concussions of intestine strife. An armed encounter between the States would be fatal to a Constitution designed to hold them in amicable association; and your Union would go down with the principle of mutual affection on which it reposes. He must be inattentive to the plainest lessons of history who does not foresee that from a bloody struggle among the States—*bellum plus-quam civile*[53]—either anarchy would emerge to brood over the land with desolating presence, or else military violence would assert its iron sway. What though the fortune of war be propitious to your arms? You must be content with nothing less than the annihilation of the South; for while she breathes, the impulse of honor will throb in her bosom, and urge her to still further resistance. Recollect the story of Ireland's wrongs and Ireland's emancipation. The remorseless conqueror doomed her to desolation; but fate reserved her as a dependent province of the British Empire. How, as a thorn in England's side, she avenged herself on the tyrant, and at last extorted from his fears the recognition of her rights, your intelligence needs not to be instructed. And so would your difficulty be our opportunity.

Imagine, then, for a moment, the complete subjugation of the South; after every spark of vitality is extinguished, and her inanimate form lies prostrate before you, tell me, what recompense do you gain for all your sacrifices, or what consolation in the tormenting memory of your fratricidal deed?

But I dismiss the humiliating thought. No matter what her inferiority of force, you cannot subjugate the South. Smitten she may be, but not subdued; defeated, but never dismayed. Already, by her determined and defiant attitude, she gives you earnest of the spirit that will animate her sons in the hour of trial. From many memorable examples of heroic resistance to wrong, they derive the consolatory assurance that a brave people battling for the right are invincible against any odds. Nine million of freemen—and heed not, I admonish you, the treacherous suggestion that the South will not oppose a united front to the foe—nine million of freemen, of a race the most energetic and indomitable recorded in history, glorying in traditions of ancestral prowess, and attached to the cause of liberty with a chivalric devotion—this people, themselves distinguished for valor and the genius of war, contending on their own soil for whatever imparts a felicity to life— this people will laugh to scorn all the imposing array of your military preparation.

Not for themselves, then, do they deprecate a conflict of arms; but from respect to the memory of our common ancestry; for the sake of a land to be torn by the cruel lacerations of the sword; and in reverence of virtues a benign religion instructs them to adore. By the persuasion of these pious and pathetic importunities we would soothe in every breast the spirit of strife, and invoke the pacific intervention of reason for the adjournment of our dispute.

And what, I pray you, is the dictate of reason? Not, surely, that a free people should be held in subjection to a Government they detest; not that the sword be employed to coerce sovereign States, and constrain them to wear the yoke of an odious and oppressive association; but rather that distinct communities be permitted to follow the bent of their peculiar nationality; and to realize the destiny indicated by their own interests and their own aspirations. You of the North hold in your grasp the elements of a great empire—a teeming population, immense resources, and a daring energy of genius which surmounts all obstacles, and dazzles the world with its exploits. For our part, in slight esteem as you affect to hold the South, we are content with our portion. Whensoever occasion shall require—and occasion does now demand it—we are prepared to assert our equality among the sovereigns of the earth, and to make good the claim against all comers.

Instead, then, of vainly essaying to counteract the designs of nature, let us heed the voice of reason; instead of lamenting the rupture of an artificial tie, as involving the ruin of all our hopes, let us lean on the wisdom of Providence, persuaded that as He has already distinguished the epoch of revolution as the most glorious in the annals of America, He intends still further to advance the cause of freedom and civilization by means of another dissevered nationality.

Source: *Congressional Globe*, 36th Cong., 2nd Sess., 601–3.

5

---•◆•---

Virginia State Convention
February–April 1861

Virginia's convention met longer than any other state convention producing both the longest record (over 3,000 published pages) and the largest number of solutions (sixteen) to the sectional crisis in the form of proposed constitutional amendments. Gathering in Richmond's Mechanics' Institute (at the intersection of Ninth and Bank Streets), the 152 elected delegates began their deliberations on February 13 after six southern states had declared their independence. Unlike her Deep South sisters, Virginia hoped for, and worked toward, a constitutional compromise that would knit the country back together. The delegates debated the exact wording of their proposed constitutional amendment up until the moment they received notice on April 12 that the Confederacy was bombarding Fort Sumter.

John Goode Jr.
February 26, 1861

John Goode Jr. (1829–1909) was born in Bedford County, graduated from Emory and Henry College in 1848, and established his law practice in Liberty, Virginia, two years later. He served as a member of the House of Delegates in 1852, voted in favor of secession, and fought for the Confederacy as a colonel before being elected twice to the Confederate Congress.

Delegate Goode advocated immediate secession on the grounds that a Black Republican had been elected to the White House "upon a Black Republican platform." In his mind, there was no question but that "the coercion of the seceded States is to be attempted by the Lincoln administration." The best way to preserve the "institution of African slavery," was to make "a Union with our Southern Sister States." By the time Goode addressed the convention, Texas had also seceded bringing the number of original states of the Confederacy to seven.

FEDERAL RELATIONS

Mr. GOODE of Bedford—Mr. President: as the reading of the resolutions has been called for, I deem it proper to state that it was not my purpose, yesterday, to speak to the resolutions but in reply to the speech of the gentleman from Rockbridge [Mr. MOORE].[1]

I regret, Mr President, that my physical condition, this morning, is such that I am wholly unable to do justice to the cause which I am endeavoring to represent upon this floor. I regret, also, that circumstances, beyond my control, prevented me, yesterday, from concluding the few remarks which I intended to submit in answer to the address of the gentleman from Rockbridge. I have no allusion to make to the occurrences of yesterday, farther than to give expression to the hope that our fellow citizens who occupy the galleries, will, in future, abstain from such demonstrations of applause. Sirs, it is a solemn work in which we are now engaged. The action of this Convention may determine, and doubtless, will determine, the destinies of Virginia in all time to come. And while it is natural, that the eagle eye, of a people jealous of their rights, and trembling for their honor, should be riveted anxiously upon us. I beg them to remember, in the language of Mirabeau to the French Assembly, that "the silence of the people is a lesson to kings."[2]

I was proceeding on yesterday, Mr. President, when interrupted, to inquire what Virginia ought to do in this the most trying and perilous hour of her history. That, sir, is the all absorbing question of the hour. It comes home to the minds and hearts of the people, and it must be answered by this convention. We must answer it before God and our country. We must answer it plainly, flatly, pointedly, and unequivocally; if we fail to answer it, we fail to meet the just expectations of our constituents.

Sir, gentlemen may sing paeans to the Union; they may discourse eloquently upon the hallowed glories, the historic memories of the Union; but the Union is already dissolved. The Union of 1789 which our fathers formed; which we have heretofore cherished with such fond devotion, and that which, in the language of the Father of his country, we have been accustomed in days that are gone, to look upon as the palladium of our liberties, safety and prosperity—that Union is already numbered with the things that were.

"Why stand we here, then, all the day, idle?"[3] Whither will we go? What will Virginia do? Will she be true to herself and her historical renown? Will she nobly vindicate her ancient fame? or is her proud blood altogether extinct, and are we prepared to lower her proud banner, and permit her to humble her pride and pass under the yoke of Northern abolition? Whither, then, will we go, sir? Will we go north, or will we go south? Will we go to the house of our enemy, or will we go to the house of our friends? Will Virginia cast her lot with her southern sister States of the South? Or will she still hope on, hope ever, hope against hope, trusting in the meantime, to the tender mercies of Mr. Abraham Lincoln?

Sir, I know not what others may think; I know not what others may do; but for myself, I feel a sense of the solemn responsibilities which now rest upon me, and appealing to the Searcher of hearts, as to the rectitude of my purpose, I have no hesitation in declaring, that in my humble opinion, Virginia ought now, promptly and without delay, to take her position at the head of the Southern column.

Sir, I believe in my inmost soul that immediate separation from the Northern Confederacy is a peace measure. If we are to believe the organs of Black Republican sentiment in the North, the coercion of the seceded States is to be attempted by the Lincoln administration. The tone of the northern press, the declarations of their representative men, the votes and speeches of their Senators and Representatives in Congress, the action of their State Legislatures, the collection of the Federal troops at the Federal Metropolis, the repeated declarations of Mr. Abraham Lincoln himself, the organization and constant drilling of Northern Wide-Awakes,[4] are sufficient in my judgment to convince the most skeptical upon this subject. He may not attempt, sir, to march his Federal myrmidons[5] into a seceded State, but he will attempt to collect the Federal revenue, and retake the captured forts. Will our Southern brethren submit to this? Submit! Why, sir, it is a slander upon their fair fame and good name to entertain the idea for one solitary moment. You may talk about your alien and sedition laws; your stamp acts; your tax upon tea, and the most abominable tyranny that ever cursed any people upon earth; but I maintain that the most abhorrent tyranny upon earth would be to attempt to wring tribute from the pockets of an unwilling people.

Sir, the union of these States can never be restored by the power of the sword. It has rested upon entirely different grounds in the past; it has rested upon public opinion, and been preserved in the hearts and affections of the people. I say, then, that threats of coercion can have no fears for freemen. The blood of the martyrs, in every age, has been the seed of the Church; and if coercion is attempted, the blood of slaughtered patriots would be like the dragons' teeth sown upon the earth, from which would come forth heroes, full grown and armed, ready to spring into life and rush to battle.

Then, sir, they will attempt, doubtless, the coercion, the coercion of the seceded States; but they will never attempt to coerce a united South. The strong, sometimes, are tempted to make war upon the weak; but the strong sit down and reflect long and well before they make war upon the strong. And, sir, when old Virginia places herself at the head of this Southern column, the other border States will wheel quickly in line, and then, and not till then, in my humble judgment, will the offensive and insulting threats of Northern coercion be abandoned. Then, sir, and not until then, will "grim-visaged war smooth his wrinkled front"[6] and all again be peace—then may the Union of our fathers be reconstructed upon fair, just and honorable principles, and our country move forward once again upon a brilliant career of prosperity and glory.

Sir, what a noble chapter would be hereafter entwined about the venerable brow of our blessed old mother, if, under the Providence of God, it should be her mission to restore peace to these dissevered, discordant, and almost belligerent States; if, in the Providence of God, it should be her destiny to appear at the mouth of the sepulchre itself of this dead Union, and say: "Lazarus, come forth"—I say, it would be a noble chapter. Not only the people of this now distracted land would with one acclaim bless her; and nations of the earth would cry all hail to her; and, what is more, we have the word of eternal truth itself, which cannot fail, that "blessed are the peace makers, for they shall be the elect of Heaven."[7] If there are among those who hear me today, who earnestly and ardently desire a re-construction of this Union upon terms of fair, just and honorable principles, I sympathize with them cordially. But I beg them to remember, that Virginia can never exert her just and proper influence with the now seceded States until she manifests her determination to cut loose from the Northern aggressor and take sides with the oppressed—until she manifests her determination to share with her gallant Southern sisters the dangers and the perils and the trying ordeal through which they are now passing.

Why, sir, when they sent their Ambassadors[8] here to defer to Virginia, to ask her to take the lead and say what was best to be done for the common good, and when old Virginia coolly spurned the offer of sympathy and turned away from her children, it was but natural that these Southern States should feel some temporary distrust towards the Old Mother. Was it not natural? They did feel it. They felt it properly. But when Virginia shall move into line and proclaim to the world that, come weal or come woe, her destinies are indissolubly linked with her sister States of the South; when she shall take this position, and this unnatural strife shall be terminated hereafter; when Virginia invites these Southern sisters to come back into the government which she has helped to reconstruct—they will come, sir, I hope, not as my friend from Rockbridge [Mr. MOORE] supposed on yesterday; they will come not like the prodigal son of old, repenting, in sack cloth and ashes, for what they have done—but they will come in the proud consciousness of virtue and right; they will come back to the Old Mother, and in the beautiful and touching language of Ruth to Naomi: "Entreat me not to leave thee or to return from following thee, for whither thou goest I will go, and where thou lodgest I will lodge; thy people shall be my people, and thy God my God. Where thou diest will I die, and there will I be buried."[9]

But if in this, sir, I shall be mistaken; if Virginia cannot reconstruct the Union, Virginia can secure a peaceable separation. Sir, if we cannot live together with our Northern Confederates, we have a right to be permitted to separate; we have a right surely to depart in peace. This would be a poor boon, and Virginia, by a prompt and decided action, in my humble judgment, would either restore the Union, or secure a peaceable and final separation; she would have a right to say, sir, as was said by one of old, "let there be no contention I pray thee, between thou and me—thou wilt go to the right, and then I will go to the left."[10]

But, sir, I say it is no longer a question of Union or disunion. The question is, will we go North, or will we go South? Every consideration of interest, of honor, of patriotism—every impulse of the heart prompts the Virginia people to cast their destiny with their sister States of the South. Sir, more than 300,000 of those Southern people have gone from Virginia. They claim Virginia as their mother; they are our brethren, our kindred; bone of our bone, and flesh of our flesh. Can Virginia desert them now? Can Virginia desert them in their hour of greatest need? As well, sir, might I ask if a mother could forget and desert her offspring.

But, Mr. President, I had intended to refer particularly to some of the points made by the gentleman from Rockbridge [Mr. MOORE]. I regret that he is not in his seat this morning.

I will, with the permission of the Convention, notice some few of the objections urged by that gentleman against a connection of Virginia with the Southern Confederacy.

He seems still determined to believe, in spite of all the evidence which can be adduced, that it is the purpose of the Southern Confederacy to re-open the African slave trade. Why, sir, not only has every State Convention of the seceded States put the heel of condemnation upon it, but the Congress at Montgomery itself has embodied in its Constitution a provision prohibiting the re-opening of the African slave trade.

But what says the gentleman? He says he is not willing to go into a Southern Confederation—in fact, into any Confederacy whose Constitution does not prohibit the re-opening of the African slave trade; and yet he prefers to adhere to this Northern Confederacy in whose Constitution no such prohibition is to be found.

We are to be oppressed, he tells us, with direct taxation. Why, sir, in answer to that it is sufficient to say that the provisional government had already adopted the tariff of the old government, and that the revenue of the government is now collected by duties upon imports, and we have the assurance of their commissioners and of their leading men throughout the South that it is not their purpose to resort to direct taxation, but to levy such duties as shall produce a sufficient revenue to carry on the government.

But the Southern States have not assigned the true cause of their withdrawal from the Union. That is the great objection urged by the gentleman [Mr. MOORE] to these Southern States. He maintains that the cause
which they have given is not the true one. Why, sir, some of them gave
notice twelve months ago, that the election of a Black Republican to the
Presidency, upon a Black Republican platform, would be with them a treaty
breach, and they would no longer remain in the Northern Confederacy. It is
upon this ground that they have taken their stand, although for years they
have submitted to acts of intolerable oppression in the way of high tariffs,
in order to attest their devotion to the Union. But, now, when a President
is elected by a party who denounce the Union of our fathers and the Constitution of the country as a league with death and a covenant with hell,[11]
those Southern people can submit no longer, but have determined to cut the
Gordian knot, and risk the issue with the god of battles.

We were told by the gentleman [Mr. MOORE] that he is unwilling to
form any connection with the seceded States, because there is a direct conflict of interest between Virginia and her sister States of the South. The
gentleman did not proceed to point out that conflict. In what does it consist?
Are we not a people of homogeneous interests? Are we not a people of like
habits, of like institutions and like religion? Are we not all deeply and vitally
concerned in the preservation of the institution of African slavery? We are,
sir, and the only Union which can yield any material benefit to us is a Union
with our Southern Sister States.

But the burdens of taxation, under the new government would be intolerable. Sir, it is humbling to me, in times like these, to be compelled to
meet the argument of taxation. Carried out to its legitimate extent, would
it benefit us to submit to any and all aggression, and to purchase exemption
from taxation at the price of honor itself? I maintain not, sir. But can the tax
be so enormous in the Southern Government? I have no doubt it would be
the most economical and virtuous government ever administered upon this
continent. I believe it would be an honest government, and that is to me a
controlling reason for the preference that I give to it over our old Northern
confederates.

But, sir, we may be taxed; and if so, are there not advantages to be reaped
from it? We would derive some benefits from this taxation. As it is now, we
are taxed for the benefit of the North; we are taxed and taxed, and they enjoy

the benefits, because the money is distributed and expended in the Northern States. We furnish two-thirds of the revenue and they get four-fifths of the expenditures; and if the South is to be taxed by any future government, we would have this assurance, that we would derive some benefits from that tax.

But, sir, if the gentleman from Rockbridge [Mr. MOORE] will not go with the South, where will he go? Will he go with the North? Look upon that side of the picture. We have been unable heretofore to secure our rights, with seven seceded States to maintain us. What hope for the future can the gentleman indulge, with nineteen Northern States against seven? If we have been taxed for the benefit with these seven States united with us — if with this advantage we were unable to uphold and maintain our equal rights and common property in the past; what, I ask, must be our fate, when left to the mercy of nineteen Black Republican non-slaveholding States in this controversy? Why, what have they already done? They have deliberately nullified and trampled underfoot the Constitution of the country. They have continued to agitate the subject of slavery in Congress and out of Congress, with a view of exciting servile insurrection and rebellion in our homes. They have elected sixty-eight of their chosen leaders to the Federal councils who have deliberately endorsed the infamous Helper book, which advised our slaves to rise at midnight and cut the throats of their masters and murder our wives and innocent little ones.[12] They have deliberately placed under the ban four hundred million of dollars worth of Southern property. They have said that there shall be no more slave States admitted into the Union, and that there shall be no peace so long as we claim the right of property in slaves.

{Delegate Goode continued here to recommend secession over remaining in the Union.}

Source: George H. Reese, ed., *Proceedings of the Virginia State Convention of 1861: February 13–May 1.* 4 vols. (Richmond: Virginia State Library, 1965), 1:193–99.

Walter Daniel Leake
March 5, 1861

Walter D. Leake (1813–1873) was born in Goochland County, graduated from Hampden-Sydney College (1832), the University of Virginia (1833), and from the College of William and Mary in 1836 with a degree in law. He was elected to the Virginia House of Delegates in 1842 and again in 1854. He voted for secession and promptly raised a company of artillery for the Confederate Army.

The day after Lincoln's inauguration, Leake argued for immediate secession because the president's inaugural speech included "sentiments which breathe war and revolution." "Black Republicans" require the collection of tariffs and the holding of forts, he asserted, but Virginia should resist those efforts out of fidelity to equal rights, and "maintain her honor" by driving back "any invasion that may be made upon her." In arguing his point that the South would not be intimidated by a northern majority, Leake asserted that with thirty-four states, a three-fourths ratification vote (required by the Constitution) for any constitutional amendment favored by the North would be impossible. If the fifteen slave states voted as a bloc, any ratification of such a "compromise" amendment would fall short of the twenty-six states needed for approval. (Some southern moderates used the same logic to argue that Republicans could not abolish slavery via a constitutional amendment if the fifteen slave states voted against it.)

Mr. LEAKE—Then I propose to offer some remarks on the subject of these resolutions.[13]

Mr. President, two sentiments have been in conflict in the bosoms of the people in reference to the condition of our national affairs. Sir, there is among them an inherent love of the Union—a Union formed by the blood of patriots and by the efforts of her best citizens; and there too, beyond that and before that, is the love of equality, is the love for all the rights of all the States. And, sir, the facts which have been developed for the last few years have satisfied the South—have satisfied Virginia that to maintain a love of equality, to maintain the rights of all the States of this Union, would bring up this conflict to that sentiment, to that attachment which has been revered by all.

But, sir, the course of Northern fanaticism, the strides which a sectional party has made towards the usurpation of the power of the Federal Government, has brought about a state of things when the people of Virginia should no longer hesitate as to what part they shall take in the conflict that is now going on between the rights of the South and a sectional majority which is claiming the power of the Federal Government for the purpose of advancing their selfish interests, and not for the purpose of saving the Constitution or advancing the rights and interests of all.

Mr. President, the devotion to the Union which exists among us has made the people of Virginia anxious that all the means of conciliation and of compromise should be used for the purpose of preserving that Union, if it could be preserved consistently with our rights, consistently with our honor, consistently with our safety. And, sir, if the people of Virginia have been anxious that our rights shall be so recognized by this Northern majority, that it would not become necessary for them to resort to any changes or measures to secure their rights and prevent them from being usurped by a Northern majority, have not passing events satisfied them that it is utterly impossible to secure our rights in a Constitutional way?

The Constitution, it is true, as was stated by the gentleman from Bedford [Mr. GOGGIN][14] provides the means for its own amendment. But it is now utterly impossible that that Constitution can be amended in the way pointed out by any resolutions which have been offered.

Sir, this Northern sectional majority headed by Lincoln, Seward and Chase,[15] are unwilling to acknowledge the right of secession. They plant themselves upon the platform that no State in any case whatsoever, has a right to secede from this Union; and so far from acknowledging the right of secession, so far from acknowledging the propriety of the conduct of any of these Southern States, the President of the United States has just proclaimed that he will exercise all the power vested in him by the laws of Congress in holding, in occupying, in possessing the public property within the seceded States, and in the collection of the revenue upon imports to the ports of these States.

Sir, to be allowed to collect the revenue in the seceded States, and to hold the forts in those States, is all that the Black Republicans ever desire the President of the United States to demand. If the President of the United States shall do this; if the seceded States will pay tribute to Black Republicans; if the Southern States are so lost to all the principles of true independence as to be unconscious of their just rights, and their equality as a nation, they have indeed played their part in this great political arena to little advantage. If they have not been in earnest in the assertion of their rights, then, sir, they will allow the President of the United States to use the means under his control for the purpose of taking possession of the forts, and of collecting the revenue. But, sir, if they are true to themselves, if they are true to the principles which they have advocated, if they are true to their professions of loyalty to equal rights, they will resist, to the last extremity, any effort on the part of the Federal authorities to hold these forts, or to collect the revenue in their ports, either in the harbor or at sea.

Sir, there was a time in Virginia when this doctrine of secession was considered a doctrine to which Virginia clung. It seems now, sir, that the time has come when this doctrine is to be denounced—it is to be regarded as something worthless, or at least something that is calculated to bring ruin and disaster upon us. I shall not enter into a discussion of the right of secession. The day for the discussion of that question has passed. Whether it be a constitutional or revolutionary right, six or seven States of the South have already exercised that right, and Virginia will exercise it if she thinks it necessary for her safety and for the protection and maintenance of her rights. She will exercise that right regardless of consequences—she will stand upon the platform of inalienable rights—to maintain her honor and drive back any invasion that may be made upon her.

Hence, sir, if the Northern States, who are in a large majority, will not acknowledge the right of secession, will not recognize the independence of those States that have withdrawn from the Union—how can you maintain the Constitution of the United States? If there was a decision upon that point; if the Northern majority was to surrender to us these things to which we are entitled—for we demand nothing to which we are not entitled—if they are unwilling to recognize the independence of these States, it is utterly impossible that a constitutional number can be obtained to ratify any amendment that may be proposed to the present Constitution. It is necessary that twenty-five States should vote for the amendment before it could become part of the Constitution. Does anybody dream that any Southern State will vote for any amendment that will meet with the approval of this Northern majority? That, sir, is out of the question. I have no idea that any Southern State would record such a vote.

Sir, do not the occurrences which have taken place in Washington within the last two days satisfy us that this Northern majority is unwilling to surrender to the South its just demands; is unwilling to acknowledge any amendment to the Constitution that would satisfy even the most submissive in Virginia? Sir, so far as I can learn anything of the sentiments of the people of this State, they are not willing to accept anything less than the Crittenden resolutions. And these have been spurned by the Black Republican majority in the Senate of the United States.

Sir, we are deceiving ourselves; we are deceiving the people of Virginia that are looking to us for prompt action, when we place ourselves upon the platform that the Constitution can be amended in a constitutional way. How is it to be done, sir? It is true, the Peace Congress, initiated by Virginia, after a long struggle, has adopted a proposition which has been offered to the Congress of the United States and to the world; but the Congress of the United States has not deigned to treat even that with any kind of respect. Neither the President of the United States, the Senate, nor the House of Representatives have considered that the action of the Peace Convention was worthy of their respect or consideration. It seems to me, sir, that the proposition of the Peace Congress, far from insuring the rights and interests of Virginia, rather involves a surrender of those rights which she now undoubtedly has, so that, so far as that Congress is concerned, it has ended in nothing.

What then will you have Virginia do? Will you have her running about these Northern States with this peace proposition in her hand, begging the North to allow her to remain with them in the Union upon the terms of this peace proposition? Would you have Virginia so far forget the high position which she occupies? Would you have Virginia so far forget the renown connected with her name? Would you have Virginia so far forget the duties which she owes to her citizens? Would you have Virginia so far forget her constitutional rights, for which she has always contended, as to go to the North on bended knees and beg Seward and Chase to condescend so far as to recommend the people of the North to adopt this peace proposition? I do not believe that there is a man in Virginia who would have the old mother occupy a position of that sort. She has stood up nobly in behalf of peace, demanding nothing but equality, and yet, sir, her demands have been denied her; and every effort which she has made for conciliation and compromise; every effort which she has made to preserve the Union has, sir, been treated with contempt by that Northern majority which controls the reins of this Government, that majority is determined to use this Government for the advancement of their own interest and prosperity.

Sir, just after this effort thus made upon the part of Virginia to secure her rights; just after this effort upon the part of Virginia to secure the rights of her sister States of the South; just after this effort upon her part to secure the rights and equality of all the States; just as Virginia was making every effort in her power to compose the difficulties which surrounded us, even before the members of the Peace Conference could fairly have returned home—notwithstanding that the Virginia Convention stood here delaying action in the hope that something might emanate from the North which would give promise of peace, and showing every sort of determination to demand nothing that was not right, to insist upon nothing that was wrong, the President of the United States, in the inaugural address which he delivered on yesterday in Washington, utters sentiments which breathe war and revolution, and treats with contempt the declarations made by the Legislature of Virginia almost unanimously—that any attempt by the Federal Government to coerce the seceded States would be met with resistance. At the very time that Virginia is occupying this position that was calculated to disarm her adversaries—a position that might cause her to be kindly and respectfully treated—this President of the United States pledges himself that the odious platform upon which he was nominated—the Chicago platform—should be his law.

He uttered sentiments which are not only calculated to excite and arouse Virginia to resistance, but which will excite every lover of freedom to resistance everywhere.

Sir, in this emergency what is the duty of Virginia? Shall she be content with mere resolutions? Is that what is demanded of Virginia at this crisis? Why, sir, for the last twenty years she has been passing resolutions of resistance to the death, and, one by one, her resolutions of resistance have been disregarded; one by one these resolutions have been treated with contempt by this Northern majority; and Virginia has not yet placed herself in that attitude of resistance which her own resolves demanded that she should have assumed long ago. Why was this Convention called? What was it called for? Was it merely for the purpose of passing resolutions? Was it not because the sentiment was deep-seated in the bosoms of the people that they should take some action? And do you now propose merely to pass resolutions that any effort at coercion will be met with resistance?

There is no time now to take that stand. Lincoln has proclaimed that he will coerce the seceded States. Sir, the question does not arise whether the collection of the revenue and the re-occupation of the forts is coercion or not. I believe the common sense of the people of Virginia understand that the collection of the revenue by the Federal authorities from an unwilling people, and the occupation of the forts against the remonstrance of the people, is coercion. It is so understood by the people, and whether it is or not, it is an act they will all resist, you may call it by what name you please.

Then, sir, it is necessary that Virginia should place herself in a position to show that she means to carry out the resolves which she has heretofore made. The President of the United States says that he means to collect the revenue and occupy the forts. Are you going to wait until he does collect the revenue and occupy the forts before you carry your resolutions into practice? Sir, is not his declaration enough? Is it to be supposed that Abraham Lincoln has used this language in his Inaugural merely for the purpose of deceiving the people of the country, and that he does not mean to carry out his threats of coercion? If such had not been his policy, he would have used language of conciliation; and the fact that the President of the United States has used language of this character, in such a document as his Inaugural, is conclusive evidence of his intention to carry out the policy which it proclaims.

{Delegate Leake continued here at length urging immediate secession in light of his perception of the impending "coercion" of the South on the part of the Lincoln administration.}

I do not desire to detain you any longer. The only thing I desire is that the Convention of Virginia will act at this particular time when our adversaries are using all the powers of a common Government to effect our ruin and degradation;[16] when they are promulgating sentiments in conflict with the sentiments of Virginia; and when they are proclaiming principles that are utterly inconsistent with our peace. Now that principles have been proclaimed which must inevitably initiate civil war, it is time for Virginia, not only to declare what she will do but to take such steps as will show that she means to place herself in the front of resistance to all the encroachments which may be made upon us. Let Virginia do that. Let Virginia show that sort of determination. Let there be no doubts as to the position which she intends to occupy. Let the world understand that she places herself upon the right. Let her announce her disposition to encroach upon nobody, and that she will never allow any encroachments to be made upon her or upon her sister States, and we may do something to drive back that tide of fanaticism which is now rolling on towards the South, and which, if not resisted, will inevitably end in the overthrow, not only of our institutions, but in blasting the best hopes of humanity. It does seem strange to me that such sentiments as are promulgated by the President of the United States in the last 24 hours have not called into existence all the resistance in our nature; I believe that the people of Virginia and of all parties will not submit to such an encroachment upon our reserved rights as that which has been threatened by those now in authority in Washington. They will lend all their power for the purpose of driving back the invaders and maintaining the blessings which have been secured to us by the Constitution which these very men have threatened to destroy, and which they are now trampling under foot by the course they are pursuing.

Source: George H. Reese, ed. *Proceedings of the Virginia State Convention of 1861: February 13–May 1.* 4 vols. (Richmond: Virginia State Library, 1965), 1:390–401.

Thomas Stanhope Flournoy
March 6, 1861

Thomas S. Flournoy (1811–1883) was educated at Hampden-Sydney College, studied for and was admitted to the bar, and set up his law practice in Halifax in 1834. He was elected as a Whig to the Thirtieth

Congress (1847–1849), but was unable to hold his seat in the Thirty-First Congress. After voting in favor of secession, Flournoy raised a company of cavalry and served the Confederate Army as a captain and later colonel.

A self-proclaimed Unionist, Delegate Flournoy believed slavery was best preserved in the Union and that compromise was the best solution to the secession crisis. In this speech, he addressed the issue of northern coercion. Because Congress had adjourned not to reconvene until December, Flournoy reasoned that a message to President Lincoln would preserve the peace. That message, thought Flourney, would be that "Virginia will never, never, never submit to see her Southern sisters coerced." "If you do not take the position that the Southern States shall not be coerced, war will come." Ironically, Flournoy expressed his concern for northern aggression on the same day that the Confederate Congress authorized the raising of 100,000 troops, and Virginia's militia totaled 18,400. The US Army on that day totaled fewer than 17,000 soldiers who were scattered across the country in forts as far from Washington as New Mexico and California.[17]

Mr. FLOURNOY, of Halifax—It is with very great reluctance, Mr. President, that I trespass this morning upon the time and the attention of this Convention. I shall be as brief as I well can be, and shall address myself to one single question, to which I desire to call the attention of this Convention, and upon which I most earnestly desire to see immediate, firm and decisive action upon the part of this body. I mean that question, which I understand has occupied the time and attention of our Committee upon Federal Relations for the last three weeks—the question of coercion. The situation of Virginia is a responsible and painful one. But, I think, I know Virginia well enough, from her sea-board to the beautiful Ohio, to know that she is equal to any responsibility that circumstances may impose upon her. I regret, Mr. President, in the course of the running debate to which we have listened in this Convention to have heard at any time the word party announced, or any allusion to the different portions of our State—East or West. Sir, I trust—and until some evidence conclusive to the contrary shall be shown by the action of gentlemen in the future, I shall believe that none but the true hearts of Virginia beat at the bosoms of our people upon every foot of our soil.

I say, Mr. President, that I desire to address myself to this single question of coercion, and I desire to see this Convention take a strong decisive, firm, unequivocal and unmistakable position upon that subject. And in urging it, I urge it upon the consideration of this body as a measure of peace. I urge it, as, in my humble judgment, the only chance and hope that is left to preserve this Government of ours, and restore it in all its parts and in all its perfection. I do not think, Mr. President, that in the course of my life I ever read with deeper interest or more painful emotion any paper that has ever come under my observation than the Inaugural Address of Abraham Lincoln, the President of the United States; and the outrage of that document is greater upon Virginia and upon us assembled here, who represent her sovereignty, than it is upon any portion of this vast Republic. The States of the South, seven of them, had seceded from this Union. They had placed themselves in hostility and in antagonism to the General Government. But was that the condition of Virginia? How did Virginia stand when this Inaugural Address of Abraham Lincoln was sent out to the country with its menaces and its threats of coercion. When this Convention, which is now assembled, was called to meet together, what was the responsibility of the people of Virginia, even though a portion of our sister States of the South had already left the Union? She responded to the call for a Convention, and she sent here upon this floor, to represent her and to protect, guard and preserve her honor and her interest, and to restore this Government to its unity, a very large majority of men, who were determined to exhaust every means to save the country. I was, and am still, among that number. I came here with an earnest desire—and the people who sent me here felt that same earnest desire—that under the Providence of God, something might occur to drive away the storm that hung over our land and save it from its final destruction. We assembled. Our Legislature in the meantime, in the spirit of peace and with a desire of preserving our Government and of bringing back our sister States of the South, appointed distinguished citizens as Commissioners to assemble in Washington, and Virginia invited all the States of the Confederacy to meet her there. A large number responded to the call made by Virginia to assemble there, and see if men fresh from the people, would not be able to settle and adjust these difficulties, upon a basis that would preserve our country and preserve the rights, honor and liberty of the South. They did assemble, sir. That Conference finally adopted measures, the Franklin propositions, not up to the standard of Virginia, not up to her desire.[18]

But, sir, even the Franklin propositions, which were adopted by that Peace Conference, when submitted to the Congress of the United States, found not a response sufficient in the hearts of the Black Republicans in Congress. The Peace Conference has adjourned; Congress has adjourned, while we in Virginia, assembled in convention, have been waiting for some action upon the part of the General Government that would drive away the clouds which now hang over us and darken our whole horizon. Upon the very adjournment of that Peace Conference and the adjournment of the Congress of the United States, the President, in his inaugural address, says to us — this Union is not dissolved; this Union cannot be dissolved; that it is his duty, to execute all the laws in every part of the land, and that he intends to hold, occupy and possess all the public property in the seceded States and collect the duties upon imports.

I have heard it said by some here that Mr. Lincoln does not mean what he has said; that his language is susceptible of different constructions, and that while, in reading his inaugural, it may appear that he intends to exercise force to carry out his purpose, no coercion will be attempted and no force resorted to. Sir, no man with a just sense of responsibility, no man, who, when called to preside over thirty millions of people, and upon whose conduct hangs the happiness of a nation, if not civilization and liberty throughout Christendom, ought to speak in doubtful language upon such a question; and I hope if his language is really susceptible of a different construction; if he really does not intend coercion; if his object really is not to attempt to re-possess himself of the public property in the seceded States by force; that a voice with unanimity, with clearness, with emphasis that does not admit of two constructions, will go up from this Convention saying to Mr. Lincoln, if coercion is attempted, that Virginia with all her power and resources, will at once be in a position to maintain her honor and her interest, and protect her sisters of the South.

In reference to the proposition submitted on yesterday,[19] I desire, when the Convention comes to take action upon it, that the question will be divided, so that we may pass that branch of the resolution requiring the Committee on Federal Affairs to report, without delay, upon the subject of coercion. I hope that they will strip off and lay aside everything else connected with the matters referred to them, and make a report to us at once upon this subject, so that the voice of Virginia may be heard, so that she may give quiet and assurance to our own people and say to this Government of the North, threatening the coercion of the Southern States, that Virginia will never, never, never submit to see her Southern sisters coerced, until an arm more powerful than any that she can raise shall crimson her soil with the blood of her children.

The time has passed, Mr. President, in my judgment, to speak in doubtful language any longer. I make this suggestion to this body in good faith, and as carrying out the views with which I was elected. I make it hoping that it will be the means of preserving harmony between the sections, and as the means of restoring the peace of the country by awarding to every portion of our land protection for all the rights and interests to which they are entitled. I make it with no view of breaking up or destroying this Government, for I trust, that sustained by the righteous omnipotent hand of Him who presides over the destinies of men and nations, the peace of this land will be preserved, and its fraternity ultimately restored. The measure that I insist this Convention shall act upon, is eminently a peace measure. It is the only way of preserving peace.

It is unnecessary for me to occupy the time of this Convention in telling you, that if the peace is broken, and war begun, the Union is at an end, and the possibility of its restoration over a free and excited people utterly impossible. I, therefore, say as a measure of peace, it addresses itself to this Convention as the only measure of peace left, and I hope that Virginia will find, from the one extremity to the other of this great old State, her sons coming up in one unanimous and undivided unbroken column, saying to the powers at Washington—"stay your hand; lay it not in wrath upon any Southern sister of ours."

When they shall do that, then, Mr. President, we can go and act upon the various questions before us. We can then go on and make an earnest and honest endeavor to settle and adjust the questions of difficulty that have divided and are still dividing and distracting our country. We can go on and adjust them upon a basis in which I trust that our sister States of the South and all of us may come again together into the Union, and keep in that great road in which we have been led by Providence to greatness, power, and a position exalted above all the other nations of the earth. But refuse to take this position; say that Mr. Lincoln has spoken in a doubtful position; that we do not believe the man means what he has said; remain here in quiet; let the struggle come; let blood be spilt; let our Southern sisters and this Government get into a bloody controversy; and, I tell you, no matter what may be our feelings, that when we get into war, God only knows how this country of ours will come out of that war. If you take a step now, in view of preserving the peace, Virginia will still occupy her commanding position, acting, as she does, for all her border sisters, for a million and half of conservative men at the North, who are looking with interest to us to-day, and for her sisters of the South, who are looking to Virginia, in the hope that she will not allow them to be coerced. If we take the position that the Southern States shall not be coerced, war may come. If you do not take the position that the Southern States shall not be coerced, war will come. Your choice, it appears to me, from the best view I can take of these questions, is between the possibility and certainty of war. If war should come, it will be attended with the loss of all that is dear to every section of this Confederacy; for I am not one of those who believe, when this Government is finally overthrown and a separation is finally made between the North and the South, that in either section, for any great length of time, republican institutions will be maintained.

I shall not go into a discussion of the question of slavery; but I desire to announce this as my conviction: that this much derided and much assailed institution is the conservative element in our Government, and that our liberty hangs upon its preservation. Sir, blot out to-morrow the four millions of Africans that occupy the position of laborers in the Southern States, and you put an extinguisher upon human liberty. Separate and divide us, throw us into a Northern and into a Southern Confederacy; let the conservatism and slaveholding representatives be taken out of the Congress of the United States, let the North be left alone to itself, and anarchy and confusion worse confounded, would, in a few years, reign throughout her borders; and the result would be that she could have no peace, no liberty but by the strong arm of power and by her standing armies to keep her disorderly population in order. And, on the other hand, cut us loose from this Union of ours and make a Southern Confederacy of all these Southern States, and I will not draw you a picture of the troubles that may come upon us of the South. Let us unite in an effort to restore this Government, to save this Union, and save it upon the terms of justice and equality to all the South. Let us bring our offending seceded sisters back, and they will come when Virginia shall make an adjustment of the difficulties, and throw around them such guards as shall protect their honor and their rights. Let us once more get together; let all our land see the troubles that spring from an improper interference with this institution of ours in the South. Let them reflect, too, that this day England, is alarmed for fear that the failure of one cotton crop may throw five millions of operatives out of employment. Restore the Government with these impressions upon the public mind, and one hundred years will pass away before the head of fanaticism will so erect itself in the North again as to disturb the peace and quiet of this land.

But in order to do this, the first step, the main step, is for this Convention now promptly and at once to take the position I have indicated in regard to the employment of coercion by the General Government—not in the spirit of menace, not in the way of threat, but with a cool, determined and deliberate purpose, expressed in such a form and in such a manner, as will show to the world that Virginia has placed herself where she means to stand, for weal or woe. If the effect of our voice is to bring peace back to our land, it will fill every heart with rejoicing; if it brings war, she has no recreant son who will refuse to buckle on his armor and fight gloriously in her defence.

Source: George H. Reese, ed., *Proceedings of the Virginia State Convention of 1861: February 13–May 1.* 4 vols. (Richmond: Virginia State Library, 1965), 1:412–16.

Report from the Washington Peace Conference
March 6, 1861

Within a week of the adjournment of the Washington Peace Conference, Virginia's five delegates presented their assessment of the conference's proposed constitutional amendment to the convention. John White Brockenbrough (1806–1877), the designated spokesman for the delegates, was a lawyer who practiced in Hanover and Rockbridge Counties. He was elected to the Confederate Provisional Congress and later became the Confederate district judge for Western Virginia.

Judge Brockenbrough analyzed the conference's amendment point by point and found that it was "clear that the Crittenden plan is far preferable to that of the late Peace Conference." Virginia's delegates "struggled" to develop an amendment based more closely on Senator Crittenden's proposal as directed by the general assembly on January 19, 1861, but were consistently voted down by the northern majority. Had the conference delegates been able to cast a vote for the entirety of the amendment, instead of only on its constituent parts, Brockenbrough would have voted for the package "as distasteful as the scheme was to me."

The PRESIDENT — The Chair has received a communication from the Commissioners of the Peace Conference at Washington, which he begs leave to present for the consideration of the Convention.

The communication was then read by the Secretary as follows:

To his Excellency JOHN LETCHER, Governor of Virginia:

The undersigned, Commissioners, in pursuance of the wishes of the General Assembly expressed in the resolutions of the 19th day of January last, repaired in due season to the city of Washington. They there found, on the 4th day of February, the day suggested in the overture of Virginia for a Conference with the other States, Commissioners to meet them from the following States, viz: Rhode Island, New Jersey, Delaware, Maryland, New Hampshire, Vermont, Connecticut, Pennsylvania, North Carolina, Ohio, Indiana, Illinois and Kentucky. Subsequently, during the continuance of the Conference, at different periods, appeared likewise Commissioners from Tennessee, Massachusetts, Missouri, New York, Maine, Iowa and Kansas, so that before the close, 21 States were represented by Commissioners, appointed either by the Legislatures or Governors of the respective States.

The undersigned communicated the resolutions of the General Assembly to this Conference, and both before its Committee appointed to recommend a plan of adjustment, and the Conference itself urged the propositions known as the Crittenden Resolutions, with the modifications suggested by the General Assembly of Virginia as the basis of an acceptable adjustment.

They were not adopted by the Conference, but in lieu thereof, after much discussion, and the consideration of many proposed amendments the article, with seven sections, extended as an amendment to the Constitution (a copy of which article is hereto adjoined),[20] was adopted by sections (not under the rules being voted on as a whole), and by a vote of the Conference (not taken by States), was directed to be submitted to Congress, with the request that it should be recommended to the States for ratification, which was accordingly done by the President of the Conference.

The undersigned regret that the journal, showing the proceedings and votes in the Conference has not yet been published or furnished them, and that, consequently, they are not able to present it with this report. As soon as received, it will be communicated to your Excellency.

In the absence of that record, it is deemed appropriate to state, that on the final adoption of the first section, two of the States, Indiana and Missouri, did not vote, and North Carolina was divided, and that the vote by States was — ayes 8, noes 8, Virginia, by a majority of her Commissioners, voting in the negative. The other sections were adopted by varying majorities (not precisely recollected) and on the 5th and 7th sections, the vote of Virginia was in the negative.

The plan, when submitted to Congress, failed to receive a recommendation, and, as that body having adjourned, can take no farther cognizance of it, the undersigned feel that the contingency has arrived on which they are required to report, as they herein do, the result of their action.

Respectfully,
JOHN TYLER,
G. W. SUMMERS,
W. C. RIVES,
JAMES A. SEDDON[21]

COMMUNICATION FROM JUDGE BROCKENBROUGH

Mr. SUMMERS — With the permission of the gentleman from Prince Edward [Mr. THORNTON],[22] who was entitled to the floor but gave way I will make a remark or two.

It will be perceived, Mr. President, that that report is signed by four of the Commissioners from Virginia, one of our Commissioners, Judge

Brockenbrough of the county of Rockbridge, not being present in the city, his name is not signed to the report. I am in possession of a communication from that gentleman, giving his views somewhat at large upon the various sections of which that document is composed, addressed to two of the members of this body. I think that justice to that gentleman, our absent colleague, as well as other points of view, make it proper that this communication shall be presented to this body.

I rise for the purpose, therefore, of presenting this communication from Judge Brockenbrough, and to ask that it be printed in connection with the report—not as part of the report. The report is complete in itself and signed by the Commissioners, who were present.

I move, sir, that the report be laid upon the table, and the usual number of copies printed. A gentleman beside me suggests that the report be referred to the Committee on Federal Relations, I have no objection to that disposition of it, if the Convention shall so decide.

I now submit the communication of Judge Brockenbrough, and move that it be laid upon the table and printed—agreed to.

The following is the communication:

WASHINGTON, March 2, 1861.
The Hon. JOHN TYLER, ex-President of the United States,
and Hon. GEORGE W. SUMMERS:

Gentlemen: I beg leave to address you, as two of the Commissioners representing the State of Virginia in the last Peace Conference at Washington, and also as members of the State Convention, now sitting in Richmond, and to state, as briefly as I can, my views in reference to the results of that Conference.

The act of the General Assembly of Virginia which originated the Conference, declares the patriotic purposes which impelled the Legislature in resorting to this extraordinary mode of adjusting the unhappy controversy which now divides the States of this Confederacy, and declares unless it be satisfactorily adjusted, "a permanent dissolution of the Union is inevitable; and the General Assembly, representing the wishes of the people of this Commonwealth, is desirous of employing every reasonable means to avert so dire a calamity, and determined to make a final effort to restore the Union and the Constitution in the spirit in which they were established by the fathers of the Republic." The act further declared the opinion of the General Assembly to be, that the resolutions submitted to the Senate of the United States by Mr. Crittenden, with several specified modifications, constitute the basis of such an adjustment of the controversy as would be accepted by the people of Virginia.

The plan of adjustment agreed upon by a majority of the Conference differs in many important particulars from the scheme of Mr. Crittenden. The main difficulty we had to contend with in the controversy, was in a satisfactory adjustment of the Territorial question. The Crittenden plan distinctly recognizes slavery of the African race South of 36 30 as existing, and precludes Congress from interfering therewith: and declares that it shall be *protected as property* by all the departments of the territorial government during its continuance. The Conference plan contains no such recognition, *eo nomine*,[23] but declares that "the status of persons held to involuntary service or labor; as it now exists, shall not be changed: nor shall any law be passed by Congress or the Territorial Legislature to hinder or prevent the taking of such persons from any of the States to said territories, nor to impair the rights arising from said relations; but the same shall be subject to judicial cognizance in the federal courts, according to the course of the common law."

Whether this provision is substantially equivalent to the corresponding clause of the Crittenden plan is a question of interpretation. The language of the latter is clear and perspicuous; of the former, vague and ambiguous. Whatever the true construction of it be, it is a most weighty objection to it, that it admits of various interpretations. The rights arising from the relations of master and slave are expressly recognized, and the Federal Courts are, required to take cognizance of them; but neither the Executive or Legislative departments are, *in terms*, required to protect them. Its advocates in the Conference insisted that while the rights arising, from the relation are referred to the judicial determination of the Courts, the recognition of them in the article, by a just implication, imports that it is the duty of the Legislature to afford them ample protection by positive enactment of laws necessary to accomplish the end. If this be the proper construction of the clauses, and in my opinion it is—the guarantee of protection of the rights of property in slaves in the territories, is equivalent to that contained in the Crittenden scheme. But we have to resort to implication to deduce it. The terms employed, to secure protection of the rights growing out of the relation of master and slave, are negative only; they shall not be changed, or the introduction of slaves hindered, or the rights of the master impaired by legislation. No duty is prescribed to hedge them round with proper enactments. It is for this reason that I made a most strenuous effort to amend the section by interpolating the words—"and it shall be the duty of the Territorial Government, in all its departments, to protect the rights arising from said relation." The effort was repeatedly and most earnestly made. It was ineffectual, but it is fair to say that the sense of the Conference was not tested on this particular question—the consideration of the amendment being precluded by the ruling of the Chair, that the section was not then amendable.

The rights of the master are made subject to judicial cognizance *according to the course of the common law*! How far can the *courts* afford protection to the rights of the master to his slave, according to the course of the common law? Where legal rights exist, that most wise and flexible system of law known as the common law always supplies the appropriate remedies for their enforcement. The invasion of a right is an injury, for the redress of which a suitable remedy was always afforded; for the common law knows no such anomaly as a wrong without a remedy. Any civil injury, therefore, to the rights growing out of the relation of master and slave would be redressed, according to the course of the common law, by supplying the appropriate remedy of detinue, trover, case, &c.[24] It is said that at common law, slavery was not recognized—that at common law, man could not have property in man; and the celebrated Somerset case, and the late Anderson case are cited,[25] in support of the proposition; to which may be added the imposing authority of W. H. Seward himself. 2 Seward's Works, vol. II, p. 453–4. But the common law is not referred to here to determine *rights*, but simply to furnish *remedies* for injustices to rights recognized by the section in explicit terms. The principle that rights always draw after them at common law the remedy for injuries to those rights, does not apply to public wrongs or crimes. Those are not punishable until defined and appropriate penalties are deduced either by the common law or by statute. But we cannot look to the common law as a source of criminal jurisdiction in the Federal Courts where those rights are made cognizable, for those tribunals have no such jurisdiction, and can only take cognizance of crimes specially created or defined by statute. Statutes prescribing police regulations are indispensable in a slaveholding country; but the duty of enacting them is not enjoined by this section, unless it be implied from the recognition of the rights arising from the relation of master and slave. Is it a fair implication from the language of the section, that it is the duty of the Territorial Legislature of New Mexico to protect the rights of slave owners by all proper enactments? In my judgment, it admits of no other fair or reasonable construction. There is much circumlocution to avoid the use of the terms "slaves" and "slavery"; but the *status* of persons held to involuntary service or labor there, is that of slavery, and the persons so held are slaves; that status — that is, the state or condition of slavery — shall not be changed, nor the importation or introduction of such persons from any of the States prevented, nor the rights arising from such relation impaired. They would be impaired without proper legislation for their protection, and the duty of such protection may therefore be inferred, since the failure to legislate may as effectually impair the rights recognized, as positive hostile legislation. But, in point of fact, there is no necessity for such legislation in New Mexico. It exists already in very ample measure, as I learn from undoubted authority. The *status* of such persons, as it now exists, is recognized as a status of slavery, and of slavery only; the rights of the master are already fully protected by law, and to repeal those laws would be a clear violation of the spirit and very words of this section, as it would certainly impair, most probably destroy, those rights. Upon every sound principle of interpretation, I think that the rights of the master to his slaves, *as property*, are protected by this section.

The second section introduces a new, and as I think, valuable principle. So far as the acquisition of future territory is concerned, it creates a dual Senate, by an equal partition of power between the two sections of the Senate. This is a practical guarantee of equal power to the weaker section, by which the South can exclude any future territory if the conditions of an admission are disadvantageous to her. But the Northern section may equally checkmate her, in her attempts to acquire future territory. True, but the only territory South of 36 deg. 30 min. which can be hereafter acquired, is Cuba and the Northern part of Mexico. Cuba is a slaveholding island already, and its great resources can only be developed by slave labor. The North is more eager to possess it than the South. If any portion of Mexico is hereafter acquired, it will be on the principle of a fair and equitable partition of the territory between the sections. This section was approved by four of the Commissioners from Virginia.

The third section embodies, substantially, I think, the provisions of the second, third and fourth sections of the Crittenden plan. It prohibits Congress from interfering with slavery within any State or Territory; or in the District of Columbia, without the consent of Maryland and of the owners, or making the owners just compensation; or with representatives or others bringing slaves for personal service with them and taking them away; or in places within the exclusive jurisdiction of the United States within those States and Territories where slavery exists; or the removal or transportation of slaves from one State or Territory to any other where slavery exists; or the right during transportation, by sea or river, of *touching* at ports, shores and landings, and of landing in case of distress. The right of *transit* through States where slavery does not exist, is not confirmed. The provision that no higher rate of taxation shall be imposed on slaves than on land, is of some value to the South.

The action prohibiting the foreign slave trade by Constitutional amendment is objectionable, simply because it was wholly unnecessary. Even the confederated States of the South now constituting an independent Government of slave States, *de facto*, if not *de jure*,[26] have prohibited this traffic. The advocates for the re-opening of it in any one of the border slave States are very few, and there was no sort of necessity for interpolating this provision, which had no connection with the pending controversy, into this scheme of adjustment.

The seventh and last section of the Conference scheme is very much less satisfactory than the corresponding one in Mr. Crittenden's plan. Each provides for the payment of the full value of fugitive slaves by the United States in all cases where the officer, charged with the duty of making the arrest, is prevented from so doing by violence or intimidation, or when after arrest, the slaves are rescued. But the former is defective in not providing for re-imbursement to the United States by clothing it with power to impose and collect a tax on the county or city where the outrage was committed, equal to the principal, interest and costs, as is provided in the Crittenden resolutions. There is a double advantage in this feature. In the first place it is more just and equitable to cast the burthen on those who committed the wrong than upon the public treasury. The South is thus made, by its omission in the Conference scheme, to pay its full proportion of a charge resulting from a wrong committed against herself. But by far the most important consideration is, that such a requirement would tend powerfully to restrain such wicked outrages by making it the interest of the offending locality to suppress all mobs and riotous assemblages, to rob and plunder the citizens of the South for no other cause than asserting an undoubted constitutional right.

I have thus endeavored to run a parallel between the two plans of adjustment. On the whole, it is clear that the Crittenden plan is far preferable to that of the late Peace Conference. It is necessary to say how earnestly, yet ineffectually, we struggled to come up to the very letter of our commission by obtaining an adjustment on the basis of the former plan, and in every variety of form. We were uniformly voted down by that inexorable majority! At length, all rival schemes being rejected, the naked question came up of the adoption or rejection of the present Conference scheme. The vote was by sections, and Virginia voted against the most important sections, particularly the first and seventh of the series; and they were all adopted *seriatim*.[27] It was supposed that, as a matter of course, the vote would be taken upon the scheme as an entirety, and I announced to one of you that after the most anxious deliberation, I had come to the conclusion that, distasteful as the scheme was to me, I felt it to be my duty to cast a representative vote, and sustain the measure as a whole. I was convinced that Western Virginia, which I in part represented, would have so voted by an immense majority, if her voice could be heard within that hall, and, acting under that strong conviction, I would have done homage to that great principle of representative government which demands that the representative yield his individual sentiments, and give utterance to those of his constituents. But no vote was taken on the plan, as a whole, the Chair having ruled that each section being successively adopted, the entire plan was adopted, and no farther vote was necessary or admissible under the parliamentary rule.

The most solemnly momentous issue that ever agitated the councils of our dear old Commonwealth is now fairly made up and must soon find its solution in the deliberations of the Convention now assembled to give expression to her sovereign will. My earnest prayer is that true wisdom may conduct her safely and honorably out of this great crisis. Every loyal son of hers awaits the issue with intense solicitude, and for myself I will say that my destiny is bound up indissolubly with hers!

I am, gentlemen, most cordially,
Your friend, W. BROCKENBROUGH.

Source: George H. Reese, ed., *Proceedings of the Virginia State Convention of 1861: February 13–May 1.* 4 vols. (Richmond: Virginia State Library, 1965), 1:417–24.

Majority Report of the Committee on Federal Relations
March 9, 1861

Reflecting its Unionist majority (prior to Lincoln's call for troops on April 15), the committee's report expressed the sentiment that "an adjustment may be reached by which the Union may be preserved in its integrity, and peace, prosperity and fraternal feelings be restored throughout the land." Without providing specific language, the report recommended that the Constitution be amended to address "exhibited defects." Recognizing that the needs of the border states were different from those of the cotton states, the committee believed the eight slave states remaining in the Union should consult together to devise a united response to the dismembered Union. Delivered less than a week after Lincoln was inaugurated, the report displayed a more moderate tone than some delegates would have preferred.

Mr. R. Y. CONRAD [28] — The Committee on Federal Relations, to whom has been referred a large number of resolutions, have had the same under consideration and have directed me to make a partial report.[29]

I will add, sir, that certain proposed amendments to the Constitution of the United States, referred to in this report, are now under consideration before the committee, and as soon as the same can be properly considered and decided upon, will be reported to the Convention. But the committee has deemed it proper to submit first this report, embodying various results, to which they have come after mature consideration, and have instructed me to move that it be laid upon the table and printed.

The motion was put and agreed to.

MAJORITY REPORT OF THE COMMITTEE
ON FEDERAL RELATIONS

The following is the report submitted by Mr. CONRAD:
Partial Report from the Committee on Federal Relations, presented March 9, 1861.

The representatives of the people of Virginia in Convention assembled are profoundly sensible of the difficulty, delicacy and importance of the duty which, in obedience to the popular will, they have assumed to perform.

They feel that the controversy which unfortunately distracts and divides our country has brought about a condition of public affairs for which history has no parallel and the experience of Governments no precedent.

They recognize the fact that the great questions which press for consideration are of entire novelty and of great intrinsic difficulty, and that their proper solution will require on the part of our Governments, State and Federal, and of our people the exercise of the utmost prudence, discretion, calmness and forbearance.

Above all other things at this time they esteem it of indispensable necessity to maintain the peace of the country, and to avoid everything calculated or tending to produce collision and bloodshed.

The grievances for which several of the States have withdrawn from the Union and overthrown the Federal Government within their limits, are such as have affected the people of Virginia to a greater extent than any of the seceded States, and it is their determined purpose to require such guarantees for the protection of the rights of the people of the slaveholding States as in the judgment of Virginia will be sufficient for the accomplishment of that object.

Virginia having initiated measures to obtain such guarantees, a proper self-respect impels her to demand of all the parties that they shall refrain, during the pendency of her efforts for amicable adjustment, from all action tending to produce a collision of forces; therefore,

1. Be it resolved and declared by the people of the State of Virginia in Convention assembled, That the States which composed the United States

of America, when the Federal Constitution was formed, were independent sovereignties, and in adopting that instrument the people of each State agreed to associate with the people of the other States, upon a footing of exact equality. It is the duty therefore, of the common Government to respect the rights of the States and the equality of the people thereof, and within the just limits of the Constitution, to protect with equal care, the great interests that spring from the institutions of each.

2. African slavery is a vital part of the social system of the States wherein it exists, and as that form of servitude existed when the Union was formed, and the jurisdiction of the several States over it within their respective limits, was recognized by the Constitution, any interference to its prejudice by the federal authority, or by the authorities of the other States, or by the people thereof, is in derogation from plain right, contrary to the Constitution, offensive and dangerous.

3. The choice of functionaries of a common government established for the common good, for the reason that they entertain opinions and avow purposes hostile to the institutions of some of the States, necessarily excludes the people of one section from participation in the administration of the Government, subjects the weaker to the domination of the stronger section, leads to abuse, and is incompatible with the safety of those whose interests are imperilled; the formation, therefore, of geographical or sectional parties in respect to federal politics is contrary to the principles on which our system rests, and tends to its overthrow.

4. The Territories of the United States constitute a trust to be administered by the General Government, for the common benefit of the people of the United States, and any policy in respect to such Territories, calculated to confer greater benefits on the people of one part of the United States than on the people of another part, is contrary to equality, and prejudicial to the rights of some for whose equal benefit the trust was created. If the equal admission of slave labor and free labor into any Territory excites unfriendly conflict between the systems, a fair partition of the Territories ought to be made between them, and each system ought to be protected within the limits assigned to it, by the laws necessary for its proper development.

5. The sites of the federal forts, arsenals, &c., within the limits of the States of this Union, were acquired by the Federal Government, and jurisdiction over them ceded by the States, as trusts, for the common purposes

of the Union, during its continuance; and upon the separation of the States such jurisdiction reverts of right to the States, respectively, by which the jurisdiction was ceded. Whilst a State remains in the Union, the legitimate use of such forts, &c., is to protect the country against foreign force, and to aid in suppressing domestic insurrection. To use, or prepare them to be used to intimidate a State, or constrain its free action, is a perversion of the purposes for which they were obtained; they were not intended to be used against the States in whose limits they are found, in the event of civil war. In a time of profound peace with foreign nations, such as now exists, and when no symptoms of domestic insurrection appear—but whilst irritating questions, of the deepest importance, are pending between the States—to accumulate within the limits of a State interested in such questions, an unusual amount of troops and munitions of war, not required for any legitimate purpose, is unwise, impolitic and offensive.

6. Deeply deploring the present distracted condition of the country, and lamenting the wrongs that have impelled some of the States to cast off obedience to the Federal Government, but sensible of the blessings of Union, and impressed with its importance to the peace, prosperity and progress of the people, we indulge the hope, that an adjustment may be reached by which the Union may be preserved in its integrity, and peace, prosperity and fraternal feelings be restored throughout the land.

7. To remove the existing causes of complaint much may be accomplished by the Federal and State Governments; the laws for the rendition of fugitives from labor and of fugitives from justice may be made more effectual, the expenditures of the Government may be reduced within more moderate limits and the abuses that have entered into the administrative departments reformed. The State authorities may repeal their unfriendly and unconstitutional legislation, and substitute in its stead such as becomes the comity and its due to the rights of the States of the same Union. But to restore the Union and preserve confidence, the Federal Constitution should be amended in those particulars wherein experience has exhibited defects and discovered approaches dangerous to the institutions of some of the States.

8. The people of Virginia recognize the American principle that government is founded in the consent of the governed, and they concede the right of the people of the several States of this Union, for just causes, to withdraw from their association under the Federal Government with the people of

the other States, and to erect new governments for their better security, and they will never consent that the federal power, which is in part their power, shall be exerted for the purpose of subjugating the people of such States to the federal authority.

9. The exercise of this right by the States of South Carolina, Georgia, Florida, Mississippi, Alabama, Louisiana and Texas, without the assent of the other States, has given rise to new conditions, and presented questions touching those conditions intimately affecting the rights and safety of the other States. Among these are the free navigation of the Mississippi river, the maintenance of the forts intended to protect the commerce of the Gulf of Mexico, and the power to restrain smuggling along the interior borders of the seceded States; but the federal authorities under the Constitution as it is, disclaim power to recognize the withdrawal of any State from the Union, and consequently to deal with these questions, holding that it is reserved only to the States as parties to the government compact to take lawful action touching them.

10. Without expressing an opinion as to the question of power, but in deference to the opinion of the federal authorities, the people of Virginia hereby declare their desire to confer upon the Government of the United States, the powers necessary to enable its proper authorities to deal peaceably with these questions, and, if it shall become necessary, to recognize the separate independence of the seceding States, and to make such treaties with them, and to pass such laws as the separation may make proper.

11. This Convention, composed of delegates elected by the people in districts, for the purpose of considering the existing difficulties in our federal relations, represents the desire and earnest request of the people of Virginia, to meet as directly as possible the people of her sister States, and to them appeal for satisfactory adjustment. Virginia, therefore, requests the people of the several States, either by popular vote, or in Conventions similar to her own, to respond, at their earliest convenience, to the positions assumed in the foregoing resolutions, and the proposed amendments to the Constitution of the United States hereunto appended. And in the event that this Commonwealth fails to obtain satisfactory responses to her requests, from the non-slaveholding States, she will feel compelled to resume the powers granted by her under the Constitution of the United States, and to throw herself upon her reserved rights.

12. The people of Virginia will await any reasonable time to obtain answers from the other States, to these propositions, aware of the embarrassments that may produce delay, but they will expect, as an indispensable condition, that a pacific policy shall be adopted towards the seceded States, and that no attempt be made to subject them to the federal authority, nor to reinforce the forts now in possession of the military forces of the United States, or recapture the forts, arsenals or other property of the United States within their limits, nor to exact the payment of imposts upon their commerce; nor any measure resorted to, justly calculated to provoke hostile collision.

13. In the opinion of this Convention, the people of Virginia would regard any action of the Federal Government, tending to produce a collision of forces, pending negotiations for the adjustment of existing difficulties, as aggressive and injurious to the interests and offensive to the honor of this Commonwealth; and they would regard any such action on the part of the seceded or confederated States as hurtful and unfriendly, and as leaving them free to determine their future policy.

14. The peculiar relations of the States of Delaware, Maryland, Virginia, North Carolina, Tennessee, Kentucky, Missouri and Arkansas to the other States, make it proper, in the judgment of this Convention, that the former States should consult together and concert such measures for their final action as the honor, the interests and the safety of the people thereof may demand, and for that purpose the proper authorities of those States are requested to appoint commissioners to meet commissioners to be appointed by this Convention on behalf of the people of this State, at Frankfort, in the State of Kentucky, on the last Monday in May next.

Source: George H. Reese, ed., *Proceedings of the Virginia State Convention of 1861: February 13–May 1.* 4 vols. (Richmond: Virginia State Library, 1965), 1:523–28.

Minority Report of the Committee on Federal Relations
March 9, 1861

Henry Alexander Wise (1806–1876) was born in Accomack County; educated at Washington College, Pennsylvania; and admitted to the bar in 1828. He served as a US representative (1833–1844), minister to

Brazil (1844–1847), and as governor of Virginia (1856–1860). He represented Princess Anne County during the convention. After voting in
favor of secession, Wise accepted an appointment by Jefferson Davis to
serve in the Confederate Army.[30]

The most irrepressible delegate to Virginia's convention, former governor Wise dissented from the majority of the Committee on Federal
Relations and penned the following opinion. Concerned that the antislavery forces of the North had "obtained the reins of federal power
and control in all departments of government," Wise continued to believe that some sort of compromise was possible. His problem with the
majority report was that it was not sufficiently specific regarding the
issues in need of resolution. He believed not only that constitutional
amendments were warranted, but also "grants of power to check abuses
or wrongs by a majority of the States." To that end, he listed fifteen
points of "difference or dissension" that needed to be addressed. While
the majority of these points dealt with issues directly related to slavery,
others concerned the appointment of federal judges, and (referencing
the still recent memory of John Brown's raid on Harpers Ferry), the
suppression of "incendiary assemblages, associations and publications
which have engendered the societal wrongs and hatred which have rent
the Union asunder and now threaten civil war."

Following the presentation of former governor Wise's report, Lewis
Harvie submitted a second minority report that called for a secession
ordinance "resuming the powers delegated by Virginia to the Federal
Government, and to make provision for submitting the same to the
qualified voters of the Commonwealth for their adoption or rejection."

REPORT BY GOV. WISE

Mr. WISE—With the assent of the gentleman from Louisa [Mr.
AMBLER],[31] I rise to a privileged question, that of making a report from
the Committee on Federal Relations, or rather a minority report. I ask leave
to present my dissenting report in the form of a minority report, and which
I now beg leave to read.

The undersigned begs leave to assign the reasons for his dissent from the

Report of the Committee on Federal Relations, and presents the following as a substitute for the plan of measures recommended thereby to be adopted by the Convention:

———————◆◆———————

Substitute offered by Mr. WISE to the Preamble and Resolutions of Mr. SCOTT,[32] as amended, in the Committee on Federal Relations, Friday, March 8, 1861:

This Convention, called by the people of the Commonwealth of Virginia, to deliberate upon the present exigencies of their federal relations, and upon the redress of their wrongs and grievances in the Confederacy of the United States, deems it necessary and proper, with a view to preserve peace, to defend the Federal Constitution, and to restore and perpetuate the Federal Union of all the States, on a basis of just and equal rights, to declare:

That for a long series of years the property of the citizens of the slaveholding States, and particularly that of her own citizens, has been assailed and endangered; that the Constitution of the United States has been broken; that the rights and comities of States and their equality in the Union have been denied to the people of the slaveholding States; that the federal laws have been nullified in respect to the protection of their property in slaves; that the separate and independent right of self-government by the border slaveholding States has been seriously impaired, and, in part, practically annulled; that their domestic tranquility and social safety have been endangered and ruthlessly disturbed by actual invasion; that associated and systematic efforts have been constantly and persistently made to enforce upon the people rules of conscience and of morals by a power without their borders, to control the family governments of their homes and their relations as masters to their domestic slaves; that their character as a people has been maligned and misrepresented to the world, in order to bring an influence to bear upon their rights and relations and their wills, rendering them odious and no less offensive and injurious to their sense of self respect and to their interests than the force of arms; that the sanctity of the federal judiciary has been threatened and set at naught, in order to destroy the only peaceful guard and guarantee of their rights of property and federal equality; and that a sectional hate which engendered these evils is continually magnifying them by every form and effort of incendiarism, until they are no longer endurable; until the people actuated by it have obtained the reins of federal authority and control in all departments of government; and until several of the sovereignties, parties to the federal compact, have been compelled to resume the powers granted by them under the independent confederacy, thereby dissolving the Union of the United States of America.

These wrongs have been perpetrated in part by the Federal Government, either by acts of omission or commission, in part by the non-slaveholding States, and in part, by their people, unrestrained by laws, such as confederates are bound to enact in respect to the rights and safety of each other.

And the secession, consequent upon these wrongs, is now met by every indication of an intention and an attempt to coerce the submission of seceding States, by the authorities of the Federal Government, who are but the mere agents of the sovereign parties to the federal compact, without even an appeal to them for the sanction of any ultimate resort to force.

Thus, under the pretext of enforcing laws of the Federal Government, the jurisdiction of which is now denied and abjured by the seceding States, the nation is imminently threatened by an unnatural and unnecessary civil war; equally unnecessary, whether the Union is to be finally dissolved or restored.

These indications are made but too plainly manifest by the failure of the Conference, inaugurated by the Legislature of this Commonwealth herself, to agree on any terms of adjustment; by the disclaimer of all power on the part of the federal authorities to negotiate for peace with the commissioners of the seceded States; by the inaugural address of the incumbent President of the United States, declaring the policy, powers and purposes of his administration of the Federal Government, and supposed to represent the sentiments of large majorities of the States constituting the major section of the United States; by his failure to suggest any mode, whilst disclaiming all powers of adjustment; by the failure of Congress to recognize the results of the Peace Conference, or to recommend any other plan of peace; and by the concentration of Federal troops at various points, and the reinforcing and holding of certain forts and arsenals, with the obvious intent and purpose of overcoming any resistance to the execution of federal laws by the seceded States, and to overawe the further secession and free action of the slaveholding States.

Under these circumstances of peril to every thing precious to a State, this Commonwealth feels compelled to appeal to her confederates still remaining in the Union, and to ask for their determinate conclusions on the following points of difference and dissension, as to which she is bound to demand, and seeks to obtain satisfactory guarantees and assurances for the future:

1. As to a full recognition of the rights of property in African slaves.

2. As to slavery in the District of Columbia.

3. As to the powers of the Federal Government over African slavery, and the employment of slave labor in the forts, arsenals, dock yards, and all places ceded by the States for federal uses.

4. As to protection against the pretension to lay and collect excessive *direct taxes* on slaves.

5. As to the rendition of fugitive slaves.

6. As to protection of the right and comity of transit with slaves through the limits of the States, by land or water; and of the right of transportation of slaves on the high seas.

7. The protection of the right of citizens of the United States, owning slaves to sojourn temporarily with their slaves in waiting, in the limits of non-slaveholding States.

8. The protection of equality of settlement by owners of slaves, with their slave property, in the common territories of the United States.

9. As to the rights of negroes or free persons of the African race to all the privileges and immunities of citizens of the several States.

10. As to the equality of the African race with the white race in the States where it may reside, and the protection of that equality by State laws, and by the laws of the United States.

11. As to the better security of the independence of the Judicial Department of the Government of the United States, by changing the mode of appointing the Federal Judges.

12. As to the protection of the slaveholding States against the abduction of their slaves, by repealing such State or Federal laws as may countenance the wrong, or by passing such laws by the States and by the Federal Government as may be necessary and proper to suppress it.

13. As to the protection of the domestic tranquility of the people of the United States, by suppressing the incendiary assemblages, associations and publications which have engendered the sectional wrongs and hatred which have rent the Union asunder and now threaten civil war.

14. The protection of the public peace by suppressing societies and individual efforts for the collection of money and other means to invade the States or territories of the United States.

15. And by suppressing all organizations seeking and introducing foreign aid and influence, to incite domestic violence in any of the States or Territories of the United States.

Upon these points, and any others which may arise requiring them, this Commonwealth needs and ought to demand additional assurances and guarantees to those now existing; and those assurances and guarantees can, on the main points of dissension and severance, only be made sure by obtaining, not merely Constitutional amendments, or the pledges of States by resolves or otherwise, but by grants of power to check abuses or wrongs by a majority of the States.

And with a view of adjusting these points and obtaining these guarantees, guarded by the necessary and proper checks and balances of power, it is recommended that this Convention shall appeal to the States still remaining in the Union, to give, at as early a day as practicable, their answers to those demands of this Commonwealth, say within the period of the present year and by the 1st day of October next, if possible.

In the mean time it is recommended that every step be taken to preserve the peace of the country.

That to that end neither the Federal Government nor the seceded States shall commence hostilities; that the States now in the Union should confer with this State upon a mode of sanctioning the claim of the right of peaceable secession, and of determining all questions arising thereupon, such as the free navigation of the Mississippi river, the maintenance of forts and arsenals, and the settlement of commercial and postal regulations, &c. And the Federal authorities should avoid all acts whatever tending to cause or to irritate the causes of civil war, by abstaining from the execution of all laws which may require the force of arms against the seceded States; by withdrawing all occupation of their forts, arsenals, dock yards and other places ceded; and by reducing the military forces at the forts, arsenals, magazines, dock yards, &c., within the limits and around and about the borders of the slaveholding States still remaining in the Union, to mere garrisons, for the purpose of guarding and preserving the public property; pending the efforts of the Commonwealth to adjust pending issues, to obtain guarantees, to preserve peace, and to restore the amity and Union, if possible, of all the States.

And it is further recommended to adopt an ordinance that this Commonwealth shall be immediately placed in a full and complete state of military organization for defence; and it shall be immediately submitted to the people to determine whether, if the just demands of this Commonwealth are not satisfactorily responded to, or are not responded to at all by her Confederates, or civil war commencing on the part of the Federal Government, within the period named, pending her efforts of adjustment, they will or will not resume the powers granted by them under the Constitution of the United States, and that this Convention shall place itself immediately in communication with the border slaveholding States for conference and co-operation.

To these ends, therefore, be it resolved—

1. That the foregoing points for adjustment or for declaration of purpose on the part of the States now in the Union, be immediately addressed to them.

2. That additional guarantees or assurances shall be demanded on the more important of these points, in the forms of checks and balances of power, to be defined by amendments to the Constitution of the United States.

3. That responses to these demands from the respective States shall be requested within a fixed and limited time, to wit: on or before the 1st day of October next, if possible.

4. That, in the mean time, it be recommended to the people of this Commonwealth, in the event the federal authorities shall, under any pretext whatever, attempt to enforce their claim of jurisdiction over the people of the seceded States, as by collecting the duties for revenue or diverting the transit or entrance of commerce, or in any other mode, by force of arms, to resist such exertion of force by all the means in their power.

5. That the federal authorities be requested to withdraw all occupation of the places ceded in the seceded States, and to reduce the forces at Fortress Monroe and Harper's Ferry, at Fort Washington and Fort McHenry, in Maryland, to garrisons on guard duty; and that the guns which have been lately mounted landwards, be removed and all other preparations for war in the limits of this Commonwealth, or on her border be at once stopped; protesting that these forces and warlike preparations are irritating causes of civil war and dangerous to the people.

6. That the Legislature of this Commonwealth be recommended and urged to make ample appropriations to place her people in a complete state of military defence.

7. That this Convention will place itself in immediate communication with the border and other slaveholding States still remaining in the Union, for conference and co-operation, whilst awaiting the responses of the other States to these requests and demands.

8. That an ordinance be adopted at once, submitting to the people of this Commonwealth to determine whether, if their just demands are not satisfactorily responded to by the non-slaveholding States, or are not responded to at all by them, or if civil war shall commence on the part of the Federal authorities, within the period named pending the efforts of this Commonwealth for adjustment, they will or will not resume the powers granted by them under the Constitution of the United States; and will or will not unite their destiny with that of the seceded slaveholding States of the South, embracing in any new Union to be formed such non-slaveholding States as will manifest a disposition and determination to respect and maintain the equal rights of all the States and their people.

All which is respectfully submitted, with the request to be permitted to assign hereafter the objections to the report entertained by the minority of the Committee, several of whom are now absent.

HENRY A. WISE

On motion of Mr. WISE, the report was laid on the table and ordered to be printed.

Mr. HARVIE[33]—With the consent of my friend from Louisa [Mr. AMBLER], I will submit a minority report from the Committee on Federal Relations, and will ask that it be laid upon the table and printed.

I concur with many portions of the report submitted by the gentleman who has just taken his seat [Gov. WISE], and I concur with the request to be allowed, with him, an opportunity of expressing the objections that I entertain to the majority report, differ from it, as I do, in many essential particulars.

I now beg leave to submit the following report:

The undersigned, a minority of the Committee on Federal Relations,

JOHN SNYDER CARLILE, MARCH 25

report that, having had under consideration the resolution referred to the said Committee, and dissenting from the report of the majority, recommend to the Convention the adoption of the following resolution:

Resolved, That the Committee on Federal Relations be instructed to report an ordinance resuming the powers delegated by Virginia to the Federal Government, and to make provision for submitting the same to the qualified voters of the Commonwealth for their adoption or rejection.

Respectfully submitted,
LEWIS E. HARVIE,
ROBT. L. MONTAGUE,
SAM'L C. WILLIAMS.[34]

Source: George H. Reese, ed., *Proceedings of the Virginia State Convention of 1861: February 13–May 1.* 4 vols. (Richmond: Virginia State Library, 1965), 1:534–40.

John Snyder Carlile
March 25, 1861

John S. Carlile (1817–1878) was born in Winchester, educated by his mother, and studied for and was admitted to the bar in 1840. He soon moved to Clarksburg where he began his political career. He served one term as a state senator in 1847–1851, and served as a US representative both in 1855–1857 and from March to July 1861 when he resigned after being elected to the US Senate to replace the secessionist senator Robert M. T. Hunter. He remained in the senate throughout the war and played a major role in drafting the bill for West Virginia statehood. On April 17, Carlile voted against the ordinance of secession.

Delegate Carlile began his speech by ruing the passage of the Kansas-Nebraska Act and by suggesting that the Republican Party did not have the power secessionists believed it had. Offering a civics lesson to his colleagues, he reminded them that "there are three departments in the government. In neither the Legislative or Judicial is the Black

Republican party in power, and the department of which they have possession is a pure Executive department, and the Executive officer is powerless for harm." When Carlile argued against the presumption that the Lincoln administration was committed to the abolition of slavery, he was interrupted by former governor Henry A. Wise.

Mr. WISE—May I ask the gentleman a question? Did I understand him to say, that he did not consider the Black Republicans were in power or ever would be? Is that so?

Mr. CARLILE—I will explain. No, sir; they are not in power, thank God, and I think it is very evident that they never will be. We were told that they would not stop with the plank in the platform declaring their opposition to the extension of slavery into the territories of the United States, but that they would advance still further and prohibit the slave trade between the States, abolish slavery in the District of Columbia, and finally interfere with slavery in the States. I ask gentlemen, if all these apprehended dangers were not provided against by the Committee at the late Peace Conference at Washington—each and every one? Now tell me, if you please, what more do you ask? Do you want remedies for the recovery of your fugitive slaves? What better remedies could you have than the remedies which the experience of centuries has perfected? What territory have we now, to which any act going to amend the Constitution of the United States, in any particular could apply? Did the Black Republican party, which had the majority in Congress at the last session, after the withdrawal of the Representatives and Senators of the seceding States, apply the Wilmot proviso to the territories, or exclude you from the territories? They did no such thing.[35] They have by their action negatived the charge which you made against them, that they would exercise the power, if it were ever in their possession, for the purpose of excluding you, by Congressional enactment, from the common territories of the land. They have organized the territories and have left to the people within them to settle and determine this question of slavery for themselves, when they should come to form their State Constitution—a power I have yet to hear a Southern man deny to the people.

What do you want as Union men? I mean as men, who are not prepared to drag this State, or rather to allow it to be dragged, at the heel of the cotton States, by their precipitate action, and who are determined, so far as their representative conduct can go, not to consent that the people against their will shall be telegraphed out of a Union which is dear to them. I ask these gentlemen what do they expect from a border slave State conference to be assembled within 60 days, to lay down, it may be an ultimatum, and to require that that ultimatum shall be accepted within a period of time within which it would be impossible to submit it to the people of the several States of the Union? Sir, have we not had a border slave State conference within the last thirty days? Was not each and all the border slave States represented in this conference at Washington? You are to have, by the report of this committee, a border slave State conference which is to meet the last Monday in May, and who will appoint commissioners to that conference. I confess I am afraid of the men in power.

A VOICE — The people.

Mr. CARLILE — No sir, they would be appointed either by the present Governors or the present Legislators of the several States. I confess I am afraid of the men in power. I would ask where are the sympathies of the Governor of North Carolina, and where are the sympathies of the present Legislature of North Carolina? I know where the people are, because they have spoken. I know where the people of Tennessee are, but I know not where the sympathies of the Governor or the present Legislature of Tennessee are. I know where the heart of Kentucky is. No man doubts that; but I know not where the sympathies of her Governor or her Legislature may be. But, sir, I know that while I adhere to the Peace Conference propositions, I am anchored and the moment I let go of them, I am again at sea.

Mr. WISE — Will the gentleman tell us about the other border States, where their sympathies are — Maryland and Virginia?

Mr. CARLILE — Judging from the fact that my friend from Princess Anne and myself are here without the people having the privilege of saying whether this body should assemble or not, I think I can tell where the sympathies of her present Legislature are. Judging from the appointment which they made of the distinguished gentlemen who represented us in the Peace Conference, I am very much inclined to think that it would not require a prophet to tell who they would appoint again. I repeat again, that standing upon the Peace Congress propositions I am anchored. I do not wish to put again to sea.

Mr. WISE — The gentleman did not answer me fully.

Mr. CARLILE — Does the gentleman want me to tell him about Maryland and Delaware?

Mr. WISE — The gentleman has referred only to one branch — the Legislature. Will he tell us where the executive officers of these States stand?

Mr. CARLILE — I trust that the Executive of Virginia and the Executive of little Maryland, are where I think all good Union men ought to be.

Mr. WISE — They suit you, then? [Laughter.]

Mr. CARLILE — Now, sir, I grant you in one department of the General Government the Black Republican party is in power. But it is known to all gentlemen here, as well as to myself, that there are three departments in the Government. In neither the Legislative or Judicial is the Black Republican party in power, and the department of which they have possession is a pure Executive department, and the Executive officer is powerless for harm. He can do no harm, unless we suspect ourselves. Do we? If we do, I fear that seceding from the Union would not increase your confidence. Are we, the representatives of the people of Virginia, to distrust our constituents? Are we to refuse to those who sent us here the right to judge for themselves, and to protect their own rights? Shall not their vote be heard? Are we to follow the example set us by these States of the Cotton Confederacy?

Sir, we are told that you can never restore the Union again. I do not admit that it is broken. But, for the sake of the argument, I will assume that it is in a condition to be reconstructed. I say to gentlemen who believe that it is in a condition to be reconstructed, that the sooner they disabuse their minds of the idea that we can reconstruct it, the better it will be for them. We cannot do it.

But there is no necessity why we should attempt it. The sovereign people, upon whose virtue and intelligence rests all free government, in each and every one of these States, will re-construct it for themselves. And that the men in power know it, is evidenced by the fact that they refuse to allow the people the opportunity to pass upon this new Government, which they have determined to impose upon them. Whenever you point me to an act on the part of that new Government, that assumed Government, showing a confidence that the people they claim to represent are truly represented by them, then I grant you that there will be some evidence that it may have permanency attached to it.

But, sir, even in Louisiana, they refused to submit an ordinance to the people, and refused to declare the vote of the people.[36] At Montgomery a Congress is constituted, composed of men claiming to be representatives of the people. Are these men the representatives of the people? No, sir. No such thing. That Congress is composed of gentlemen selected by the several Conventions that met in the several States; and they, in the name of the people, presume to construct for them a Government, and have resolved to force it upon the people, and to refuse to the people the right and the privilege of saying whether they desire the Government or not. Sir, there is no necessity—nor if there was a necessity, have we the ability—so to shape our action here as to re-construct—to use the language of the gentleman—the old Union.

But, sir, there is another fact to which I would respectfully call the attention of gentlemen who are so enamored of this report from the Committee on Federal Relations, and with its various propositions. After occupying nearly eight pages with what I conceive to be pretty much generalities and abstractions, it begins to talk a little practically. I mean nothing at all disrespectful when I speak of this report. It is a very able report, and one, sir, that I regret exceedingly I cannot approve by my action here. The report says:

> Virginia, therefore, requests the people of the several States, either by popular vote, or in Convention similar to her own, to respond, at their earliest convenience, to the positions assumed in the foregoing resolutions, and the proposed amendments to the Constitution of the United States hereunto appended. And in the event that this Commonwealth fails to obtain satisfactory responses to her requests, from the non-slaveholding States, she will feel compelled to resume the powers granted by her under the Constitution of the United States, and to throw herself upon her reserved rights.

By what authority, gentlemen, do we, the advisory representatives of Virginia, make this decision?

The report goes on to say:

> The people of Virginia will await any reasonable time to obtain answers from the other States, to these propositions, aware of the embarrassments that may produce delay, but they will expect, as an indispensable

condition, that a pacific policy shall be adopted towards the seceded States, and that no attempt be made to subject them to the Federal authority, nor to reinforce the forts now in possession of the military forces of the United States, nor recapture the forts, arsenals or other property of the United States within their limits, nor to exact the payment of imposts upon their commerce; nor any measure resorted to, justly calculated to provoke hostile collision.

In the opinion of this Convention, the people of Virginia would regard any action of the Federal Government, tending to produce a collision of forces, pending negotiations for the adjustment of existing difficulties, as aggressive and injurious to the interests and offensive to the honor of this Commonwealth; and they would regard any such action on the part of the seceded or confederated States as hurtful and unfriendly, and as leaving them free to determine their future policy.

Mr. Chairman, will gentlemen be good enough to inform us how long they propose to wait? Or rather, how long will they have to wait for this report of the Conference which they desire to inaugurate, and then for the action of the people of the several States, in the event that Conference should agree upon the propositions that it would submit? It certainly will take months, if not years, to get a final settlement of the matter.

But let us say it takes but a twelve month—I want gentlemen to tell me how they are going to prevent this collision in the mean time? How are you going to prevent this collision? And if it takes place, you commit me and mine, the destinies of my children and of the people I represent, to the destinies of these seceded States—aye, rather, to the destiny that may be provided for them by the seceded States. You link my fortunes with theirs, and you bring upon me and Virginia, so far unoffending, all the evil consequences that may possibly come upon those who have offended.

Sir, we have no representatives in Congress now. Many of the States have not elected representatives. The last Congress expired upon the 4th of March. The President of the United States has sworn to see that the laws are faithfully executed. The United States have a tariff, and the Southern Confederacy, down South, pretends to have a tariff. Tell me, gentlemen, how long are you going to wait and how long do you expect it will be before those two tariffs come into collision? And when they do come into collision, how long do you expect that it will be before something very near akin to civil war will come? And then Virginia is to take part and parcel in that civil war—not part and parcel, sir, but here upon the border, she is to be the victim.

There are a few other considerations that weigh upon my mind why we should have action, and prompt action, if we would save the Union, if we would save our people from all the horrors of civil war, if we would save the institutions of our State, of our section of the Union; and if we would afford an opportunity to the people in the seceded States, to declare their wishes as to the maintenance of what gentlemen term the old Union—why we should take that proposition which will the soonest bring quiet and peace to the country. How long, sir, will it be?

We know by this time, Mr. Chairman, that it is not the intention, nor is it the desire of the Executive at Washington to do anything by which a collision will be provoked. We know, sir, what has been given out as to the policy of that Administration. However much we may have differed about the Inaugural Address, we know that the policy of the Executive is peace.

Ex-Governor WISE—Will the gentleman allow me a moment? He keeps me alternating between a fever and an ague. One moment he tells us that there is imminent danger of a violent collision between the Federal Government and the seceded States. In the next breath almost, he announces that the policy of the Federal Executive is peace. Finally he assures us that we need entertain no apprehension. Now, leaving out of view the apparent incongruity of those positions, I would ask him, how he knows that the policy of the administration is peace?

Mr. CARLILE—I will tell you how I know.

Ex-Governor WISE—There is no apprehension about a collision if the President does mean peace.

Mr. CARLILE—I will explain, I will tell you. Mr. Chairman, I can say perhaps what even my friend from Princess Anne cannot say—during a term in Congress I did not speak to them, and while I have seen gentlemen who now hold high positions in this new Government, walking side by side in Pennsylvania Avenue, with Joshua R. Giddings, I never spoke to him; and I have never spoken to Mr. Lincoln, or any one belonging to his Administration.

Mr. WISE—I hope the gentleman will pardon me for interrupting him. I wish to tell him that I was eleven years in Congress, and I learned there not to call a spade a spade—we learn curious things you know in Congress?

[Laughter.] There were sometimes terms of four years when I did not speak to anybody in the Administration. Very often, however, I knew what they were going to do. What is this administration going to do? The gentleman from Harrison [Mr. CARLILE], knows somehow or other, what they are going to do. Are they going to slough off the Southern States? Are they going to be disunionists? Are they going intentionally to slough off those Southern States, and form a new Union? Is that their acknowledged position—the position of disunion? I put the question.

Mr. CARLILE—Mr. Chairman, when I spoke of what we knew as to the policy of the Administration, I spoke from facts before the public, from information that is before not only the representatives of the people in this hall, but before the whole people of the United States. I felt authorized so to speak from the fact that has been announced that Fort Sumter was to be evacuated; from the fact that we have it repeated day after day that it is to be the effort on the part of the Executive to preserve peace if he can do so, as long as he can; and I believe that he may be able to do so for a short period of time, but I do not believe that he can very long discharge the duties imposed upon him under and by virtue of the solemn oath that he has taken, without a collision being brought about between these two tariffs. And hence, sir, I advocate that proposition which can be acted upon within the shortest period of time. If we adopt the substitute and the people of Virginia shall, at the polls in May next, ratify our action; these Peace Conference propositions will go before the several States of this Union and will be acted upon by the first day of August next, and if accepted by the States as a fair adjustment of our difficulties, peace will be restored to the country; and upon the meeting of Congress the adjustment will be placed before the States in a constitutional mode, to be acted upon and adopted by them as an amendment to the Constitution.

Ex-Gov. WISE—Will you allow me to interrupt you again? I want information. Whilst they are evacuating Fort Sumter—perhaps at this time; I hope they are—does the gentleman know that an order came this day to Junius Archer, of the Bellona Arsenal,[37] from the Ordinance Department at Washington to have all the new guns at that arsenal sent to Fortress Monroe?[38] Does the gentleman know that?

Mr. CARLILE—No, sir.

Ex-Gov. WISE—And whilst they are sloughing off the Cotton States of the South, they are making every preparation now to force Virginia to remain with the Northern Confederacy.

Mr. CARLILE — I ask the gentleman if he apprehends danger?

Ex-Gov. WISE — Apprehend it, sir? It is fearful. So much, that I would be this moment demanding that that armament at Fortress Monroe should be reduced.

Mr. CARLILE — Well, sir, if the Federal Government were to order all its arms and all its men to Fortress Monroe to-day or to-morrow, I would feel as secure in all my rights as I feel at this hour. Sir, how is it possible that gentlemen can suppose for one moment that there can be, by any man or any set of men, the slightest design to make war upon or otherwise injure or invade the right of a single citizen in this State? These sensation articles, these alarming telegraphic orders, never have disturbed my peace for a single moment, for I know, that up to this hour, Virginia has done nothing to bring down upon her the power of the Federal Government to be used against her; and I would be more willing to believe that these arms are ordered there to protect and defend Virginia. But, sir, I will say, although I disclaim any extra bravery, that the people of Virginia never could, standing alone, be subjected or subdued, by any power on this continent.

{Delegate Carlile concluded his address with yet another plea for the conference to support the constitutional amendment proposed by the Washington Peace Conference and submit it to a popular vote.}

Source: George H. Reese, ed., *Proceedings of the Virginia State Convention of 1861: February 13–May 1.* 4 vols. (Richmond: Virginia State Library, 1965), 2:313–22.

William Marshall Tredway
April 1, 1861

William M. Tredway (1807–1891) was born near Farmville, Prince Edward County, educated at Hampden-Sydney College, admitted to the bar in 1830, and established his law practice in Danville. He served one term as a US representative (1845–1847), represented Pittsylvania County in the state convention, and voted for secession.

Three and a half weeks after Lincoln's inauguration, Delegate Tredway lectured his colleagues that there was no urgent need to secede. The grievances the South complained of had existed since the end of the war with Mexico, and, with a Democratic majority in both houses of Congress for the next two years, Lincoln could do nothing "without the aid of Congress." There was still plenty of time to affect a political compromise with the North. Only after all "means of saving this Union" had been exhausted, would he agree to go with the southern Confederacy.

Mr. TREDWAY, of Pittsylvania, addressed the Committee as follows:

It is with sincere reluctance and very great distrust that I presume to throw myself upon the attention of this Committee under the circumstances which surround me. I know, notwithstanding the clamor made here, and notwithstanding that a conflict has arisen upon this floor in regard to the length and freedom of debate, that the people of Virginia are tired and sick of debate. I know that my own people, while they desire that I should stand and counsel freely with the distinguished and wise men who have been sent up to this Convention, while they expect me to take part in its deliberations yet, they would hold me inexcusable if I was to consume too much of its time by speaking, and thereby, in some measure, prevent the body from coming to some conclusion.

In the position which I shall take, Mr. Chairman, I shall agree with very much of what has been said by the gentleman from Culpeper [Mr. {James} BARBOUR], who has so ably and eloquently addressed the Committee.[39] I shall have the misfortune to disagree with some with whom it has been my pride and fortune to associate politically in times gone by, and I shall have the misfortune to disagree with the other extreme wing in this body. While it would afford me great pleasure to agree with both, if I could, I dissent from them with great pain.

The gentleman {James Barbour} who has just taken his seat has told us that it becomes a statesman to survey all the circumstances surrounding him when he is called upon to act, and to determine his action by the circumstances which surround him, and adapt himself to them. It is true, sir; and one strong and controlling reason why I have not been able to agree with the gentlemen with whom I have formally associated, and who have been denominated the precipitators from the inception of this revolution is, that I have felt the force of that sentiment, and I desired to accommodate my action not only to the circumstances which had transpired, but I felt that I ought to await the development of others. In my opinion, the great fault with my friends on that side is that they have not adhered to that principle. They have wandered from that wise maxim which was reiterated by Edmund Burke,[40] and which was actuated by my friend who has just taken his seat. If that principle had governed the South; if South Carolina, who commenced this revolution, had acted upon that principle, and those Southern States who have associated with her, we would not have been placed in the alarming condition in which we have found ourselves since the 20th of December last. I do not believe, sir, that they acted advisedly, and I do not believe that their course was justified by the circumstances.

Let me be understood. As a States Rights man, I hold to the doctrine of peaceable secession as a right which belongs to the people; but I hold that it is a right which ought to be exercised only under extreme circumstances, and that it cannot be justified unless it is done under circumstances stronger than any which have occurred yet. I ask, sir, why was it that South Carolina first resorted to this remedy? In view of all the tremendous consequences which have resulted, and of those untold and incalculable results which may yet come and which the wisest men cannot foresee, how is she to stand justified before a Christian world for the act which she has done? Take any and all of the grievances of which we now complain—take the Personal Liberty bills—those outrageous infractions of our rights which have been passed by some of the Northern States—take their continued interference, their unjustifiable warfare upon the institutions of the South, in every mode and every form to which they have resorted—take the invasion of Virginia in October, 1859—take all, and, even after all, by a resort to the constitutional, legal mode of resistance, without resorting to secession, we might have corrected the evil.

I point, sir, to one fact: Every grievance under which South Carolina and the other States of the Southern Confederacy have suffered, and on account of which they justify that revolution to which they have resorted, has existed for a period of from twelve to fourteen years. We have lived under that Union—aye, more, sir, that Union had prospered—and the people of the Southern States, as well as of the Northern States, enjoyed a degree of tranquility and prosperity, personal and political, which no other people on the earth did enjoy. After every grievance had operated upon the States for years; after every wrong had been inflicted and borne for years; even with these operating upon us and grinding us, as gentlemen say they have ground us, to the dust, before the election of a President, in November last, every party of every political hue proclaimed, at least in Virginia, that they were not ready for secession, and that that crowning act, the only one which has transpired since all the wrongs to which I have alluded have existed—the election of a Black Republican President—did not justify secession on the part of the South. We were a unit, sir. As a Douglas man, as one of that wing of the Democratic party, I agreed with my Breckinridge Democratic friends in the last canvas. Nothing, sir, beyond that election has been alleged to justify this course on the part of the Southern States, which threatened to engulf not only all that was valuable and dear in Southern institutions, but all that was valuable, venerable and glorious in our Union, and to destroy the hopes of liberty throughout the world.

But gentlemen tell us that secession, resorted to under such circumstances, which already has produced consequences most disastrous—they tell us now, and have told us for months past, that secession on the part of Virginia is to cure the mischiefs which have resulted entirely from secession on the part of the other States.

Sir, up to the moment of the secession of those States, the prosperity of this country was great; all was calm and tranquil; there was no ripple on our political surface; no disturbance of our commercial or social systems; but as soon as secession was resorted to, a panic has spread over this broad land, which has not only addressed itself in fearful tones to the statesman who could stand in his position and view the causes, look to the results, and see the effects which certain causes have produced; not only to the capitalist, with his keen eye, who looks to political causes when he undertakes to invest his money; not only to the workshop, where the operations have been stopped; not only has enterprise everywhere been thwarted and brought to a stand, but panic has gone into the very dwellings of our citizens; it has sought the fireside of our household, and spread terror and consternation among the women and the children of the nation. Until secession occurred, there was no evil known in this land.

Now, sir, that was precipitate action, mark you. And those gentlemen who now justify that precipitate action, the results of which are not now matters of speculation, but are facts written in woeful characters upon the face of the country, these gentlemen tell us, and have been telling us for months, that the only remedy for these evils is immediate secession on the part of Virginia. Sir, when the election was progressing, I took little part in the canvass; but when I defined my position as one who was not willing to act precipitately—when I stood appalled in view of the fearful scene which was then spread out before me, and I could not speak advisedly to my people; for I told them I had not wisdom enough to do it—then I met with gentlemen who were wise enough to tell me that if Virginia would secede immediately, peace would be restored to the country, and prosperity within our borders. I could not see it then. I did not see the force of their position. I did not agree with them. I made up an issue with them. They said boldly and defiantly, and a panic was gotten up. "If you don't secede before the 4th of March; if you permit a Black Republican President to take his seat, and hold his sceptre over you, war is inevitable; you will surely bring desolation and ruin to all the interests of this country." I did not believe that, sir. I did regard the election of Abraham Lincoln as a most unfortunate occurrence, as a fearful thing, when I saw even the possibility of it; and I did really fear when I saw that he was elected.

But I rested upon one strong arm of the government, which I knew had more power than he, and without whose concurrence, even the President did not have power to make war upon us, seriously to injure us. I looked to the fact that he had a minority of the votes cast in that election, that there were a majority of a million of the voters of the United States against him; I looked to the fact that the Congress of the United States elected up to that time, contained a majority against him, and he, the President, could do nothing without the aid of Congress. I mention these things as facts which I suppose will not be controverted.

Now, sir, what has been the effect of secession up to this period? It is plain, it is incontrovertible, it is seen and felt in the deplorable condition of every department of enterprise; it is holding us here in deliberation—I regret to say, in divided council; it is holding the people of Virginia and the people of the other States in fearful, in awful suspense, as to what will be the final issue. Now, sir, in view of that fact, I ask, shall we listen, even for the very powerful reasons given by the gentleman who has just taken his seat [Mr. BARBOUR, of Culpeper], to those who have wholly deceived themselves when they said, if we did not secede before the 4th of March, we would have bloodshed, and all the fearful evils attendant upon civil war?

Mr. Chairman, this is the day of panics; the age is adapted to them. The excitable and inflammable material which now exists, ignites and rises in a terrific flame at the slightest touch from the hands of the panic-maker. The telegraphic wires have played an important part in extending this excitement. All will remember how difficult it was until recently, while Congress was in session, and about the time of the inauguration of the present President, to receive from Washington a dispatch, which did not either excite the precipitators or gratify the peace-makers. It is a remarkable fact, that whatever came from Washington upon the telegraphic wire, saying that war was probable, saying that Lincoln had taken up a position of hostility to the seceded States—whatever came which ministered to that spirit—I had like to have said, that wild spirit of fanaticism (but on account of my respect for gentlemen who labor under that infatuation, I will not say so)—whatever came here of that character, elated the hearts of the precipitators. Well, now, sir, I point to the calm and quiet now restored, in justification of my course in waiting to deliberate—in waiting, when we were warned by the gentleman from Bedford [Mr. GOODE],[41] who sits near me, who played so beautifully on the expression *wait*, but who, somehow or other, has changed his tune, and I believe is struggling now to *wait*, while the other side of the house are for bringing matters to a speedy termination.

Mr. GOODE, of Bedford—The 4th of March has come and gone.

Mr. TREDWAY—Yes, sir, the 4th of March has come and gone, and I wonder that the gentleman alludes to the fact that it has come and gone, for as it has passed by it has proclaimed that my friend was no prophet. Now, sir, I maintain that while on the one hand the practical results of secession stand out in broad, in living and in fearful characters before the country, the very time we have taken to deliberate has relieved us of many difficulties, put us in a better position for adjustment, than we have ever been in before. You were told, sir, that the Peace Conference was a failure. I admit that it was a failure so far as it was designed to accomplish a settlement such as I would have been willing to have taken; but I will not admit that the Peace Conference was an entire failure. I ask, sir, as one important thing result- ing from this Peace Conference, if we did not get in a proposition which, I understand, was supported by the Northern members of that Peace Con- ference, a proposition which they never did tolerate before at the North? In that article of the Peace Conference, a proposition which allows the General Government to pay the owners of a slave for his property which would be wrested from the marshal, I maintain there is a distinct recognition of the right of property in the slaveholder. Otherwise, how would they agree to pay the owner?

I am not arguing, and I do not intend to argue, that the propositions of that Peace Conference, as a settlement, were sufficient to meet the demands we ought to make upon the North by any means. But I say that the agree- ment to that one article did, at least, settle that the portion of the North represented in that Peace Conference were willing to make that distinct ad- mission, which was never before obtained from the North — nay, sir, which they had always refused.

{Delegate Tredway continued on at some length making his point that secession did not solve any of the grievances the South claimed against the North. Every effort must be made at compromise, he counseled, before Virginia should consider leaving the Union.}

Well, sir, the question has been asked, if the North do not choose to ac- cept those propositions, where is Virginia to go? I can answer that question. My mind has been made up upon that subject long ago. I am going to ex- haust every means of saving this Union, that does not sacrifice or endanger the interests or honor of Virginia; but if they refuse to give us that which is right; if they will not give us such a platform as the Southern States which have gone out of the Union can stand upon; such a platform as we can go upon to reconstruct the Union, I say that Virginia ought to go, and must go, with the Southern Confederacy.

{Tredway here emphasized his opinion that Virginia ought to exhaust all efforts to resolve the crisis before voting in favor of disunion. He concluded his speech as follows.}

I assure I do it {present his views} with diffidence; I do it with humiliation, with distrust of my own judgment. I feel my weakness. I feel my inadequacy to propose any remedy that shall meet all the difficulties that surround us. I pledge myself if any gentleman can bring forward any plan that can restore this great and mighty government, and preserve the honor of Virginia, I will waive all the opinions which I entertain and most heartily and cordially unite with him in the patriotic and noble purpose. I am ready to sacrifice every thing to save the country and restore the Union.

Source: George H. Reese, ed., *Proceedings of the Virginia State Convention of 1861: February 13–May 1*. 4 vols. (Richmond: Virginia State Library, 1965), 2:704–29.

Jeremiah Morton
April 4, 1861

Jeremiah Morton (1799–1878) was born in Fredericksburg, Spotsylvania County, and graduated from the College of William and Mary in 1819. Admitted to the bar, he began his law practice in Raccoon Ford, in nearby Culpeper County. He served one term as a US representative (1849–1851) elected as a Whig. During the convention, Morton represented Greene and Orange Counties, and on April 17, voted in favor of secession.

Because of the "irrepressible conflict" between free institutions and slave institutions, Delegate Morton proposed that the "South should have the *political power* to protect herself." He called for alterations to the United States Constitution that would create equity between the South and the North. (The rising population in the West did not seem to factor into his calculations.) Morton proposed that no law should be passed by Congress that did not have a "majority of votes from the free States, and a majority of votes from the slave States." Additionally, federal judges should not be confirmed without the same balance of votes, nor should a president be elected without a "majority of the electoral votes from the North and a majority from the South." If these conditions could not be met, and maintained, Virginia should seek her destiny with the South.

FEDERAL RELATIONS

The hour of half past ten having arrived, the Convention resolved itself into Committee of the Whole [Mr. SOUTHALL[42] in the Chair], and resumed the consideration of the report of the Committee on Federal Relations, the question being on the 4th resolution, as follows:

"The Territories of the United States constitute a trust to be administered by the General Government, for the common benefit of the people of the United States, and any policy in respect to such Territories calculated to confer greater benefits on the people of one part of the United States, than on the people of another part, is contrary to equality and prejudicial to the rights of some for whose equal benefit the trust was created. If the equal admission of slave labor and free labor into any Territory, excites unfriendly conflict between the systems, a fair partition of the Territories ought to be made between them, and each system ought to be protected within the limits assigned to it, by the laws necessary for its proper development."

Mr. RICHARDSON[43] resumed and concluded his remarks.

Mr. MORTON — It had been my wish to address the committee on topics discussed in the general range of debate; but in the very limited time that will elapse before the hour arrives when this debate is to close — not more, I believe, than 30 minutes — I shall confine my remarks to a very few points, and I desire the attention of the majority, as well as of the minority; for, permit me to say, that while the minority have generally been in their seats, extending a close attention to gentlemen of the majority who have addressed them, yet when a minority man has occupied the floor, I have found the seats on the other side of the House very generally vacant.

When I presented myself to my fellow citizens as a candidate for a seat in this Convention, or rather when I accepted an almost unanimous invitation

of the people of the county of Greene to become a candidate for a seat in this
Convention, to that invitation I made a response, from which I will read a
couple of lines. I said "the South should be satisfied with nothing short of
equal rights, and the political power to protect them." This equality was the
great principle which I announced to my constituents, and it is a principle
which has resounded from every section of this Commonwealth, and every
quarter of this hall, that we are entitled to equal rights. But when we come
to carry the principle into practice, the very men who proclaim it, in the
next breath tell you they are willing that there should be a division of the
common territory of the United States, by the line of 36 degrees 30 minutes,
above which slavery shall be excluded, and south of which slavery may be
permitted, and *that*, we are told, is equality. Sir, I say that is not the equality
of the present Constitution; it is not the equality declared by the Supreme
Court of the United States. That tribunal has declared that all the territory
belonging to the common government, shall be occupied by the citizens of
the common government, with the right of protection for all their property.
That I deem to be equality. Sir, is it to be said that it is a degradation to
the Northern man to go South because my son or my neighbor may have a
plantation of slaves by his side? Is the Northern man a better or a purer man
than the slaveholder from the Southern States? I think not. It is no more a
degradation for him to settle by a planter, a man his equal and generally his
superior, than it is for a Southern man to go North of that line, and settle by
the Northern man. I say then, Mr. Chairman, while this principle of equality is proclaimed in our Constitution, as construed by the Supreme Court
of the United States, that the Northern man and the Southern man should
go to all the territories together upon terms of perfect equality, the majority
of the Committee of Twenty-one[44] have agreed to a compromise which is
a sacrifice of Southern rights if not of Southern honor.

So much, Mr Chairman, for that branch of the subject. For one I say that
if we come together again we must come by a re-construction, and I am
never for re-constructing this government unless it is done upon the foundation stone of equality and unless that equality is carried to the very cap of
the edifice.

Mr. Chairman, the next great principle that I enunciated to my constituents was that the South should have the *political power* to protect herself. The South is in a minority. We have seen what is the efficacy of paper

guarantees. The distinguished gentleman from Fauquier [Mr. {Robert Eden} SCOTT] who has been the Ajax of the Union party upon this floor, yesterday made the manly declaration, the manly concession, that the eight slave States could not remain in a Union with the Northern States even if the free States permitted Virginia and the other border States to write a Constitution with all the guarantees that we might consider necessary for our protection. You cannot be safe, write the Constitution as you will; cross every "t" and dot every "i," because of the hostility existing between the nineteen free States and the slave States—because, I suppose, of that irrepressible conflict between the free institutions and slave institutions. With that concession, coming from any quarter, but especially so distinguished a quarter as it emanated from yesterday, I ask if there should not be political power to protect us. I regretted very much that the gentleman's indisposition deprived us of hearing his argument upon the very point to which I am now directing the attention of the Committee, for, if he thinks, as I think, I know it would come with more power and influence from that gentleman than it will from me. But, sir, I say that we ought to have political power to protect ourselves; and at this point I am solicitous of having the ear of my distinguished friend from Bedford [Mr. {William L.} GOGGIN], for I am desirous of having his co-operation. I desire also the attention of the gentleman from Kanawha [Mr. {George W.} SUMMERS]. Can we have these guarantees? If I can make it palpable to my distinguished friend from Montgomery [Mr. {William Ballard} PRESTON], from the very principles which he laid down I think he will concede it. Now, sir, these questions have been shadowed forth by the Committee of 21 in part, when they propose that no laws shall be passed in respect to the acquisition of territory without a majority vote of each section. I will illustrate the point by the action of clerical and lay deputies in Episcopal conventions. Gentlemen who have paid any attention to our ecclesiastical policy know that there have been dissensions and jealousies existing between the clergy and laity. We have a house of bishops. Then we have a lower house, composed of clergy and laity. Whenever any question arises in the lower House, as to whether the clergy are jealous of the laity, or the laity jealous of the clergy, they call for a vote by orders, and it must pass by a majority of the clergy and a majority of the laity.[45] That is the principle which I ask now to have applied to both Houses of Congress on any or on all questions on which either a Northern or a Southern member shall call for a vote by sections. Let nothing become a law that has not a majority of votes from the free States, and a majority of votes from the slave States.

Then, Mr. Chairman, as respects the Judiciary! Let there be no confirmation of the appointment of a judge, whose tenure is for life, or during good behavior, except by a majority of Senators from the South, and a majority from the North. In that way, you will have national men filling the judicial bench, and not Black Republicans, as the present prospect is.

So much for Congress, and so much for the Judiciary. Then, as to the Executive! That can be effected by requiring any man who is elected president, to receive a majority of the electoral votes from the North and a majority from the South. The effect of that amendment would be that you would never see an Abe Lincoln dishonoring the presidential mansion. You would never see a worse man than him, Wm. H. Seward, presiding in the presidential mansion. You would find moderate men from either North or South. You would find such a man as Dickinson in the North or one of his type in the South. You would not find an extreme man in either section.

If we have these political guarantees, if the North be willing to concede to us guarantees of political power, then I think, we might safely see reconstruction under the expectation and hope that the high destinies of the Union will be worked out with all of the distinction which the fathers of the Republic anticipated when they established our Government. You will then have security to a minority, and the majority cannot trample down and oppress the minority.

In throwing out these suggestions, I do not say that I have done more than shadow forth the general ideas. Whether or not these particular guarantees of power in one branch of Congress would suffice, whether they could be dispensed with in the Executive Department or in the Judiciary Department, is a matter which is for the Convention to decide. My own belief is, that if we acknowledge the principle in theory, we ought to apply that principle to every department of the Government.

Mr. Chairman, I will not, in the few moments that I have left, expend more time on that branch of the subject. The distinguished gentleman from Fauquier [Mr. SCOTT] made the confession that Virginia and the border slave States could not find security with the North even though she were to give us a *carte blanche* to write such a Constitution as we choose. He confessed also that when he came from home he had a confident hope that this

Union could be reconstructed, and reconstructed with safety and with honor to all parties, but that that confident hope and expectation had "vanished into thin air." And he made another confession which I should be glad to hear echoed by my distinguished friend from Kanawha [Mr. SUMMERS] and by all the trans-Alleghany range and the seaboard of Virginia—that if this Union cannot be reconstructed the destiny of Virginia is with the South. I believe that that sentiment will have, and has, a response in the bosom of an overwhelming majority in this Convention. With these confessions, the point of difference to which I wish to call the gentleman's [Mr. ROBERT E. SCOTT's] attention and the attention of this Committee is as to the policy of Virginia, whether she is to seek cooperation with the border States in the Union or out of the Union? The gentleman seemed to argue, with a confident and triumphal manner, that if we are to have consultation with the border States, that consultation had better be before than after the withdrawal of Virginia. I think that my friend from Culpeper [Mr. {James} BARBOUR], demonstrated, with as much mathematical precision as a moral question is susceptible of, that the true policy of Virginia is to act for herself and not to go into conference with the border States. If we are to have a border conference, this Convention is to nominate the delegates to that border Conference. You may judge from what has been the action of this body and of its President—all honorable men, all seeking to act for the best—what would be the stripe and type of the delegation from Virginia. My opinion is, that it would not represent the popular sentiment of Virginia—and there is the beginning point. Where will you find Maryland? Maryland has a Black Republican Governor, or one who is cousin-german[46] to a Black Republican, and he would depute submissionists from Maryland. What would you expect from Delaware—a State which has not as many slaves as there are in the city of Richmond—not one third as many as there are in my county?[47] What would you expect from Kentucky? If there is a vote, of which I shall for ever be proud, it was that by which I refused a vote of thanks to John J. Crittenden. As much as I venerated and honored him in time past, I saw enough of him in Washington to satisfy me that he would rather give up the institution of slavery than give up the Union. You find him to-day proclaiming in Kentucky that the interest of Kentucky is in union with the North.[48] Then what can you expect from Missouri and Tennessee, sir? If you were to go into council with those States you will find that they would bring you down to the lowest demand of the lowest submissionist in this Convention. I am against it. I want Virginia to act, and to act for herself. I would be willing to rest this question, if it were a new question, on the argument with the gentleman from Fauquier [Mr. SCOTT]; or, if I had not successfully met it myself, I say his argument was answered before it was delivered, by my friend from Culpeper [Mr. BARBOUR].

But, Mr. Chairman, we have something more than theory, and something better than theory. The very policy which the gentleman from Fauquier is urging upon this convention is that which caused the struggle in the Confederate States before there was separate State action. I was there when this question agitated those States. In the struggle in Alabama, in Louisiana, and in Georgia you did not find a man who said that the State should submit to the rule of the Black Republicans—not one that did not say that Southern rights had been invaded, and that they must be vindicated. But the co-operationists there, as the co-operationists here insisted that no State ought to act until five of the Southern States would agree to act together, and go out together. That was the struggle. The secessionists insisted on going at once, and co-operating afterwards.

Well, what has been the result, the signal result of this experiment? No man could pay it a higher compliment than my distinguished friend from Fauquier did yesterday, when he said, that though the Confederate Government has had but a short existence, it is conducted by wise men, by statesmen. It is a stable Government, and commands to-day more of the respect and confidence of the capitalists of the world than the miserable, crumbling, corrupt Government under which Virginia is yet seeking to find protection and shelter.

There is experience against theory. There you find secession first, and co-operation afterwards. Who doubts, who is bold enough to doubt, that if Virginia retires and unites her destiny with the South, the border States will not follow? I have not seen an intelligent man from any one of those States who expresses any doubt of it. We will solve the difficulty by our own action. If we retire now, we will have, by another year, a republic of fifteen slave States.

At this point, Mr. Chairman, permit me to say that we should form our own Constitution with none but slave States, and admit such of the border States as may affiliate with us in sentiment, as will purge themselves of abolitionism, as will acknowledge the right of a Southern man to go into those

States with his servant in the same manner as Northern men are permitted to go into the Southern States with his white servant.

I say, until they come to this point, I will not go into union with them. Permit me to say another thing, sir, that, never in this new Confederacy, would I ask or permit the introduction of any free State unless they would not only acknowledge me their equal politically but socially. A friend told me, that last year, speaking of this same question, a man visited the State of Minnesota with a black servant to wait upon a dying wife; and he petitioned the Legislature to permit the servant to remain in the State until the fall to nurse that dying wife, and that pure, immaculate body considered that their soil and their social institutions would be contaminated, and they unanimously rejected the application.

Now, what do you want? Do you not humble yourselves by seeking an association with these men? I humbly submit that you do. While I admire much that fell from my young friend who has just taken his seat, I have no idea of a necessity for 120,000 men to guard our border. I do not believe it will require more soldiers to guard that than our Canadian border. It is more to their interest to preserve the peace than it is to our interest. Now, sir, I will say, in the few moments left to me—are we men, or are we children? Can we not look to facts as facts exist? Where is the man that has any hope, or ought to have any rational hope, of a re-construction of this Union? Your "Peace Conference" resolutions were rejected, I may say, in Washington, because if the New York delegation had voted, they would not have passed them.[49] It would have been nine to nine—this proposition, which the House of Representatives trampled under foot—this proposition which was scorned by the Senate, with Wm. H. Seward at its head; and when it is brought to this Union-loving body, it is consigned to the silent grave, with my friend from Franklin [Mr. EARLY],[50] leading a few sad mourners. And even as mean as it was; as despised as it was; it was too good for the South.

They tell you of the re-action in public sentiment; and this, whilst Abraham Lincoln has formed his Cabinet with five abolitionists from the free States and two renegades from the South.

At this stage, the hour of 12 arrived, when, under a resolution adopted a few days ago, debate, in the Committee of the Whole, should cease.

Source: George H. Reese, ed. *Proceedings of the Virginia State Convention of 1861: February 13–May 1.* 4 vols. (Richmond: Virginia State Library, 1965), 3:116–23.

6

Proposed Constitutional Amendments
December 1860–April 1861

When the Thirty-Sixth Congress convened on December 3, 1860, it became clear that the passage of laws by Congress would not calm southern anxiety over Lincoln's election. Constitutional amendments alone would satisfy the South's concerns over the future security of slavery. Beginning with President Buchanan's suggested amendment on the session's opening day, the elected officials of the country proposed, over the next four and a half months, a total of sixty-nine additions to the United States Constitution. Virginians offered the largest number with sixteen, followed by Tennessee with nine; Kentucky and Pennsylvania presented six each.[1]

Virginians submitted proposed amendments to Congress, the Washington Peace Conference, the state general assembly, and Virginia's state convention. The eighty-three sub-parts (or articles) of the sixteen amendments provide a clear window into the critical issues plaguing the country over Secession Winter. All sixteen included a proposed settlement of the territorial issue, thirteen dealt with the subject of fugitive slaves, eleven concerned the transit of slaves and slavery in the District of Columbia, and ten were designed to protect slavery in federal installations in the South. Eight prohibited Congress from interfering with slavery in the states, six would have deprived all free Blacks of the right to hold office, and four would have nationalized slavery. Only two proposed prohibitions on protective tariffs. Governor Letcher's proposed amendment is included in chapter 1, while former governor Henry A. Wise's March 9 amendment is included in chapter 5 under the title "Minority Report of the Committee on Federal Relations."

Representative Shelton Farrar Leake
(Independent Democrat)
December 12, 1860

Resolved, That the Constitution of the United States ought to be amended, so as to provide:

1. That Congress shall have no power or jurisdiction over the subject of domestic slavery, either in the States, the Territories of the United States, or the District of Columbia, or over the trade in slaves in or between them, except so far as hereinafter provided.

2. That where domestic slavery may exist in any Territory or district of the United States, it shall be the duty of Congress to protect it by adequate and efficient legislation.

3. That no Territorial Legislation, or other territorial authority, shall have power or jurisdiction over such subject.

4. That the rights of masters or owners to their slaves, while sojourning in, or *in transitu* through, any State or Territory of the United States, shall be guaranteed and protected; and,

5. That fugitive slaves shall be given up on demand of their owners or masters, and that all such fugitives as may be lost by reason of the legislation of any State, or the act of its constituted authorities, shall be paid for by such State.

[Note: Leake's amendment was the first of twenty-seven that would have protected slavery in the states from congressional interference.]

Source: *Congressional Globe*, 36th Cong., 2nd Sess., 77.

Representative Albert Gallatin Jenkins
(Democrat)
December 12, 1860

Resolved, That the committee of one from each State, recently appointed by this House, be instructed to inquire into the expediency of so amending the fugitive slave law as best to promote the rendition of fugitives under the operation of the same, the more adequate punishment of its infraction, and the affording *proper* compensation to the owners of those who are not returned; also, to inquire into the propriety of providing, either by constitutional amendment or legislative enactment, for the better security of the rights of slaveholders in the common Territories of the United States; also, to inquire what further constitutional checks are demanded by a sense of self-preservation on the part of the slaveholding States against the operation of the Federal Government, when about to be administered by those who have avowedly come into power on the ground of hostility to their institutions, and to consider whether this fact does not of itself so isolate and antagonize the slaveholding interest as to make it necessary to its own security that its concurrent voice, separately and distinctly given, should be required to sanction each and every operation of the Federal Government; and to consider whether a dual Executive, or the division of the Senate into two bodies, or the making a majority of Senators from both the slaveholding and non-slaveholding States necessary to all action on the part of that body, or the creation of another advisory body or council, or what other amendments to the Federal Constitution would best promote that result, and to report thereon.

Source: *Congressional Globe*, 36th Cong., 2nd Sess., 77.

Representative John Singleton Millson
(Democrat)
December 31, 1860

On motion of Mr. Nelson, the committee agreed to lay aside the joint resolution to amend the Constitution of the United States, in order to consider the following proposition presented by Mr. Millson to amend the Constitution, to wit:

The Congress may provide for the government of the territory now belonging to the United States, or which may hereafter be acquired by them, and may establish inferior legislatures therein, with such powers of legislation, consistent with the Constitution, as Congress may limit and prescribe; but neither Congress nor such inferior legislature shall prohibit the migration or introduction of such persons as may be held to service or labor under the laws of any State into any part of the territory which may lie south of thirty-six degrees thirty minutes north latitude, nor by any law or regulation therein discharge such persons from such service or labor. But the claim of the party to whom such service or labor may be due shall be recognized by all departments of the territorial government, and protected by apt and proper regulations therein. But into all other territory not included within the limits of any State the migration of such persons shall be prohibited.

Source: 36th Cong., 2nd Sess., House of Representatives Report No. 31, 22. (Journal of the Committee of Thirty-Three).

Senator Robert Mercer Taliaferro Hunter
(Democrat)
January 11, 1861

I say, therefore, sir, that the South is bound to take this course unless it can get some guarantees which will protect it in the Union, some constitutional guarantees which will serve that end; and I now ask, what should be the nature of the guarantees that would effectually prevent the social system from such assaults as these? I say, they must be guarantees of a kind that will stop up all the avenues through which they have threatened to assail the social system of the South. There must be constitutional amendments which shall provide: first, that Congress shall have no power to abolish slavery in the States, in the District of Columbia, in the dock-yards, forts, and arsenals of the United States; second, that it shall not abolish, tax, or obstruct the slave trade between the States; third, that it shall be the duty of each of the States to suppress combinations within their jurisdiction for armed invasions of another; fourth, that States shall be admitted with or without slavery, according to the election of the people; fifth, that it shall be the duty of the States to restore fugitive slaves when within their borders, or to pay the value of the same; sixth, that fugitives from justice shall be deemed all those who have offended against the laws of a State within its jurisdiction, and who have escaped therefrom; seventh, that Congress shall recognize and protect as property whatever is held to be such by the laws or prescriptions of any State within the Territories, dock-yards, forts, and arsenals of the United States, and wherever the United States has exclusive jurisdiction; with the following exceptions: First, it may leave the subject of slavery or involuntary servitude to the people of the Territories when a law shall be passed to that effect with the usual sanction, and also with the assent of a majority of the Senators from the slaveholding States, and a majority of the Senators from the non-slaveholding States. That exception is designed to provide for the case where we might annex a Territory almost fully peopled, and whose people ought to have the right of self-government, and yet might not be ready to be admitted as a State into the Union.

The next exception is, that "Congress may divide the Territories, to the effect that slavery or involuntary servitude shall be prohibited in one portion of the territory, and recognized and protected in another; provided the law has the sanction of a majority from each of the sections as aforesaid," and that exception is designed to provide for the case where an unpeopled Territory is annexed and it is a fair subject of division between the two sections.

Such, Mr. President, are the guarantees of principle, which, it seems to me, ought to be established by amendments to the Constitution; but I do not believe that these guarantees alone would protect the social system of the South against attack, and perhaps overthrow, from the superior power of the North.

Source: *Congressional Globe*, 36th Cong., 2nd Sess., 328–29.

State Senator Alexander Hugh Holmes Stuart
(Constitutional Unionist)
January 19, 1861

Mr. Stuart submitted the following joint resolution, which lies over under the rules:

Resolved, That in the opinion of the General Assembly of Virginia the following would constitute a satisfactory basis of adjustment of the unhappy controversies which now distract and threaten to destroy the peace of the United States.

The territories having been acquired by the common efforts, blood and treasure of all the States, are of right the common property of all the States, and neither the slaveholding nor nonslaveholding States have any just claim to appropriate all of them to their exclusive use.

By existing provisions of the Constitution of the United States, Congress is the trustee of all the States in regard to the territories. Experience, however, has shown, that in consequence of irreconcilable differences of opinion between members of Congress representing the slaveholding and nonslaveholding States, the common property cannot be so regulated and administered by that body as to do full justice to all the beneficiaries of the common property; it is therefore necessary to provide new agencies for its regulation and administration.

To this end the Constitution of the United States should be so amended, so as to withdraw the trust in regard to the territories entirely from the hands of Congress, and to provide for the equitable partition of the territories between the slaveholding and nonslaveholding States, by assigning to the former, as an outlet for its increasing population, all that portion of the common territory now held, or to be hereafter acquired, situated south of the parallel of thirty-six degrees thirty minutes, north latitude, and assigning to the latter as an outlet for its increasing population all that part of the common territory now held, or hereafter to be acquired, situated north of said parallel.

It should further be provided by a similar amendment, that the slaveholding States shall be constituted trustees in regard to the territory south of thirty-six degrees thirty minutes, with full power, through their representative Legislatures or delegates in Congress, to determine and regulate the States in regard to slavery of such territory, and that the nonslaveholding States shall be constituted in like manner trustees of the territory north of said line with like power, through their respective Legislatures or delegates in Congress, to determine and regulate the States of said territory.

States created out of territory north or south of the parallel of thirty-six degrees thirty minutes, shall be admitted into the Union with or without slavery, as their respective Constitutions may ordain.

Source: *Journal of the Senate of the Commonwealth of Virginia: Begun and Held at the Capitol in the City of Richmond, on Monday, the Seventh of January, 1861, in the Year One Thousand Eight Hundred and Sixty-One—Being the Eighty-Fifth Year of the Commonwealth. Extra Session* (Richmond: James E. Goode, Senate Printer, 1861), 90.

Delegate James Alexander Seddon
(Democrat)
February 15, 1861

Mr. SEDDON:—The report presented by the majority, I think, is a wide departure from the course we should have adopted. Virginia has prepared and presented a plan, and has invited this Conference to consider it. I think we ought to take up her propositions, amend and perfect them if need be, and then adopt or reject them. To avoid all misconstruction as to my individual opinions or position, I have reduced my views to writing, which, with the leave of the Conference, I will now read.

No objection being made, Mr. Seddon proceeded to read the following:

REPORT OF MR. SEDDON.

The undersigned, acting on the recommendation of the Commissioners from the State of Virginia, as a member of the committee appointed by this Convention to consider and recommend propositions of adjustment, has not been so happy as to accord with the report submitted by the majority; and as he more widely dissents from the opinions entertained by the other dissenting members, he feels constrained, in vindication of his position and opinions, to present on his part this brief report, recommending, as a substitute for the report of the majority, a proposition subjoined. To this course he feels the more impelled, by deference to the resolutions of the General Assembly of his State, inviting the assemblage of this Convention, and suggesting a basis of adjustment.

These resolutions declare, that "in the opinion of the General Assembly of Virginia the propositions embraced in the resolutions presented to the Senate of the United States by the Hon. John J. Crittenden, so modified as that the first article proposed as an amendment to the Constitution of the United State shall apply to all territory of the United States now held or hereafter acquired south of latitude 36°30', and provided that slavery of the African race shall be effectively protected as property therein during the continuance of the territorial government, and the fourth article shall secure to the owners of slaves the right of transit with their slaves between and through the non-slaveholding States or Territories, constitute the basis of such an adjustment of the unhappy controversy which now divides the States of this Confederacy, as would be accepted by the people of the Commonwealth."

From this resolution, it is clear that the General Assembly, in its declared opinion of what would be acceptable to the people of Virginia, not only required the Crittenden propositions as a basis, but also held the modifications suggested in addition essential. In this the undersigned fully concurs. But, in his opinion, the propositions reported by the majority do not give, but materially weaken the Crittenden propositions themselves, and fail to accord the modifications suggested. The undersigned therefore, feels it his duty to submit and recommend, as a substitute, the resolutions referred to, as proposed by the Hon. JOHN J. CRITTENDEN, with the incorporation of the modifications suggested by Virginia explicitly expressed, and with some alterations on points which, he is assured, would make them more acceptable to that State, and, as he hopes, to the whole Union. The propositions submitted are appended, marked as No. 1.

The undersigned, while contenting himself, in the spirit of the action taken by the General Assembly of his State, with the proposal of that substitute for the majority report, would be untrue to his own convictions, shared, as he believes, by the majority of the commissioners from Virginia, and to his sense of duty, if he did not emphatically declare, as his settled and deliberate judgment, that for permanent safety in this Union, to the slaveholding States, and the restoration of integrity to the Union and harmony and peace to the country, a guarantee of actual power in the Constitution and in the working of the Government to the slaveholding and minority section is *indispensable*. How such guarantee might be most wisely contrived and judiciously adjusted to the frame of the Government, the undersigned forbears now to inquire. He is not exclusively addicted to any special plan, but believing that such guarantee might be adequately afforded by a partition of power in the Senate between the two sections, and by a recognition that *ours* is a Union of freedom and consent, not constraint and force, he respectfully submits, for consideration by members of the Convention, the plan hereto appended, marked No. 2.

Whether he shall feel bound to invoke the action of the Convention upon it, may depend on the future manifestations of sentiment in this body.

All which is respectfully submitted,

JAMES A. SEDDON,
Commissioner from Virginia.

NO I.

February 15th, 1861.

*Joint Resolutions proposing certain amendments
to the Constitution of the United States.*

Whereas, serious and alarming dissensions have arisen between the Northern and Southern States, concerning the rights and security of the rights of the slaveholding States, and especially their rights in the common territory of the United States; and *whereas*, it is eminently desirable and proper that those dissensions, which now threaten the very existence of this Union, should be permanently quieted and settled by constitutional provisions, which shall do equal justice to all sections, and thereby restore to the people that peace and good will which ought to prevail between all the citizens of the United States: Therefore,

Resolved, by this Convention, that the following articles are hereby approved and submitted to the Congress of the United States, with the request that they may, by the requisite constitutional majority of two-thirds, be recommended to the respective States of the Union, to be, when ratified by Conventions of three-fourths of the States, valid and operative as amendments of the Constitution of the Union.

Article 1. In all the territory of the United States, now held or hereafter acquired, situate north of latitude thirty-six degrees and thirty minutes, slavery or involuntary servitude, except as a punishment for crime, is prohibited, while such territory shall remain under territorial government. In all the territory south of said line of latitude, slavery of the African race is hereby recognized as existing, and shall not be interfered with by Congress, but shall be protected as property by all the departments of the territorial government during its continuance; and when any territory, north or south of said line, within such boundaries as Congress may prescribe, shall contain the population requisite for a member of Congress, according to the then federal ratio of representation of the people of the United States, it shall, if its form of government be republican, be admitted into the Union on an equal footing with the original States, with or without slavery, as the Constitution of such new State may provide.

Article 2. Congress shall have no power to abolish slavery in places under its exclusive jurisdiction, and situate within the limits of States that permit the holding of slaves.

Article 3. Congress shall have no power to abolish slavery within the District of Columbia, so long as it exists in the adjoining States of Virginia and Maryland, or either, nor without the consent of the free white inhabitants, nor without just compensation first made to such owners of slaves as do not consent to such abolishment. Nor shall Congress at any time prohibit officers of the Federal Government, or members of Congress, whose duties require them to be in said District, from bringing with them their slaves, and holding them as such during the time their duties may require them to remain there, and afterwards taking them from the District.

Article 4. Congress shall have no power to prohibit or hinder the transportation of slaves from one State to another, or to a Territory in which slaves are by law permitted to be held, whether that transportation be by land, navigable rivers, or by sea. And if such transportation be by sea, the slaves shall be protected as property by the Federal Government. And the right of transit by the owners with their slaves, in passing to or from one slaveholding State or Territory to another, between and through the non-slaveholding States and Territories, shall be protected. And in imposing direct taxes pursuant to the Constitution, Congress shall have no power to impose on slaves a higher rate of tax than on land, according to their just value.

Article 5. That, in addition to the provisions of the third paragraph of the second section of the fourth article of the Constitution of the United States, Congress shall provide by law, that the United States shall pay to the owner who shall apply for it, the full value of his fugitive slave, in all cases, when the marshal, or other officer, whose duty it was to arrest said fugitive, was prevented from so doing by violence or intimidation, or when, after arrest, said fugitive was rescued by force, and the owner thereby prevented and obstructed in the pursuit of his remedy for the recovery of his fugitive slave, under said clause of the Constitution and the laws made in pursuance thereof. And in all such cases, when the United States shall pay for such fugitive, they shall reimburse themselves by imposing and collecting a tax on the county or city in which said violence, intimidation, or rescue was committed, equal in amount to the sum paid by them, with the addition of interest and the costs of collection; and the said county or city, after it has paid said amount to the United States, may, for its indemnity, sue and

recover from the wrong-doers, or rescuers, by whom the owner was prevented from the recovery of his fugitive slave, in like manner as the owner
himself might have sued and recovered.

Article 6. No future amendment of the Constitution shall affect the five
preceding articles, nor the third paragraph of the second section of the first
article of the Constitution, nor the third paragraph of the second section of
the fourth article of said Constitution, and no amendment shall be made
to the Constitution which will authorize or give to Congress any power to
abolish or interfere with slavery in any of the States, by whose laws it is or
may be allowed or permitted.

Article 7, Sec. 1. The elective franchise and the right to hold office,
whether federal, State, territorial, or municipal, shall not be exercised by
persons who are, in whole or in part, of the African race.

And *whereas*, also, besides those causes of dissension embraced in the
foregoing amendments proposed to the Constitution of the United States,
there are others which come within the jurisdiction of Congress, and may
be remedied by its legislative power: and *whereas*, it is the desire this Convention as far as its influence may extend, to remove all just cause for the
popular discontent and agitation which now disturb the peace of the country, and threaten the stability of its institutions: Therefore,

---

{Seddon included herein the four resolutions Crittenden included in his
proposal of December 18. Note that Seddon did not include the second part of section 7 authorizing Congress to purchase land in Africa
and South America for the removal of "negroes and mulattos" that he
(Crittenden) had borrowed from Stephen Douglas's proposal of December 24, 1861.}

NO. 2.

Proposed Amendments by Mr. Seddon.

To secure concert and promote harmony between the slaveholding and
non-slaveholding sections of the Union, the assent of the majority of the

Senators from the slaveholding States, and of the majority of the Senators from the non-slaveholding States, shall be requisite to the validity of all action of the Senate, on which the ayes and noes may be called by five Senators.

And on a written declaration, signed and presented for record on the Journal of the Senate by a majority of Senators from either the non-slaveholding or slaveholding States, of their want of confidence in any officer or appointee of the Executive, exercising functions exclusively or continuously within the class of States, or any of them, which the signers represent, then such officer shall be removed by the Executive; and if not removed at the expiration of ten days from the presentation of such declaration, the office shall be deemed vacant and open to new appointment.

The connection of every State with the Union is recognized as depending on the continuing assent of its people, and compulsion shall in no case, nor under any form, be attempted by the Government of the Union against a State acting in its collective or organic capacity. Any State, by the action of a convention of its people, assembled pursuant to a law of its Legislature, is held entitled to dissolve its relation to the Federal Government, and withdraw from the Union; and, on due notice given of such withdrawal to the Executive of the Union, he shall appoint two Commissioners, to meet two Commissioners to be appointed by the Governor of the State, who, with the aid, if needed from the disagreement of the Commissioners, of an umpire, to be selected by a majority of them, shall equitably adjudicate and determine finally a partition of the rights and obligations of the withdrawing State; and such adjudication and partition being accomplished, the withdrawal of such State shall be recognized by the Executive, and announced by public proclamation to the world.

But such withdrawing State shall not afterwards be readmitted into the Union without the assent of two-thirds of the States constituting the Union at the time of the proposed readmission.

Source: Lucius E. Chittenden, ed., *A Report of the Debates and Proceedings in the Secret Sessions of the Conference Convention, for Proposing Amendments to the Constitution of the United States, Held at Washington, D.C., in February, A.D. 1861* (New York: D. Appleton & Company, 1864), 47–52.

Delegate James Alexander Seddon
February 23, 1861

I move to amend the substitute offered by the gentleman from Pennsylvania, by the insertion after the clause providing for the division of the territory, of the following:

"All appointments to office in the Territories lying north of the line 36°30', as well before as after the establishment of Territorial governments in and over the same, or any part thereof, shall be made upon the recommendation of a majority of the Senators representing, at the time, the non-slaveholding States. And, in like manner, all appointments to office in the Territories which may lie south of said line of 36°30', shall be made upon the recommendation of a majority of the Senators representing, at the time, the slaveholding States. But nothing in this article shall be construed to restrain the President of the United States from removing, for actual incompetency or misdemeanor in office, any person thus appointed, and appointing a temporary agent, to be continued in office until the majority of Senators as aforesaid may present a new recommendation; or from filling any vacancy which may occur during the recess of the Senate; such appointments to continue *ad interim*.[2] And to insure, on the part of the Senators, the selection of the most trustworthy agents, it is hereby directed that all the net proceeds arising from the sales of the public lands, shall be distributed annually among the several States, according to the combined ratio of representation and taxation; but the distribution aforesaid may be suspended by Congress, in case of actual war with a foreign nation, or imminent peril thereof."

[Note: Seddon's amendment was offered as additional language to an amendment proposed by Thomas E. Franklin from Lancaster, Pennsylvania; 288–91]

Source: Lucius E. Chittenden, ed., *A Report of the Debates and Proceedings in the Secret Sessions of the Conference Convention, for Proposing Amendments to the Constitution of the United States, Held at Washington, D.C., in February, A.D. 1861* (New York: D. Appleton & Company, 1864), 328–29.

Delegate James Alexander Seddon
February 26, 1861

Mr. SEDDON:—The substitute which I propose embodies the Crittenden resolutions, with the modifications suggested by Virginia. These are principally confined to the first section, which is made to apply to our future as well as our present territory. I have modified the form of the substitute in several particulars, and now offer it without farther introduction. These are the amendments which I understand the delegation from Virginia is instructed to insist upon:

JOINT RESOLUTIONS

PROPOSING CERTAIN AMENDMENTS TO THE CONSTITUTION OF THE UNITED STATES.

WHEREAS, serious and alarming dissensions have arisen between the Northern and Southern States, concerning the rights and security of the rights of the slaveholding States, and especially their rights in the common territory of the United States; and whereas, it is eminently desirable and proper that those dissensions, which now threaten the very existence of this Union, should be permanently quieted and settled by constitutional provisions, which shall do equal justice to all sections, and thereby restore to the people that peace and good will which ought to prevail between all the citizens of the United States: therefore,

Resolved, by this Convention, that the following articles are hereby approved and submitted to the Congress of the United States, with the request that they may, by the requisite constitutional majority of two-thirds, be recommended to the respective States of the Union, to be, when ratified by conventions of three-fourths of the States, valid and operative as amendments of the Constitution of the Union.

Article 1. In all the territory of the United States now held or hereafter acquired, situate north of latitude 36°30', slavery or involuntary servitude, except as a punishment for crime, is prohibited, while such territory shall remain under territorial government. In all the territory now or hereafter acquired south of said line of latitude, slavery of the African race is hereby recognized as existing, and shall not be interfered with by Congress; but

shall be protected as property by all the departments of the territorial government during its continuance; and when any territory, north or south of
said line, within such boundaries as Congress may prescribe, shall contain
the population requisite for a member of Congress, according to the then
federal ratio of representation of the people of the United States, it shall,
if its form of government be republican, be admitted into the Union on an
equal footing with the original States, with or without slavery, as the constitution of such new State may provide.

Article 2. Congress shall have no power to abolish slavery in places under
its exclusive jurisdiction, and situate within the limits of States that permit
the holding of slaves.

Article 3. Congress shall have no power to abolish slavery within the
District of Columbia, so long as it exists in the adjoining States of Virginia
and Maryland, or either, nor without the consent of the free white inhabitants, nor without just compensation first made to such owners of slaves as
do not consent to such abolishment. Nor shall Congress at any time prohibit
officers of the Federal Government or members of Congress, whose duties
require them to be in said District, from bringing with them their slaves
and holding them, as such, during the time their duties may require them
to remain there, and afterwards taking them from the District.

Article 4. Congress shall have no power to prohibit or hinder the transportation of slaves from one State to another, or to a Territory in which
slaves are by law permitted to be held, whether that transportation be by
land, navigable rivers, or by the sea. And if such transportation be by sea,
the slaves shall be protected as property by the Federal Government. And
the right of transit by the owners with their slaves in passing to or from
one slaveholding State or Territory to another, between and through the
non-slaveholding States and Territories shall be protected. And in imposing
direct taxes pursuant to the Constitution, Congress shall have no power to
impose on slaves a higher rate of tax than on land, according to their just
value.

Article 5. That in addition to the provisions of the third paragraph of the
second section of the fourth article of the Constitution of the United States,
Congress shall provide by law, that the United States shall pay to the owner
who shall apply for it, the full value of his fugitive slave, in all cases, when

the marshal, or other officer, whose duty it was to arrest said fugitive, was prevented from so doing by violence or intimidation, or when, after arrest, said fugitive was rescued by force, and the owner thereby prevented and obstructed in the pursuit of his remedy for the recovery of his fugitive slave, under the said clause of the Constitution and the laws made in pursuance thereof. And in all such cases, when the United States shall pay for such fugitive, they shall reimburse themselves by imposing and collecting a tax on the county or city in which said violence, intimidation, or rescue was committed, equal in amount to the sum paid by them, with the addition of interest and the costs of collection; and the said county or city, after it has paid said amount to the United States, may, for its indemnity, sue and re-cover from the wrong-doers, or rescuers, by whom the owner was prevented from the recovery of his fugitive slave, in like manner as the owner himself might have sued and recovered.

Article 6. No future amendment of the Constitution shall affect the five preceding articles, nor the third paragraph of the second section of the first article of the Constitution, nor the third paragraph of the second section of the fourth article of said Constitution, and no amendment shall be made to the Constitution which will authorize or give to Congress any power to abolish or interfere with slavery in any of the States by whose laws it is or may be allowed or permitted.

Article 7. Sec. 1. The elective franchise and the right to hold office, whether Federal, State, territorial, or municipal, shall not be exercised by persons who are, in whole or in part, of the African race.

And whereas, also, besides those causes of dissension embraced in the foregoing amendments proposed to the Constitution of the United States, there are others which come within the jurisdiction of Congress, and may be remedied by its legislative power: and whereas it is the desire of this Convention, as far as its influence may extend, to remove all just cause for the popular discontent and agitation which now disturb the peace of the country, and threaten the stability of its institutions: Therefore,

---

{Seddon included the four resolutions that John Crittenden attached to the end of his December 18 proposal to amend the Constitution.

This amendment is almost identical to the proposal Seddon made on February 15. Crittenden added article 7 to his original amendment on January 3, having borrowed it from Senator Stephen Douglas's proposal of December 24, 1861. Seddon did not include section 2 of article 7.}

Source: Lucius E. Chittenden, ed., *A Report of the Debates and Proceedings in the Secret Sessions of the Conference Convention, for Proposing Amendments to the Constitution of the United States, Held at Washington, D.C., in February, A.D. 1861* (New York: D. Appleton & Company, 1864), 418–20.

Representative Sherrard Clemens
(Democrat)
February 27, 1861

The SPEAKER. The question now recurs upon the resolutions offered by the gentleman from Virginia, [Mr. CLEMENS.]

The resolutions were read, as follows:

JOINT RESOLUTION.

Whereas the Union is in danger; and owing to the unhappy divisions existing in Congress, it would be difficult, if not impossible, for that body to concur, in both its branches, by the requisite majority, so as to enable it either to adopt such measures of legislation, or to recommend to the States such amendments to the Constitution, as are deemed necessary and proper to avert that danger; and whereas, in so great an emergency, the opinion and judgment of the people ought to be heard, and would be the best and surest guide to their Representatives; Therefore,

Resolved by the Senate and House of Representatives of the United States of America in Congress assembled, That provision ought to be made by law, without delay, for taking the sense of the people, and submitting to their vote the following resolutions as the basis for the final and permanent settlement of those disputes that now disturb the peace of the country and threaten the existence of the Union.

JOINT RESOLUTIONS PROPOSING CERTAIN AMENDMENTS
TO THE CONSTITUTION OF THE UNITED STATES.

Whereas serious and alarming dissensions have arisen between the northern and southern States, concerning the rights and security of the rights of the slaveholding States, and especially their rights in the common territory of the United States; and whereas it is eminently desirable and proper that those dissensions, which now threaten the very existence of this Union, should be permanently quieted and settled by constitutional provisions which shall do equal justice to all sections, and thereby restore to the people that peace and good will which ought to prevail between all the citizens of the United States: Therefore,

Resolved by the Senate and House of Representatives of the United States of America in Congress assembled, (two thirds of both Houses concurring,) That the following articles be, and are hereby, proposed and submitted as amendments to the Constitution of the United States, which shall be valid to all intents and purposes as part of said Constitution, when ratified by conventions of three fourths of the several States.

Art. 1. In all the territory of the United States now held or hereafter acquired, situate north of the southern boundary of Kansas and the northern boundary of New Mexico, slavery or involuntary servitude, except as a punishment for crime, is prohibited, while such territory shall remain under territorial government. In all the territory south of said line now held or hereafter acquired, slavery of the African race is hereby recognized as existing, and shall not be interfered with by Congress; but shall be protected as property by all the departments of the territorial government during its continuance; and when any Territory, north or south of said line, within such boundaries as Congress may prescribe, shall contain the population requisite for a member of Congress, according to the then Federal ratio of representation of the people of the United States, it shall, if its form of government be republican, be admitted into the Union on an equal footing with the original States, with or without slavery, as the constitution of such new State may provide.

Art. 2. Congress shall have no power to abolish slavery in places under its exclusive jurisdiction, and situate within the limits of States that permit the holding of slaves.

Art. 3. Congress shall have no power to abolish slavery within the District of Columbia so long as it exists in the adjoining States of Virginia and Maryland, or either, nor without the consent of the inhabitants, nor without just compensation first made to such owners of slaves as do not consent to such abolishment. Nor shall Congress at any time prohibit officers of the Federal Government, or members of Congress, whose duties require them to be in said District, from bringing with them their slaves, and holding them as such, during the time their duties may require them to remain there, and afterwards taking them from the District.

Art. 4. Congress shall have no power to prohibit, or hinder the transportation of slaves from one State to another, or to a Territory in which slaves are by law permitted to be held, whether that transportation be by land, navigable rivers, or by the sea.

Art. 5. That, in addition to the provisions of the third paragraph of the second section of the fourth article of the Constitution of the United States, Congress shall have power to provide by law, and it shall be its duty so to provide, that the United States shall pay to the owner who shall apply for it, the full value of his fugitive slave, in all cases, when the marshal, or other officer, whose duty it was to arrest said fugitive, was prevented from so doing by violence or intimidation, or when, after arrest, said fugitive was rescued by force, and the owner thereby prevented and obstructed in the pursuit of his remedy for the recovery of his fugitive slave, under the said clause of the Constitution and the laws made in pursuance thereof. And in all cases, when the United States shall pay for such fugitive, they shall have the power to reimburse themselves by imposing and collecting a tax on the county or city in which said violence, intimidation, or rescue was committed, equal in amount to the sum paid by them, with the addition of interest and the costs of collection; and the said county or city, after it has paid said amount to the United States, may, for its indemnity, sue and recover from the wrong-doers or rescuers, by whom the owner was prevented from the recovery of his fugitive slave, in like manner as the owner himself might have sued and recovered.

Art. 6. No future amendment of the Constitution shall affect the five preceding articles, nor the third paragraph of the second section of the first article of the Constitution, nor the third paragraph of the second section of the fourth article of said Constitution; and no amendment shall be made to the Constitution which will authorize or give to Congress any power to abolish or interfere with slavery in any of the States by whose laws it is or may be allowed or permitted.

Art. 7. Sec. 1. The elective franchise and the right to hold office, whether Federal, State, territorial, or municipal, shall not be exercised by persons who are, in whole or in part, of the African race.

Sec. 2. The United States shall have the power to acquire, from time to time, districts of country in Africa and South America, for the colonization, at the expense of the Federal Treasury, of such free negroes and mulattoes as the several States may wish to have removed from their limits, and from the District of Columbia, and such other places as may be under the jurisdiction of Congress.

And whereas also, besides those causes of dissension embraced in the foregoing amendments proposed to the Constitution of the United States, there are others which come within the jurisdiction of Congress, and may be remedied by its legislative power; and whereas it is the desire of Congress, as far as its power will extend, to remove all just cause for the popular discontent and agitation which now disturb the peace of the country and threaten the stability of its institutions: Therefore,

---

[Note: The amendment Clemens proposed here is a close replica of John J. Crittenden's of December 18, including the four resolutions that Crittenden attached to the end of his amendment. Article 7 was added by Crittenden to his own amendment on January 3. The House defeated these resolutions by a vote of 113 to 80.]

Source: *Congressional Globe*, 36th Cong. 2nd Sess., 1260–261.

State Convention's Committee on Federal Relations
March 19, 1861

REPORT OF THE COMMITTEE ON FEDERAL RELATIONS

Mr. R. Y. CONRAD—The Committee on Federal Relations have had under further consideration the reports referred to them, and have directed me to make a report upon the subject of the proposed amendments to the

Constitution of the United States, which I will send to the Clerk's desk. These amendments, I may state, in general, are neither of the schemes precisely which have been submitted for the consideration of the Convention, to the extent of being properly termed either the one or the other. They are Virginia's propositions of amendments to the Constitution, combining, in view of the Committee, all the advantageous features of both of Virginia's schemes that have hitherto been before the public mind.

I move that the report be printed and referred to the Committee of the Whole.

The report was then read by the Secretary as follows:

The Committee on Federal Relations have, according to order, had under consideration sundry resolutions to them referred, and amendments proposed to the Federal Constitution, and beg leave to report the following amendments to be proposed to the Constitution of the United States, to be appended to their former report:

ARTICLE XIII

SECTION 1. In all the present territory of the United States, North of the parallel of thirty-six degrees and thirty minutes of North latitude, involuntary servitude, except in punishment of crime, is prohibited. In all the present territory South of that line, involuntary servitude, as it now exists, shall remain and shall not be changed; nor shall any law be passed by Congress or the Territorial Legislature to hinder or prevent the taking of persons held to service or labor from any of the States of this Union to said territory, nor to impair the rights arising from said relation; nor shall said rights be in any manner affected by any pre-existing law of Mexico;[3] but the same shall be subject to judicial cognizance in the federal courts, according to the remedies and the practice of the common law. When any territory North or South of said line, within such boundary as Congress may prescribe, shall contain a population equal to that required for a member of Congress, it shall, if its form of government be republican, be admitted into the Union on an equal footing with the original States, with or without involuntary servitude, as such Constitution of the State may provide. In all territory which may hereafter be acquired by the United States involuntary servitude is prohibited, except for crime, North of the latitude of 36 deg. and 30 min.; but shall not be prohibited by Congress or any Territorial Legislature South of said line.

SECTION 2. No territory shall be acquired by the United States, except by discovery and for naval and commercial stations, depots and transit routes, without the concurrence of a majority of all the Senators from States which allow involuntary servitude, and a majority of all the Senators of States which prohibit that relation; nor shall territory be acquired by treaty, unless the votes of a majority of the Senators from each class of States herein before mentioned be cast as a part of the two-thirds majority necessary to the ratification of such treaty.

SECTION 3. Neither the Constitution, nor any amendment thereof, shall be construed to give Congress power to legislate concerning involuntary servitude in any State or Territory wherein the same is acknowledged or may exist by the laws thereof, nor to interfere with or abolish the same in the District of Columbia without the consent of Maryland and Virginia, and without the consent of the owners, or making the owners who do not consent just compensation; nor the power to interfere with or prohibit representatives and others from bringing with them to the District of Columbia, retaining and taking away, persons so held to labor or service, nor the power to interfere with or abolish involuntary service in places under the exclusive jurisdiction of the United States within those States and Territories where the same is established or recognized; nor the power to prohibit the removal or transportation by land or water of persons held to labor, or involuntary service in any State or Territory of the United States to any other State or Territory thereof where it is established or recognized by law or usage; and the right during transportation, by sea or river, of touching at ports, shores and landings, and landing in case of need, shall exist, but not the right of sojourn or sale in any State or Territory, against the laws thereof. Nor shall Congress have power to authorize any higher rate of taxation on persons held to labor or service than on land.

The bringing into the District of Columbia persons held to labor or service for sale, or placing them in depots to be afterwards transferred to other places for sale as merchandise, is prohibited.[4]

SECTION 4. The third paragraph of the second section of the fourth article of the Constitution shall not be construed to prevent any of the States, by appropriate legislation, and through the action of their judicial and ministerial officers, from enforcing the delivery of fugitives from labor to the person to whom such service or labor is due.

SECTION 5. The importation of slaves, coolies or persons held to service or labor in the United States and the Territories, from places beyond the limits thereof, is hereby forever prohibited.

SECTION 6. Congress shall provide by law that the United States shall pay to the owner the full value of his fugitive slave from labor, in all cases where the marshal, or other officer, whose duty it was to arrest such fugitive, was prevented from so doing by violence or intimidation from mobs, or riotous assemblages, or by violence, or when, after arrest, such fugitive was rescued by like intimidation or violence, and the owner thereby deprived of the same.

SEC. 7. The elective franchise and the right to hold office, whether Federal or Territorial, shall not be exercised by persons who are of the African race.

SEC. 8. No one of these amendments nor the third paragraph of the second section of the first article of the Constitution, nor the third paragraph of the second section of the fourth article thereof, shall be amended or abolished without the consent of all the States.

The report was laid on the table and ordered to be printed.

Source: George H. Reese, ed., *Proceedings of the Virginia State Convention of 1861: February 13–May 1*. 4 vols. (Richmond: Virginia State Library, 1965), 2:34–37.

Delegate Robert H. Turner (Warren County)
March 26, 1861

The preamble I desire, shall be as follows:

"Seven States having withdrawn from the Federal Union and formed a new and distinct Government, it has become necessary for Virginia, if she remains in the present Federal Union, to obtain guarantees by way of amendments to the Constitution of the United States, upon the following points."

The fact of the withdrawal, I desire to be stated as the cause of the necessity for the guarantees. That is all I wish to be stated in the preamble; that the position of Virginia, in the Northern Confederacy or the Union as it now exists, compels her to demand guarantees for her future safety. In arriving at those guarantees, I wish that they shall be such that she can remain in this Union alone; that if every other sister slave State shall withdraw, she may retain self-protecting power. I propose to show the manner in which that self-protecting power may be secured. The first point I propose is:

"1st. A recognition, that by virtue of the Constitution, African slavery does exist in all the territory of the United States, and must be protected by the Federal Government."

That by virtue of the Constitution of the United States, African slavery, sir, not "involuntary servitude," not "persons held to labor," or anything else, but that "African slavery does exist in all the territory of the United States, and must be protected by the Federal Government."

The second proposition is:

2d. Upon all questions relating to the acquisition of territory a concurrent majority of the Senators in Congress from the slaveholding and non-slaveholding States shall be required.

Sir, I am opposed to compromising away our rights. We may compromise the question of the division of the territory—the mere division of the land—but a right within the Territory is an entirely different thing. I am opposed to compromising our rights as citizens of a confederacy or citizens of a State. But, sir, I am in favor of a compromise in regard to the settlement of the Territory itself, as far as the possession of the Territory is concerned.

The third section I propose is as follows:

3d. With a view to settle the vexed question of the territories it is agreed that in all the territory of the United States, now held or hereafter acquired, situate North of 36 degrees 30 minutes north latitude, slavery is prohibited, and in all the territory of the United States now held or hereafter acquired South of said line, African slavery is recognized as existing, and shall receive its necessary protection as property from the various departments of the Government.

But sir, there is one other proposition which I deem of more importance to Virginia if she remains in this Union—a proposition which I believe, if any guarantee can bring back the seceded States, will produce that result. It was not the mere question of slavery that has carried off the seceded States of the South. It was a question of taxation, a question of tariff. They knew well what they were doing. They knew, the very best means to prosecute this irrepressible conflict against slavery was by means of taxation, to make that species of property valueless; and they knew that the Black Republican party would inaugurate a system of taxation which would deprive them of the benefit of that property. And they were not mistaken, for, as soon as that party has come into power, we find them inaugurating a tariff imposing the most oppressive taxation that was ever inflicted on any people.[5] In order to prevent that oppression, I offer this as the fourth proposition:

4th. On all questions relating to laying taxes, duties, imposts and excises, or any other means necessary to raise revenue for the support of the General Government, a concurrent vote of a majority of the Senators in Congress, from the slaveholding and non-slaveholding States, shall be required.

I think the gentleman from Montgomery, [Mr. {William Ballard} PRESTON], will find a tangible guarantee in this: that upon all questions relating to laying duties, imposts and excises, or any other means necessary to raise revenue, for the support of the General Government, a concurrent vote of a majority of the Senators in Congress from the slaveholding and non-slaveholding States, shall be required, and if that is done Virginia may remain satisfied that she cannot be imposed upon.

The other points are as follows:

5th. The right of transit by the citizens of the several States with their property, slaves included, through the States and Territories.

6th. The rendition of fugitive slaves, and in case of their loss by violence or intimidation, remuneration by the General Government to the owner; and Congress shall provide for its reimbursement by laying and collecting a tax upon the State, city, or county in which said loss occurred.

7th. That Congress shall not abolish or interfere with slavery, as it now exists, in the District of Columbia; nor shall it abolish or interfere with slavery in any of the States, by whose laws it is or may be allowed or permitted.

8th. The withholding from persons who are in whole or in part of the African race, the elective franchise and the right to hold office whether Federal, State, Territorial or Municipal.

9th. Congress shall have no power to abolish slavery in places under the exclusive jurisdiction of the Federal Government, and situate within the limits of States that permit the holding of slaves.

10th. That the importation of slaves from foreign countries into the United States shall be forever prohibited.[6]

11th. That Congress shall have no power to interfere with the slave trade between the States.

12th. That the foregoing amendments shall not be subject to repeal or modification except with the consent of all the States of the Union.

Source: George H. Reese, ed., *Proceedings of the Virginia State Convention of 1861: February 13–May 1.* 4 vols. (Richmond: Virginia State Library, 1965), 2:389–91.

Delegate Henry Alexander Wise (Democrat)
March 29, 1861

The evening session began with a short discussion on the obstacles in the way of agreement on resolutions that had been proposed. Former governor Wise quickly changed the subject.

Mr. WISE—I wish to enquire whether a Committee of the Whole can order any printing to be done.

The PRESIDENT—I presume not.

Mr. WISE—My impression was that they could not, and desiring to offer a series of amendments for the second part of the report of the Committee of Twenty-one, and to have these amendments, consisting of some nine or ten sections, in lieu of their eight or nine sections, I ask that the House will receive the amendments, order them to be printed for their information, and have them referred to the Committee of the Whole with the report, to be offered by me at the proper time. I ask this as a courtesy from the House for their own benefit as well as mine, that they may have an opportunity of seeing the competing propositions before they come before the Committee for consideration. I move, sir, that these amendments be received by the House, referred to the Committee of the Whole, and ordered to be printed.

The motion was agreed to.

Amendments were proposed by Mr. WISE, to propositions of the second part of the report of the Committee of Twenty-one on Federal Relations, so as to make the same read as follows:

AMENDMENT 1st—Amend by striking out the first and second sections of the report, and inserting:

SECTION 1. In all the present territory of the United States, involuntary servitude, as it now exists, shall remain and shall not be changed; nor shall any law be passed by Congress or the territorial legislatures to hinder or prevent the taking of persons held to service or labor, from any of the States of this Union to said territory; nor to impair the rights arising from said relation; nor shall said rights be in any manner affected by any pre-existing law of Mexico in the part acquired from her; but the same shall be protected as other rights, and be subject to judicial cognizance in the Federal Courts, according to the existing laws, and to the remedies and practice of the common law, so far as they may be consistent with each other. And when any territory, within such boundary as Congress may prescribe, shall contain a population equal to that required for a member of Congress, it shall, if its form of government be republican, be admitted into the Union on an equal footing with the original States, with or without involuntary servitude, as such Constitution of the State may provide. In all territory which may hereafter be acquired by the United States, involuntary servitude is prohibited, except for crime, north of thirty-six degrees thirty minutes; but shall not be prohibited by Congress or any territorial legislature south of that line.

AMENDMENT 2.—Amend by striking out the 3rd section of the report and inserting:

SECTION 2. Neither the Constitution, nor any amendment thereof, shall be construed to give Congress power to abolish involuntary servitude in any territory; nor in the District of Columbia; nor in the sites of forts, magazines, arsenals or other places ceded by the States to the Federal Government, within the limits of those States where involuntary servitude is established or recognized; nor within any forts, magazines, arsenals, or other places reserved within the limits of any territory for the uses of the Government of the United States; but Congress shall pass all laws necessary and proper to protect the property in persons held to service or labor, in said territory, District, or other places ceded or reserved to the United States. Nor shall any law be passed by Congress to hinder or prevent the taking of persons held to service or labor to or from the District of Columbia, or to hinder or prevent the retaining of the same within the limits thereof. Nor shall Congress have the power to prohibit the removal or transportation, by land or water, of persons held to service or labor in any State or Territory of the United States to any other State or Territory thereof, where it is established or recognized by law or usage; and the owner of property in persons held to service or labor, or his agent, shall have the right of transit through any State or Territory of the United States with such property and persons, to and from any State or territory recognizing said property by law or usage, and the right during transportation, by sea or river, of touching at ports, shores and landings, and of landing and sojourning with said property, in cases of need, temporarily, any law of any State or Territory to the contrary notwithstanding. And Congress shall not have the power to lay on persons held to service or labor in any of the States or territories of the United States any other tax than a capitation tax, to be apportioned as capitation or other direct taxes are directed to be apportioned throughout the United States according to the fourth clause of section nine of article first of the Constitution of the United States.

AMENDMENT 3.—Amend by inserting:

SECTION 3. In all cases where the property in persons held to service or labor in any State or Territory of the United States, or in the District of Columbia, has been or hereafter may be taken for public use, as in cases of impressment in war or otherwise, the owner thereof shall be justly compensated as in cases of other property so taken; and in all cases involving questions of property in said persons, the rights of property in them shall be recognized and protected by the United States and their authorities as the rights of other property are recognised and protected.

AMENDMENT 4.—Amend section 4th of the report, by adding, after the word "due," the words "and it shall be the duty," *et seq.*—so that the 4th section, as amended, shall read:

SECTION 4. The third paragraph of the second section of the fourth article of the Constitution shall not be construed to prevent any of the States, by appropriate legislation, and through the action of their judicial and ministerial officers, from enforcing the delivery of fugitives from labor to the person to whom such service or labor is due.

And it shall be the duty of all the States, to pass all laws necessary and proper to aid, by their authorities, judicial and ministerial, in the execution of the laws passed by Congress for the delivery of fugitives from service or labor to the person to whom such service or labor is due. And in case the owner, or his agent, of the person held to service or labor, shall be unlawfully deprived of his property in such person by force or violence, by mobs or riotous assemblages, or by secret associations or conspiracies, in the limits of any State, such States shall make just compensation therefor, and it shall be the duty of Congress to provide by law for the enforcement of such compensation.

AMENDMENT 5. Amend the 5th section of the report, by adding, after the word "prohibited," the words "Provided that" *et seq.*—so that the 5th section, as amended, shall read:

SECTION 5. The importation of slaves, coolies or persons held to service or labor, into the United States, and the territories from places beyond the limits thereof is hereby forever prohibited. Provided, that nothing herein contained shall be deemed to apply to the Southern States which have declared, or may hereafter declare, their separation from the Confederacy, in case their separate independence shall be acknowledged and continued.

AMENDMENT 6. Amend by striking out the 6th section of the report.

AMENDMENT 7. Amend by changing section 7th of the report to section 6th; and by adding, after the word "race," the words "and no person" *et seq.*—so that the section, as amended, shall read:

SECTION 6. The elective franchise and the right to hold office, whether federal or territorial, shall not be exercised by persons who are of the African race.

And no person of the African race shall be deemed and held entitled, under the Constitution of the United States, to the privileges and immunities of citizens in the several States. And the several States are prohibited from passing any laws establishing equality of the African with the white race within their limits.

AMENDMENT 8th. Amend by inserting:

SECTION 7. The second clause of the second section of the second article of the Constitution of the United States shall be so amended as to take from the President of the United States the power of nominating and appointing the judges of the Supreme and other Federal Courts of the United States, and their nomination and appointment shall be vested in the Senate of the

United States alone; and three-fourths of the whole number of Senators shall be required to confirm the appointments.

AMENDMENT 9th. Amend by inserting:

SECTION 8. It shall be the duty of the several States, and of the Congress of the United States, within their respective jurisdictions, to pass all laws necessary and proper, to protect and preserve the domestic tranquility of the people of the several States, by suppressing all attempts of individual persons, or of assemblages, or associations to excite any portion of the people of the States to acts which will cause, or tend to cause, animosity or hostility between the various sections, or any invasions of any of the States or territories of the United States, or which will introduce or invite foreign influence to divide the Union, or which may tend to destroy the same.

AMENDMENT 10. Amend by changing section 8th of the report to section 9th, viz:

SECTION 9. No one of these amendments, nor the third paragraph of the second section of the first article of the Constitution, nor the third paragraph of the second section of the fourth article thereof, shall be amended or abolished without the consent of all the States.

Source: George H. Reese, ed., *Proceedings of the Virginia State Convention of 1861: February 13–May 1.* 4 vols. (Richmond: Virginia State Library, 1965), 2:575–79.

Delegate William Leftwich Goggin (Unionist)
April 4, 1861

Mr. GOGGIN's amendment was then read, as follows:

AN ORDINANCE OF THE STATE OF VIRGINIA

"Whereas, the State of Virginia has made every honorable effort to restore the friendly relations which should exist between the General Government and the several States of the Union—upon terms perfectly just to all, but deeming it unnecessary to refer to the causes of complaint which have existed for a series of years, still more aggravated as those causes now are by the declared purposes of a mere sectional majority—and as all the efforts so made have proved unavailing—without reciting the differences of opinion which exist in regard to the powers of the State Government, or those of the Government of the United States, as derived from the reserved rights of the one, the constitutional authority of the other, or the inherent rights of the people, constituting a Government which seeks to protect the persons and property of those who compose and who have ordained and established it, against the abuses of such Government itself, or which arise from its connection with the Government of other States, or that of an association of States, the people of Virginia, in Convention assembled, deem it proper now to declare that the time has arrived when it becomes them to assume, as they do, their position as the people of a *sovereign independent State.*

1. Be it, therefore, ordained by the people of Virginia, and they do hereby declare, That the said State is no longer one of the Union of States known as the United States of America, and that the people of the said State owe no allegiance or duty to any Government whatever.

{Goggin's second, third, and fourth points elaborated on the separation of Virginia from the United States; called a convention of the border slave states to meet in late May 1861; and recognized the establishment of the Confederate States of America.}

---

5. Be it further declared, That the people of Virginia have ever cherished an ardent attachment for the Union and the Constitution of the United States while it was the bond of peace and fraternity; and that it can now only be restored upon the original basis by an amendment of the Constitution through the primary agency of the non-slaveholding States themselves proposing suitable and sure guarantees, and by a full and unconditional, plain and positive recognition of the rights of property in slaves, as held under the laws of any of the States; so as also to obtain satisfactory assurances and guarantees, for the future, as to slavery in the District of Columbia; as to the powers of the Federal Government over African slavery, and the employment of slave labor in the forts, arsenals, dock yards, and all places ceded by the States for Federal uses; as to protection against excessive direct taxes on slaves; as to the rendition of fugitive slaves; as to the transit with slaves through any of the States by land or water, and of the right of transportation on the high seas of slaves from one State to another State or Territory; as to the protection of slave property in the common territories of the United

States; as to the better security of the independence of the judiciary, and for protection against unjust taxation in the form of excessive imposts laid upon foreign importations.

{Goggin's sixth, seventh, and eighth points warned against aggressive behavior toward Virginia either by the United States of America or the Confederate States of America, provided for the election of commissioners to the called convention, and suspended the declaration of separation in section 2 until the state was prepared to enforce its desired independence. Elected as a Unionist, Goggin advocated for secession following Lincoln's inaugural address. Delegate Goggin offered his amendment as a substitute to Lewis E. Harvie's secession ordinance. Upon reflection, Goggin withdrew his amendment so that the convention could vote on Harvie's proposal which the delegates defeated by a vote of 88 to 45.}

Source: George H. Reese, ed., *Proceedings of the Virginia State Convention of 1861: February 13–May 1.* 4 vols. (Richmond: Virginia State Library, 1965), 3:155–58.

Amendments as Approved by Virginia's State Convention
April 13, 1861

AMENDMENTS TO THE CONSTITUTION

"ART. XIII—Section 1. In all the present territory of the United States, north of the parallel of thirty-six degrees and thirty minutes of North latitude, involuntary servitude, except in punishment of crime, is prohibited. In all the present territory south of that line, involuntary servitude, as it existed on the first day of March, 1861, shall remain, and shall not be changed; nor shall any law be passed by Congress or the Territorial Legislature to hinder or prevent the taking of persons held to service or labor from any of the States of this Union to said territory, nor to impair the rights arising from said relation; nor shall said rights be in any manner affected by any pre-existing law of Mexico; but the same shall be subject to judicial cognizance in the Federal courts, according to the remedies and the practice of the common law. When any territory north or south of said line, within such boundary as Congress may prescribe, shall contain a population equal to that required for a member of Congress, it shall, if its form of government be republican, be admitted into the Union on an equal footing with the original States, with or without involuntary servitude, as such Constitution of the State may provide. In all territory which may hereafter be acquired by the United States involuntary servitude is prohibited, except for crime, north of the latitude of thirty-six degrees and thirty minutes; but shall not be prohibited by Congress, or any Territorial Legislature south of said line. {Approved April 13, 1861: vol. III, 659–92.}

The second section was reported as follows:

"Section 2. No territory shall be acquired by the United States, except by discovery and for naval and commercial stations, depots and transit routes, without the concurrence of a majority of all the Senators from States which allow involuntary servitude, and a majority of all the Senators of States which prohibit that relation; nor shall territory be acquired by treaty, unless the votes of a majority of the Senators from each class of States hereinbefore mentioned be cast as a part of the two-thirds majority necessary to the ratification of such treaty." {Approved April 13, 1861: vol. III, 692–710.}

The third section was reported as follows:

"Section 3. Neither the Constitution, nor any amendment thereof, shall be construed to give Congress power to legislate concerning involuntary servitude in any State or Territory wherein the same is acknowledged or may exist by the laws thereof, nor to interfere with or abolish the same in the District of Columbia without the consent of Maryland and Virginia, and without the consent of the owners, or making the owners who do not consent just compensation; nor the power to interfere with or prohibit representatives and others from bringing with them to the District of Columbia, retaining and taking away, persons so held to labor or service, nor the power to interfere with or abolish involuntary service in places under the exclusive jurisdiction of the United States within those States and Territories where the same is established or recognized; nor the power to prohibit the removal or transportation by land or water, of persons held to labor, or involuntary service in any State or Territory of the United States to any other State or Territory thereof, where it is established or recognized by law or usage; and the right during transportation, by sea or river, of touching at ports, shores and landings, and landing in case of need shall exist, but not the right of sojourn or sale in any State or territory against the laws thereof. Nor shall Congress have power to authorize any higher rate of taxation on persons held to labor or service than on land.

"The bringing into the District of Columbia persons held to labor or service for sale, or placing them in depots to be afterwards transferred to other places for sale as merchandise, is prohibited. {Approved April 13, 1861: vol. III, 710–11.}

Section 4. In all cases where property in persons held to service or labor in any State or Territory of the States or in the District of Columbia has been or hereafter may be taken for public use as in the case of impressment in war or otherwise, the owner thereof shall be justly compensated as in the case of other property taken; and in all cases involving the question of property in said persons, the rights of property in them shall be recognized and protected by the United States and other authorities, as rights to any other property are recognized and protected. {Approved April 13, 1861: vol. III, 711–13.}

Section 5. The third paragraph of the second section of the fourth article of the Constitution shall not be construed to prevent any of the States, by appropriate legislation, and through the action of their judicial and ministerial officers, from enforcing the delivery of fugitives from labor to the person to whom such service or labor is due. {Approved April 13, 1861: vol. 3, 713–14.}

Section 6. The importation of slaves, coolies or persons held to service or labor, in the United States, and the territories, from places beyond the limits thereof, is hereby forever prohibited. Provided that nothing herein contained shall be deemed to apply to the Southern States which have declared, or may hereafter declare their separation from this Confederacy, in case their separate independence shall be acknowledged and continued.

{The convention was debating this section when it received word of the fall of Ft. Sumter; vol. 3, 714–30.}

Source: George H. Reese, ed. *Proceedings of the Virginia State Convention of 1861: February 13–May 1.* 4 vols. (Richmond: Virginia State Library, 1965), 3:659–730.

7

Secession
April–May, 1861

Ordinance of Secession
April 17, 1861

While the convention worked to craft a constitutional compromise for most of its session, once word of the bombardment of Fort Sumter reached Richmond, the delegates immediately stopped working to avoid secession. Lincoln's call for 75,000 troops to suppress the rebellion on April 15 pushed Virginia over the edge prompting the convention to pass an ordinance of secession two days later. While the ordinance specifically made the vote conditional upon a popular referendum scheduled for May 23, the state, now dominated by secessionists, rushed to join the Confederacy. The day after the secession vote, Virginia militiamen from Charles Town, directed by former governor Wise, captured the United States Arsenal in Harpers Ferry. On April 25, the convention approved a military alliance with Montgomery and adopted the Provisional Constitution of the Confederate States of America, neither action requiring the approval of Virginia's electorate. Two days later, the convention invited Jefferson Davis "to make the city of Richmond or some other place in Virginia, the seat of government of the Confederacy." Welcoming these measures, the Confederate Congress officially admitted the Old Dominion into the Confederacy on May 7, 1861, two weeks before the scheduled referendum to approve the ordinance of secession.[1] Once the secession vote became a reality, citizens in the northwestern section of the state began assembling with the intent of separating from Virginia. Various conventions starting with gatherings in Wheeling in May and June of 1861, led to the creation of the "Restored Government of Virginia" and the eventual creation of the state of West Virginia in 1863.[2]

William Ballard Preston representing Montgomery County introduced the ordinance of secession on April 14 with the following comments.

Mr. Wm. B. Preston, of Montgomery—I arise, with feelings of the deepest pain, to offer something to the House that is tangible, and to express my opinion in this exigency. I hold in my hand what I am compelled to offer, and what, in a measure, circumstances have accidentally made me the origin of. It is an ORDINANCE OF SECESSION. I offer it to the House, and I trust that God shall extend his mercy to me on this occasion. He is my witness that I am devoting every service of my heart to the Commonwealth of Virginia. That Ordinance has not been offered under the influence of circumstances or telegraphic information. It is offered on the basis of the report we brought here from Washington,[3] and the proclamation of the President. I cannot, I will not recede now from the grounds I have taken. I feel that I would be unworthy of the position I occupy here, were I to take one step backwards. Those who choose this lead may follow. Those who don't choose have a right to take whatever course their judgments may dictate. I will not upbraid them if they choose to take a position different from that which I have marked out for myself. I shall go through all these struggles with a consciousness that I have done my duty to my country, and I believe I have done it to God, and I feel that in this contest God himself will be with us. I now submit the Ordinance:

———◆———

AN ORDINANCE *to repeal the ratification of the Constitution of the United States of America, by the State of Virginia, and to resume all the rights and powers granted under said Constitution.*

The people of Virginia, in their ratification of the Constitution of the United States of America, adopted by them in Convention, on the twenty-fifth day of June, in the year of our Lord one thousand seven hundred and eighty-eight, having declared that the powers granted under the said Constitution were derived from the people of the United States, and might be resumed whensoever the same should be perverted to their injury and oppression, and the Federal Government having perverted said powers, not only to the injury of the people of Virginia, but to the oppression of the Southern slaveholding States,

Now, therefore, we, the people of Virginia, do declare and ordain, That the ordinance adopted by the people of this State in Convention, on the twenty-fifth day of June, in the year of our Lord one thousand seven hundred and eighty-eight, whereby the Constitution of the United States of America was ratified; and all acts of the General Assembly of this State ratifying or adopting amendments to said Constitution, are hereby repealed and abrogated; that the union between the State of Virginia and the other States under the Constitution aforesaid, is hereby dissolved, and that the State of Virginia is in the full possession and exercise of all the rights of sovereignty, which belong and appertain to a free and independent State.

And they do further declare, That said Constitution of the United States of America, is no longer binding on any of the citizens of that State.

This ordinance shall take effect and be an act of this day, when ratified by a majority of the votes of the people of this State, cast at a poll to be taken thereon, on the fourth Thursday in May next, in pursuance of a schedule hereafter to be enacted.

Done in Convention in the city of Richmond, on the seventeenth day of April, in the year of our Lord one thousand eight hundred and sixty-one, and in the eighty-fifth year of the Commonwealth of Virginia.

[Note: The convention approved the ordinance of secession on April 17, 1861, by a vote of 88 to 55; White male voters of the state ratified the ordinance on May 23, 1861, by 86 percent to 14 percent.]

Source: George H. Reese, ed., *Proceedings of the Virginia State Convention of 1861: February 13–May 1.* 4 vols. (Richmond: Virginia State Library, 1965), 4:24–25, 144.

John Brown Baldwin Dissents
April 25, 1861

John B. Baldwin (1820–1873) was born in Augusta County, studied at
the University of Virginia from 1836 to 1839, and was admitted to the
bar in 1842. While opposing the war, he served briefly in the Confederate Army and then became a member of the Confederate House of
Representatives from 1861 to 1865. Following the war he was elected
to the Virginia House of Delegates (1865–1867) where he presided as
speaker.

A staunch Unionist, Baldwin voted against secession on April 17 and
in this speech argued against the military alliance with the Confederacy without confirmation from the public that they agreed with the
conference's decision to secede. Believing the convention delegates had
no authority to "supercede the Executive functions of the Governor
of this State," and that Virginia was "surrendering too much in this
alliance," Baldwin felt compelled to vote against the proposed affiliation. Upon the completion of his comments, the convention voted
upon the military alignment with the Confederacy which passed 80 to
16. Baldwin was joined by John Janney, the president of the convention,
and fourteen other delegates in expressing their opposition to joining
the Confederacy.

Mr. BALDWIN, of Augusta—It seems to me, sir, that the subjects before
this Convention are of too vast importance to be dealt with in the very brief
and hasty way that they are dealt with here. I don't propose to go into any
discussion on the question of the power of this Convention to make an arrangement of this sort. I think I entered into a stipulation some days back in
this Convention not to debate in this body any more questions as to its powers. I deem it to be but just to myself to say, that I have no idea at all that this
Convention has any power to make such an agreement as proposed by this
paper. I understand that although we have revolutionized the government
of the United States, and separated ourselves from that government and the

other states composing it, that we have not as yet undertaken to revolution-ize the State government. But I take it that every member of this body will recognize the fact that we are assembled here under the Constitution of the State, subject to the Constitution of the State in all our actions—having the power to change the Constitution, it is true, when the changes we make are ratified by the people of the State—but having no other power to change the Constitution of Virginia. I have never understood that this Convention had, as yet, come to revolutionize the State Government. It is true that we have, in a number of instances, assumed, under the pressure of the circum-stances by which we have been surrounded, to exercise power which could not be justified by a fair construction of the Constitution of the State, and which could only be excused by the press of the emergency; but we never have undertaken yet to go as far as is undertaken by this agreement. I take it, sir, that the authority of this Convention is plainly limited, so that we shall not change the relations between this State and the General Government of the United States without the assent of the people of the State; and I take it that we have no right any more to enter into new governmental connections with another Government without a like consent of the people; and if we had the power, so far as I am concerned, I would not be willing to exercise it, because it so plainly affects the rights of the people without consulting them at the polls.

But, sir, I don't propose to discuss that question at all. I merely wish to state my own opinion and belief that this Convention has no power what-ever to do any one of a number of things that are proposed in this paper.

In the first place, we have no authority, as was stated by the gentleman from Frederick {Robert Y. Conrad}, to supersede the Executive functions of the Governor of this State. In the next place, we have no authority whatever to undertake to place our people under the military control of any foreign potentate whatever, even with the Governor's consent. The Governor him-self and all the authorities of the State have no right to demand of our people that they shall give supreme obedience to another government. It is true that under the treaty making power as an independent sovereignty, we have a right to contribute our forces to a common, offensive and defensive alliance; but our government has not a right to depart with the power of governing our own people. It is not merely a power and a right, but government is a duty as well, and our government has no right to depart from the duty of governing every citizen of the Commonwealth, according to the Constitution and laws of Virginia; and we assume a fearful responsibility when we undertake to say that all the military strength of this Commonwealth, by which we mean that the life, the blood, the muscle, the spirit, the energy of every man in the Commonwealth is to be transferred and made subject to the supreme control of a foreign power. We undertake a fearful responsibility; and, as it seems to me, we undertake to let go a high duty when we abandon the government of the people of this State and the protection of their rights.

So far as I am concerned, I am not willing to do that. I am perfectly willing, and think it desirable on every ground whatever, that as a sovereign, independent State, in peril of a great conflict just at hand, we should have the alliance of other sovereign States in a like situation with ourselves, of like interests and like sympathies. But, sir, the world's history is full to overflowing of instances of alliances between sovereign States for offensive and defensive warfare, without either one undertaking to place its entire military force and all its citizens under the supreme control of the government of the other. I can see no reason, sir, assigned why, in the exercise of the treaty-making power, the State of Virginia on the one part and the Confederate States upon the other, may not agree to the terms upon which, as equals, as co-equal sovereignties, they shall wage a common war for a common cause. I have never heard of an instance—I venture to say there is no instance in the history of the world—where, between equal States, the power of governing the people of the one is to be surrendered over to the control of the other. How was it with England and France in the Crimean war?[4] They co-operated together, and I suppose that the terms of that co-operation were agreed upon between them, and carried out according to the terms of the convention. Who ever heard that the people of England agreed that the Empire of France should have the supreme control and direction, according to the laws of France, of the whole military of England? Or *vice versa*, that the people of France agreed that England should have the supreme control and direction, according to the laws of England, of the whole military power of France?

Sir, it seems to me that this is a matter unnecessary, wholly unnecessary.

It may be said—and I have no doubt that that is the chief consideration in this matter—that the Confederate States undertake to bear the whole burden of this conflict. That certainly is a very important affair. But if they bear the expenses of the war, and we become part of the Confederate States, we will have to bear, after all, a very large portion of the expenses. But it seems to me that there is no necessity at all for this course. A mere pecuniary and financial necessity cannot justify this Convention, cannot justify this government in parting with a responsibility which God Almighty has placed under these circumstances, in their hands—the responsibility of guiding and governing the destinies of the people of this Commonwealth. You may talk about resisting civil power, but, in flagrant war, he who has the unrestrained military control of the land and naval forces—not only of those called into the field, but the power to call as many more as they want—wields a power which it is vain to attempt resisting.

I want to know from the committee whether Virginia has any more discretion in this matter.

Mr. HOLCOMBE[5]—That provision to which the gentleman refers, making the President of the Confederate States the Commander-in-Chief of the military and the naval forces, is a provision that will last only for four or five days. It will last only until we go into the Provisional Government, or until our own application to go into that Government is granted, and it confers upon the President of the Confederate States only the direction of the military power of the Commonwealth, and no authority at all except through our own Governor and officers, and in accordance with our own laws.

Mr. BALDWIN—I understand the matter. I do not understand it to be in contemplation that we shall go immediately into the Provisional Government.

Mr. HOLCOMBE—The ordinance before the Convention is merely upon this stipulation. The treaty stipulation and the ordinance adopting the Constitution of the Provisional Government have been brought in together, and, as it seems to me, with due deference to the Chair, should have been voted upon together in the Convention. All the stipulations are merely, intended to cover the brief interval of time that will elapse between the ratification of the treaty, and the action of the Provisional Government of the

Confederate States. The Congress of that Confederacy meets on Monday, and we propose to follow this proposition with a proposition to send Commissioners to that Congress.

Mr. BALDWIN — I don't so read it. It reads, "Until the union of said Commonwealth with said Confederacy shall be perfected, and said Commonwealth shall become a member of said Confederacy according to the Constitution of both powers, the whole military force and military operations, offensive and defensive of said Commonwealth in the impending conflict with the United States, shall be under the chief control and direction of the President of said Confederate States, upon the same principles, basis and footing as if said Commonwealth were now, and during the interval, a member of said Confederacy."

Do I understand that it is proposed to take this Government into the control of the Confederate States in anticipation of the vote at the polls in May?

Mr. HOLCOMBE — It says that if the ordinance is rejected, this whole subject goes to the ground.

Mr. BALDWIN — I understand it is proposed to take us into the Confederate States and place us under the power of the Confederate States in advance of the decision of the question to be submitted to the people at the polls. So far as I am concerned, I do not believe that we have any such power under the Heavens — none whatever.

But, sir, there are some other matters that I do not understand in regard to this Convention. I have not been able to see at all where is the necessity which impels us to become members of the Confederacy prior to the action of our people.

I have been under the impression, and am now, that the result has been brought about which cannot be avoided; that sooner or later the entire South must be united under a common government. All that I desire now in regard to this matter is that Virginia shall go into that government under circumstances that give her the best possible advantage in the terms on which she goes in. And, sir, as a part of the advantages which she is to derive by going into that government, I take it that the matter which we have been contemplating ever since the passage of the ordinance of secession, was to have a conference with our sister border slave States in regard to our common interests; and, so far as I am concerned, whilst I recognize the fact that we are in a position that compels us to make an alliance offensive and defensive in behalf of a common cause, yet I am unwilling to let go the power of negotiation; the right of acting as equal in any assemblage of the States South, and of taking a position of just equality in all forms of negotiation. I object to that, mainly as a matter of policy. I say nothing of the matter of power that I have suggested. It seems to me that this is an unnecessary exercise of power which does not belong to us, and an inexpedient exercise of it besides. This is one thing we ought to retain, subject to our own action.

The future, as yet, is not sufficiently developed to enable us to see what is the true policy of the war in which we are engaged. I have a very recent conviction in regard to the policy of that war; but I am not military man enough to say how far it may be right or wrong. I do not wish to be venturing opinions upon subjects with which I am not acquainted. But Virginia, it seems to me, ought to have the determination of this question. I think that Virginia ought not now nor at any time to give up, for even a single day, any attribute of a sovereign State, dealing with a sovereignty, that she ought not go into the Confederate States and give up her voice as a sovereign State dealing with a sovereign nation; that she ought not to give up to four or five other States a question which involves the integrity of her soil and the safety of all her people. It seems to me that we are surrendering too much in this alliance. As to the assistance that we are to expect from these Confederate States, I look to their assistance with pleasure and satisfaction always.

I am perfectly willing to reciprocate that assistance to the full extent of our power. I have no wish to do anything—God forbid I would do anything—to impair the efficiency of the military associations of these different governments. But I don't wish Virginia to be so far overcome by the anticipations of the conflict as to lose all prudential considerations in regard to her future destiny. I want her to look this question in the face calmly. She has, I am satisfied, the strength of will to defend her soil and to repel any invasion that may be attempted upon her. She is not in so helpless a situation as to give up everything like a prudential regard for her own safety. I prefer that a matter of this importance should be gone on with more cautiously, leaving Virginia, meanwhile, to defend the rights of her citizens.

I have not seen this convention, except by a mere casual reading of it. I am not prepared to say that there may not be other objections which have not come under my notice; but because we have no power to overthrow the Constitution of the State, because our rights, as a class, are not recognized in this Convention, and because we refuse to Virginia her equal and full voice in the future management of the war, I shall be compelled to vote against the ratification of this Convention; and, while I do so, I am very anxious to unite in every measure and sustain every policy which shall, in my judgment, best subserve the interests of the State in this emergency.

So far as the capacity of the President of the Confederate States is concerned, I know he has a very high reputation; but as regards his capacity for a war of this character, that is to be tried. I am satisfied to see him tried, if compatible with the sovereignty, the independence and the safety of Virginia.[6]

Source: George H. Reese, ed., *Proceedings of the Virginia State Convention of 1861: February 13–May 1.* 4 vols. (Richmond: Virginia State Library, 1965), 4:487–93.

Alliance with the Confederate States of America
April 25, 1861

The President — The first business now in order, is the report of the committee appointed to wait on the Commissioner from the Confederate States.

Mr. SHEFFEY[7] — The pending question was upon the ordinance which I offered last evening, and which I shall now read again, for the information of the House.

"AN ORDINANCE *ratifying and confirming the Convention entered into between the Commissioner of the Confederate States and the Commissioners of the State of Virginia.*"

"Be it ordained, That the convention entered into on the twenty-fourth of April, eighteen hundred sixty-one, between Alexander H. Stephens, Commissioner of the Confederate States, and John Tyler, Wm. Ballard Preston, S. McD. Moore, James P. Holcombe, James C. Bruce and Lewis E. Harvie, Commissioners of Virginia, for a temporary union of Virginia with said Confederate States, under the provisional government, adopted by the said Confederate States, be, and the same is hereby ratified and confirmed on the terms agreed upon by said Commissioners."

Mr. {George} BAYLOR, of Augusta—I desire again to have the convention reported.

The Secretary again read the report of the committee, which is as follows:

The Commonwealth of Virginia, looking to a speedy union of said Commonwealth and the other slave States with the Confederate States of America, according to the provisions of the Constitution for the Provisional Government of said States, enters into the following temporary convention and agreement with said States for the purpose of meeting pressing exigencies affecting the common rights, interests and safety of said Commonwealth and said Confederacy:

1st. Until the Union of said Commonwealth with said Confederacy shall be perfected, the said Commonwealth shall become a member of said Confederacy according to the Constitutions of both powers, the whole military force and military operations, offensive and defensive, of said Commonwealth, in the impending conflict with the United States, shall be under the chief control and direction of the President of said Confederate States, upon the same principles, basis and footing as if said Commonwealth were now, and during the interval, a member of said Confederacy.

2d. The Commonwealth of Virginia will, after the consummation of the union contemplated in this Convention, and her adoption of the Constitution for a permanent government of said Confederate States, and she shall become a member of said Confederacy, under said permanent Constitution, if the same occur, turn over to said Confederate States all the public property, naval stores and munitions of war, etc., she may then be in possession of, acquired from the United States, on the same terms and in like manner as the other States of said Confederacy have done in like cases.

3d. Whatever expenditures of money, if any, said Commonwealth of Virginia shall make before the union under the Provisional Government, as above contemplated, shall be consummated, shall be met and provided for by said Confederate States.

This convention, entered into and agreed to in the city of Richmond, Virginia, on the twenty-fourth day of April, eighteen hundred and sixty-one, by Alexander H. Stephens, the duly authorized Commissioner to act in the matter for the said Confederate States, and John Tyler, William Ballard Preston, Samuel McD. Moore, James P. Holcombe, James C. Bruce and Lewis E. Harvie, parties duly authorized to act in like manner for said

Commonwealth of Virginia—the whole subject to the approval and ratification of the proper authorities of both Governments respectively.

In testimony whereof, the parties aforesaid have hereto set their hands and seals, the day and year aforesaid, and at the place aforesaid, in duplicate originals.

JOHN TYLER,
WM. BALLARD PRESTON,
S. MCD. MOORE,
JAMES P. HOLCOMBE,
JAMES C. BRUCE,
LEWIS E. HARVIE,
Committee of the Convention.

ALEXANDER H. STEPHENS,
Commissioner of Confederate States.

[Note: The convention adopted the military alliance with the Confederacy by a vote of 80 to 16.]

Source: George H. Reese, ed., *Proceedings of the Virginia State Convention of 1861: February 13–May 1.* 4 vols. (Richmond: Virginia State Library, 1965), 4:479–81, 493.

Adoption of the Provisional Constitution of the Confederate States
April 25, 1861

Mr. {Timothy} RIVES, of Prince George—Before I vote I desire to know whether the ordinance is intended only to ratify the Convention which has been reported, or whether it is intended also to adopt the provisional government.

The PRESIDENT—It is intended only to ratify the Convention, and not the ordinance adopting the provisional Constitution.

Mr. RIVES—Under these circumstances I vote aye.

Mr. {Thomas Stanhope} FLOURNOY—I understand from the explanation of the Chair, that the ordinance just adopted did not embrace the ordinance reported by the committee, which proposes to adopt the provisional Constitution.

I ask the previous question upon that ordinance.

The call was sustained, and the main question ordered to be put, which was as follows:

AN ORDINANCE *for the adoption of the Constitution of the Provisional Government of the Confederate States of America.*

We, the delegates of the people of Virginia, in Convention, assembled, solemnly impressed with the perils which surround the Commonwealth, and appealing to the Searcher of Hearts for the rectitude of our intentions in assuming the grave responsibility of this act, do, by this ordinance, adopt and ratify the Constitution of the Provisional Government of the Confederate States of America, ordained and established at Montgomery, Alabama, on the eighth day of February, eighteen hundred and sixty-one: Provided, That this ordinance shall cease to have any legal operation or effect if the people of this Commonwealth, upon the vote directed to be taken on the ordinance of secession passed by this convention on the seventeenth day of April, eighteen hundred and sixty-one, shall reject the same.

Mr. CONRAD—I call for the yeas and nays: upon that question.

The call was sustained, and the vote being taken, resulted yeas 76, nays 19.

Source: George H. Reese, ed., *Proceedings of the Virginia State Convention of 1861: February 13–May 1.* 4 vols. (Richmond: Virginia State Library, 1965), 4:493–94.

Wheeling Convention's Report of the Committee on State and Federal Relations
May 15, 1861

Western Virginia's response to the convention's passage of the ordinance of secession was fast and direct. Several counties passed resolutions calling for a convention to be held in Wheeling to determine next steps. The recommended gathering took place in Wheeling from May 13 to 15 over a week before the scheduled popular vote on the secession ordinance. Four hundred and twenty-nine delegates represented twenty-nine counties. The Report of the Committee on State and Federal Relations condemned the passage of the ordinance of secession by the state convention as "unconstitutional, null and void" and its subsequent agreements with the Confederacy "plain and palpable violations of the Constitution of the United States, and are utterly subversive of the rights and liberties of the people of Virginia." The report recommended that if secession was ratified by the voters on May 23, a second gathering of the northwestern counties should be scheduled for early June to determine the course best suited for that part of the state.[8]

---

1. *Resolved*, That in our deliberate judgment the ordinance passed by the Convention of Virginia, on the 17th day of April, 1861, known as the ordinance of secession, by which said convention, undertook in the name of the State of Virginia, to repeal the ratification of the Constitution of the United States by this State, and to resume all the rights and powers granted under said Constitution, is unconstitutional, null and void.

2. *Resolved*, That the schedule attached to the ordinance of secession suspending and prohibiting the election for members of Congress from this State, is a manifest usurpation of power to which we ought not to submit.

3. *Resolved*, That the agreement of the 24th of April, 1861, between the Commissioner of the Confederate States and this State, and the ordinance of the 25th of April, 1861, approving and ratifying said agreement by which the whole military force and military operations offensive and defensive, of this Commonwealth are placed under the chief control and direction of the President of the Confederate States, upon the same principles, basis and footing as if the Commonwealth were now a member of said Confederacy, and all the acts of the executive officers of our State in pursuance of said agreement and ordinance are plain and palpable violations of the Constitution of the United States, and are utterly subversive of the rights and liberties of the people of Virginia.

4. *Resolved*, That we earnestly urge and entreat the citizens of the State everywhere, but more especially in the Western section, to be prompt at the polls on the 23d inst.; and to impress upon every voter the duty of voting in condemnation of the Ordinance of Secession, in the hope that we may not be involved in the ruin to be occasioned by its adoption, and with the view to demonstrate the position of the West on the question of secession.

5. *Resolved*, That we earnestly recommend to the citizens of Western

Virginia to vote for members of the Congress of the United States, in their several districts, in the exercise of the right secured to us by the Constitutions of the United States and the State of Virginia.

6. *Resolved*, That we also recommend to the citizens of the several counties to vote at said election for such persons as entertain the opinions expressed in the foregoing resolutions, for members of the Senate and the House of Delegates of our State.

7. *Resolved*, That in view of the Geographical, social, commercial and industrial interests of Northwestern Virginia, this Convention are constrained in giving expression to the opinion of their constituents to declare that the Virginia Convention in assembling to change the relation of the State of Virginia to the Federal Government, have not only acted unwisely and unconstitutionally, but have adopted a policy utterly ruinous to all the material interests of our section, severing all our social ties and drying up all the channels of our trade and prosperity.

8. *Resolved*, That in the event of the Ordinance of Secession being ratified by a vote, we recommend to the people of the Counties here represented, and all others, disposed to co-operate with us, to appoint on the 4th day of June, 1861, delegates to a General Convention, to meet on the 11th of that month, at such place as may be designated by the Committee hereafter provided, to devise such measures and take such action as the safety and welfare of the people they represent may demand, — each County to appoint a number of Representatives to said Convention equal to double the number to which it will be entitled in the next House of Delegates; and the Senators and Delegates to be elected on the 23rd inst., by the counties referred to, to the next General Assembly of Virginia, and who concur in the views of this Convention, to be entitled to seats in the said Convention as members thereof.

9. *Resolved*, That inasmuch as it is a conceded political axiom, that government is founded on the consent of the governed and is instituted for their good, and it cannot be denied that the course pursued by the ruling power in the State, is utterly subversive and destructive of our interests, we believe we may rightfully and successfully appeal to the proper authorities of Virginia, to permit us peacefully and lawfully to separate from the residue of the State, and form ourselves into a government to give effect to the wishes, views and interests of our constituents.

10. *Resolved*, That the public authorities be assured that the people of the North West will exert their utmost power to preserve the peace, which they feel satisfied they can do, until an opportunity is afforded to see if our present difficulties cannot receive a peaceful solution; and we express the earnest hope that no troops of the Confederate States be introduced among us, as we believe it would be eminently calculated to produce civil war.

11. *Resolved*, That in the language of Washington in his letter of the 17th of September, 1787, to the President of Congress; "in all our deliberations on this subject we have kept steadily in view that which appears to us the greatest interest of every true American, the consolidation of our Union, in which is involved our prosperity, felicity, safety, and perhaps our national existence." And therefore we will maintain and defend the Constitution of the United States and the laws made in pursuance thereof, and all officers acting there-under in the lawful discharge of their respective duties.

12. *Resolved*, That John S. Carlile, James S. Wheat, Chester D. Hubbard, Francis H. Pierpont, Campbell Tarr, George R. Latham, Andrew Wilson, S. H. Woodward and James W. Paxton be a Central Committee to attend to all the matters connected with the objects of this Convention; and that they may have power to assemble this Convention at any time they may think necessary.

13. *Resolved*, That the Central Committee be instructed to prepare an address to the people of Virginia in conformity with the foregoing resolutions and cause the same to be published and circulated as extensively as possible.

MR. POLSLEY[9] suggested that instead of acting to-night on the report of the committee, it be laid upon the table and printed, in order that every member might have an opportunity to inspect it.

GEN. JACKSON[10] objected; he wanted to go home. It was corn planting time.

MR. CARLILE asked Mr. P. to withdraw his motion. He was satisfied that nothing more than was now incorporated in the report could be obtained from the Convention at that time, and he was happy to state that since the adjournment this evening a resolution had been adopted by the committee which he regarded worth all the rest, and which would in a short time realize all their hopes of a New Virginia. That resolution provides for the appointment of a committee possessing all the powers this Convention can exercise, so far as they can be exercised by the committee.

The question on the adoption of the report of the Committee was then put, and the report was adopted with an almost unanimous "aye," only two dissenting voices being heard.

The announcement that the motion had carried, was received with tremendous cheering.

Source: Virgil A. Lewis (state historian and archivist), *How West Virginia was Made. Proceedings of the First Convention of the People of Northwestern Virginia at Wheeling May 13, 14 and 15, 1861, and the Journal of the Second Convention of the People of Northwestern Virginia at Wheeling, Which Assembled, June 11th, 1861, and Continued in Session Until June 25th. Adjourned Until August 6th, 1861. Reassembled on that Date and Continued in Session Until August 21st, When it Adjourned sine die. With Appendices and an Introduction, Annotations and Addenda* (Charleston: News-Mail Company Public Printers, 1909), 62–64.

APPENDIX

Timeline for Secession Winter

—1860—

November 6   Abraham Lincoln elected President of the United States
December 3   Second session of the Thirty-Sixth Congress convenes
December 17   South Carolina convenes secession convention
December 18   Senator John J. Crittenden introduces compromise amendment
December 20   South Carolina secedes

—1861—

January 3   Florida convenes secession convention
January 7   Mississippi convenes secession convention
January 7   Alabama convenes secession convention
January 9   Mississippi secedes
January 9   The *Star of the West* repulsed off Morris Island, South Carolina
January 10   Florida secedes
January 11   Alabama secedes
January 16   Georgia convenes secession convention
January 19   Georgia secedes
January 23   Louisiana convenes secession convention
January 26   Louisiana secedes
January 28   Texas convenes secession convention
February 4   Secessionist convention convenes in Montgomery, Alabama
February 4   Washington Peace Convention convenes
February 4   Virginia elects delegates to its state convention
February 8   Provisional Confederate States of America established
February 9   Jefferson Davis elected Provisional President of the CSA
February 13   Virginia convenes state convention
February 18   Jefferson Davis inaugurated President of the CSA
February 23   Texas secedes
February 27   Washington Peace Convention concludes
February 28   Missouri convenes state convention
March 4   US Senate approves Thomas Corwin's compromise amendment
March 4   US Senate rejects Washington Peace Convention amendment

March 4	Abraham Lincoln inaugurated President of the USA
March 4	Arkansas convenes secession convention
March 6	Confederate Congress authorizes raising 100,000 troops
March 11	Permanent Confederate Constitution created in Montgomery, Alabama
March 19	Missouri votes against secession
March 26	Permanent Confederate Constitution ratified
April 4	Virginia ordinance of secession defeated 90 to 45
April 12	Bombardment of Fort Sumter begins
April 15	Lincoln calls for 75,000 troops
April 17	Virginia convention votes to secede 88 to 55
April 18	Virginia militia capture the US Harpers Ferry Arsenal
April 22	Clarksburg gathering initiates call to consider secession of western Virginia
April 25	Virginia convention ratifies treaty with the CSA by a vote of 80 to 16
April 25	Virginia convention ratifies Provisional Constitution of CSA, 76 to 19
May 6	Arkansas secedes
May 7	Virginia admitted into the Confederate States of America
May 13–15	First Wheeling convention calls for an assembly of Unionists to convene June 11 should Virginia's electorate vote for secession
May 20	North Carolina convenes secession convention
May 20	North Carolina secedes
May 23	Virginia secedes: popular vote approves ordinance of secession, 86 percent to 14 percent
June 8	Tennessee secedes
June 11	Second Wheeling convention convenes and establishes the Reorganized Government of Virginia
July 20	Confederate government reconvenes in Richmond

—1863—

| March 26 | West Virginia voters ratify state constitution that includes a provision for compensated emancipation |
| June 20 | State of West Virginia admitted to the United States |

—1865—

| February 3 | West Virginia ratifies Thirteenth Amendment |
| February 9 | Virginia ratifies Thirteenth Amendment |

NOTES

Introduction

Epigraph. Brent Tarter, "Part II: Confederate Monuments and Christopher Columbus," *Virginia Forum* (blog), accessed 2020 (post since removed).

1. Jefferson Davis, *The Rise and Fall of the Confederate Government* (1881; repr., New York: Thomas Yoseloff, 1958), 1:80–83.

2. Jefferson Davis, *A Short History of the Confederate States of America* (New York: Belford Company Publishers, 1890), 19.

3. David Blight, *Race and Reunion: The Civil War in American Memory* (Cambridge: Harvard University Press, 2001). For Davis's views of the war, see pages 258–64. See also Michael Kammen, *Mystic Chords of Memory: The Transformation of Tradition in American Culture* (New York: Vintage Books, 1991), 101–31, 590–610; Robert Penn Warren, *The Legacy of the Civil War* (1961; repr., Lincoln: University of Nebraska Press, 1998); Robert J. Cook, *Troubled Commemoration: The American Civil War Centennial, 1961–1965* (Baton Rouge: Louisiana State University, 2007); W. Stuart Towns, *Enduring Legacy: Rhetoric and Ritual of the Lost Cause* (Tuscaloosa: University of Alabama Press, 2012).

4. Benjamin J. Hillman, ed., *Virginia's Decision: The Story of the Secession Convention of 1861* (Richmond: Virginia Civil War Commission, 1964). A 1992 study of Virginia's legal statutes governing slavery determined that the first principle was to "presume, preserve, protect, and defend the ideal of the superiority of whites and the inferiority of blacks." A. Leon Higginbotham Jr., and Anne F. Jacobs, "The Law Only as an Enemy: The Legitimization of Racial Powerlessness through the Colonial and Antebellum Criminal Laws of Virginia," *North Carolina Law Review* 70, no. 4 (1992): 975.

5. Allan Nevins, *The Emergence of Lincoln: Prologue to Civil War, 1859–1861* (New York: Charles Scribner's Sons, 1950), 470.

6. William G. Shade, *Democratizing the Old Dominion: Virginia and the Second Party System, 1824–1861* (Charlottesville: University Press of Virginia, 1996), 20.

7. Alison Goodyear Freehling, *Drift Toward Dissolution: The Virginia Slavery Debate of 1831–1832* (Baton Rouge: Louisiana State University Press, 1982), 77. See also Christopher M. Curtis, "Reconsidering Suffrage Reform in the 1829–1830 Virginia Constitutional Convention," *Journal of Southern History* 74, no. 1 (February 2008): 89–124.

8. Freehling, *Drift Toward Dissolution*, 158. See also Marie Tyler-McGraw, *An African Republic: Black and White Virginians in the Making of Liberia* (Chapel Hill: University of North Carolina Press, 2007), 105–11.

9. Freehling, *Drift Toward Dissolution*, 148–49, 165.

10. Freehling, *Drift Toward Dissolution*, 238–40.

11. Freehling, *Drift Toward Dissolution*, 240. See also Brent Tarter, *Constitutional History of Virginia* (Augusta: University of Georgia Press, 2023), 121; George Ruble Woolfolk, "Taxes and Slavery in the Ante Bellum South," *Journal of Southern History* 26, no. 2 (May 1960): 200.

12. Freehling, *Drift Toward Dissolution*, 241.

13. For a smart account of this tumultuous decade, see Elizabeth R. Varon, *Disunion: The Coming of the American Civil War, 1789–1859* (Chapel Hill: University of North Carolina Press, 2008), 235–335.

14. Leonard L. Richards, *The California Gold Rush and the Coming of the Civil War* (New York: Knopf, 2007), 97–110.

15. Stephen E. Maizlish, *The Strife of Tongues: The Compromise of 1850 and the Ideological Foundations of the American Civil War* (Charlottesville: University of Virginia Press, 2018); Nicole Etcheson, *Bleeding Kansas: Contested Liberty in the Civil War Era* (Lawrence: University Press of Kansas, 2004).

16. Williamjames Hull Hoffer, *The Caning of Charles Sumner: Honor, Idealism, and the Origins of the Civil War* (Baltimore: Johns Hopkins University Press, 2010).

17. Brooks soon resigned from the House of Representatives, but was quickly reelected. Sumner slowly recovered from his injuries not returning to the Senate until December 1859.

18. Heather Cox Richardson, *To Make Men Free: A History of the Republican Party* (New York: Basic Books, 2014), 1–13.

19. Jean H. Baker, *James Buchanan* (New York: Henry Holt and Company, 2004), 68–74; Paul Finkleman, *Millard Fillmore* (New York: Henry Holt and Company, 2011), 132–34.

20. James M. McPherson, *Battle Cry of Freedom: The Civil War Era* (New York: Ballantine Books, 1988), 153–62.

21. For a concise rendering of Buchanan and the election, see Baker, *James Buchanan*, 67–74. Buchanan's administration is closely analyzed in John W. Quist and Michael J. Birkner, eds., *James Buchanan and the Coming of the Civil War* (Gainesville: University Press of Florida, 2013).

22. Michael F. Holt, *The Election of 1860: "A Campaign Fraught with Consequences"* (Lawrence: University Press of Kansas, 2017), 191–92.

23. The surname "Lemon" was changed to "Lemmon" by the New York press and courts.

24. Marie Tyler-McGraw and Dwight T. Pitcaithley, "The Lemmon Slave Case: Courtroom Drama, Constitutional Crisis and the Southern Quest to

Nationalize Slavery," *Commonplace: The Journal of Early American Life*, http://commonplace.online/article/lemmon-slave-case/. See also Paul Finkelman, *An Imperfect Union: Slavery, Federalism, and Comity* (Chapel Hill: University of North Carolina Press, 1981), 296–338; Craig M. Simpson, *A Good Southerner: The Life of Henry A. Wise of Virginia* (Chapel Hill: University of North Carolina Press, 1985), 185–86.

25. William W. Freehling, *The Road to Disunion*, vol. 2, *Secessionists Triumphant, 1854–1861* (New York: Oxford University Press, 2007), 12.

26. David S. Reynolds, *John Brown, Abolitionist: The Man Who Killed Slavery, Sparked the Civil War, and Seeded Civil Rights* (New York: Vintage Books, 2005), 419–24.

27. Matthew Karp, *The Vast Southern Empire: Slaveholders at the Helm of American Foreign Policy* (Cambridge: Harvard University Press, 2016), 185–86.

28. The abolition of slavery would have to depend (as it did in 1865) on the ratification of a constitutional amendment to that effect. Ratification required approval by three-fourths of the states. In 1860, the country was divided between fifteen slave states and eighteen non-slave states. If the slave states voted as a bloc, there would have had to be twenty-five states supporting the amendment to ensure passage.

29. Joseph Howard Parks, *John Bell of Tennessee* (Baton Rouge: Louisiana State University Press, 1950), 357–88.

30. Holt, *The Election of 1860*, 194–95; Daniel W. Crofts, *Reluctant Confederates: Upper South Unionists in the Secession Crisis* (Chapel Hill: University of North Carolina Press, 2016), 81.

31. W. G. Bean, "John Letcher and the Slavery Issue in Virginia's Gubernatorial Contest of 1858–1859," *Journal of Southern History* 20, no. 1 (February 1954): 22–49; *American National Biography* (New York: Oxford University Press, 1999), 13:526–28.

32. *Journal of the Senate of the Commonwealth of Virginia: Begun and Held at the Capitol in the City of Richmond, on Monday, the Seventh Day of January, in the Year One Thousand Eight Hundred and Sixty-One—Being the Eighty-Fifth Year of the Commonwealth. Extra Session* (Richmond: James E. Goode, Senate Printer, 1861), 9–27. See also F. N. Boney, *John Letcher of Virginia: The Story of Virginia's Civil War Governor* (Tuscaloosa: University of Alabama Press, 1966), 100–104.

33. See Dwight T. Pitcaithley, *The U.S. Constitution and Secession: A Documentary Anthology of Slavery and White Supremacy* (Lawrence: University Press of Kansas, 2018), 77–91.

34. *Journal of the House of Delegates of the State of Virginia, for the Extra Session, 1861* (Richmond: William F. Ritchie, Public Printer, 1861), 65–66.

35. Howard C. Westwood, "The Real Lost Cause: The Peace Convention of 1861," *Military Affairs* 27, no. 3 (Autumn 1963): 119–30; Robert Gray

Gunderson, *Old Gentlemen's Convention: The Washington Peace Conference of 1861* (Madison: University of Wisconsin Press, 1961); Jesse L. Keene, *The Peace Convention of 1861* (Gainesville: University of Florida, 1955); and Mark Tooley, *The Peace That Almost Was: The Forgotten Story of the 1861 Washington Peace Conference and the Final Attempt to Avert the Civil War* (Nashville: Nelson Books, 2015).

36. Lucius E. Chittenden, ed., *A Report of the Debates and Proceedings of the Secret Sessions of the Conference Convention, for Proposing Amendments to the Constitution of the United States, Held at Washington, D.C., in February, A.D. 1861* (New York: D. Appleton & Company, 1864), 43–45.

37. *American National Biography*, 19:575–77.

38. Chittenden, *A Report of the Debates*, 418–20. Seddon's seventh article had earlier been suggested by Crittenden on January 3 as an addition to his (Crittenden's) initial constitutional amendment. Crittenden acknowledged borrowing the language from an amendment proposed on December 24, 1860, by Senator Stephen A. Douglas of Illinois. See *Congressional Globe*, 36th Cong., 2nd Sess., January 3, 1861, 237.

39. It should not pass notice that of the eighteen "free" states in 1860, only five (Maine, New Hampshire, Vermont, Massachusetts, and Rhode Island) allowed Black men unrestricted voting rights, while three others (New York, Ohio, and Michigan) allowed the vote, but with certain restrictions—restrictions not binding on White voters. For an insightful analysis of the role white supremacy played over Secession Winter, see Ulrich B. Phillips, "The Central Theme of Southern History," *American Historical Review* 34, no. 1 (October 1928): 30–43.

40. Chittenden, *A Report of the Debates*, 440–45.

41. *Congressional Globe*, 36th Cong., 2nd Sess., March 1, 1861, 1310.

42. *Congressional Globe*, 36th Cong., 2nd Sess., March 2, 1861, 1316.

43. *Congressional Globe*, 36th Cong., 2nd Sess., March 1, 1861, 1333, 1344.

44. House Committee of Five, *Seizure of Forts, Arsenals, Revenue Cutters, and Other Property of the United States*, H.R. 91, 36th Cong., 2nd Sess., February 28, 1861, 1–27.

45. Robert Gray Gunderson, "Letters from the Washington Peace Conference of 1861," *Journal of Southern History* 17, no. 3 (August 1951): 386.

46. *Congressional Globe*, 36th Cong., 2nd Sess., March 1, 1861, 1307.

47. *Congressional Globe*, 36th Cong., 2nd Sess., March 1, 1861, 1307.

48. *Congressional Globe*, 36th Cong., 2nd Sess., March 2, 1861, 1405; March 1, 1861, 1333.

49. *Congressional Globe*, 36th Cong., 2nd Sess., 1285, 1403. The amendment would eventually be ratified by Kentucky, Ohio, Rhode Island, Maryland, and Illinois before federal efforts during the war turned from protecting slavery to abolishing it. For a detailed history of the Seward/Corwin Amendment,

see Daniel W. Crofts, *Lincoln and the Politics of Slavery: The Other Thirteenth Amendment and the Struggle to Save the Union* (Chapel Hill: University of North Carolina Press, 2016).

50. Crofts, *Lincoln and the Politics of Slavery*, 235–36; Eric Foner, *The Fiery Trial: Abraham Lincoln and American Slavery* (New York: Norton, 2010), 157–58.

51. William A. Link, *Roots of Secession: Slavery and Politics in Antebellum Virginia* (Chapel Hill: University of North Carolina Press, 2003), 227–28; William W. Freehling and Craig M. Simpson, *Showdown in Virginia: The 1861 Convention and the Fate of the Union* (Charlottesville: University of Virginia Press, 2010), xi.

52. George H. Reese, ed., *Proceedings of the Virginia State Convention of 1861: February 13–May 1* (Richmond: Virginia State Library, 1965), 1:6. See also Anne Sarah Rubin, "Between Union and Chaos: The Political Life of John Janney," *Virginia Magazine of History and Biography* 102, no. 3 (July 1994): 381–416.

53. The workings of the convention are well told in Freehling and Simpson, *Showdown in Virginia*; Link, *Roots of Secession*, 226–44; Edward L. Ayers, *In the Presence of Mine Enemies: The Civil War in the Heart of America 1859–1863* (New York: Norton, 2003), 119–42; and Nelson D. Lankford, *Cry Havoc!: The Crooked Road to Civil War, 1861* (New York: Viking, 2007), 45–58, 113–25.

54. Reese, *Proceedings*, 1:50–62. Mississippi had seceded on January 9, the second state to do so, announcing in its declaration of secession that "Our position is thoroughly identified with the institution of slavery—the greatest material interest in the world. . . . There was no choice left us but submission to the mandates of abolition, or a dissolution of the Union, whose principles had been subverted to work out our ruin."

55. Reese, *Proceedings*, 1:62–75.

56. Reese, *Proceedings*, 1:76–93.

57. Charles B. Dew, *Apostles of Disunion: Southern Secession Commissioners and the Causes of the Civil War* (Charlottesville: University of Virginia Press, 2001), 74–81, 89. White supremacy, as a motivating factor in the secession of the South, was also emphasized three years after Appomattox by Edward A. Pollard, editor of the Richmond *Examiner*, in *The Lost Cause Regained* (New York: G. W. Carleton & Co., 1868), 13–14, 112–28. For a contemporary view of the relationship between slavery and secession, see Thomas Ellison, *Slavery and Secession in America, Historical and Economical* (London: Sampson Low, Son & Co., 1861).

58. Reese, *Proceedings*, 2:176. The political distinctiveness of Augusta Country is highlighted in the University of Virginia's digital project *The Valley of the Shadow* which compares the two Shenandoah Valley counties of Augusta in Virginia and Franklin in Pennsylvania. See https://valley.lib.virginia.edu/.

59. *Congressional Globe*, 36th Cong., 2nd Sess., January 22, 1861, Appendix, 105.

60. Carlile, Willey, and Stuart were later instrumental in the conventions that led to the creation of the state of West Virginia. Willey, elected to the US Congress by the "Restored Government of Virginia" to replace Senator James M. Mason, presented the petition for the creation of West Virginia, and served as one of the first two senators from the newly created state. Eric J. Wittenberg, Edmund A. Sargus, Jr., and Penny L. Barrick, *Seceding from Secession: The Civil War, Politics, and the Creation of West Virginia* (El Dorado Hills, California: Savas Beatie, 2020), 35–76.

61. Reese, *Proceedings*, 1: 366; 3:170; 1:469. An important sub-theme that ran throughout the conference was that of taxation. The Virginia constitution of 1851 stipulated that slaves under the age of twelve were not to be taxed and those over twelve would not be valued at more than $300 for purposes of taxation. Delegates from the mountainous regions of Virginia where slaves were few resented the exclusion and believed they were being treated as unequal citizens. They voiced their discontent repeatedly throughout the conference even suggesting that they might secede from Virginia if the convention voted for disunion without addressing their concerns. Ultimately, the convention agreed to an *ad valorem* tariff on all property. Freehling and Simpson, *Showdown in Virginia*, xix, 133–52, 204–6.

62. Among the eleven states that seceded, Lincoln was on the ballot only in Virginia.

63. *Congressional Globe*, 36th Cong., 2nd Sess., January 28, 1861, 602.

64. Reese, *Proceedings*, 1:240.

65. Reese, *Proceedings*, 1:345.

66. Reese, *Proceedings*, 2:529–33. Speaking on March 28, 1861, Goode was aware that Congress had not been in session since March 4 (Inauguration Day), and that in the Thirty-Seventh Congress, Democrats would control the Senate, and its confirmation authority, as they had during the Thirty-Sixth Congress.

67. Reese, *Proceedings*, 3:576.

68. On February 2, 1860, Davis had proposed six resolutions relevant to the status of slavery in the country. They included propositions to the effect that slavery was an important element in southern society and that any "inter-meddling" with it was a violation of the Constitution; that the union of the states rested upon the "equality of rights and privileges" of all and that nei-ther Congress nor territorial legislatures possessed the right to interfere with the right of slave owners from taking their slaves into the western territories. Indeed, if necessary, Congress should ensure that right. Only the inhabitants of a territory, when applying for statehood, could determine whether slavery would be allowed or prohibited. Emphasizing the importance of returning fugitive slaves to their owners, Davis concluded by stating that without the Constitution's fugitive slave clause, the "Union could not have been formed." On May 25, 1860, after lengthy debate, the United States Senate approved

all six resolutions. *Congressional Globe*, 36th Cong., 1st Sess., 2321–352. See William J. Cooper, *Jefferson Davis, American* (Baton Rouge: Louisiana State University, 2000), 327–29.

69. *Congressional Globe*, 36th Cong., 2nd Sess., December 12, 1860, 77.
70. *Congressional Globe*, 36th Cong., 2nd Sess., December 12, 1860, 77.
71. *Biographical Directory of the United States Congress*, "Jenkins, Albert Gallatin," http://bioguide.congress.gov/scripts/biodisplay.pl?index=J000081.
72. *Congressional Globe*, 36th Cong., 1st Sess., January 31, 1860, Appendix, 104–5; Richard R. Moore, "Robert M. T. Hunter and the Crisis of the Union, 1860–1861," *The Southern Historian* 13 (Spring 1992): 25–35; William S. Hitchcock, "Southern Moderates and Secession: Senator Robert M. T. Hunter's Call for Union," *Journal of American History* 59, no. 4 (March 1973): 871–84.
73. *Congressional Globe*, 36th Cong., 2nd Sess., January 11, 1861, 328–29.
74. *Biographical Directory of the United States Congress*, "Hunter, Robert Mercer Taliaferro," http://bioguide.congress.gov/scripts/biodisplay.pl?index=H 000988.
75. *Congressional Globe*, 36th Cong., 2nd Sess., February 27, 1861, 1260–261.
76. Reese, *Proceedings*, 1:523–28.
77. Lankford, *Cry Havoc!*, 50.
78. Reese, *Proceedings*, 1:535–36.
79. Reese, *Proceedings*, 1:537.
80. Reese, *Proceedings*, 1:536–39. Like a number of Democrats over Secession Winter, Wise attempted to be comprehensive out of a desire to protect slavery in the Constitution. Articulating every possible situation where slavery might be threatened, the former governor presented a laundry list of desired constitutional "guarantees and assurances." A less enthusiastic Wise might have realized that a focus on his first point, the constitutional "recognition of the rights of property in African slaves" protected under the due process clause of the Fifth Amendment, would have made most of his other protections for the institution redundant.
81. Reese, *Proceedings*, 2:35–37.
82. Reese, *Proceedings*, 2:389–91.
83. Reese, *Proceedings*, 2:575–79. It is unclear whether Wise was aware that nationalizing slavery by protecting it under the Fifth Amendment was inconsistent with his proposal that territories could prohibit the institution upon admission as a state.
84. On December 22, 1860, Senator Jefferson Davis had proposed an amendment to the Constitution which stated that "property in slaves, recognized as such by the local law of any of the States of the Union, shall stand on the same footing in all constitutional and federal relations as any other species of property so recognized." *Congressional Globe*, 36th Cong., 2nd Sess., Senate Report 288, 3.
85. Reese, *Proceedings*, 2:578.

86. Virginia was the largest exporter of slaves during the antebellum period selling nearly 300,000 slaves to slave owners further south between 1830 and 1860. Kenneth M. Stampp, *The Peculiar Institution: Slavery in the Ante-Bellum South* (New York: Vintage Books, 1956), 238. For a graphic accounting of the slave trade in Richmond, see Charles B. Dew, *The Making of a Racist: A Southerner Reflects on Family, History, and the Slave Trade* (Charlottesville: University of Virginia Press, 2016), 87–167.

87. Reese, *Proceedings*, 2:578.

88. Reese, *Proceedings*, 3:155–58.

89. Reese, *Proceedings*, 2:672–77. See also Freehling and Simpson, *Showdown in Virginia*, 101–12.

90. Reese, *Proceedings*, 3:161–63; Link, *Roots of Secession*, 235.

91. Reese, *Proceedings*, 3:711–13.

92. Reese, *Proceedings*, 3:713–14. For a fascinating history of the actual secession parchment, see Marianne E. Julienne and Brent Tarter, "The Virginia Ordinance of Secession," *Virginia Magazine of History and Biography* 119, no. 2 (2011): 154–81.

93. Reese, *Proceedings*, 3:730.

94. Reese, *Proceedings*, 4:144–46.

95. Link, *Roots of Secession*, 240–42; Lankford, *Cry Havoc!*, 114–16, 123, 125, 129; Simpson, *A Good Southerner*, 245, 251–52.

96. Reese, *Proceedings*, 4:124.

97. Fort Monroe, designed to protect the entrance to Hampton Roads, was never seriously threatened by Confederate troops. Like Fort Pickens in Pensacola, it remained under United States command throughout the war.

98. *The Statutes at Large of the Provisional Government of the Confederate States of America, From the Institution of the Government, February 8, 1861, to its termination, February 18, 1862, Inclusive . . .* , ed. James M. Matthews (Richmond: R. M. Smith, Printer to Congress, 1864), 104.

99. Cooper, *Jefferson Davis, American*, 368. A detailed treatment of the Confederate capital's move from Montgomery to Richmond can be found in Davis, *"A Government of our Own": The Making of the Confederacy* (Baton Rouge: Louisiana State University, 1994), 371–400. See also James M. McPherson, *Embattled Rebel: Jefferson Davis as Commander in Chief* (New York: Penguin Press, 2014), 33–37. In his July 4 message to the first session of the Thirty-Seventh Congress, President Lincoln commented on the Confederate government's relocation to Richmond by observing: "The people of Virginia have thus allowed this giant insurrection to make its nest within her borders." *Congressional Globe*, 37th Cong., 1st Sess., July 4, 1861, Appendix, 2.

100. James W. Hunnicutt, *The Conspiracy Revealed. The South Sacrificed; or, The Horrors of Secession* (Philadelphia: J. B. Lippincott & Co., 1863), 269–70. See also Steven E. Nash, "'The Devil Let Loose Generally': James W.

Hunnicutt's Conceptualization of the Union in Fredericksburg," *Virginia Magazine of History and Biography* 126, no. 3 (2018): 298–333.

101. Freehling, *The Road to Disunion*, 526.

102. Link, *Roots of Secession*, 243–44; Wittenberg, et al., *Seceding from Secession*, 35–124.

103. Granville D. Hall, *The Rending of Virginia: A History* (1902; repr., Knoxville: University of Tennessee Press, 2000), 102.

Chapter One: Governor John Letcher

1. See Boney, *John Letcher of Virginia*.

2. John Floyd (1783–1837) served as Virginia's governor from 1830 to 1834.

3. Joanna Baillie (1762–1851), *The Bride: A Drama in Three Acts*, act II, scene VI (1828). Walter Scott called Baillie the best dramatic writer in Britain since Shakespeare and Massinger.

4. The Mesilla Valley was, and is, a fertile agricultural area along the Rio Grande extending from El Paso, Texas, to just north of Las Cruces, New Mexico. It was part of the Gadsden Purchase acquired by the United States from Mexico in 1853.

5. Christopher Gustav Memminger (1803–1888) later served as the Confederacy's first secretary of the treasury. In January 1860, Memminger had been dispatched to Richmond by South Carolina to encourage the Virginia legislature to lead the southern states into independence. Speaking only weeks after John Brown's execution for his Harpers Ferry raid, Memminger, nevertheless, failed to move the state's representatives. Peter Burwell Starke (1813–1888).

6. United States Constitution, Article V.

7. William Henry Gist (1807–1874), message to South Carolina's general assembly, November 27, 1860, in *Journal of the Senate of South Carolina During the Annual Session of 1860* (Columbia, 1860), 9–25.

8. Christopher G. Memminger.

9. John Jones Pettus (1813–1867), message to Mississippi's general assembly, November 26, 1860, in *Journal of the Senate of the State of Mississippi, Called Session* (Jackson: E. Barksdale, State Printer, 1860), 5–12. In 1940, Alabama dedicated the Edmund Pettus Bridge in Selma, in honor of Pettus's brother. Edmond Pettus served as a senior officer in the Confederate Army, and after the war, as a Grand Dragon in the Ku Klux Klan.

10. John Jones Albion (1818–1867).

11. Ohio governor William Dennison, Jr. (1815–1882); Iowa governor Samuel Jordan Kirkwood (1813–1894).

12. Meaning "with an equal step" or "on equal footing."

13. Imbalance in the Senate occurred in 1850 when California was admitted as a non-slave state.

14. When admitted as a state in 1845, Texas retained the right to divide itself into as many as five states if it wished.

15. On January 7, 1861, the New Mexico Territory, by virtue of territorial legislation, was a slave territory. The slave code for the territory was repealed in December 1861.

16. From Lincoln's "House Divided" speech accepting the Republican nomination to run against Stephen A. Douglas for his seat in the United States Senate, June 16, 1858.

17. This quote, attributed to Lincoln at the time, cannot be found in Lincoln's papers. It is a comment he most assuredly did not make.

18. The declarations of secession from South Carolina, Georgia, Mississippi, and Texas all complained of hostility to slavery on the part of the northern states, not of the federal government.

19. Benjamin Watkins Leigh (1781–1849) was a lawyer and politician from Richmond who was commissioned by the Legislature in 1833 to mediate the nullification crisis of that year.

20. Years later, the country's foremost historian of the South, Ulrich B. Phillips, wrote when slavery was attacked, "It was defended not only as a vested interest, but with vigor and vehemence as a guarantee of white supremacy and civilization. . . . Otherwise it would be impossible to account for the fervid secessionism of many non-slaveholders and the eager service of thousands in the Confederate army." See Phillips, "The Central Theme of Southern History," 31. See also James Dunwoody Brownson De Bow's, "The Non-Slaveholders of the South: Their Interest in the Present Sectional Controversy Identical with That of the Slaveholders" De Bow's Review 30, no. 1 (January 1861): 67–77.

21. Written by James Madison in response to the restrictive Alien and Sedition Acts of 1798. The resolutions and report argued in favor of free speech and press, and of state sovereignty under the US Constitution.

22. Meeting in Hartford, Connecticut, from December 15, 1814, until January 5, 1815, the New England Federalist Party expressed its dissatisfaction with President James Madison and his economic policies which had led to the War of 1812. The convention's threat of secession quickly abated when the war ended with Andrew Jackson's victory in New Orleans on January 8. The convention is cited as a major factor in the collapse of the Federalist Party.

23. Ruth 1:16.

Chapter Two: Washington Peace Conference

1. Reverdy Johnson (1796–1876) had served as US senator (1845–1849) and US attorney general (1849–1850) before becoming a delegate to the Peace Conference. He gained fame as a defense attorney in the Dred Scott case. Johnson

was reelected to the US Senate and served from 1863 to 1868 when he was appointed minister to the United Kingdom.

2. The Missouri Compromise did not apply to slavery in territories yet to be acquired. Enacted on March 6, 1820, its primary provision prohibited slavery north of the 36°30" parallel, excepting Missouri, throughout the remainder of the Louisiana Purchase.

3. Boston's Faneuil Hall was constructed between 1740 and 1742. It became the site of pro-independence speeches favoring separation from Great Britain on the eve of the American Revolution. It is presently managed by the National Park Service as a part of Boston National Historical Park.

4. William Curtis Noyes (1805–1864), moments earlier, had observed that the Constitution provided the "proper" manner by which amendments could be considered, and since the calling of a national convention by a single state was not envisioned by the Founders, the Washington conference was, by his lights, "unconstitutional." Article V of the Constitution stipulates that amendments can be proposed by "two thirds of both Houses" of Congress, or by a national convention called by two-thirds of the "several States."

5. On the threshold or at the beginning.

6. Jacob Collamer (1791–1865) from Vermont.

7. Called by Virginia, the Annapolis Convention met September 11–14, 1786, to discuss interstate commercial matters and concluded by issuing an invitation to gather in Philadelphia to revise the Articles of Confederation. The resulting Constitutional Convention in May 1787 drafted the United States Constitution.

8. Roger Sherman Baldwin (1793–1863), governor (1844–1846) and US senator (1849–1851). He notably participated in the *Amistad* slave case in 1841. In the 1997 movie by the same name, Baldwin was portrayed by actor Matthew McConaughey.

9. George Sewell Boutwell (1818–1905) from Massachusetts, later US representative (1863–1869), secretary of the Treasury (1869–1873), and US senator (1873–1877). In 1868, Boutwell was one of the House managers in the impeachment of President Andrew Johnson.

10. Alexander Hamilton (1755–1804) from New York; delegate to the 1786 Annapolis Convention and promoter of the Constitutional Convention; first secretary of the Treasury under George Washington. He was killed in a duel by Aaron Burr on July 12, 1804, in Weehawken, New Jersey.

11. At the end of 1860, the United States Army had an authorized strength of 18,000, but only 16,367 were on the rolls. Clayton R. Newell, *The Regular Army Before the War: 1845–1860* (Washington, D.C.: Center of Military History, 2014), 50.

12. George S. Boutwell.

13. Nathaniel Gorham (1738–1796) was a delegate to the 1787 Constitutional

Congress. On August 27, 1787, Charles Cotesworth Pinckney of South Carolina proposed that the date for an end to the foreign slave trade be extended from 1800 to 1808. The change was seconded by Nathaniel Gorham.

14. George S. Boutwell.

15. Lot Myrick Morrill (1813–1883), served as governor of Maine (1858–1860) and later as US senator (1861–1876) and secretary of the Treasury (1876–1877).

16. James A. Seddon's February 26, 1861, proposal is reproduced in chapter 6.

17. Kentucky senator John J. Crittenden first introduced his amendment on December 18, 1860.

18. On February 4, White male voters in Virginia elected delegates to the state's convention. More than two-thirds of the delegates elected opposed secession.

19. A passing or incidental remark.

20. Charles Anderson Wickliffe (1788–1869) from Bardstown, Kentucky. He served as governor of Kentucky from 1839 to 1840.

21. A reference to George Washington's birthday, February 22, 1732 (or February 11 in the Julian dating of Washington's day).

22. A reference to Frederick T. Frelinghuysen who on February 20 made an impassioned address in favor of compromise.

23. David Wilmot (1814–1868). On August 8, 1846, while serving as a congressional representative from Pennsylvania, Wilmot had authored the famous Wilmot Proviso. Introduced while the House of Representatives was debating a bill to fund the declared war with Mexico, the Proviso provided that slavery would not be allowed to exist in any land acquired from Mexico as a result of the war.

24. The paragraphs referenced in the first and fourth articles of the United States Constitution refer to the counting of three-fifths of slaves for each state's representation in the House of Representatives, and the return of fugitive slaves respectively.

Chapter Three: United States Senate

1. See Moore, "Robert M. T. Hunter and the Crisis of the Union, 1860–1861," 25–35.

2. A reference to New York senator William Henry Seward's October 25, 1858, address titled "On the Irrepressible Conflict."

3. A reference to the Missouri Compromise of 1820 that prohibited slavery from the Louisiana Territory north of the 36°30' parallel.

4. Georgia senator Robert Augustus Toombs (1810–1885).

5. As a result of the 1860 election, Democrats would have controlled both houses of Congress for the first two years of the Lincoln administration had the South not seceded. The Supreme Court was still dominated by the

proslavery chief justice Roger B. Taney. Republicans would have controlled only the executive branch.

6. Hinton Rowan Helper's *Compendium of the Impending Crisis of the South* (1860) argued that nonslaveholding White southerners should unite to abolish slavery because the institution disadvantaged them economically, socially, and culturally. "The truth is, slavery destroys, or vitiates, or pollutes, whatever it touches. No interest of society escapes the influence of its cling- ing curse." Helper, from North Carolina, believed that African Americans should be removed from the United States and shipped to Africa or Mex- ico or South America. Dozens of Republicans endorsed the publication. Southern Democrats made frequent references to Helper's book throughout the Thirty-Sixth Congress. Arkansas representative Thomas Carmichael Hindman (1828–1868) titled one of his addresses, "That Black Republican Bible—The Helper Book." See *Congressional Globe*, 36th Cong., 1st Sess., January 19–20, 1860, 81–88; and David Brown, *Southern Outcast: Hinton Rowan Helper and The Impending Crisis of the South* (Baton Rouge: Louisiana State University Press, 2006).

7. On March 4, 1850, John C. Calhoun delivered his Fourth of March speech opposing what would become the Compromise of 1850. At the conclusion of his remarks he suggested an amendment to the Constitution that would give equal authority to the North and South through the creation of a dual executive. See *Congressional Globe*, 31st Cong., 1st Sess., 455; and Richards, *The California Gold Rush*, 105–6.

8. With the passage of the Slavery Abolition Act of 1833, the British Parliament formally ended slavery in Jamaica on August 1, 1834.

9. See Robert W. Young, *James Murray Mason, Defender of the Old South* (Knox- ville: University of Tennessee Press, 1998).

10. James Dixon (1814–1873) proposed printing Lincoln's Inaugural Address for the use of the Senate on March 6, 1861. See *Congressional Globe*, 36th Cong., 2nd Sess., 1436.

11. Stephen A. Douglas. See *Congressional Globe*, 36th Cong., 2nd Sess., March 6, 1861, 1436–443.

12. The day before Mason addressed the Senate, the Confederate Congress had authorized the enlistment of 100,000 troops. As he spoke, Virginia's militia numbered 18,400 and the US Army fewer than 17,000 assigned to forts scat- tered across the country.

13. A reference to Senator William H. Seward's speech of March 11, 1850, on the admission of California wherein he argued that slavery was governed by a higher law than the Constitution, it was governed by the "moral law created by the Creator of the universe." See *Congressional Globe*, 31st Cong., 1st Sess., Appendix, 260–69.

14. The Seward/Corwin Amendment passed the Senate on March 4, 1861, and

declared that Congress had no authority to interfere with or abolish slavery in the states in which it already existed.

15. In Greek mythology, Cerberus, often referred to as the hound of Hades, is a multiheaded dog that guards the gates of the Underworld to prevent the dead from leaving.

16. From Lincoln's Inaugural Address on March 4, 1861.

17. This passage is in quotation marks for rhetorical emphasis not attribution. Lincoln's reference to the Corwin amendment in his inaugural speech read as follows: "I understand a proposed amendment to the Constitution, which amendment, however, I have not seen, has passed Congress, to the effect that the Federal Government shall never interfere with the domestic institutions of the States, including that of persons held to service. To avoid misconstruction of what I have said, I depart from my purpose not to speak of particular amendments, so far as to say that, holding such a provision to now be implied constitutional law, I have no objection to its being made express and irrevocable." See *Congressional Globe*, 36th Cong., 2nd Sess., 1433–435.

18. Senator Stephen Douglas was the northern Democratic candidate for president in the election of 1860. Douglas came in second in the popular vote, but fourth in the Electoral College.

Chapter Four: United States House of Representatives

1. Organized during the early 1850s, the Know Nothing Party (also known as the American Party) adopted an anti-immigrant and anti-Catholic philosophy.

2. According to Michael Holt, Lincoln garnered 1,865,593 popular votes while votes for Douglas, Breckinridge, and Bell totaled 2,821,157. See Holt, *The Election of 1860*, 173.

3. James Gillespie Birney (1792–1857) was an abolitionist, politician, and attorney born in Danville, Kentucky. He ran on the Liberty Party ticket in the election of 1840.

4. John Parker Hale from New Hampshire was the candidate of the Free Soil Party in 1852. He received only 156,149 popular votes nationwide and no electoral votes. Democrat Franklin Pierce won handily over the Whig candidate, Winfield Scott. Hale's daughter, Lucy Lambert Hale, was secretly engaged to John Wilkes Booth. A photograph of Lucy was found on Booth's body after he was killed in April 1865.

5. William Henry Seward (1801–1872), "An Irrepressible Conflict" speech, delivered in Rochester, New York, on October 25, 1858.

6. Seventh debate with Stephen A. Douglas, October 15, 1858, in Alton, Illinois. Asterisks indicating ellipses are in the original.

7. As a result of the 1856 election, James Buchanan (Democrat) won 1,836,072

popular votes, John C. Fremont (Republican) 1,342,345 votes, and Millard Fillmore (American Party) 873,053 votes. The American party was more anti-Catholic than antislavery.

8. Seventh debate with Stephen A. Douglas, October 15, 1858, in Alton, Illinois.

9. Congress ultimately carved the remaining western territories into fourteen additional states. With a total of forty-eight states (and later fifty), if the fifteen slave states voted as a block, they could have prevented passage of a constitutional amendment abolishing slavery.

10. Representative Garnett voted in favor of the Corwin Amendment on February 28.

11. Jeremy Bentham (1748–1832), a British philosopher and social reformer. In his *A Fragment on Government* (1776) he included his famous belief, "It is the greatest happiness of the greatest number that is the measure of right and wrong."

12. Thomas Corwin (1794–1865). See *Congressional Globe*, 36th Cong., 2nd Sess., January 21, 1861, Appendix, 72–75.

13. Representative Millson may have been referring to Wisconsin's governor, Alexander W. Randall, who in his annual address to the general assembly on January 10, 1861, directed the assembled legislators to revise the state's personal liberty laws if they were "in conflict with the Constitution." *Journal of the Assembly of Wisconsin, Annual Session, A.D. 1861* (Madison: E. A. Calkins & Co., State Printers, 1861), 35–36. On January 25, 1861, Rhode Island's legislature repealed the state's 1854 personal liberty law which had discouraged the capture of fugitive slaves. *New York Times*, January 26, 1861.

14. For an assessment of the three-fifths clause and the advantage it gave the South, see Garry Wills, *"Negro President": Jefferson and the Slave Power* (New York: Houghton Mifflin Company, 2002), 1–13.

15. Link, *Roots of Secession*, 70–71.

16. Mrs. Grundy is a figurative name for an extremely conventional or priggish person.

17. Or shuttlecock, as used in the game of badminton.

18. On December 28, 1860, Massachusetts representative Charles Francis Adams had proposed an amendment to the Constitution that would have prohibited Congress from interfering with slavery in the States. During Secession Winter, twenty-eight amendments suggested similar prohibitions. Republican Thomas Corwin, chair of the Committee of Thirty-Three, ultimately substituted language proposed by Senator William Seward on December 24, 1860. The Seward-Adams-Corwin amendment passed the US Senate on March 4, 1861.

19. A reference to the *Dred Scott* decision of March 6, 1857.

20. Peter the Hermit (1050–1115), also known as Peter of Amiens, was one of the promoters of the First Crusade in 1096.

21. George Thompson was a British abolitionist, writer, and lecturer who visited New England in 1834–1835 at the request of the Boston abolitionist William Lloyd Garrison. He lectured extensively throughout New England, delighting northern abolitionists, but antagonizing antiabolitionists to the extent that, in Boston, he had to be hidden between speaking engagements. C. Duncan Rice, "The Anti-Slavery Mission of George Thompson to the United States, 1834–1835," *Journal of American Studies* 2, no. 1 (April 1968): 13–31. See also Henry Mayer, *All On Fire: William Lloyd Garrison and the Abolition of Slavery* (New York: St. Martin's Griffin, 1998), 197–203.

22. Saturn was a god in Roman mythology. According to the myth, Saturn, aware that it was foretold that a son of his would overthrow him, devoured all of his children by his wife/sister/consort Ops, a goddess of fertility and the earth. Saturnalia, one of the most popular public festivals in ancient Rome coinciding with the winter solstice, was named after Saturn.

23. The HMS *Guerriere* was defeated by the USS *Constitution* on August 19, 1812; the HMS *Java* was defeated by the USS *Constitution* on December 13, 1812.

24. Thomas Jefferson to John Taylor, June 1, 1798, during the 1798–1800 undeclared naval war with France.

25. According to Otis's biographer, it was George Thacher from Maine who proposed the prohibition on slavery in the Mississippi Territory. Otis is quoted as advising his northern colleagues that it should not be "in their disposition to interfere with the Southern States as to the species of property referred to." See Samuel Eliot Morison, *Harrison Gray Otis, 1765–1848: The Urbane Federalist* (Boston: Houghton Mifflin Company, 1969), 425.

26. Thomas Jefferson to John Holmes, congressman from Massachusetts, April 22, 1820.

27. An occasion for war.

28. George Washington's Farewell Address, published September 19, 1796.

29. The final argument.

30. David Campbell (1779–1859), governor from 1837 to 1840.

31. William Dennison Jr. (1815–1882), governor (1860–1862); later US postmaster general (1864–1866).

32. John Sherman (1823–1900), younger brother of William Tecumseh Sherman (1820–1891).

33. Thomas Walker Gilmer (1802–1844), governor of Virginia from 1840 to 1841.

34. Abolitionists William Lloyd Garrison (1805–1879), Joshua Reed Giddings (1795–1864), and Wendell Phillips (1811–1884).

35. Caius Marius (157 BCE–86 BCE) was a Roman general and statesman. Leake may have been referring here to Pierre-Nolasque Bergeret's 1807 painting *Marius Meditating on the Ruins of Carthage* currently in the possession of the Dayton (Ohio) Art Institute.

36. Hurrah for the Triumph.

37. Unionist Thomas Amos Rogers Nelson (1812–1873). In late May 1861, Nelson was elected president of the East Tennessee Convention which attempted to secede from Tennessee after that state joined the Confederacy. Nelson spoke just before Leake. See *Congressional Globe*, 36th Cong., 2nd Sess., January 25, 1861, Appendix, 106–11. See also Dwight T. Pitcaithley, *Tennessee Secedes: A Documentary History* (Knoxville: University of Tennessee Press, 2021), 22–23.

38. New York representative Charles Henry Van Wyck (1824–1895).

39. Howell Cobb (1815–1868); governor of Georgia (1851–1853) and secretary of the Treasury under President James Buchanan (1857–1860). Cobb was one of the founders of the Confederacy and served as president of the Provisional Congress of the Confederate States.

40. New York representative Emory Bemsley Pottle (1815–1891).

41. Robert S. Holzman, *Adapt or Perish: The Life of General Roger A. Pryor, C.S.A.* (Hamden, Connecticut: Archon Books, 1976), 20.

42. Holzman, *Adapt or Perish*, 42. Pryor was in Charleston on April 12, and was given the opportunity to fire the first shot of the war. He declined. Holzman, *Adapt or Perish*, 58–59.

43. From Edmund Burke's "Speech on the Nabob of Arcot's Debts," February 28, 1785.

44. While the House of Representatives deliberated the passage of a Force Bill that would have given the president power to suppress the obstruction of federal authority in any state, no such bill gained approval. Less interest in a Force Bill was displayed by Senate Republicans. (Such a Force Bill had been approved by Congress in 1833 to deal with South Carolina's threat of nullification over the tariff acts of 1828 and 1832.)

45. In William Shakespeare's *King Lear*, the protagonist divides his power and land between his daughters, Goneril and Regan. They, in time, turn against Lear which leads to his insanity and death.

46. In 1860, the US Census Bureau determined that the total value of the southern slave population amounted to $3 billion or more than the capital value of manufacturing, railroads, and banks combined. Joseph C. G. Kennedy, *Preliminary Report of the Eighth Census, 1860* (Washington: Government Printing Office, 1862), 190, 193–94, 197, 199, 231. Historians like Charles Dew place the total value of slaves at $4 billion. Dew, *The Making of a Racist*, 138–40. A 1975 study of wealth in the United States determined that the average value of a slave in 1860 was $900, making the total value $3.6 billion. See Lee Soltow, *Men and Wealth in the United States, 1850–1870* (New Haven: Yale University Press, 1975), 182.

47. The total number of fugitive slaves reported by southerners in 1860 was 803. Kennedy, *Preliminary Report*, 137. If the average value of a slave were $900, the total loss to the South would have been $722,700.

48. The Glorious Revolution (1688–1689) refers to the deposition of James II and VII, king of England, Scotland, and Ireland, and his replacement by his daughter Mary II and her husband, William III of Orange. With the passage of the Bill of Rights, the following year, the revolution stamped out once and for all any possibility of a Catholic monarchy, and ended moves toward absolute monarchy in the British kingdom. Virginia's College of William and Mary, founded in 1693, was named for the new monarchs.

49. The Hungarian Revolution of 1848 against Austria resulted in the establishment of a representative type of parliament. Although the revolution ultimately failed, it is considered the cornerstone of modern Hungarian national identity.

50. Sicily and the Italian states desired independence from the Austrian Empire in 1848. Austrian authority was established the following year. Modern Italy became a nation state in 1861.

51. On December 4, 1860, Virginia representative Alexander Robinson Boteler (1815–1892), recommended the establishment of the Committee of Thirty-Three. *Congressional Globe*, 36th Cong., 2nd Sess., 6.

52. Senator Lazarus W. Powell of Kentucky proposed the creation of the Committee of Thirteen.

53. From the Roman poet Lucan's *Pharsalia*, a treatise on the civil war between Julius Caesar and Pompey. Translation: "a war more than civil." In other words, there would be nothing civil about the approaching "civil" war.

Chapter Five: Virginia State Convention

1. Samuel McDowell Moore (1796–1875). On January 25, Moore spoke on the concerns and interests of the cotton states being different from those of the border states. See Reese, *Proceedings*, 1:172–84.

2. Honoré Gabriel Riqueti, Count of Mirabeau (1749–1791), was a leader of the early stages of the French Revolution.

3. Matthew 20:6.

4. The Wide Awakes was a youth organization cultivated by the Republican Party during the 1860 presidential campaign. They were noteworthy for their precision marching and cadenced cheering accompanied by brass bands during torch-light parades.

5. Soldiers who willingly obey unscrupulous commands.

6. William Shakespeare, *The Tragedy of Richard the Third*, Act 1, scene 1.

7. Variation on Matthew 5:9.

8. On February 18 and 19, secession commissioners from Mississippi, Georgia, and South Carolina addressed the convention. Fulton Anderson (1820–1874), Henry Lewis Benning (1814–1875), and John Smith Preston (1809–1861) attacked the Republican Party as an abolitionist party; staying in the United

States would ultimately lead to the abolition of slavery, they argued. Despite
the passion of the three speeches, Virginia's convention delegates remained
pro-Union until the Confederate attack on Fort Sumter and Lincoln's call
for troops. Fort Benning, Georgia is named after Henry Benning. Reese,
Proceedings, 1:50–93. See also Dew, *Apostles of Disunion*, 59–73.

9. Ruth 1:16.
10. Genesis 13:8.
11. At a Fourth of July picnic in 1854, sponsored by the Massachusetts Anti-
Slavery Society to protest the passage of the Kansas-Nebraska Act, abolitionist
William Lloyd Garrison (1805–1879) famously lit a match to the US Constitution calling it "a covenant with death and an agreement with hell." See Mayer,
All on Fire: William Lloyd Garrison and the Abolition of Slavery, 443–45.
12. Hinton Rowan Helper (1829–1909) published *The Impending Crisis of the
South, and How to Meet It* in 1857. A native of North Carolina, Helper
believed slavery was an impediment to southern economic growth and
recommended that non-slave owners work to displace the slave-owning oligarchy and abolish slavery. Two years later he published a condensed version
titled *Compendium of the Impending Crisis of the South* which was endorsed by
prominent northerners including William Seward, Charles Sumner, Ralph
Waldo Emerson, and Harriet Beecher Stowe. Neither edition recommended
or promoted slave revolts.
13. The "resolutions" refer to instructions to the newly formed Committee on
Federal Relations suggested by Leake minutes earlier. Leake proposed that
the committee develop an ordinance that recognized the "hopeless condition
of New England fanaticism, the blind hate of Black Republicanism, and
the coercive policy indicated by the President [Lincoln] of a dismembered
Union." The only hope for Virginia in the present circumstance was to "declare her independence."
14. William Leftwich Goggin (1807–1870) represented Bedford County. Goggin
had served as a US representative on four occasions: 1839–1843, 1844–1845,
and 1847–1849. After voting in favor of the ordinance of secession, Goggin became a captain of the Home Guards in the Confederate Army. See
Goggin's speech in Reese, *Proceedings*, 1:381–86.
15. Salmon Portland Chase (1808–1873) served as governor of Ohio (1855–1860),
US senator (1849–1855), secretary of the treasury (1861–1864), and chief justice
of the Supreme Court (1864–1873).
16. Upon the conclusion of Abraham Lincoln's inauguration the day before
Leake spoke, Congress was functionally adjourned and not scheduled to
reconvene until December. Without a Congress to approve its actions, the
"common Government" was powerless to carry out the "ruin and degradation" Leake envisioned.
17. *Acts and Regulations of the First Session of the Provincial Congress of the*

292   NOTES TO PAGES 168–182

Confederate States. 1861 (Montgomery, Ala.: Barrett, Wimbish & Co.,
Printers and Binders, 1861), 35–38; Reese, *Proceedings*, 4:90–94; Newell, *The
Regular Army Before the Civil War*, 50.

18. Thomas Emlen Franklin (1810–1884) was a delegate from Pennsylvania.
Franklin was neither a vocal participant in the proceedings nor a major contrib-
utor to the convention's approved amendment to the Constitution. Once that
amendment was adopted, Franklin offered this resolution: "*Resolved*, As the
sense of this convention, that the highest political duty of every citizen of the
United States is his allegiance to the Federal Government created by the Constitution of the United States, and that no State of this Union has any constitutional right to secede therefrom, or to absolve the citizens of each State from
their allegiance to the Government of the United States." It was not adopted by
the conference. Chittenden, *A Report of the Debates and Proceedings*, 446.

19. On March 5, Delegate William L. Goggin representing Bedford County introduced a resolution that read, in part, "That any attempt on the part of the
General Government to use coercive measures for the collection of revenue
from imports, at or near any of the ports within the States which have seceded, will be regarded by Virginia as furnishing just cause for apprehension
of danger to the whole South, Virginia inclusive." See Reese, *Proceedings*,
1:385–86.

20. The final amendment adopted by the Peace Conference is reproduced in
chapter 2.

21. John Tyler (1790–1862), president of the United States (1841–1845); George
William Summers (1804–1868); William Cabell Rives (1793–1868); James
Alexander Seddon (1815–1880), Confederate secretary of war (1862–1865).

22. John T. Thornton represented Prince Edward County.

23. By that name.

24. Detinue, trover, and case were actions at common law to recover personal
property wrongfully taken, or to recover damages for the loss of personal
property. Derived from English law, they were familiar features of American
legal practice in the nineteenth century.

25. In *Somerset v. Stewart* (1772), the English court ruled that because British
common law did not recognize slavery, a slave (James Somerset) brought to
England by Charles Stewart could not be compelled to leave the country.
In *Anderson v. Poindexter* (1856), the Ohio Supreme Court held that Henry
Poindexter, a Kentucky slave, was free the moment he crossed over the Ohio
River.

26. In fact, if not in law.

27. Literally, "in series." In this case, each section of the amendment was voted
on separately.

28. Robert Young Conrad (1805–1875) represented Frederick County.

29. The committee included Robert Y. Conrad, Henry A. Wise (Princess

Anne County), John B. Baldwin (Augusta), Robert E. Scott (Fauquier),
William B. Preston (Montgomery), Lewis E. Harvie (Amelia), John J.
Jackson (Wood), William H. Macfarland (Richmond), William McCo-
mas (Cabell), Robert L. Montague (Matthews and Middlesex), Samuel
Price (Greenbrier), Valentine W. Southall (Albemarle), Waitman T. Wiley
(Monongalia), James C. Bruce (Halifax), William W. Boyd (Botetourt),
James Barbour (Culpeper), Samuel C. Williams (Shenandoah), Timothy
Rives (Prince George and Surry), Samuel McD. Moore (Rockbridge),
George Blow Jr., (Norfolk City), Peter C. Johnston (Lee and Scott).

30. See Simpson, *A Good Southerner.*
31. William Marshall Ambler (1813–1896) represented Louisa County.
32. Robert Eden Scott (1808–1862) represented Fauquier County.
33. Lewis E. Harvie represented Amelia and Nottoway Counties.
34. Robert Latané Montague (1819–1880) represented Matthews and Middlesex
    Counties. Montague served as Virginia's lieutenant governor (1860–1864)
    and in the Second Confederate Congress from (1864–1865). Samuel C.
    Williams (1812–?) represented Shenandoah County.
35. After the secession of seven states, the Republican-controlled Congress or-
    ganized the territories of Dakota, Colorado, and Nevada without providing
    for the exclusion of slaves.
36. By March 25, secession conventions in Louisiana and Mississippi had
    specifically voted against proposals to require ordinances of secession to be
    ratified by the White male voters of those states. Later, Arkansas and North
    Carolina would follow suit. Only Texas, Tennessee, and Virginia submitted
    the issue of disunion to a popular vote.
37. Founded in 1810, the Bellona Foundry, located on the south shore of the
    James River, fourteen miles west of Richmond, manufactured weaponry for
    the US Department of War. In 1856, Dr. Junius L. Archer purchased the
    arsenal and, during the war, leased it to the Confederacy.
38. Located at the confluence of the Elizabeth, Nansemond, and James Rivers,
    Fort Monroe remained in United States hands throughout the war. In 2011,
    President Obama designated it a National Monument. Today it is managed
    by the National Park Service.
39. James Barbour had urged his fellow delegates to recognize reality (as he
    understood it) and cast the state's lot with the Confederacy in Montgom-
    ery, believing that Virginia's interests were more "bound up in it" than the
    financially "bankrupt" government in Washington. See Delegate Barbour's
    comments in Reese, *Proceedings*, 2:671–704.
40. Edmund Burke (1729–1797) was an Irish-British statesman, economist, and
    philosopher. Burke's maxim as quoted by James Barbour was "Statesmanship
    is the science of circumstances. He who ruled over mankind has a different
    part to play from him who is a Professor in a College. The Professor may

deal with abstract principles, the statesman has to look at the circumstances by which he is surrounded, and to endeavor to shape the action of his people in accordance with the circumstances that surround him."

41. John Goode Jr. (1829–1909). During the war Goode served in the Confederate Congress and on the staff of General Jubal Early.

42. Valentine Wood Southall (1793–1861) represented Albemarle County.

43. George W. Richardson represented Hanover County.

44. Committee on Federal Relations.

45. For an interesting examination of the Episcopal Church and slavery in one Richmond congregation, see Christopher Alan Graham, *Faith, Race, and the Lost Cause: Confessions of a Southern Church* (Charlottesville: University of Virginia Press, 2023).

46. Another name for cousin. Thomas Holliday Hicks served as Maryland's governor from 1858 until 1862. He was proslavery, but antisecession.

47. In 1860, Delaware listed 1,798 slaves, the smallest number among the fifteen slaveholding states. Virginia recorded the most with 472,494.

48. For Senator Crittenden's perspective over Secession Winter, see Dwight T. Pitcaithley, *Kentucky and the Secession Crisis: A Documentary History* (Knoxville: University of Tennessee Press, 2022).

49. The vote of the New York delegation was divided on sections 1, 2, 3, 4, 6, and 7. It voted in favor of section 5 prohibiting the foreign slave trade.

50. Jubal Anderson Early (1816–1894) voted against Virginia's ordinance of secession, and then joined the Confederate Army. General Early became the Confederacy's key defender of the Shenandoah Valley before being routed by General Philip Sheridan at Winchester in the fall of 1864. After Appomattox, Early fled to Mexico, then Cuba and Canada. Eventually returning to the United States, he became one of the founders of the Southern Historical Society in 1869.

Chapter Six: Proposed Constitutional Amendments

1. See Pitcaithley, *The U.S. Constitution and Secession*, 161–275.

2. For the intervening time, or temporarily.

3. Mexico had abolished slavery in 1829.

4. The slave trade, but not slavery, had been prohibited in the District of Columbia since 1850. The ban was part of the Compromise of 1850.

5. On March 2, Congress had passed the Morrill Tariff named after Representative Justin Smith Morrill of Vermont. The tariff significantly raised taxes on imports. Its passage was made possible by the departure from Congress of senators and representative from seven southern states which placed Republicans in the majority in both houses.

6. The foreign slave trade had been abolished by Congress on March 2, 1807, effective January 1, 1808.

Chapter Seven: Secession

1. *The Statutes at Large of the Provisional Government of the Confederate States of America*, 104.
2. Wittenberg, et al., *Seceding From Secession*, 35–75.
3. At the bidding of the convention, George W. Randolph, William Ballard Preston, and Alexander H. H. Stuart met with President Lincoln on April 12–13 to determine his intentions and persuade him against coercion of the seceded states. See Crofts, *Reluctant Confederates*, 309–10; Lankford, *Cry Havoc!*, 100–102; and Link, *Roots of Secession*, 239–40.
4. The Crimean War, sparked by religious and nationalistic issues, was fought from October 1853 to February 1856 in which Russia lost to an alliance of France, the Ottoman Empire, the United Kingdom and Sardinia.
5. James Philemon Holcombe represented Albemarle County.
6. For a close analysis of Jefferson Davis as military leader, see McPherson, *Embattled Rebel*.
7. James W. Sheffey represented Smyth County.
8. The Committee on State and Federal Relations included Campbell Tarr (Brooke County), Waitman Thomas Willey (Monongalia), John Snyder Carlile (Harrison), General John Jay Jackson (Wood), Charles Hooton (Preston), Daniel Lamb (Ohio), George McC. Porter (Hancock), Joseph S. Machir (Mason), Daniel D. Johnson (Tyler), James Scott (Jackson), George W. Bier (Wetzel), R. C. Holliday (Marshall), Alexander Scott Withers (Lewis), E. T. Graham (Wirt), Franklin Harrison Pierpont (Marion), Spencer Dayton (Barbour), George S. Senseney (Frederick), John S. Burdett (Taylor), A. R. McQuilkin (Berkeley), Friend Cochran (Pleasants), Irwin C. Stump (Roane), S. Martin (Gilmer), C. P. Rohrbaugh (Upshur), Captain Owen D. Downey (Hampshire), and James A. Foley (Doddridge).
9. Daniel Polsley represented Mason County.
10. John J. Jackson Sr. represented Wood County.

BIBLIOGRAPHY

Primary sources

Acts and Regulations of the First Session of the Provincial Congress of the Confederate States. 1861. Montgomery, Ala.: Barrett, Wimbish & Co., Printers and Binders, 1861.

Chittenden, Lucius E., ed. *A Report of the Debates and Proceedings in the Secret Sessions of the Conference Convention, for Proposing Amendments to the Constitution of the United States, Held at Washington, D.C., in February, A.D. 1861.* New York: D. Appleton & Company, 1864.

Freehling, William W., and Craig M. Simpson, eds. *Showdown in Virginia: The 1861 Convention and the Fate of the Union.* Charlottesville: University of Virginia Press, 2010.

Journal of the House of Delegates of the State of Virginia, for the Extra Session, 1861. Richmond: William F. Ritchie, Public Printer, 1861.

Journal of the Senate of the Commonwealth of Virginia: Begun and Held at the Capitol in the City of Richmond, on Monday, the Seventh of January, 1861, in the Year One Thousand Eight Hundred and Sixty-One—Being the Eighty-Fifth Year of the Commonwealth. Extra Session. Richmond: James E. Goode, Senate Printer, 1861.

Reese, George H., ed. *Proceedings of the Virginia State Convention of 1861: February 13–May 1, 1861.* 4 vols. Richmond: Virginia State Library, 1965. https://secession.richmond.edu.

The Statutes at Large of the Provisional Government of the Confederate States of America, From the Institution of the Government, February 8, 1861, to its termination, February 18, 1861, Inclusive. Arranged in Chronological Order. Together with the Constitution for the Provisional Government, and the Permanent Constitution of the Confederate States, and the Treaties Concluded by the Confederate States with Indian Tribes. Edited by James M. Matthews. Richmond: R. M. Smith, Printer to Congress, 1864.

United States, *Congressional Globe*, 36th Cong., 2nd Sess., December 3, 1860–March 1861. https://memory.loc.gov/ammem/amlaw/lwcglink.html#anchor36.

Suggestions For Further Reading

Ayers, Edward L. *In the Presence of Mine Enemies: The Civil War in the Heart of America 1859–1863.* New York: W. W. Norton & Company, 2003.

———. *What Caused the Civil War? Reflections on the South and Southern History.* New York: W. W. Norton & Company, 2005.

Blight, David W. *Race and Reunion: The Civil War in American Memory.* Cambridge: Harvard University Press, 2001.

Cooper, William J. *We Have the War Upon Us: The Onset of the Civil War, November 1860–April 1861.* New York: Vintage Books, 2012.

Crofts, Daniel W. *Lincoln and the Politics of Slavery: The Other Thirteenth Amendment and the Struggle to Save the Union.* Chapel Hill: University of North Carolina Press, 2016.

———. *Reluctant Confederates: Upper South Unionists in the Secession Crisis.* Chapel Hill: University of North Carolina Press, 1989.

Davis, William A. *"A Government of Our Own": The Making of the Confederacy.* Baton Rouge: Louisiana State University Press, 1994.

Dew, Charles B. *Apostles of Disunion: Southern Secession Commissioners and the Causes of the Civil War.* Charlottesville: University of Virginia Press, 2001.

Freehling, Alison Goodyear. *Drift Toward Dissolution: The Virginia Slavery Debate of 1831–1832.* Baton Rouge: Louisiana State University Press, 1982.

Freehling, William W. *The Road to Disunion.* Vol. 2, *Secessionists Triumphant, 1854–1861.* New York: Oxford University Press, 2007.

Holt, Michael. *The Election of 1860: "A Campaign Fraught with Consequences."* Lawrence: University Press of Kansas, 2017.

Holzman, Robert S. *Adapt or Perish: The Life of General Roger A. Pryor, C.S.A.* Hamden, Connecticut: Archon Books, 1976.

Lankford, Nelson D. *Cry Havoc!: The Crooked Road to Civil War, 1861.* New York: Viking, 2007.

Link, William A. *Roots of Secession: Slavery and Politics in Antebellum Virginia.* Chapel Hill: University of North Carolina Press, 2003.

McPherson, James M. *Embattled Rebel: Jefferson Davis as Commander in Chief.* New York: Penguin Press, 2014.

Moore, R. Randall. "Robert M. T. Hunter and the Crisis of the Union, 1860–1861." *Southern Historian,* vol. 13 (Spring 1992), 25–35.

Morris, Thomas D. *Free Men All: The Personal Liberty Laws of the North, 1780–1861.* Baltimore: Johns Hopkins University Press, 1974.

Pitcaithley, Dwight T. *The U.S. Constitution and Secession: A Documentary Anthology of Slavery and White Supremacy.* Lawrence: University Press of Kansas, 2018.

Rubin, Anne Sarah. "Between Union and Chaos: The Political Life of John Janney," *The Virginia Magazine of History and Biography* 102, no. 3 (July 1994), 381–416.

Seidule, Ty. *Robert E. Lee and Me: A Southerner's Reckoning with the Myth of the Lost Cause.* New York: St. Martin's Griffin, 2020.

Shade, William G. *Democratizing the Old Dominion: Virginia and the Second Party System 1824–1861.* Charlottesville: University of Virginia Press, 1996.

Simpson, Craig M. *A Good Southerner: The Life of Henry A. Wise of Virginia.*
    Chapel Hill: University of North Carolina Press, 1985.
Tooley, Mark. *The Peace That Almost Was: The Forgotten Story of the 1861 Washington
    Peace Conference and the Final Attempt to Avert the Civil War.* Nashville: Nelson
    Books, 2015.
Varon, Elizabeth R. *Disunion: The Coming of the American Civil War 1789–1859.*
    Chapel Hill: University of North Carolina Press, 2008.
Wittenberg, Eric J., Edmund A Sargus, Jr., and Penny L. Barrick. *Seceding from
    Secession: The Civil War, Politics, and the Creation of West Virginia.* El Dorado
    Hills, California: Savas Beatie, 2020.
Young, Robert W. *James Murray Mason, Defender of the South.* Knoxville: Univer-
    sity of Tennessee Press, 1998.

QUESTIONS FOR DISCUSSION

1. Governor Letcher clearly placed the blame for the country's ills on "fanatics in the Northern States." If southern "grievances" were against the action of northern legislatures and not the federal government, was his solution of a conference of states and a constitutional amendment the proper solution? Representative John S. Millson believed northern personal liberty laws should be challenged in the courts. With whom do you most agree? Why?
2. Senator Robert M. T. Hunter proposed a constitutional amendment as an alternative to secession which would have greatly expanded federal authority over slavery at the expense of state authority. How does that square with the popular notion that states' rights lay at the heart of the secession crisis? Does it?
3. Like many other elected officials, Senator James M. Mason pronounced President Lincoln's Inaugural Address, a "proclamation of war." Delegate John S. Carlile, on the other hand, argued that the official "policy of the Executive is peace." Do you find Mason's or Carlile's interpretation the more reasonable? Why?
4. Compare the speeches of Sherrard Clemens and Roger Pryor in the US House of Representatives. With which of the speakers do you most agree? Why?
5. Delegates John S. Carlile and William M. Tredway offered a logical corrective to the secessionist argument that the Republican Party controlled the federal government and would limit or abolish slavery in the near future. Their evidence was that more votes were cast against Lincoln than for him, that Democrats would control Congress for the first two years of his administration, and that the Republican-controlled Congress had just organized three territorial governments and prohibited slavery in none of them. Nevertheless, the claim that Republicans were abolitionists continued. How do you explain the popularity of Democrats' counterfactual claims in the face of evidence to the contrary? What does that tell us about the dangers posed by political misinformation?
6. The Convention approved an ordinance of secession to regain "all the rights of (state) sovereignty." How do you balance that statement against the almost immediate relinquishment of the state's military authority to the Confederacy, followed by the Convention's adoption of a Confederate Constitution

nationalizing slavery? How was the retention of states' rights affected by those actions? Was Delegate John Baldwin correct to caution against giving up "any attribute of a sovereign State" until secession had been confirmed by the scheduled popular vote?

7. Consider that slavery was abolished throughout the United States by the Thirteenth Amendment following the war. If the South had not seceded, how would slavery have been abolished? Could slavery have been abolished by any means short of war? Given that the notion of white supremacy undergirded the institution, might slavery have existed into the twentieth century and beyond? Does the prevalence of white supremacy in the twenty-first century affect your thinking about this question?

8. The South's primary concern over Secession Winter was the future of slavery in the western territories. Since the *Dred Scott* decision had formally settled the issue, why did White southerners take so seriously Republican opposition to it? With the New Mexico Territory officially proclaimed "pro-slavery," and Democrats firmly in control of the next Congress, why did the Republican "non-extension" ideology create such political unrest?

9. It is obvious from many of the constitutional amendments proposed over Secession Winter that the Lemmon Slave Case weighed heavily on in the minds of Virginia's elected officials. With the *Dred Scott* decision allowing slaveowners to move into the western territories with their slaves, a favorable decision in the Lemmon case would have allowed slaveowners to move freely with their slaves into and through any state. If the case had been pursued to the Supreme Court, and decided in Virginia's favor, how might that have shifted the discussion over the future of slavery throughout the country?

10. Suppose that Virginia had appealed the Lemmon Slave Case to the Supreme Court and embraced the Seward/Corwin amendment which would have prevented Congress from interfering with slavery in the states. How might this avenue have better served Virginia's interests during the secession crisis?

11. The two pressing complaints of the South were the Republican Party's opposition to the emigration of slaveowners with their slaves into the western territories and the reluctance of northern states to return fugitive slaves. In light of this, was secession the logical solution to the problem? Why or why not?

12. Compare and contrast Virginia's sixteen proposed constitutional amendments. How are they similar? Different? If they represent Virginia's solution to the secession crisis, how would you define the problem? Given that the five articles approved by Virginia's convention were designed to protect slavery at the federal level, what does that say about the popular notion that the South seceded to protect states' rights?

INDEX